A Simple Introduction to Data and Activity Analysis

by Rosemary Rock-Evans

Published by Computer Weekly Publications
Quadrant House, Sutton, Surrey, SM2 5AS

Publications Manager: John Riley
Publications Executive: Robin Frampton
Publications Assistant: Katherine Canham

REED BUSINESS PUBLISHING

© 1989

British Library Cataloguing in Publication Data

Rock-Evans, Rosemary
 A simple introduction to data and activity analysis.
 1. Mathematical statistics – Data processing
 I. Title
519.4   QA276.4

ISBN 1-85384-001-7

All rights reserved. No part of this publication may be reproduced, stored in a retrieval system, or transmitted, in any form or by any means, electronic, mechanical, photocopying, recording and/or otherwise, without the prior written permission of the publishers.

Typeset by Kudos Graphics, Horsham, West Sussex
Printed in England by Redwood Burn, Trowbridge, Wiltshire

Contents

Preface	vii
Acknowledgements	ix

Chapter 1 Introduction to Analysis	**1**
1.1 What does 'Analysis' mean?	1
1.2 Why is Data and Activity Analysis different from traditional 'Systems Analysis'?	1
1.3 What is its purpose?	2
1.4 Where can it be used in a traditional Systems Development Cycle?	4
1.5 How are the results of the analysis used?	8
1.6 What about the other 'methods' I've heard about?	9
1.7 Summary	10

Chapter 2 Data Analysis	**11**
2.1 Introduction	11
2.2 Main concepts	11
Entities	11
Attributes	12
Relationships	14
2.3 Diagrammatic techniques	15
Degree of Relationships	16
One-to-one Relationships	16
One-to-many Relationships	16
Many-to-many Relationships	16
Optionality	17
Exclusivity	20
Entities identified by Relationships	20
Entity sub-types	21
2.4 Other deliverables of Data Analysis	26
2.5 An example model	30
2.6 Fundamental rules of Data Analysis	32
2.7 Summary	33

Chapter 3 How to do Data Analysis	**35**
3.1 Introduction	35
Real World Abstractions and Real World Occurrences	35
Design Abstractions and Occurrences	35
3.2 Analysis	37
Using forms and record layouts	37
Using conceptual descriptions	44
Using Occurrences	53
Using Design Occurrences	60
3.3 Merging the models	72
3.4 Refining the Data Model	76
Removing Synonyms	77
Check for Attribute duplication	79
Generalisation – Entities	83
Looking for Patterns	84
Exclusivity Case	84
Generalising – Relationships	85
Removing Redundancy	91

Contents

	Resolving many-to-many Relationships	92
	Investigating one-to-one Relationships	98
	Remove 'code only' Entities	99
	Degree Verification	100
3.5	Summary	101

Chapter 4 Activity or Function Analysis — 105
4.1	Introduction	105
4.2	Main concepts of Activity Analysis	105
	Activity	105
	Event	106
	Sources and Sinks	106
	Data Flow	108
	Data Store	108
4.3	Diagrammatic representation	109
	Activity Decomposition Diagram	110
	Data Flow Diagram	113
	Conditions, repetition and sequence	119
	Conditions	119
	Repetition	122
	Sequence and Parallel	124
4.4	Other deliverables of Activity Analysis	124
4.5	Summary	125

Chapter 5 How to do Activity Analysis — 131
5.1	Introduction	131
	Real World Abstractions and Real World Occurrences	131
	Design Abstractions	132
5.2	Analysis	133
	Using Real World Abstractions	133
	Using Design Abstractions	143
	Using 'actions' or Activity Occurrences	165
5.3	Refining the results	170
5.4	Verification methods	173
	Inner consistency checks	173
	'Outer consistency' checks	176
5.5	Summary	179

Chapter 6 Improving a System Using the Analysis Methods — 181
6.1	Introduction	181
6.2	Problems, Causes and Effects	181
	Problems	181
	Cause	182
	Effect	182
6.3	Objectives, Obligations and Events	186
	Objectives	186
	Obligations	186
	Events	186
6.4	Summary	189

Chapter 7 Elementary Activities — 191
7.1	Introduction	191
7.2	Definition and purpose	191
	Definition of Elementary Activities	191
7.3	Structured Text and Access Paths	193
	Example commands to describe Elementary Activities	195
7.4	Common Procedures, Messages and embedded Elementary Activities	205
	Common Procedures	205
	Messages	206
	Embedded Elementary Activities	207
7.5	Examples of Elementary Activities	207

7.6	Updating the Data Model	208
7.7	Other useful detailed deliverables of an Elementary Activity	225
	Response required	225
	User/Activity responsibility: represented by matrix	225
	Usage figures	229
	Examples of Elementary Activity Access Path Usage	232
7.8	Summary	242

Chapter 8 Summary — **243**

8.1	Introduction	243
8.2	Packaging the results – Data Dictionaries, Analyst Workbenches and IPSEs	243
8.3	The next step – design	245
8.4	Summary of contents	248

Index — **251**

Notes — **255**

Computer Weekly Publications — **259**

Preface

In 1981 a small red book entitled *Data Analysis* was published by *Computer Weekly*. It was based on a series of about 27 articles which had appeared in *Computer Weekly* and were written by myself. The book was short and was intended as a brief introduction to some of the main concepts embodied in the new analysis techniques.

The book has been credited with arousing the interest of a huge number of people now using these new analysis techniques and has certainly changed the career course of many people I have met.

Since then, the book has gone out of print. Furthermore, there have been many advances in analysis methods since then which make it, in some ways, out of date. Even so, *Computer Weekly* is still getting enquiries, asking if copies are still available.

It is because of the success of this first book, and the immense surge in interest that has taken place recently in new analysis techniques that *Computer Weekly* again contacted me – this time to ask me if I would write a book, rather than articles which could become a book.

At the time, I was about to have released a series of four books I had written on Analysis called *Analysis within the Systems Development Cycle*, and published by Pergamon Infotech. Nevertheless, I was most enthusiastic about the suggestion.

Even though these four books cover the same topic of Analysis, I saw that there was still a need for a simple introductory book on the subject – just as *Data Analysis* had been – but updated with the new ideas and techniques which have been invented since the late 1970s.

The four books on Analysis go into some detail on all the deliverables of Analysis, their uses and how you do Analysis to get all these deliverables. It was deliberately written to be extremely comprehensive. They cannot, however, in all honesty be said to be a simple introduction to the subject.

A Simple Introduction to Data and Activity Analysis is intended for anyone greatly interested in the subject, but who wants to find out what it's about on a simple level, before they delve into any detail.

In a way, this and the other four books are complementary. Those of you whose interest is aroused by this book will be tempted to turn to the other books for the detailed help and information they contain.

I find it fascinating to think back to the early days of the techniques and consider how many advances have been made since the late 1970s when that first introductory book was written. The UK Government has adopted new analysis techniques using SSADM. In fact, big UK firms are now using these more 'modern' analysis techniques. Any firm not using them is the exception rather than the rule.

We have also seen an extraordinary rise in interest in methodologies – complete systems development cycles – embodying analysis techniques, but also starting to include new design techniques as well. This area is worth keeping an eye on, as it is the focus of effort for many leading edge consultancies, where numerous significant advances are being made.

Perhaps more important within the context of this book, we have seen advances in the methods of analysis (the 'how to do' part) as opposed to the deliverables (the 'how to structure the results'). My first book concentrated almost entirely on the deliverables – what concepts were used, how these concepts were diagrammatically represented and how they all fitted together. There was little help on how you obtained these deliverables.

This book aims to provide a more balanced picture by showing what deliverables are collected as well as how you obtain them.

You will also notice that the name of the techniques has changed from 'Data Analysis' to 'Data and Activity Analysis' to give greater emphasis to the fact that both aspects are equally important.

Ian Palmer, in his preface to the first book, mentioned that Data Analysis (as it was then known) helped to identify where data sharing could take place. This is still true, although there is possibly more emphasis given to the fact that the data would not be there in the first place if it were not for the activities, and that while we may want to share data across applications, it must be shown to have a use somewhere.

You will also notice that the term 'function' has been changed to that of 'activity'. In reality, no suitable word exists in the English language to describe concisely the concept of 'what a business does', but activity is a better word than function which is too closely tied in many people's minds to user's jobs and organisation units.

For the other changes, I suggest that you start reading this book. For those who have seen the original little red book, you will find some that is the same, but you will also notice much that has advanced during these past seven or eight years.

Acknowledgements

Many of the advances seen in this book in the methods and methodologies have been made whilst I have been working for my present company, DCE Information Management Consultancy Ltd, based in Woking. In fact, many of the advances are theirs and theirs alone. I wish therefore to express my thanks to DCE, particularly its Directors, Chairman and Chief Executive Officer, for their help and assistance, without which this book would not have been possible.

Lincoln Steffens (1866–1936)
'I have seen the future and it works!'

Francis Bacon (1561–1626)
'Read not to contradict and confute, nor to believe and take for granted nor to find talk and discourse, but to weigh and consider.'

'For all knowledge and wonder (which is the seed of knowledge) is an impression of pleasure in itself.'

Introduction to Analysis

1.1 WHAT DOES "ANALYSIS" MEAN?

Data and Activity Analysis are usually lumped together under the general term of 'Business Analysis'.

Business analysis is a method for determining what the business does now (its activities) and what data is needed to support those activities.

For Example:

Activity	Data
Collect Tax	Tax Data
	People Data
Pays People	People Data
	Pay Data
	Tax Data
	Bonus Data
	Deduction Data

Here, the business (in this case the Government) has as one of its activities the collection of tax. To collect tax it needs data on people and tax itself.

The business will want to pay people (its employees). To pay people it must have data about people: the bonuses they are to be paid, the deductions which must be made and so on. The activity will generate pay and tax data.

Activities thus both use and generate data.

Business analysis is not only a method for determining what the business does and the data it needs now; it is also a method for finding out what it should be doing and what extra data it needs to do these things.

These additional activities could be those it needs to keep up with the competition, or give it a leading edge or help it provide a better service if it is non-profit making. We will learn more about what the business should be doing in Chapter 7.

Finally, business analysis is also a method for finding out which of the business's activities are obsolete. In this context we may find that because the objectives no longer exist, the activities which are there to carry them out are now redundant. Again, Chapter 7 will be looking at this in more detail.

Since business analysis is a method for determining the activities and data needed by a business the method is usually split into "Activity Analysis" and "Data Analysis". They are interdependent methods, however, and (as we shall see) integrated, each providing output to the other.

1.2 WHY IS DATA AND ACTIVITY ANALYSIS DIFFERENT FROM TRADITIONAL "SYSTEMS" ANALYSIS?

A fundamental distinction needs to be made between the task of analysis which tells you what is required and that of design, which deals with how to achieve it.

For example, to collect tax (what I want to do) my design may use people or it may use computers, both of which we call 'mechanisms' – the means of achieving what we want to do.

If I want to pay people (requirements), I could use as one design solution a computer system together with some pay clerks to enter and distribute the information, or I could just use the pay clerks with calculators and tax tables.

For one statement of requirements about what the business does and wants to do, the designer has a large number of options on how to achieve it, and that decision depends on costs and benefits. The skill of all designers is in choosing the best, most cost effective solution within the constraints.

Business analysis is thus primarily used in a systems development cycle to determine the "User Requirements" (its place in the cycle will be discussed in more detail later in this chapter); it is not at all concerned with how those requirements are achieved.

To free itself of any concerns about the "how" aspect – the mechanisms of achievement – the concepts used in business analysis are deliberately different from those used in design.

Some term this view of the world "logical"; some call it "conceptual". It is a view which provides

2   A Simple Introduction to Data and Activity Analysis

immense power to express what is really required without making too premature a decision on how it is to be achieved.

It is this concentration on the logical rather than on the mechanisms themselves which makes this form of analysis different to the more traditional approaches.

The traditional systems analysis task would be of the form:

* Find out what the existing design is (user jobs, forms, records, programs);
* Try to find out in design terms what the user would like (how fast, how accurate, how big, what cost); then
* Invent a new design.

This, to borrow a phrase, was "one giant leap" for an analyst. It was prone to error and rarely a method which tackled the real problems.

The more modern view is as follows:

* Find out what the existing design is (if one exists);
* Find out what the business does now in logical terms;
* Work out what the business *should* be doing, again in logical terms (this is effectively a logical statement of requirements);
* Find out the design requirements (how fast, how accurate, what cost) and
* Invent a new design, using the logical statement of requirements and the design requirements to come up with the new design.

This may be a longer process, but the most important point about it is that it tackles the real issues – what a business should be doing and not simply the mechanisms of how it achieves it.

The former method enabled you to produce a system which simply encapsulated all the problems which the business had. Furthermore, its concentration on design targets simply made the problems appear faster!

The new methods concentrate on tackling what, in 99 per cent of the cases, are the real reasons why a systems is being studied, and these are logical problems not design ones. Once they have been solved, then and only then is a design produced.

This introductory book will show you how to:

* Find out what the business is doing now in logical terms (Chapters 3, 5 and 6); and
* Work out what the business should be doing in logical terms (Chapter 7).

Chapter 8 describes what you do directly before you tackle the design task.

1.3   WHAT IS ITS PURPOSE?
We have already seen that business analysis techniques help you to improve the underlying or inherent business system before you start the design. One of the purposes of business analysis is thus to help you help your business to improve. It should, however, also help you as an analyst trying to develop systems, as you are more likely to succeed by putting in a system which is what the business needs and is free of problems, than one which is riddled with residual ones.

The techniques of business analysis also aim to provide much more structure to analysis results. At one time, most analysis work was described in text. Text to record factual information is a highly inefficient and counter-productive form of fact recording. It is long winded, can hide errors, cannot easily be checked for omissions and cannot be manipulated.

An example will help to illustrate this point. Figure 1.1 shows two sets of analysis results. The text shows how old-fashioned analysis results might have been produced. There are nearly 70 words in the text and it took me about three minutes to write. The result is both difficult to visualise or check for accuracy – it is certainly not clear whether the results are logically sound or correct. Furthermore, it is not clear whether any facts are missing.

Below it is a Data Model – a deliverable of business analysis. I had to write only a few words and draw a few boxes and lines. It took me less than a minute to produce. I can easily check it because I can use the picture to see if any facts are missing and whether my conclusions are illogical or incorrect.

Structuring the results has thus helped me to produce facts more quickly, more thoroughly, more accurately and more completely. What could once have taken three weeks can now take one.

The Data Model also gives me an at-a-glance idea of how big the project is. This should help me in estimating and costing the project development.

Furthermore, business analysis techniques are ideally suited to producing both efficient databases and system designs. This is not only because the analysis results are a more accurate reflection of what the business needs, but also because the facts produced are all usable in the design process, making design much less prone to trial and error and so less risky. Section 1.5 shows how the

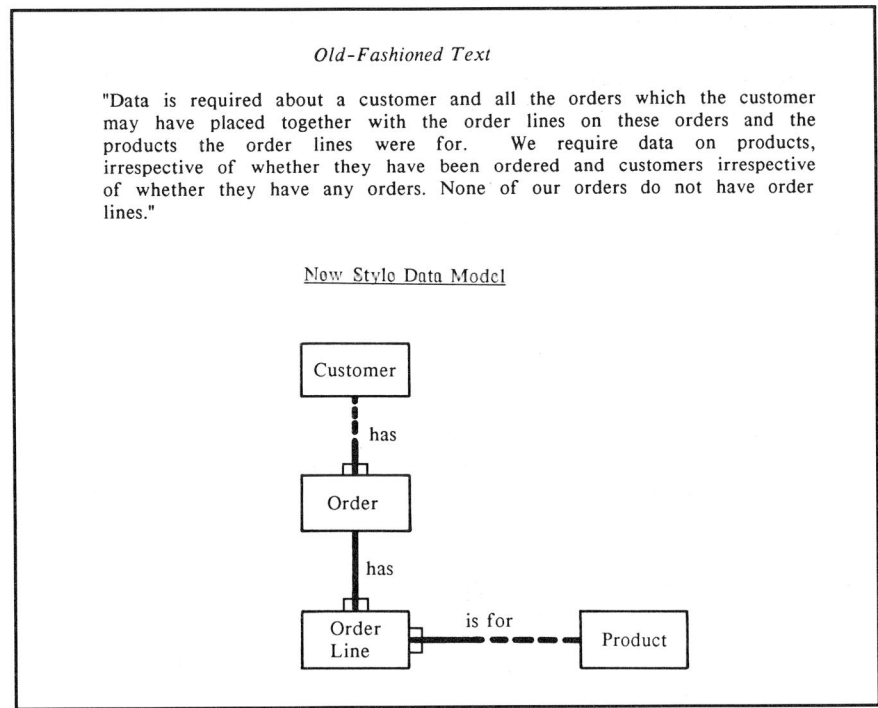

Figure 1.1 The difference between structured and unstructured information

analysis results are used in overview. Assuming you have good design methods in place, the new business analysis techniques enable you to produce an effective and efficient design.

So business analysis techniques help us to produce good designs, allow us to improve our results to reflect business needs more accurately, enable us to see the scope of the project and thus help us plan and cost the project, and help us to improve the quality of the analysis results themselves while saving effort in producing them.

Last, but not least, the techniques also enable us to share our diagrams with other members of the team. They can use and add to it as they get to know more about our "Order Processing" system.

Pooling text descriptions is nowhere near as easy.

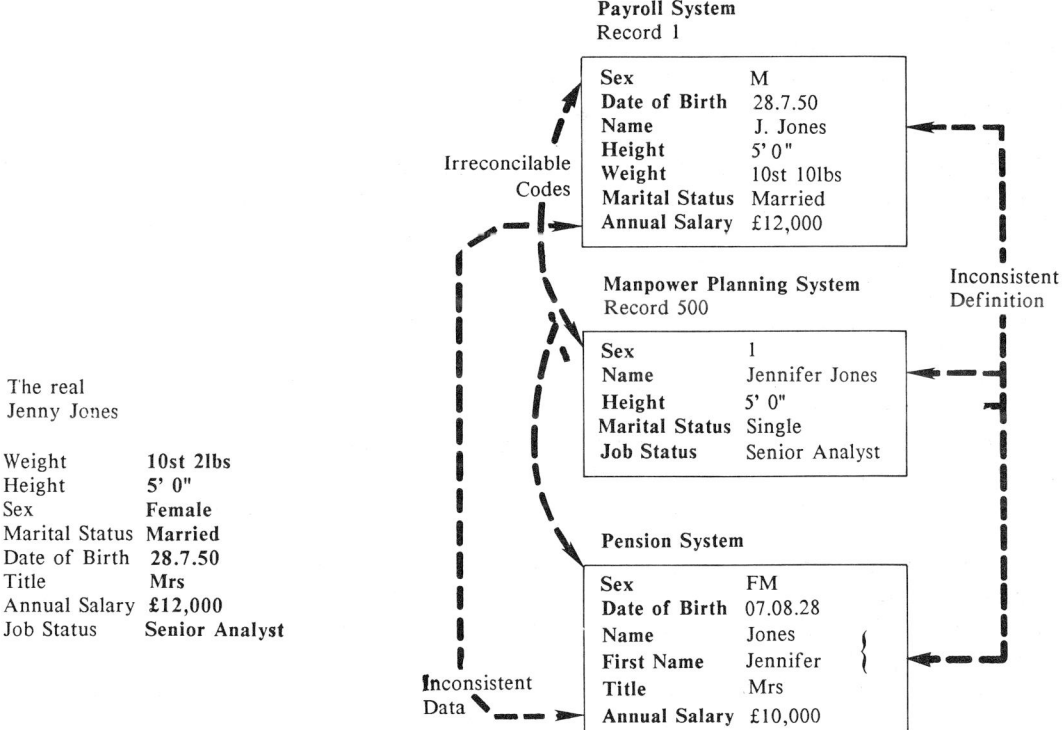

Figure 1.2 Data-sharing

4 A Simple Introduction to Data and Activity Analysis

This important feature is the first step towards data sharing. Sharing data saves you and your company effort, time and money. Without the commitment of project teams to achieve it, it can be extraordinarily hard to achieve, but once the benefits both to the company and to the teams themselves are realised, data-sharing rapidly takes off. If you share data, you save yourselves the effort of having to create interface systems; you save the company money and you also go a long way towards giving the company accurate and timely data.

But what happens when you don't share data?

Let us look at Figure 1.2. Three systems hold data about Jenny Jones. The Payroll System believes she was born on 28/7/50. The Pension System has her date of birth as 7/8/28. Although all three systems have a field called "name", what is actually recorded in "name" is different in each case. Furthermore, when we look at the field called "sex" we can see that different coding systems have been used.

Both transfer of data and cross-system queries are likely to be horrendously complex and even the actual system functions themselves are going to produce incorrect results – probably owing to successive transcription of the same data (a bit like the Chinese Whisper effect) and partly because of timeliness problems, such as out-of-date data, for example the salary data in the Pension System.

Sharing data these days has thus generally become accepted as a 'good thing', but it cannot be achieved unless you use the new analysis techniques, as they provide the means whereby data can be managed.

1.4 WHERE CAN IT BE USED IN A TRADITIONAL SYSTEMS DEVELOPMENT CYCLE?

There is no single standard Systems Development Cycle (SDC) recognised industry-wide, so to try to relate business analysis to one systems development cycle is liable to cause confusion, more particularly as some SDCs are still based on out-of-date ideas.

We at DCE like the sort of SDC shown in Figure 1.3, so I will use this one but will also attempt to give synonyms and explanations which may help you to relate yours to this.

1. Strategy Study

A Strategy Study aims to determine for a large area of the business what its main areas of activity should be and what its major objectives are.

At the same time, the types of mechanisms needed to support these activities and objectives (considering the organisation, jobs and computer systems) are also identified. The overall scope of the business is split into prime "application" areas requiring further study, these areas having been identified as being of major benefit to the company and therefore worthy of further study.

2. Tactical Study

Once termed a feasibility study, the Tactical Study now encompasses far more than the old-fashioned Feasibility Study used to.

The objective is to determine in more detail whether actual mechanisms exist which can support the application areas as identified by the Strategy Study. One design solution is NOT chosen. Instead, a number may be "carried forward" for detailed study if all are feasible and can be justified in broad terms on cost/benefit grounds. It is only at the more detailed level of study that feasibility can be assessed and cost/benefit calculated with any certainty.

3. Detailed Systems Study

This is sometimes also called the Detailed Requirements Study.

The aim here is to choose *one* design solution to be carried forward for further, more detailed "external design". Business analysis is completed during this stage, but the design solutions carried forward from the tactical study are only developed further to a point where a particular solution can be chosen with reasonable confidence, without wasting excessive effort developing very detailed solutions. Bearing in mind that one or more of these solutions could be a package, it should be obvious that if you do a very detailed design, you will have lost all the benefits of buying a package. Some detailed evaluation has to be performed on the package to assess the tailoring requirements and to make the final choice between package and in-house, but not to the detailed level required in a full "external design".

4. External Design

This is also called the Specification Stage, but this time encompassing more than many specification stages in old-fashioned SDCs.

This stage develops the outline design solution produced at the Detailed Systems Study stage into a detailed design which is "user-oriented", that is, it is what the user will see or experience as opposed to what the machine/computer will know about. Thus an external design will include the online design, and show dialogues, screens and exchanges; batch design and show listings, forms and

Introduction to Analysis 5

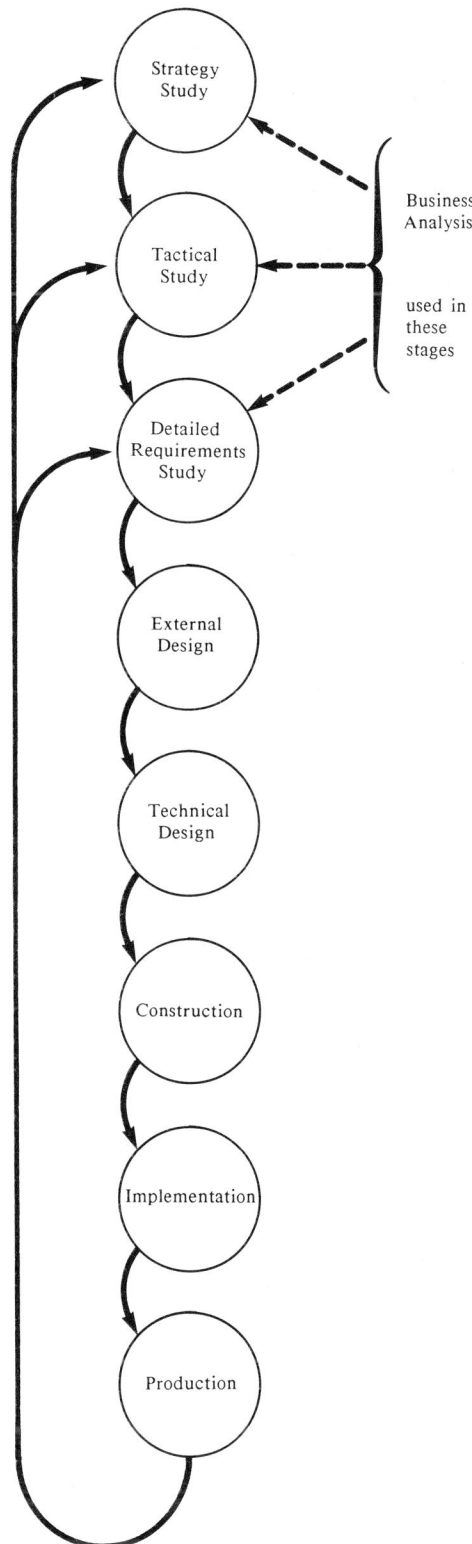

Figure 1.3 A Systems Development Cycle

jobs; clerical design and show user tasks and forms. In addition, where real-time systems are being included, the real-time processes, signals and messages will also be included.

Ideally, database and file design will also be completed to the level where the feasibility of the external design to meet the design requirements can be tested. This is where many "traditional" SDCs are lacking as this essential need to test the external design is often omitted.

5. Internal or Technical Design

Technical design uses the external design and converts it into the design which the machine will see. Technical design includes both database and systems/program design.

6 *A Simple Introduction to Data and Activity Analysis*

6. Construction
Programs and systems are written, compiled and tested. Database/files are created.

7. Implementation
The system is put into the business to replace the "old" system.

8. Production
The system is used.

Business analysis, you will remember, is used to find out what the user requirements are, and user requirements are of relevance during Strategy Studies, Tactical Studies and Detailed Requirements Studies. After the Detailed Requirements stage, we have all we need to know about the user's business requirements. What we continue to develop in the latter stages of the SDC is how these requirements are to be achieved (the mechanisms).

Why, you may ask, is business analysis performed so many times? The reason is one of "level of detail". A Strategy Study has a very wide scope and does not aim for extensive detail or absolute accuracy – the objectives can be achieved without this being available. A Tactical Study aims for slightly more detail and greater accuracy. A Detailed Requirements Study aims for all the detail and absolute accuracy (as far as it is possible to obtain).

To try to put this another way, a Strategy Study should not produce models big enough to cover a

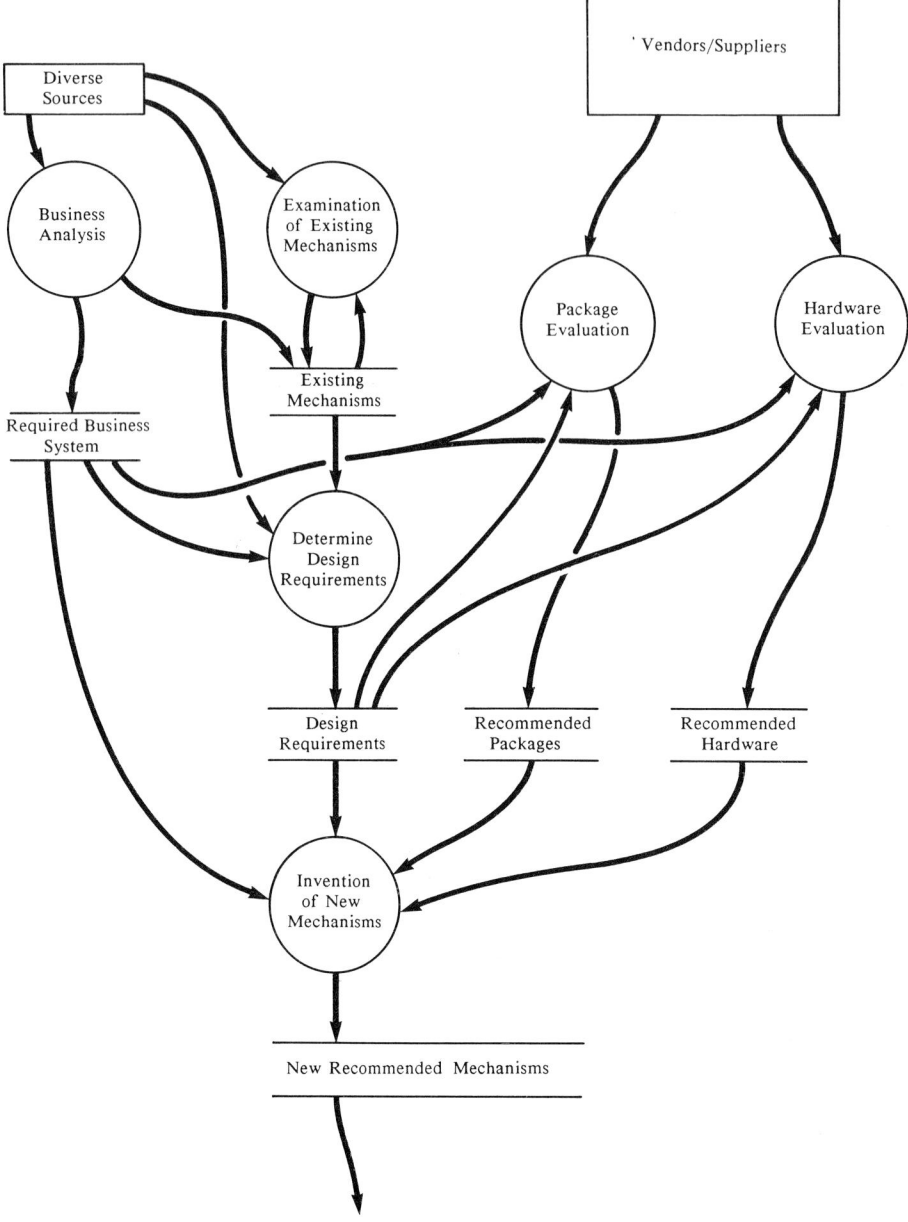

Figure 1.4 A breakdown of the main tasks

Introduction to Analysis 7

wall! It should produce models of manageable size which are capable of being further broken down in the Tactical Study stage when prime areas of study are known.

To help understanding of what part business analysis plays within a Strategy, Tactical or Detailed Requirements Study, Figure 1.4 shows a breakdown of tasks where a similar pattern emerges at every level.

1. Examination of existing mechanisms

Find out what the existing design is (if one exists).

2. Business Analysis

Find out what the business does now in logical terms and then work out what the business should be doing, again in logical terms (the logical statement of requirements).

3. Find out the design requirements (how fast, how accurate, what cost).

4. Evaluate packages against the design requirements and, more importantly, the business analysis requirements (sometimes called evaluation of functionality).

5. Evaluate hardware against the design and analysis requirements.

6. Invent a new design

Using the logical statement of requirements, recommended hardware and software and the design requirements, to come up with the new design.

You should be able to see the connection between this breakdown and the one described earlier on page 5.

The breakdown I have shown above won't be found in any SDC, as it is unique to DCE. It does represent, however, a much more "modern" view of the real tasks of systems people today and, unlike most SDCs, takes packages and hardware into account.

So far, we have been looking at the task of business analysis within the context of an SDC.

In Figure 1.5, I have provided a breakdown of the activities of business analysis itself.

As you can see, business analysis consists of five main activities:

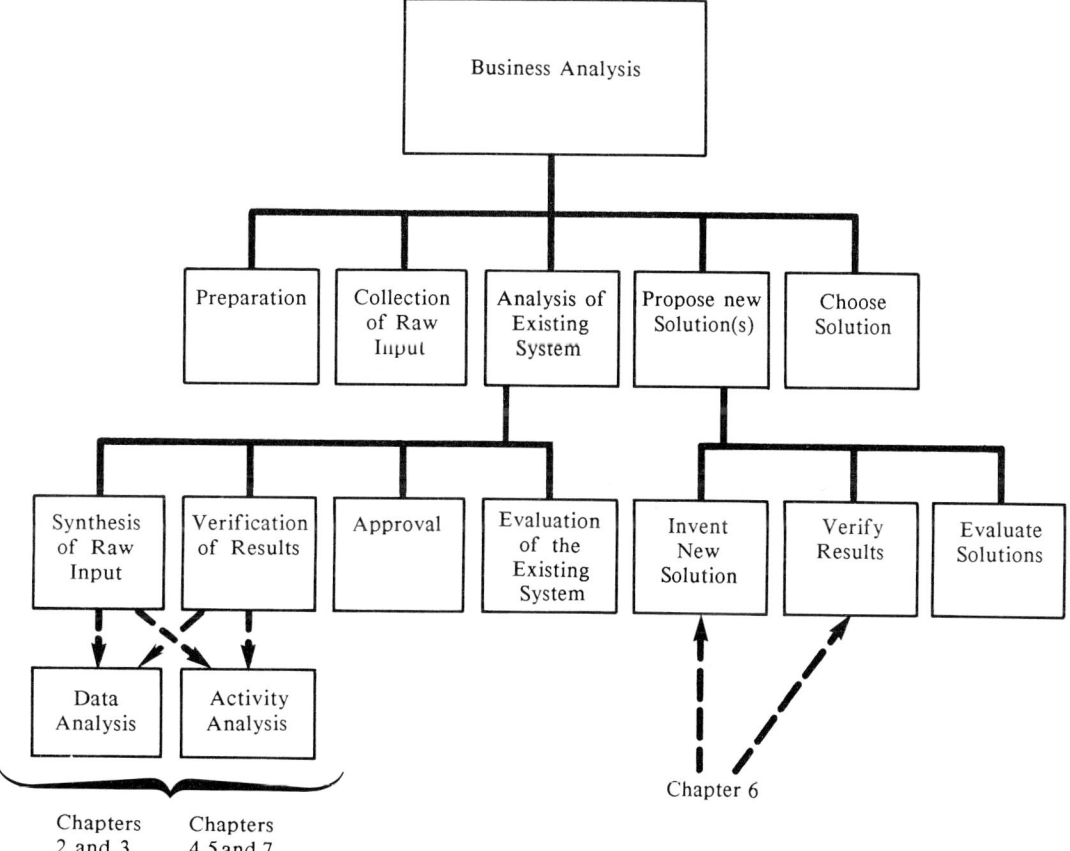

Figure 1.5 A breakdown of the business analysis task

8   *A Simple Introduction to Data and Activity Analysis*

1. Preparation
During this task, the best sources for the raw input you will need to collect are identified, together with the method of collection you intend to use;

2. Collection
The raw input you will be analysing is collected from the sources you have identified;

3 Analyse the Existing System
The existing system is analysed to find out what "logically" exists. This existing logical system is then evaluated to find out where it is deficient;

4. Propose New Business System
A new logical system is suggested, or possibly a number of alternatives which would solve the problems of the existing logical system. These are then evaluated in the same sort of way as the existing system was evaluated, except that, of course, the problems which might occur will be hypothetical ones or risks; and

5. Choose Solution
The solution which looks the best of those proposed (and here the existing one is included in the evaluation), is chosen, based on the results of the evaluations.

In this book I will not be describing the Preparation, Collection or Choose tasks, or how new solutions are invented. I will concentrate on the tasks of Analysis of the Existing system and, more particularly, how to "synthesise" the raw data together with some of the easier verification checks you can do. I have shown the Chapter heading against the task boxes for ease of reference. In Chapter 7, the way the existing system can be evaluated is described and a little of what is involved in logical change.

The four books I have written on Analysis with the Systems Development Cycle cover all these tasks in some detail. This book should give you the main threads of the tasks I have mentioned.

1.5   HOW ARE THE RESULTS OF ANALYSIS USED?
The results of Data Analysis – the Data Model and the extra facts collected about it such as the volume of Entities, size of Attributes and so on – are used in Database and File design.

The Data Model can be used as the input for any type of database or file design – computer or human paper systems – just as effectively. I have designed my own paper filing system using forms and files to record the data I need and I used a Data Model to work out what I wanted.

A Data Model is also capable of being turned into a computer database or file design using all sorts of DBMSs (Database Management Systems), "flat" files, VSAM-type files or File-Handling type packages. In other words, whatever the file handling software you have, you can use a Data Model as the start point for your file design. There are "rules" which you can use to turn the Data Model into a File Design. They tend to be more complicated for the more complex DBMSs (such as IMS) and simpler for the less complex DBMSs. The family of DBMSs known as the "two level network" – such as IMAGE and TOTAL sit somewhere in the middle – not complex, but on the other hand not as easy as, say, Codasyl-based DBMSs.

The results of Activity Analysis are used to design the system.

We will see that we produce Data Flow Diagrams, Activity Decomposition Diagrams and Elementary Activity descriptions, all of which form the basis of the Batch Jobs, Online Systems and Dialogues produced in design. Again, we can equally well use the results to produce human systems. When I produced my own paper filing system using a Data Model, I also produced my own "job description" on how to use and enter the data I was collecting. To do this I used Data Flow Diagrams and the Elementary descriptions as my start point.

Unlike database design, you can do quite a lot of outline systems design without needing to know which software, eg application builder/generator or screen painter, you intend to use. At the detailed design stage, however, you do need to know which software you will be using, as you should be building the system using this software, putting the screens and skeleton dialogues in the machine and the beginnings of your batch jobs. I call this sort of design "building in situ". It means that you are building the system on your target machine (or the same type of machine) using your target software. It also means you are getting it checked by the user as you go along – getting the user to approve the dialogue and screens and agree the listing designs.

Your analysis results form the basis of what goes into the design, but the design process can be completed with the user. This method of design produces very good system designs.

This book will not show you how to produce a design from analysis results, only how to get the analysis results in the first place. It is important to realise that *all* the things I will be describing in the rest of the book do have a use in the design process; they are not "ornamental".

1.6 WHAT ABOUT THE OTHER "METHODS" I'VE HEARD ABOUT?

Ever since the early 1970s people have been inventing ways of doing analysis better. It probably started with Bachman, who showed us how we could document the data used by a system and its relationships with a picture. His technique was the forerunner of what we now know as the Data Model.

Chen and Merise helped to develop the Data Modelling idea further. Chen's work goes back to 1970.

Matt Flavin, in 1981, used Chen and Merise's work to try to develop the Entity Relationship approach further, and you may hear of his approach which he called "Information Modelling Methodology". His approach is highly complex and unnecessarily long-winded, and has not been developed further.

In contrast, the Data Model as we know it today largely owes its existence to several European consultancies (DCE, CACI, BIS, LBMS, Inforem and so on) who have produced a set of concepts and conventions which are now fairly widely accepted and in use. These build and improve on the work of Bachman, Chen and Merise, but add concepts and deliverables which have a direct use in design.

It is this Data Model – the more modern complete version – which will be described in this book.

Those of you using SSADM, LDMS or BIS's methods may find that the Data Model I describe has fewer restrictions and slightly more "richness" than the ones you are used to.

The growth in Activity Analysis methods for a time took a quite separate course. The first methods did not use Data Models or attempt to pull the two sorts of analysis together.

The first attempts at better Activity Analysis methods were made by Tom de Marco, Gane and Sarson and, to a lesser extent, Yourdon. Their data flow diagrams (Gane and Sarson simply use a different diagramming convention to de Marco) paved the way for most of the methods we now use today. Yourdon added "events" to the picture, providing a valuable contribution. All this work goes back to the mid 1970s.

Yourdon has developed the basic techniques which he devised in those early days, and has added a form of Data Modelling, but not the full Data Model you will see in this book and not the integration between the Data Model and the activities which you will also see.

IBM's BSP (Business System Planning) was the early forerunner of Activity Decomposition diagrams.

The ISAC (Information Systems and Analysis of Change) method provided useful ideas on problem analysis and was developed at Stockholm University in about 1979.

The SADT (Systems Analysis and Design Technique) was invented in the 1970s and marketed by Softech Inc. It was used as an alternative to Data Flow diagrams for some time, and variations of it are still to be found in some consultancies' methods – notably Systems Designer's CORE and J.M.A.'s Information Engineering Method. It has some concepts such as activities and data flows which are shared by Data Flow Diagrams themselves, but it lacks the ability of Data Flow diagrams to show 'shared' data and hence provide the means to show the vital link with the Data Model. It is because of this weakness that I have not described it in this book and have shown the much richer and more powerful diagramming technique of data flow diagrams.

(Those of you who remember my first book will notice that I am a convert to data flow diagrams from SADT diagrams.)

Those of you who use Jackson structured methods may be interested to know how these have evolved. The Jackson method was developed in the days when programmers received unstructured specifications from their analysts or designers which then had to be made to work. The original Jackson structured programming method helped the programmer's job in a dramatic way and represents a significant achievement in programming methods.

Jackson subsequently extended the method to design. It has been extended to analysis to support a form of entity life history and a diagram called the network diagram, which bears a remarkable similarity to a data flow diagram but uses different diagrammatic conventions to represent the data stores and the activities. The integration between the 'conceptual data' and the activities in the network diagram is good, although the absence of a Data Model to complete the picture is a severe limitation. You will see that this book may help to complete the picture if you are using Jackson techniques.

It is possible that, in time, Jackson structured programming techniques will be used less and less, as more people move over to newer analysis and design techniques. How long this takes, however, depends on how fast these newer techniques are adopted.

There is no doubt that in their time most of these methods represented a real advance in thinking.

10   A Simple Introduction to Data and Activity Analysis

It is important to realise, however, that they were steps on the path to what we have now – and what we have now is far more powerful and useful because it draws on the work of these pioneers. We should be grateful to them and recognise their achievements, but there is no point in looking back.

What we have now is an amalgam of the best of these methods. We have been able to integrate the Data and Activity analysis approaches as well as adding deliverables to this basic framework to provide us with more and better information with which to do better and higher quality design.

Furthermore, we have started to integrate these methods into full systems development cycles, which take advantage of the newer techniques as opposed to those used and developed in the 1970s before the methods were either known or had evolved to their present state.

More important still, we have been able to put more actual method into these methods. Method is, after all, what you do to produce the actual output. Many of these methods did not tell you what to do. They explained the diagrams, how to draw them, what they meant, hints and guidelines on how to use them – but they did not show you how you obtained them, where they came from.

We are only now beginning to really develop the way in which these deliverables are produced – to put real method into the methods.

I will show you in this book the essence of what you do, but a fuller explanation is provided in my four books on Analysis within the Systems Development Cycle.

1.7 SUMMARY

Business analysis involves the two related activities of Data Analysis and Activity Analysis. Activity Analysis is the study of what the business does now and of what it should be doing. Data Analysis is the study of what data the business needs to enable these activities to be completed.

Business analysis is used during Strategy Studies, Feasibility or "Tactical" Studies and during Detailed Systems/Detailed Requirements Studies.

It involves five main activities – preparation (determine the best sources for collection); collection of the "raw" data for analysis; analysis of the "existing system" (if one exists); and proposing one or more new solutions and choosing the solution. Of these, the book will concentrate on aspects of the analysis of the existing system and the proposing of a new system, and more specifically on the actual "synthesis" task itself (how to turn the raw input into the analysis deliverables) together with the evaluation and verification methods.

Business analysis results are used both to help a business improve its activities and provide the deliverables needed in design. In the latter case, the Data Analysis deliverables are used for database and file design and the Activity Analysis deliverables are used in system design.

These new techniques have evolved from work which started as long ago as 1970. They represent the culmination of years of pioneer work in different aspects of business analysis, which you now see drawn together in this one book.

2 Data Analysis

2.1 INTRODUCTION

This chapter describes the most important concepts and diagrammatic conventions used in Data Analysis.

These concepts are the main *deliverables* from Data Analysis. It is possible to collect additional facts about these basic concepts – much of this extra information is quantifiable, for example size and volume data. All these extra facts are used to help produce a good, solid design.

As we shall see, however, it is still possible to produce powerful and extremely useful data models with just the main set of building blocks.

2.2 MAIN CONCEPTS

There are three main concepts used in Data Analysis:

1. The Entity (Type)
2. The Attribute (Type)
3. The Relationship (Type)

To be precise in naming these concepts, the word 'type' should be included, because all of these concepts describe *classes* of different sorts. To make things simpler in the book, and to keep the explanations short I will omit the word type and simply refer to Entities, Attributes and Relationships. This is actually in line with what has tended to happen in most firms using the techniques. The nuisance of having to say Entity type and Attribute type every time a Data Model was discussed, for example, has caused the full names to be abbreviated in practice.

2.2.1 Entities

An Entity is a *classification* of things, which can be given a precise definition showing whether or not any one thing is within that class.

The importance of definition of an Entity cannot be overstressed. Without a definition, it will never be clear whether or not a 'thing' in your system is included in a class. This means that when you want to populate your files and databases, you won't know which bits of information go where. Is Joe Bloggs a patient or a doctor? Is he an employee or a pensioner? Only the definition will tell you. The definition is also essential when describing how the activities are to act. Are they to act on all the occurrences in the class or only some of them? Do we pay a salary only to employees or to pensioners as well?

What is or is not an Entity depends on what the business does – it is the context of the business which determines the important classes of things to it.

To a hospital, Patient, Hospital, Doctor, Illness, Symptom, Disease and so on might all be important Entities, Entities which would have no relevance in, for example a chocolate factory where they might talk about Consignments, Product Types, Processes, Orders, Invoices and Chocolate Recipes.

When I talk about context, I am talking essentially about the business activities – what the business does and wants to do. Even in these first stages of discovering the concepts of Data Analysis, we are already seeing the dependence the Data Analysis has on the Activity Analysis.

For example:

Activity	Data
Pay the Employees	*Employee (Entity)*
Invoice the Customer	*Customer (Entity)*
Receive an Order	*Order (Entity)*
Deliver the Consignment	*Consignment (Entity)*
Register the Patient	*Patient (Entity)*
Record the Accident	*Accident (Entity)*
Determine the Illness	*Illness (Entity)*

Entities can be 'concrete' (things we can hear, touch, see and smell) – such as the Patient, Employee, Hospital, Doctor and so on above – or they can be 'abstract'. Abstract Entities tend to be the most numerous. This is because the human race thinks in terms of concepts in order to achieve most of its objectives. Examples above include the Illness, Symptom, Disease, Product type and Process. Even Order and Invoice are abstract concepts; it's just that we've got used to seeing them on paper and tend to think of them as real. In fact, an order is a request for goods and services and an invoice is a demand for payment for goods or services received, both of which are abstract concepts.

When we do a design, Entities are potentially the records in our file or database design. There may be reasons why the mapping is not exactly one for one, but these reasons are to do with the limitations of our DBMS, file-handling package or even paper filing systems. In an ideal world, we wouldn't need to make these compromises.

To help us understand which Entities are of interest to a business we build them into a picture called the "Data Model". A Data Model is a diagram which shows how the concepts fit together in our system – how the Entities relate to one another.

The Data Model is an ideal vehicle for discussion, not only with other members of your team, but with the user. The user doesn't have to be shown the Data Model; it can be used as a means of 'walking around' the facts with him or her. Some users who have asked to see what is being used to arrive at such a clear picture of their business, have even taken a liking to the picture itself – some have become better at data modelling than the analysts! On the whole, however, it is more likely that the Model will remain a powerful means of feeding back to the user what he or she has told you.

An Entity is represented in the Data Model by a box. What shape of box you use doesn't actually matter, but try to make it different to those you use for *other* concepts used in development, such as records or programs, to avoid confusion. I will be using a rectangular box. Write the Entity name in the box in the singular.

An example is given in Figure 2.1.

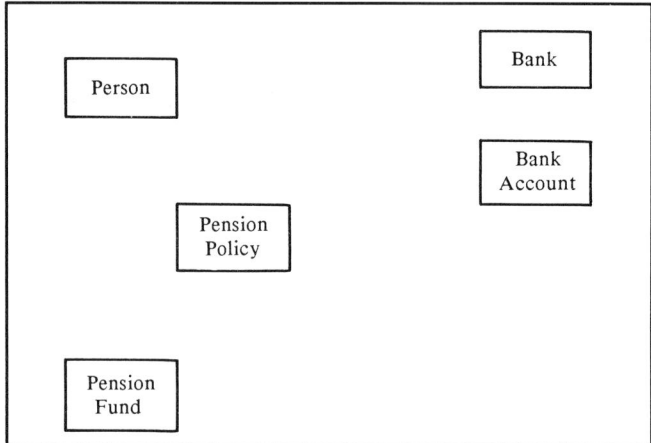

Figure 2.1 Entities are shown on a Data Model using boxes

Before describing Attributes, it may help if I draw an analogy with language at this point. When we are analysing systems we are actually analysing language. Think of the Entities as the *Noun* of our language of systems.

2.2.2 Attributes

An Attribute is a classification of the properties of the occurrences of an Entity. Figure 2.2 is an example. In the table are shown lots of 'occurrences' of the Entity Person. It also shows some actual properties about them: Smith is 6' 10"; is a Miss; is a Lily and is female. The Attributes classify these properties.

Attributes can become data items in the records we choose during design. Again, we may find that the particular software or 'mechanism' we are using gives a mapping which is not entirely one to one, but it is the limitations of the mechanism which cause this.

We will see later on, in the chapter on Activity Analysis, that Attributes are also to be found in 'Data Flows'. These are packets of data which are input to or output from activities. When we design systems these data flows can be implemented as forms, listings, transaction records, electronic mail messages and several other sorts of mechanism. Attributes in their guise as the contents of a data flow can thus also become the data items on these other sorts of media as well.

Where a particular Attribute is allowed to have only certain values, we can describe these either

Attributes	Surname	Height	Title	First name	Sex
Entity = Person	Smith	6'10"	Miss	Lily	Female
	Jones	5'9"	Mr	John	Male
	Eland	4'2"	Doctor	Hugo	Male
	White	5'8"	Mrs	Faith	Female
	Brown	6'2"	Mr	Walter	Male
	Purple	6'4"	Mr	William	Male
	Liffy	5'0"	Sir	Hugh	Male
	Long	4'11"	Miss	Patience	Female
	Marple	5'2"	Miss	Winifred	Female

Figure 2.2 Attributes are classes of Properties of an Entity

as *Permitted Values* or *Permitted Ranges*. Sex of a person, for example, has two permitted values – male and female. Permitted values can also be codes. If we had given a code to the Attribute Sex of a person, then we might have had the permitted values as 'M', say, and 'F'. Where permitted values are coded we would expect to see a description of their meaning and possibly a definition for the less obvious cases.

Permitted ranges enable us to describe the permitted values of an Attribute in a shortened way.

Suppose I had an Attribute Salary of Person. I could describe the permitted values of Salary of Person by showing that they must come within the range of +£50 000 to +£6000. Obviously, if I had to write down every permitted value to describe this fact I would have to write down 44 001 values!

Permitted values and ranges are used to validate and manipulate the data.

For example:

IF Sex of Person = 'F'
  Add '£2000' to Salary of Person (!)

There can be times when some Attributes don't apply to some of the occurrences of the Entity. In other words, the Attributes aren't necessarily classifications of the properties of *all* the occurrences of an Entity. I might decide, for example, that Date Person Married is a useful Attribute. From the Figure, it is clear that there are some of our people who are not married, so that particular Attribute doesn't apply to them. When an Attribute applies to only some of the population, we call the Attribute 'optional' (as opposed to mandatory, which means that it must have a value) and that Attribute is allowed to have a *Null* value – a value which effectively means 'not applicable' or 'not yet applicable'.

Generally speaking, we tend to use space and zero to represent the null value.

Attributes describe only *one* Entity and are thus the property of that Entity, with a precise definition, validation rules and code values applicable to that Entity. This is fundamentally important. It is only when an Attribute is described in the context of its 'owning' Entity that it *can* be given a precise definition, validation rules and Permitted Values. To give an example, let us suppose that we had two Entities in our system (a zoo system, say) of Keeper and Animal. Then let us assume that we allowed Attributes to describe more than one Entity and one of the Attributes we were interested in was Sex. Now the Sex of a Person can be Male or Female, but it is conceivable that the Sex of an Animal could be Male, Female or possibly Hermaphrodite! Clearly, we have a set of Permitted Values which is different for an Animal and for a Keeper. There is therefore a good reason to have two Attributes – Sex of Person and Sex of Animal with different Permitted Values and Different Definitions.

What do we do, however, if we find some Attributes which share codes or even part of their definitions with other Attributes? Ideally, we want to save ourselves the effort of having to repeat the codes, code meanings and that part of the definition which is common.

What we can use to get over this problem are what are called *General Attributes*.

For example, Date of Birth, Date of Placing Order, Date Employee Leaves, all use 'Date'. We can define 'Date' as a General Attribute, give it a format – YYMMDD, for example – and also describe some general validation rules, such as months between 01 and 12, days between 01 and 31 except for months 04, 06, and so on.

When we describe a specific Attribute, such as Date of Birth, we can then refer to the general definition, validation rules and format defined for 'Date', but add to this the more precise rules we may wish to apply to the Date of Birth itself (for example, it cannot be in the future).

Attributes are not shown on the Data Model. They remain as additional facts about the Entities, which are not shown pictorially.

Finally, to continue our comparison with language and the components of language, the Attribute can be thought of as the *Adjective* of our language of systems.

14   *A Simple Introduction to Data and Activity Analysis*

Customer	sent	Order	⎫
Order	has	Order Line	
Order Line	is for	Product	⎬ Relationships between two entities
Product	has	Price	
Customer	has	Address	⎭
Product	is made from	Product	⎫
Person	is married to	Person	⎬ Relationships between an Entity with itself
Course	is preceded by	Course	
Employee	reports to	Employee	⎭

Figure 2.3 Relationships

2.2.3 Relationships

A Relationship is a type of association between two Entities or of an Entity with itself. It is expressed using a verb. This is shown in Figure 2.3.

Relationships are classifications of the actual Relationship 'occurrences' between the Entity 'occurrences'. We can see this better by looking at an example, and a simple one is shown in Figure 2.4.

Relationships can be implemented in many ways.

In Relational-type DBMSs, they are implemented using a mixture of 'foreign keys' (the key of another record) and indexes or their equivalent. If you were to use ADABAS, for example, which is a Relational-like DBMS, you would use Descriptors and Superdescriptors.

In IMS, we may use the 'logical' and 'physical' pointers/links together with secondary indexes. (IMS is probably one of the more complicated DBMSs to design.)

In Codasyl-type DBMSs they become 'sets' (the implementation of Relationships is probably the most straightforward using Codasyl-type DBMSs).

In two-level networks, Relationships primarily become link paths and where the two-level nature of the mapping rules defies direct mapping, indexes can be used.

Conventional files are treated in the same way as Relational-like DBMSs. The difference is that

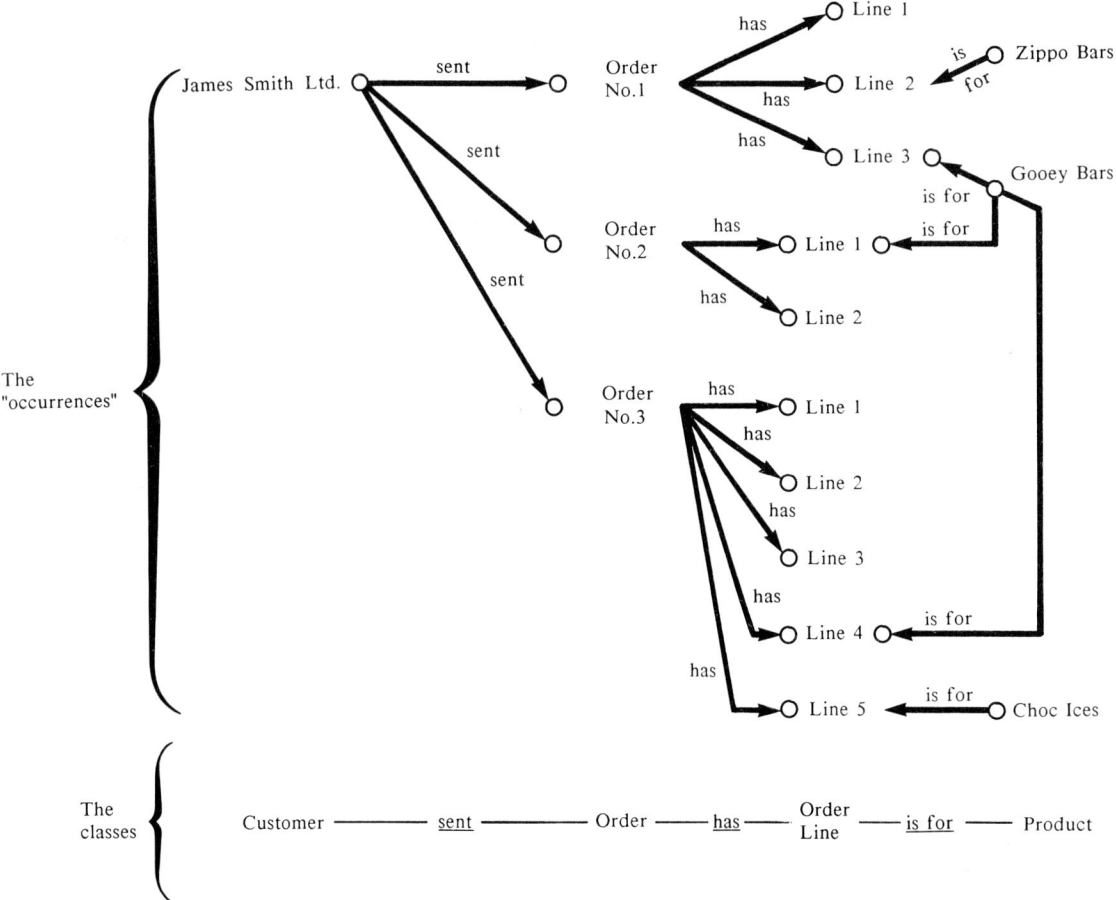

Figure 2.4 Relationships classify actual associations between the entity 'occurrences'

you will have to maintain the indexes you create, whereas by using the DBMS the indexes are maintained for you.

The same sort of approach is also applicable to paper-based files.

Relationships are shown on the Data Model by a line linking the Entity or Entities. The name of the Relationship can be written beside the line.

A Relationship can always be 'read' in two ways by using the 'active' and 'passive' voice of the verb.

If you want to make it clear on the Model, you can (although this is only a guideline) use a 'clockwise' naming convention, whereby you read the names in a clockwise direction.

Figure 2.5 shows the use of the diagrammatic convention and the naming rule.

Again, to continue our comparison between language and the concepts of Data Analysis, Relationships are the *Verbs* of our language of systems.

In Figure 2.6, the Bank and Pension Model shown earlier is expanded to provide another example.

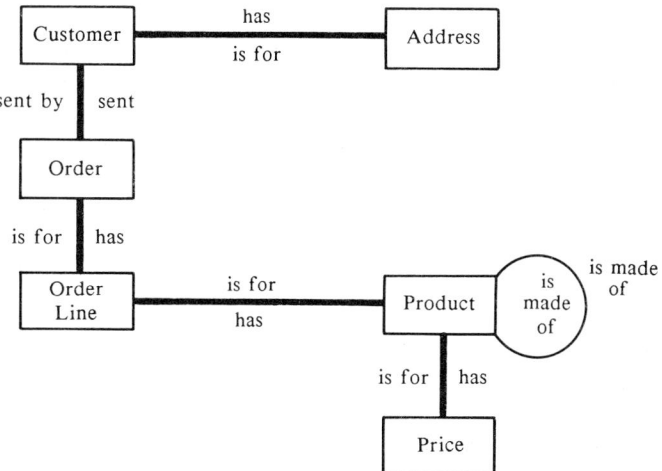

Figure 2.5 Relationships shown on the Data Model

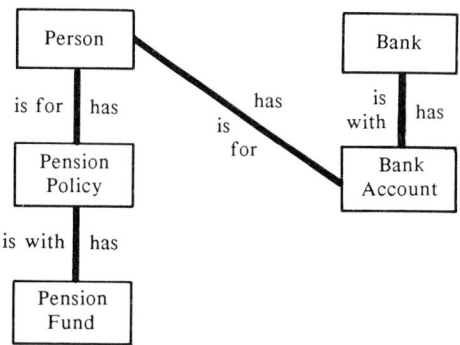

Figure 2.6 Relationships using the Bank and Pension example from Figure 2.1

2.3 DIAGRAMMATIC TECHNIQUES

Now we have all the basic diagrammatic conventions in place, we can use the Model to describe additional deliverables which will not only strengthen our picture of the system we are modelling, but provide valuable extra information of direct use in design. These additional conventions will be described next.

Our Data Model so far has simply shown the main concepts, and is missing some necessary and important additional deliverables. These are:

a) The degree of the Relationship
b) The optionality of the Relationship
c) Exclusivity of Relationships
d) Entities identified by Relationships
e) Entity sub-types

We will now explore each of these new deliverables using our Data Model to build up a picture.

16 *A Simple Introduction to Data and Activity Analysis*

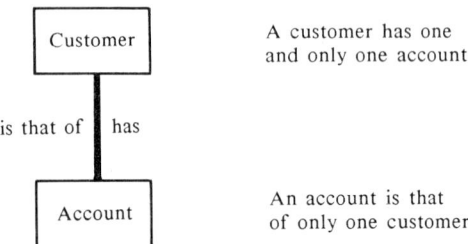

Figure 2.7 One-to-one relationships

2.3.1 Degree of Relationships
The Data Model in Figure 2.6 does not tell us how many of one Entity is related to how many of another Entity.

This understanding of the number involved is termed the degree of a Relationship and there are three sorts of degree:

    One-to-one   1:1
    One-to-many   1:N
    Many-to-many   M:N

One-to-one Relationships
When Entities are related on a one-to-one basis, it means that one of an Entity (A) has the Relationship with only one of Entity (B) and vice versa.

An example is shown in Figure 2.7.

In general, one-to-one Relationships are not very common. Even the example used is not very true to life. Most firms allow for a customer to have more than one account. We will assume for the purposes of this example, however, that our business rules state that a customer can have only one account, and in this case the Data Model would look as shown in Figure 2.7.

One-to-many Relationships
This is by far the most common degree. When Entities are related on a one-to-many basis, it means that one of an Entity (A) has the Relationship with one or more of an Entity (B), but one of an Entity (B) has the Relationship with only one of an Entity (A).

An example is shown in Figure 2.8.

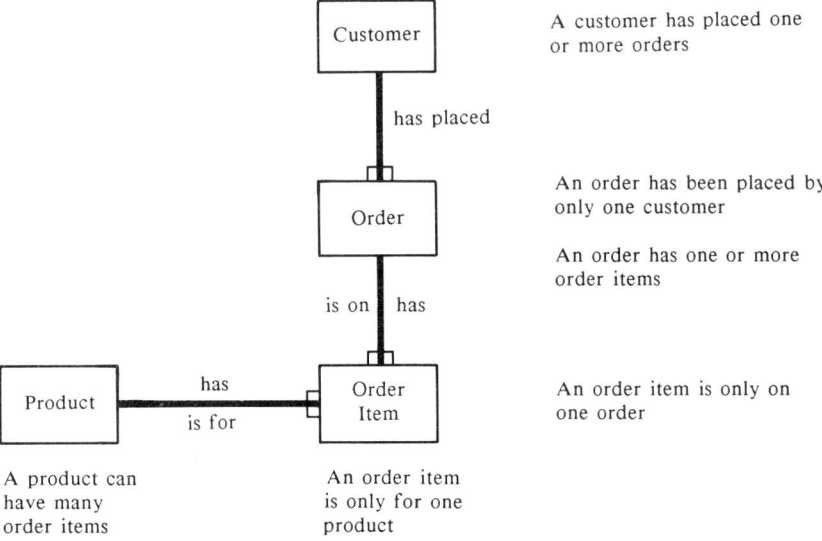

Figure 2.8 One-to-many relationships

The diagrammatic convention I will be using in this book is the trident, or 'crow's foot' symbol to represent the idea of 'many'.

You can use whatever symbol you like, as long as you use it consistently in your projects and organisation. It doesn't matter as long as it is clear. In Figure 2.9 I have shown some other examples of conventions which you could be using.

Many-to-many Relationships
When Entities are related on a many to many basis, it means that one of an Entity A has the Relationship with *one or more* of an Entity B and one of an Entity B could have the Relationship with one or more of an Entity A.

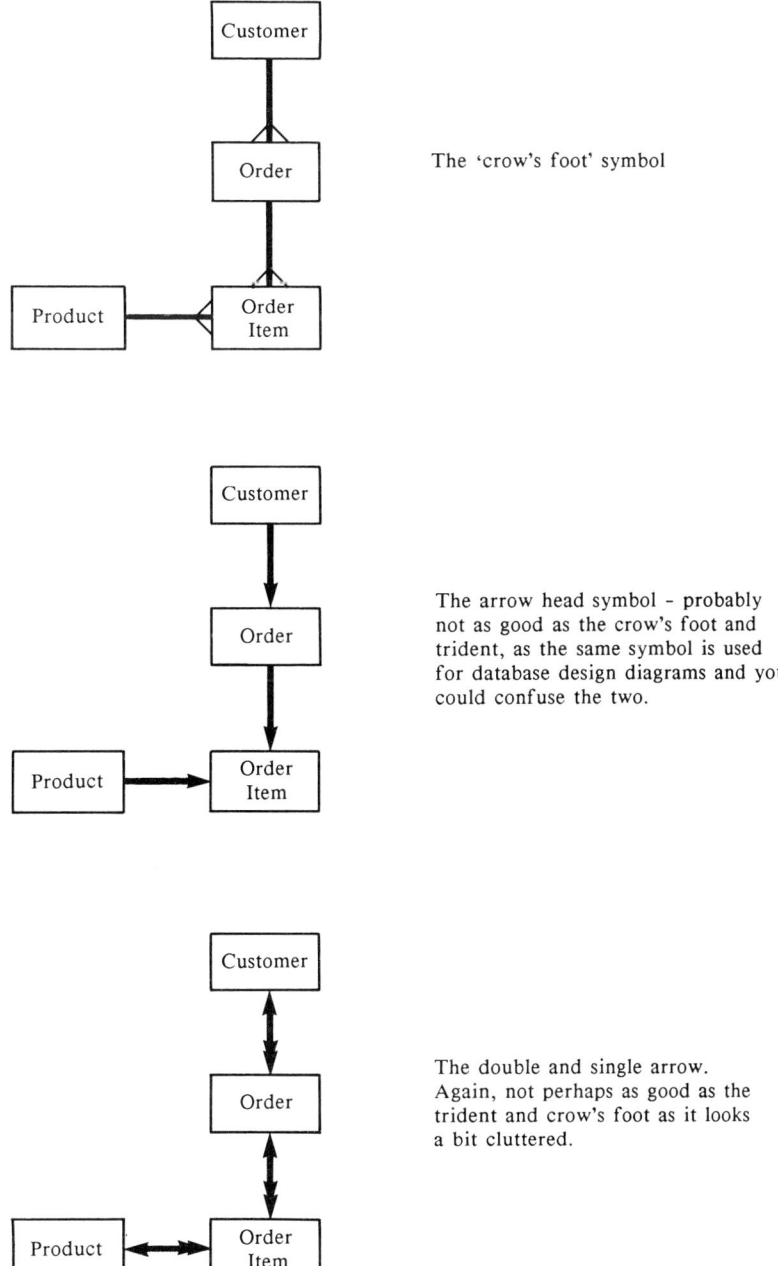

Figure 2.9 The diagrammatic conventions do not matter

An example is shown in Figure 2.10.

Note that there is nothing wrong with many-to-many Relationships in a Data Model. Some methods require you to 'remove' them all by adding artificial Entities which sit in between the two original Entities. We will be seeing in a later chapter how we need to investigate many-to-many Relationships, but your Data Model could still have them after this test and there is nothing wrong about this.

Optionality

Until now, we have assumed that there is always a Relationship between our Entities. What happens, however, when there are some of our 'occurrences' which do not have a Relationship with others? We say then that the Relationship is *optional*. Optionality allows us to model the part of language which is the word *may*. A customer *may* have placed orders; a product *may* have order items.

The opposite of optional is mandatory. This concept allows us to model the part of language which is the word *must*. An order *must* always have been placed by a customer; an order item *must* always be for a product.

18   *A Simple Introduction to Data and Activity Analysis*

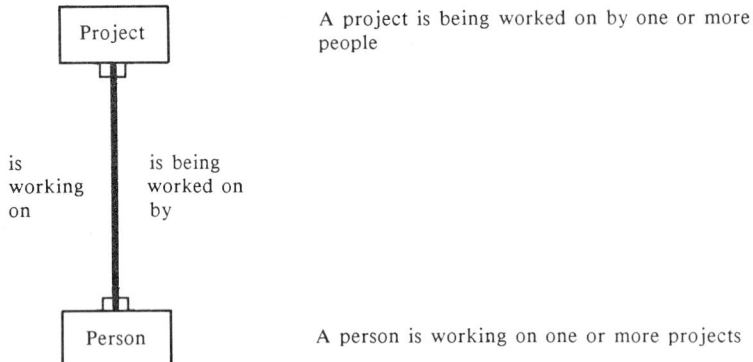

Figure 2.10 Many-to-many relationships

The Relationship is split into two to examine optionality. This is because a Relationship can be optional when viewed in one way and mandatory when viewed from the 'other end'.

A customer MAY have placed orders
An order MUST always have been placed by a customer

I will be representing optionality by using a dotted line. In Figure 2.11, we see the three types of optionality described using examples.

* Totally mandatory   [A purchase order always has order items. An order item is always on a purchase order]

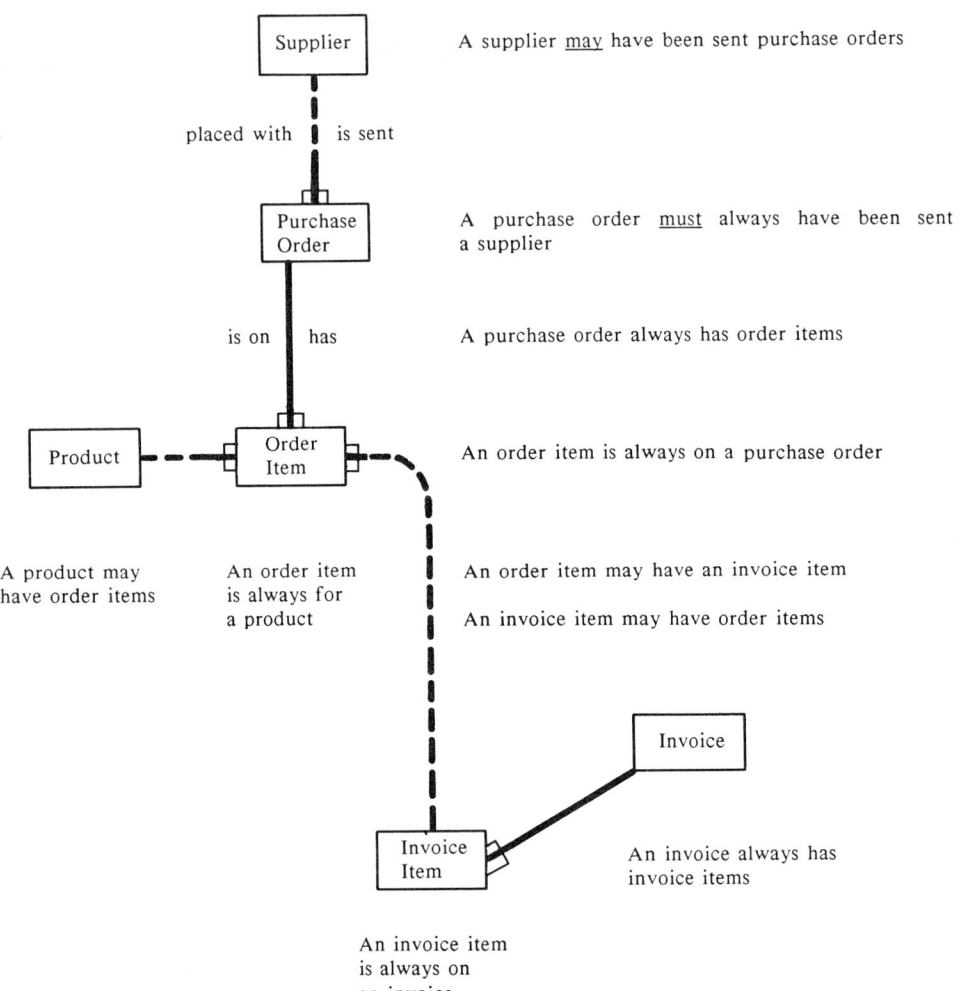

Figure 2.11 Examples of optionality

Data Analysis 19

"Contingent" or partially optional   [A supplier may have been sent purchase orders, but a purchase order must always have been sent to a supplier]

* Totally optional   [An order item may have an invoice item, an invoice item may have order items. This latter example describes the case where we may have sent a purchase order, but it hasn't been invoiced yet and we may have received the invoice, but haven't yet matched it with the order we sent]

A summary of the diagrammatic conventions is shown in Figure 2.12.

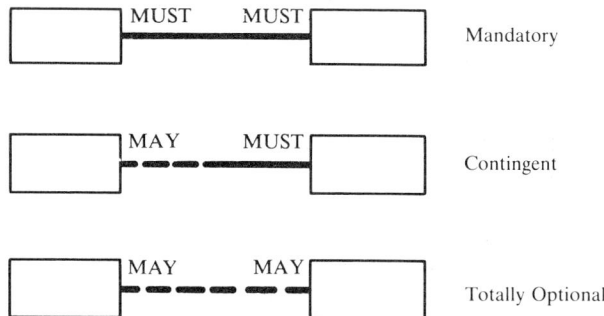

Figure 2.12 Summary of the diagrammatic conventions

Now just as you have different diagrammatic conventions for degree, you may also find different diagrammatic conventions for optionality. The most common is the little 'o' symbol used on the line. [Those using SSADM and LDMS are warned here that their Data Models are not as good at expressing optionality – the 'o' in their Models sits on the middle of the relationship and it is not clear whether the Relationship is contingent or totally optional.]

Ideally, the little 'o' should be placed on the side where the 'May' part of the name starts. In Figure 2.13 the same example is shown but using the little 'o' convention.

Again, it doesn't matter what convention you use as long as it's clear, can represent what you need to show [i.e. contingent, mandatory or totally optional] and is used as standard in your firm.

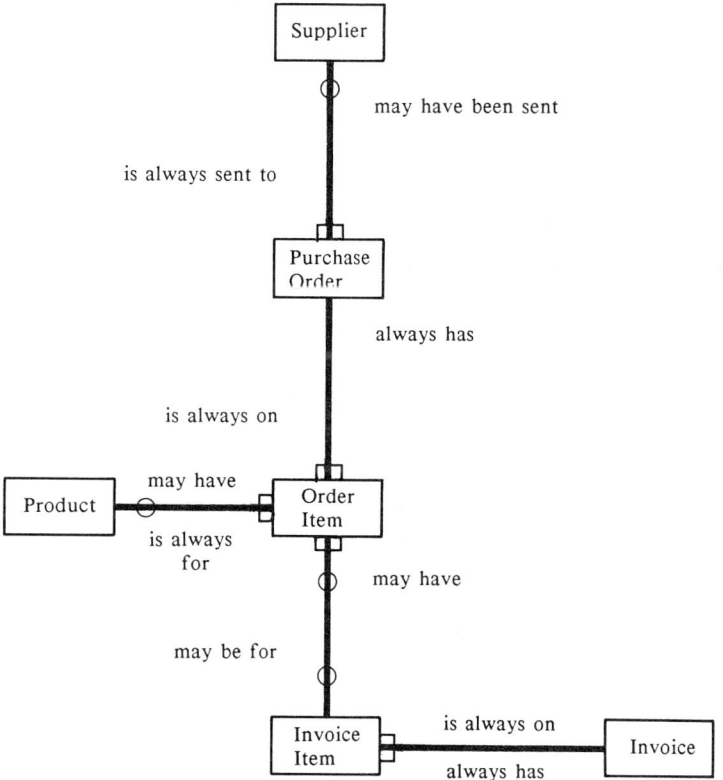

Figure 2.13 Optionality shown using the little 'o' symbol

20   *A Simple Introduction to Data and Activity Analysis*

Exclusivity

Exclusivity is best explained using examples. The two main types of exclusivity are shown in Figures 2.14 and 2.15.

Figure 2.14 shows mandatory exclusivity.

An occurrence of Entity A is related *either* to an occurrence of Entity B *or* to an occurrence of Entity C but *cannot* be *neither*.

Figure 2.15 shows optional exclusivity.

An occurrence of Entity A is related *either* to an occurrence of Entity B *or* to an occurrence of Entity C *or* neither.

You can get more complicated types of exclusivity, particularly when many Entities are involved. It is best to describe these in words. You can use the symbol shown in Figure 2.16 to indicate it is complex and that you need to refer elsewhere for a description of the business rules.

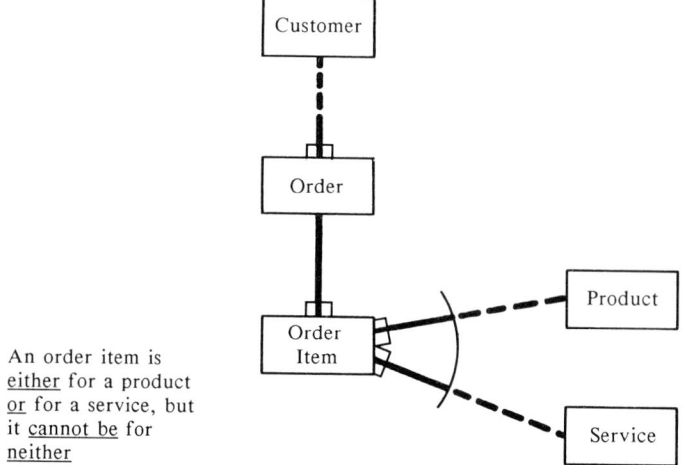

Figure 2.14 Mandatory exclusivity

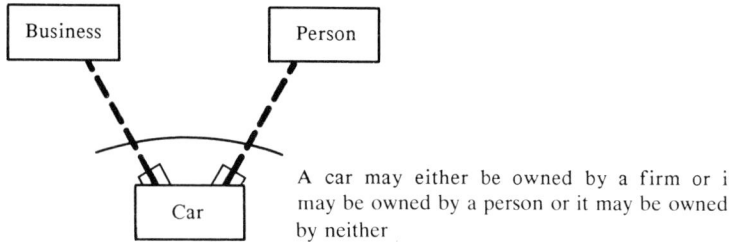

Figure 2.15 Optional exclusivity

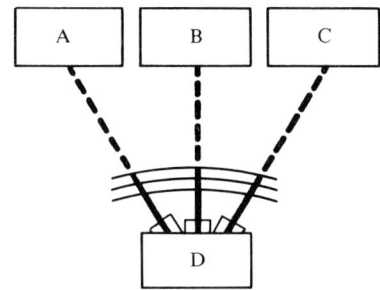

Figure 2.16 Complex exclusivity

Entities identified by relationships

This is not an easy concept to grasp, but is very powerful and useful in design. We can identify an Entity using an Attribute or a combination of Attributes:

Example

        A patient could be identified by his National Health Service Number

        A business might be identified by its VAT number

Furthermore, an Entity can have more than one identifier. When we list the Attributes of an Entity we *never* duplicate Attributes across Entities, thus the following is wrong:

Customer
Customer Code (Identifier 1)
Customer Name
Customer Address
VAT Number (Identifier 2)

Order
Customers Order Number
Customer Code INCORRECT
Order Date
Our Order Number (Identifier)

We must always ensure that Attributes *describe only the Entity*. We have *no need* to add "foreign" attributes to describe Relationships – that is what relationships are for.

Sometimes, however, we find we need to be able to identify an Entity but it has no obvious identifier of its own.

An example is shown in Figure 2.17. The Performance's Attributes are as shown, but it has no obvious identifier: none of these Attributes, singly or in combination, would identify the Entity.

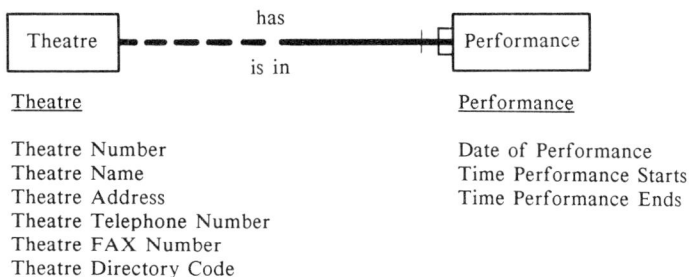

Theatre

Theatre Number
Theatre Name
Theatre Address
Theatre Telephone Number
Theatre FAX Number
Theatre Directory Code

Performance

Date of Performance
Time Performance Starts
Time Performance Ends

Figure 2.17 Identifying relationships – example 1

Now we know that a performance "owes its existence", as it were, to the existence of the theatre. We know this partly because the relationship is mandatory – a performance is always in a theatre. We can go a bit further than this, though.

If a *change of theatre would create a different performance*, then that performance is identified by its Relationship to the theatre. We show this on the model by a dash.

The underlined phrase is the important bit.

"If it is not possible to change an occurrence of an Entity A to a different occurrence of an Entity B then Entity A is identified by its Relationship to Entity B"

This has important uses in design.

Using Codasyl DBMSs, your database design could have a mandatory automatic set and the attributes as shown could all become data items. There is *no need* to place the Theatre Code or any other 'foreign key' in the Performance record, unless direct access is required – in which case the key required will be added to the data items of the Performance record. This *might* involve duplicating the Theatre Code if this is part of the key required.

This principle is also true of IMS designs, using segments and physical pointers.

Using other sorts of DBMS – Relational, two-level network etc. – you will need a key irrespective of whether or not you access the entity directly. But you may have a choice. For example, the theatre has two possible identifiers – the Theatre Code and The Theatre Directory Code. In this case the key of the Performance may be based on one of these two identifers *or* it may itself have more than one identifier, depending on the direct accesses required. This can be determined during design.

At the business analysis stage, it is useful to leave your options open, but provide the deliverable on which a choice can be made. This is what the 'identified by' symbol does.

Another example is shown in Figure 2.18, where the Stock Entity is identified by its Relationship to both Product and Depot. Stock cannot 'move' Depots without being a different occurrence of Stock, nor can it 'move' products without being a different occurrence. Notice the Attributes which are shown.

2.3.2 Entity Sub-Types

Entity sub-types are mutually exclusive groups of Entity occurrences within the main Entity class,

Example
        Entity : Person
        Entity Sub-types : Employee
                Not Employee

22 A Simple Introduction to Data and Activity Analysis

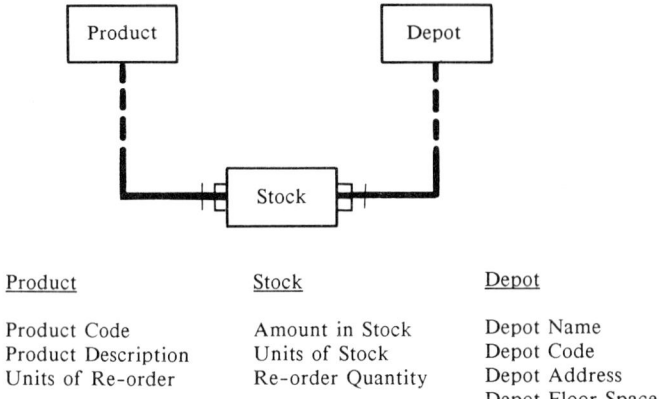

Product	Stock	Depot
Product Code	Amount in Stock	Depot Name
Product Description	Units of Stock	Depot Code
Units of Re-order	Re-order Quantity	Depot Address
		Depot Floor Space

Figure 2.18 Identifying relationships – example 2

The most important part of the definition is that they are *mutually exclusive* and that the resulting sub-types cover the whole Entity population.

Figure 2.19 illustrates this using a sports club as an example. The sports club has members, and the actual members are shown in the figure. The entity sub-types are full member, student member and day member, and our 'occurrences' can *all* be classified by these sub-types.

Where you are not sure, you can always use the method of logical division of classes which is simply as shown in Figure 2.20. If Not Day Member is empty, you have your subdivision.

It is important that we create an attribute to enable our sub-types to be identified.

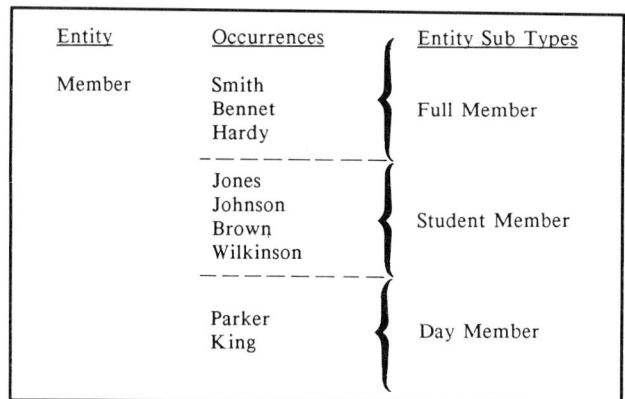

Figure 2.19 Entity sub-types

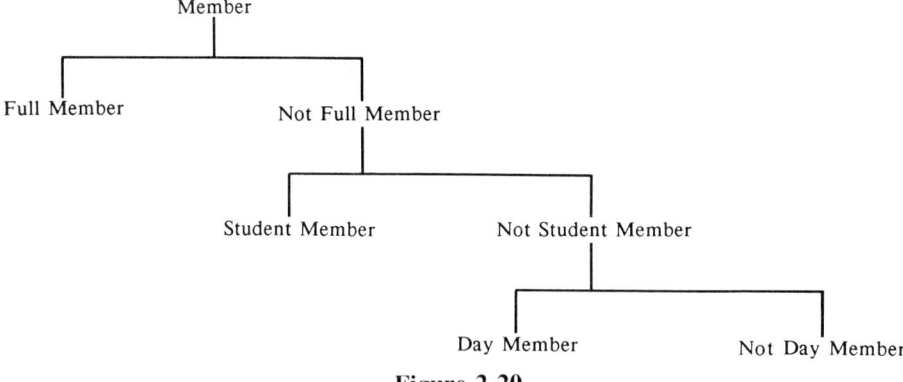

Figure 2.20

Figure 2.21 shows the Attributes of the Entity 'Member' and some occurrences. An Attribute Type of Member has been created to describe the sub-types as a whole and a code created for each sub-type – f = full; d = day; s = student.

The table also shows another important property of Entity sub-types – some Attributes may be applicable to only one sub-type. In the example, Hours of Play is applicable only to Day Members.

This is important in design as this knowledge will help us to decide, depending on the power of our DBMS, whether we will need variable length records or compression, or have to split records to save wasted space.

Member

Attributes   occurrences

Type of Member	(F = Full)	(D = Day)	(S = Student)	(F = Full)
Name	Smith	King	Jones	Bennet
Date of Birth	21.6.50	20.5.40	9.9.79	11.10.55
Sex	M	F	M	F
Hours of Play	—	9 to 5	—	—

Figure 2.21 Representing entity sub-types – attribute

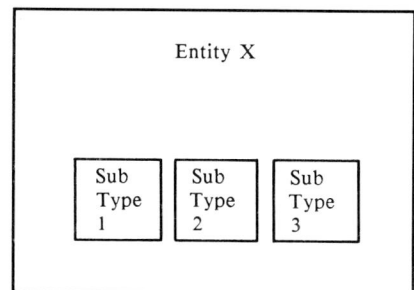

Figure 2.22 Entity sub-types – diagrammatic representation

An Entity may have many important categories of sub-type. In effect, most of our Attributes are describing sub-types. Sex, for example, describes the sub-types of 'Male' and 'Female'.

Where the sub-types have *different relationships* with other Entities, however, it is important to show them on the Data Model and they are represented diagrammatically, as shown in Figure 2.22.

An alternative representation is shown in Figure 2.23. This is now appearing in some Analyst Workbench products and has the advantage that many different groups of sub-types can be shown. This is not always possible with the convention used in Figure 2.22. The disadvantage of that shown in Figure 2.23 is that it can clutter the diagram and become unclear in large Models.

The club example is shown in Figure 2.24. This shows the advantage of sub-types in helping you express business rules.

A member is either a full member, day member or student.
Students pay no subscription, but their school must be known.
A school may have many student members.
Day members pay a daily subscription (each time they turn up)
Full members pay an annual fee.
[Because day members may not yet have appeared and full members may not yet have paid, the relationships here are optional] *All* members may become the player in a game. The game is organised first for a date and the players subsequently found.
Furthermore, all the members belong to a club.
It can be seen from this example that by recognising sub-types, we have enhanced the ability of the Data Model to express business rules.
Entity sub-types have an important role to play when activities are described. It should be clear from the Data Model that our activities – such as sending out subscriptions, organising games and

24   *A Simple Introduction to Data and Activity Analysis*

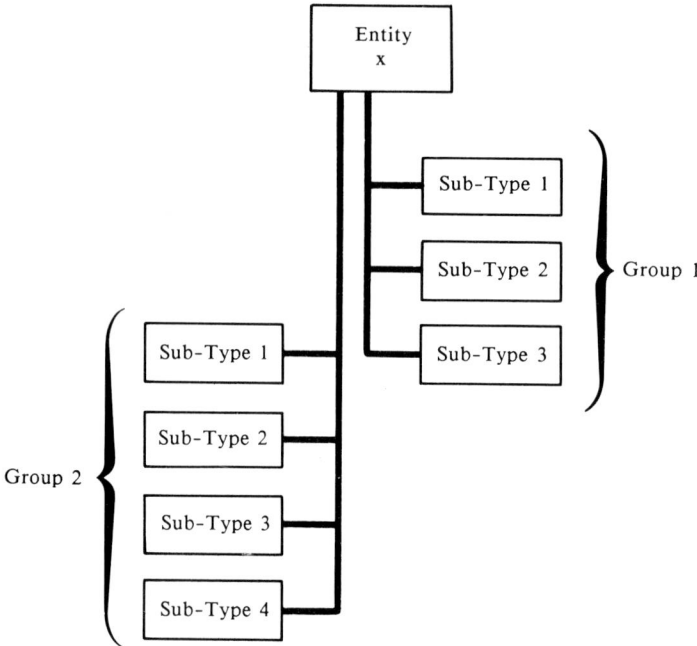

Figure 2.23 Alternative representation

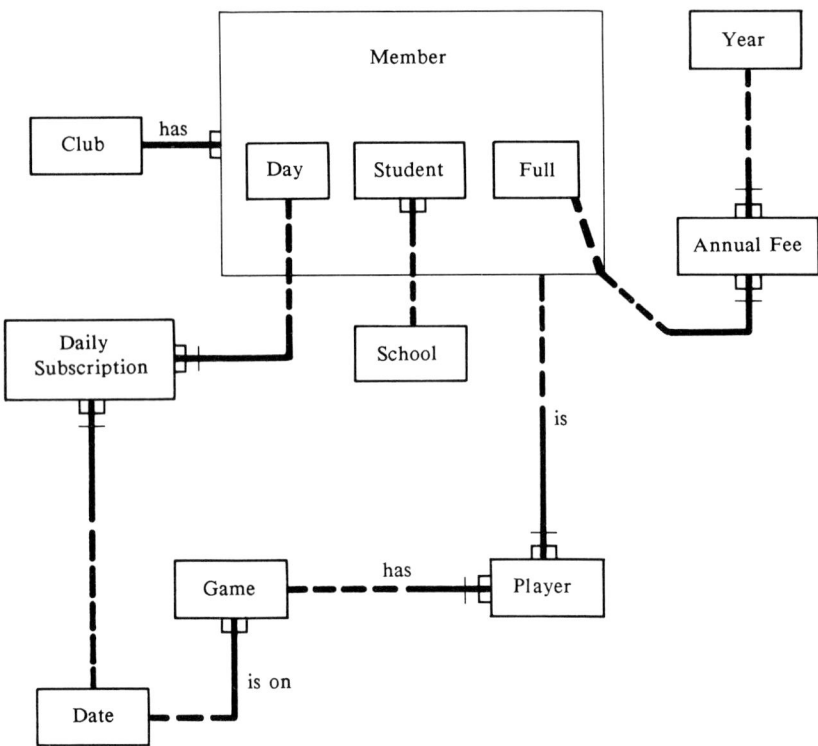

Figure 2.24 Entity sub-types

enrolling new members – are going to be influenced by the fact that students don't have to pay subscriptions, and when enrolling students you will need to know their school.

Interestingly, sub-types and exclusivity are interchangeable on the Data Model and it is really up to you whether you use one or the other.

The reason is quite logical. Exclusivity describes the case where any one Entity (occurrence) is related *either* to one Entity or another Entity (and so on). This means that we could create sub-types for each of the mutually exclusive groups to which the Entity is related. The example in Figure 2.25 perhaps explains this more easily. The sub-types are created with names related to the things they describe.

Another example is shown in Figure 2.26.

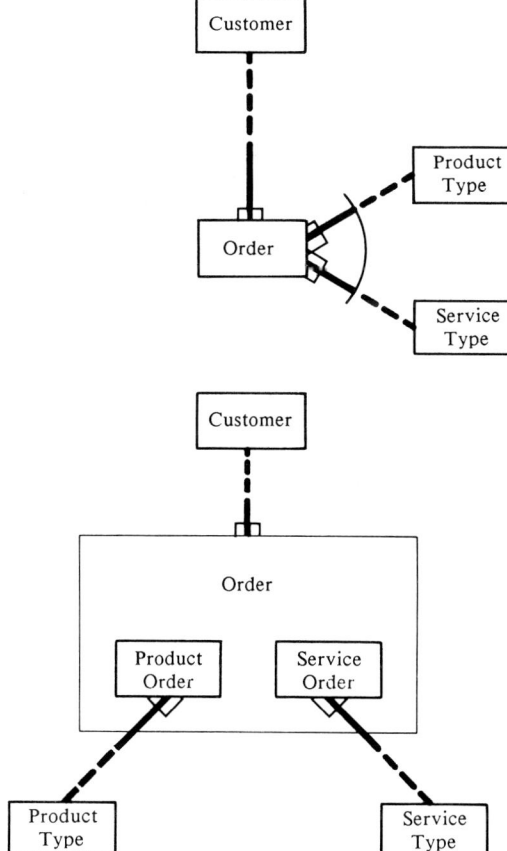

Figure 2.25

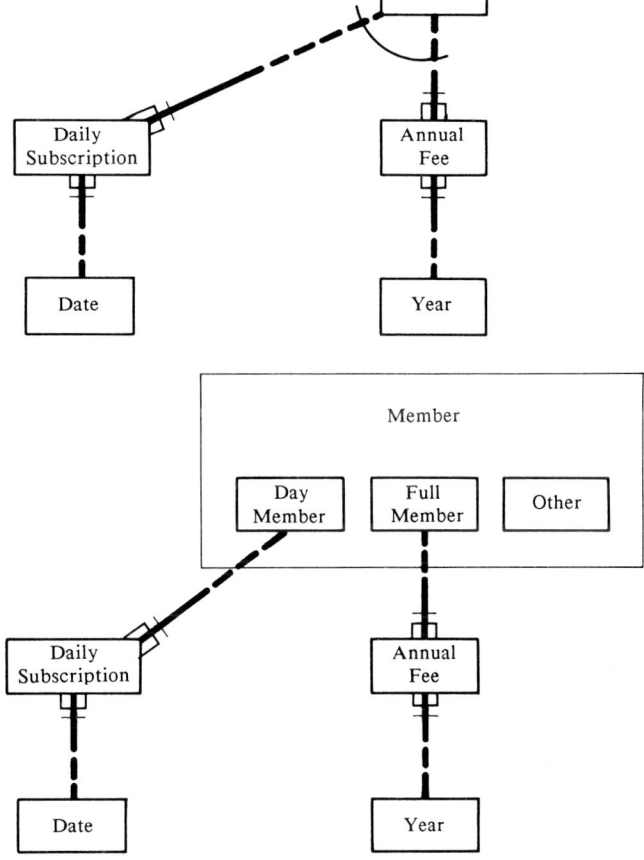

Figure 2.26

2.4 OTHER DELIVERABLES OF DATA ANALYSIS

In a short introductory book such as this, it is not possible to describe all the other deliverables (facts) which can be collected during Data Analysis. There are, however, a considerable number of extremely useful deliverables which can be collected during Strategy Studies, Tactical/Feasibility Studies and Detailed Requirements Studies.

To give you some idea of the additional facts that can be collected, I have extracted a list of all the deliverables from Book 1 of the Analysis within the Systems Development Cycle series. I have also shown the applicability of each deliverable to a particular System Development Cycle stage. This information is shown as Figures 2.27, 2.28, 2.29, 2.30. 2.31, 2.32 and 2.33.

Book 1 provides a definition for all of these deliverables and explains their purpose.

		Strategy	Tactical	Detailed
2.	Responsibility			
	3 Analyst responsible for update/allowed to look	✓	✓	✓
	4 Chief/Deputy	✓	✓	✓
	5 Type of Access Allowed	✓	✓	✓
	6 Date last updated/looked at	✓	✓	✓
7.	Versions			
	7 Version	✓	✓	✓
8.	Names			
	9 Standard Name	✓	✓	✓
	10 Abbreviated Name	✓	✓	✓
	11 Other Names (Synonyms)	✓	✓	✓
12	Definition	✓	✓	✓
13	Entity Sub-Types			
	13 Sub-Type		✓	✓
14.	Identifiers			
	14 Identifier		✓	✓
15.	User Access/Authorisation to Entity Types			
	16 User Allowed Access	✓	✓	✓
	17 Type of Access Allowed		✓	✓
	18 Range of entities Allowed to Access/partitioning criteria		✓	✓
	19 Proposed/Current		✓	✓
	20 Date of Change		✓	✓
29.	Level of Organisation Unit at which Entity Type Applicable			
	29 Organisation Unit	✓	✓	✓
30.	Partitioning			
	31 Organisational Unit at which Partitioning occurs	✓	✓	✓
	32 Range of Entities/Partitioning Criteria		✓	✓
	33 Volumes at this Unit			
	34 Total Population of Entities of this Type, Partition and Organisation Unit on this Date	Approx.	✓	✓
	35 Figures Projected or Actual		✓	✓
	36 Date/Month/Year/Time Measurements taken	Approx.	✓	✓
37.	Archiving Rules at this Unit			
38.	Event Signalling End of Life			✓
39.	Attribute Type and Value Representing Event			✓
40.	Time Span After Event Entity to be kept			✓

Figure 2.27 Entity type

		Strategic	Tactical	Detailed
101	<u>Responsibility</u>			
	102 Analyst Responsible/Allowed to look	✓	✓	✓
	103 Date last updated/looked at	✓	✓	✓
	104 Chief/Deputy	✓	✓	✓
	105 Type of Access Allowed	✓	✓	✓
106	<u>Versions</u>			
	106 Version	✓	✓	✓
107	<u>Abbreviated Name</u>	✓	✓	✓
108	<u>Definition</u>	Brief	✓	✓
109	<u>Relationship Type End</u>			
	110 Name of Relationship Type from this End		✓	✓
	111 Synonyms from this End		✓	✓
	112 Basic Optionality (Y/N)		✓	✓
	113 Basic Type of Degree (1:1, 1:N, M:N)		✓	✓
	115 Total Population Sampled			✓
	114 <u>Degree Detail</u>			
	116 Number of Owner Entities with this Degree			✓
	117 Percentage with this degree			✓
	118 Degree			✓
	119 Certainty Indicator			✓
	120 Maximum/mode Indicator			✓
121	<u>Relationship Type End Association</u>			
	122 Exclusivity Rules		✓	✓
	123 Inclusivity Rules		✓	✓

Figure 2.28 Relationship type

		Strategic	Tactical	Detailed
201	<u>Responsibility</u>			
	202 Analyst Responsible/Allowed to Look		✓	✓
	203 Date Last updated/looked at		✓	✓
	204 Chief/deputy		✓	✓
	205 Type of Access Allowed		✓	✓
206	<u>Versions</u>			
	206 Version		✓	✓
207	<u>Names</u>			
	208 Standard Name		✓	✓
	209 Abbreviated Name		✓	✓
	210 Other Names (Synonyms)		✓	✓
211	<u>Definition</u>		Brief	✓
212	<u>Entity Type or Sub-Type Described</u>		✓	✓
213	<u>Attribute Type Association</u>			
	213 Type of Association Generic			✓
	Sub-Attribute			
	Redefines			
214	<u>Format</u>			
215	Format			✓
216	Units of Measurement			✓
217	Units Scale			✓
218	Precision Required			✓
219	<u>Access Authorisation</u>			
	220 Type of Access Allowed			✓
	221 User/Job Allowed Access			✓
	222 Range of Values Allowed to Access			✓
223	<u>Validation Rules</u>			
	223 Validation Rule			✓
224	<u>Derivation Rules</u>			
	224 Derivation Rule			✓
225	<u>Archiving Rule</u> (Longevity)			
226	Time span before Entity end of life Event that			
	Attribute Type must be Archived			✓
227	Time Span before Deletion of Entity that Attribute			
	Type must be deleted			✓

Figure 2.29 Attribute type

28 *A Simple Introduction to Data and Activity Analysis*

		Strategic	Tactical	Detailed
501	Permitted Values			
502	Value (Code or Other)			✓
503	Value Name			✓
504	Value Meaning/Definition			✓
505	Value Abbreviated Name			✓
506	Start Date			✓
507	End Date			✓
508	Not Known Value? (Y/N)			✓
509	Null Value? (Y/N)			✓
510	Initial or Default Value? (Y/N)			✓
511	Permitted Ranges			
512	Maximum Value			✓
512	Minimum Value			✓
513	Start Date			✓
514	End Date			✓

Figure 2.30 Permitted values and ranges

		Strategic	Tactical	Detailed
401	Version Number	✓	✓	✓
402	Date From	✓	✓	✓
403	Date To	✓	✓	✓
404	Agreed/Under Discussion/Rejected	✓	✓	✓
405	Users Agreeing/Rejecting	✓	✓	✓
406	Abbreviated Name	✓	✓	✓
404	Advantages	✓	✓	✓
405	Disadvantages	✓	✓	✓
406	Proposed By (Users)	✓	✓	✓
413	Responsibility			
414	Analyst Responsible/Allowed to look	✓	✓	✓
415	Type of Access Allowed	✓	✓	✓
416	Chief/Deputy	✓	✓	✓
417	Date Last Accessed	✓	✓	✓
418	Descriptive Name	✓	✓	✓
419	Type of Model Fuzzy	✓		
	Overview		✓	
	Detailed			✓

Figure 2.31 Model version

	Strategy	Tactical	Detailed
DATA ITEM			
301 Name of Data item			✓
302 Descriptive name			✓
303 Format			✓
304 <u>Codes/Ranges</u>			
304 Code/Range			✓
305 <u>Responsibility</u>			
306 Designer			✓
307 Type of Access			✓
308 Date Last Accessed			✓
309 Chief/Deputy			✓
RECORD TYPE			
601 Name		✓	✓
602 Descriptive name		✓	✓
603 <u>Responsibility</u>			
604 Designer		✓	✓
605 Type of Access		✓	✓
606 Date last Accessed		✓	✓
607 Chief/Deputy		✓	✓
FILE TYPE			
701 Name	✓	✓	✓
702 Descriptive name	✓	✓	✓
703 <u>Responsibility</u>			
704 Designer	✓	✓	✓
705 Type of Access	✓	✓	✓
706 Date Last Accessed	✓	✓	✓
707 Chief/Deputy	✓	✓	✓
710 <u>Record-File Usage</u>			
710 Usage		✓	✓
721 <u>Record Partitioning</u>			
722 Partitioning Criteria		✓	✓
723 Maximum Records for that partition		✓	✓
<u>File/Record Occurrences</u>			
725 Number of Records of that Type		✓	✓
726 Date on which figures Apply		✓	✓
711 <u>File Implementations</u>			
712 Type of Implementation		✓	✓
713 Implementation Name		✓	✓
714 File Implementation Name		✓	✓
715 Descriptive name		✓	✓
716 <u>File Mapping</u>			
717 File Mapping name			✓
718 Physical File Identifier			✓
719 Date From			✓
720 Date To			✓

Figure 2.32 Design and design mapping

30   *A Simple Introduction to Data and Activity Analysis*

	Strategy	Tactical	Detailed
SET/LINK			
801 Name		✓	✓
802 Descriptive Name		✓	✓
803 <u>Ends</u>			
803 End Name		✓	✓
804 <u>Responsibility</u>			
805 Designer		✓	✓
806 Type of Access		✓	✓
807 Date Last Accessed		✓	✓
808 Chief/Deputy		✓	✓
IMPLEMENTATION			
901 Name	✓	✓	✓
902 Full Descriptive Name	✓	✓	✓
903 <u>Responsibility</u>			
904 Designer	✓	✓	✓
905 Type of Access Allowed	✓	✓	✓
906 Date last Accessed	✓	✓	✓
907 Chief/Deputy	✓	✓	✓
SYSTEM			
1001 <u>Usage</u>	✓	✓	✓
1002 Proposed/Current	✓	✓	✓
1003 Name	✓	✓	✓
1004 Short name	✓	✓	✓
1005 Description	✓	✓	✓
1006 <u>Responsibility</u>			
1007 Designer	✓	✓	✓
1008 Type of Access allowed	✓	✓	✓
1009 Date last Accessed	✓	✓	✓
1010 Chief/Deputy	✓	✓	✓
MAPPING OF ANALYSIS TO DESIGN CONCEPTS			
1101 <u>Attribute Mapping</u>			
1102 Most Reliable Source			✓
1103 <u>Code Mapping</u>			
1104 Mapping Match			✓
1105 <u>Entity Mapping</u>			
1106 Most Reliable Source		✓	✓
1107 <u>Relationship Type Mapping</u>			
1108 Most Reliable Source		✓	✓
1109 <u>Entity Group Mapping</u>			
1110 Mapping	✓		
1111 <u>Record Partitioning/Entity Type Partitioning Mapping</u>			
1112 Most Reliable Source		✓	✓
1113 <u>Entity Occurrence Mapping</u>			
1114 Mapping		✓	✓

Figure 2.33 Design and design mapping – continued

2.5 AN EXAMPLE MODEL

In order to pull all these concepts and diagrammatic conventions together, I have drawn an example Model in Figure 2.34.

The Data Model shown is for zoos – a number of imaginary zoos. We can 'walk around' to find out more about what these imaginary zoos need information about and how the zoos work.

Zoo is our main Entity, and all our zoos have one or more employees, of which there are only two sub-types (of which we need information on the Data Model) – keepers and non-keepers (other).

Our zoos always have a number of animal areas – fields, enclosures and the like – which, obviously, are places where animals are kept.

Some zoos also have buildings. But these are not buildings where animals are kept; they are administrative or public amenity buildings, such as cafes and toilets.

Some animal areas have cages in them and we always site cages in animal areas – for example, the tiger enclosure may have several cages in it. Some of these cages are empty, some have animals in

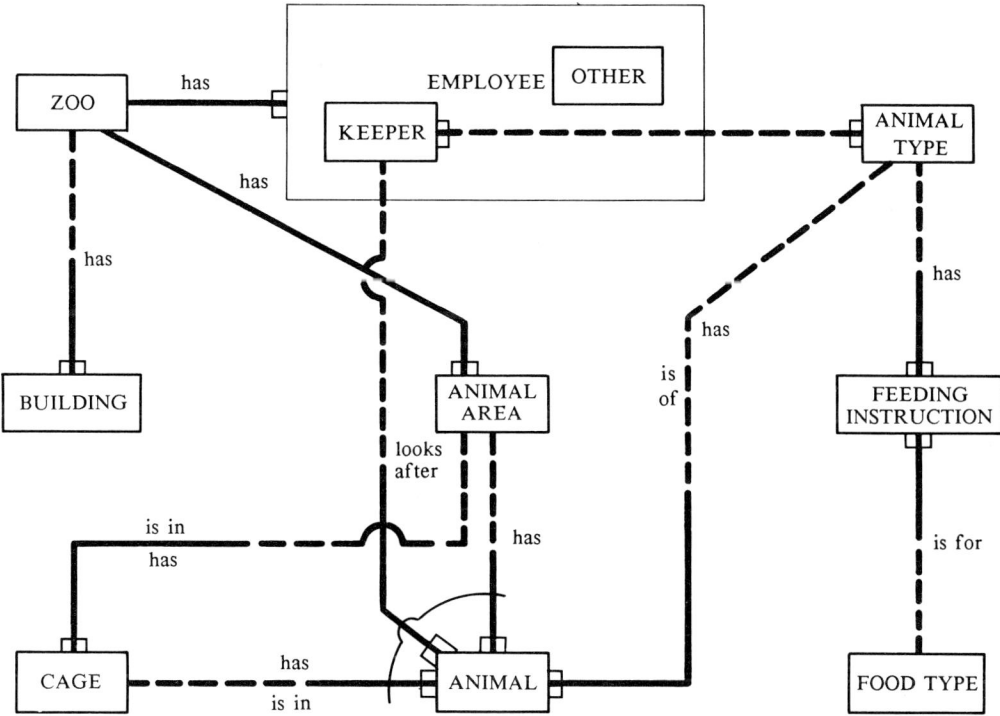

Figure 2.34 The zoo data model

them and we can put more than one animal in a cage. All of our animals are tagged (identifiable) – this means that even the gazelles in our larger enclosures are all individually identifiable and we have records on them – date purchased or born, name (if it has one) and so on.

Animals are either in cages (and hence we know which animal area they are in- or they are in an animal area roaming free – e.g. the gazelles, antelopes and wolves.

Every animal we have is allocated a keeper who is responsible for that animal. Keepers may be made responsible for a number of animals. Not all keepers look after animals – juniors and trainees undergo a training programme before allocation, and new keepers when they first start won't have been allocated animals.

We keep a record of what each animal actually is and every animal we have is classified in this way.

Thus, for example, Bimbo is an elephant, Lofty is a giraffe, Leo a lion and Mr. Chips a chimpanzee.

This classification enables us both to keep general data on the type and species of our animals and build up records about them as a group. We do keep records of species we haven't got, partly to help us decide whether to acquire that species and partly for historical reasons – for those animal types we no longer keep, but once did. It also helps us to keep records which our general hands use on feeding instructions.

Feeding instructions don't apply to every animal type we have, but it provides us with useful data on the type and quantity of food the animals need. This gives us a picture of the proper nutritional balance we must provide for each animal. We try to provide as varied a diet as possible by using details about each food type, such as calorific value, contents, vitamin content, carbohydrate content etc.

Notice that we don't have individual diets for each animal.

Notice also that we don't reserve animal areas for one animal type. This means that in practice we mix animals in an animal area (although obviously we use our common sense here).

Finally, it helps us to know which types of animal the keepers are capable of looking after. Each keeper may be looking after only a subset of this range of types at any one time. But it is useful to know, if a keeper leaves or is sick, who else is capable of looking after the animals which were in his care.

This simple Data Model should have demonstrated the power of the diagram to convey a large amount of information. I have woven a story around it, adding examples and Attributes to give a wider picture, but I have essentially worked around the Data Model describing it.

This is exactly the same technique you can use to verify your findings with a user – he need not even see the Data Model.

32 A Simple Introduction to Data and Activity Analysis

This Data Model also again highlights the 'optimal' fact-recording nature of a Model – a minimum of words and symbols, but equivalent to over a page of text.

2.6 FUNDAMENTAL RULES OF DATA ANALYSIS

Before summarising the contents of this chapter, it is important that the main rules of Data Analysis are stated. They are simple, but immensely important.

a) *Each Element in the environment must be classified as either one Entity, one Attribute or one Relationship.*
   In other words you must classify the things you find in the scope of your study in only one way – something can't be an Attribute and an Entity, or an Attribute and a Relationship.
b) *An Entity must have Attributes.*
   In other words an Entity cannot be so unless it has Attributes.
c) *Relationships may only exist between Entities.*
d) *Only Entities have Attributes.*
   In other words Relationships cannot have Attributes.

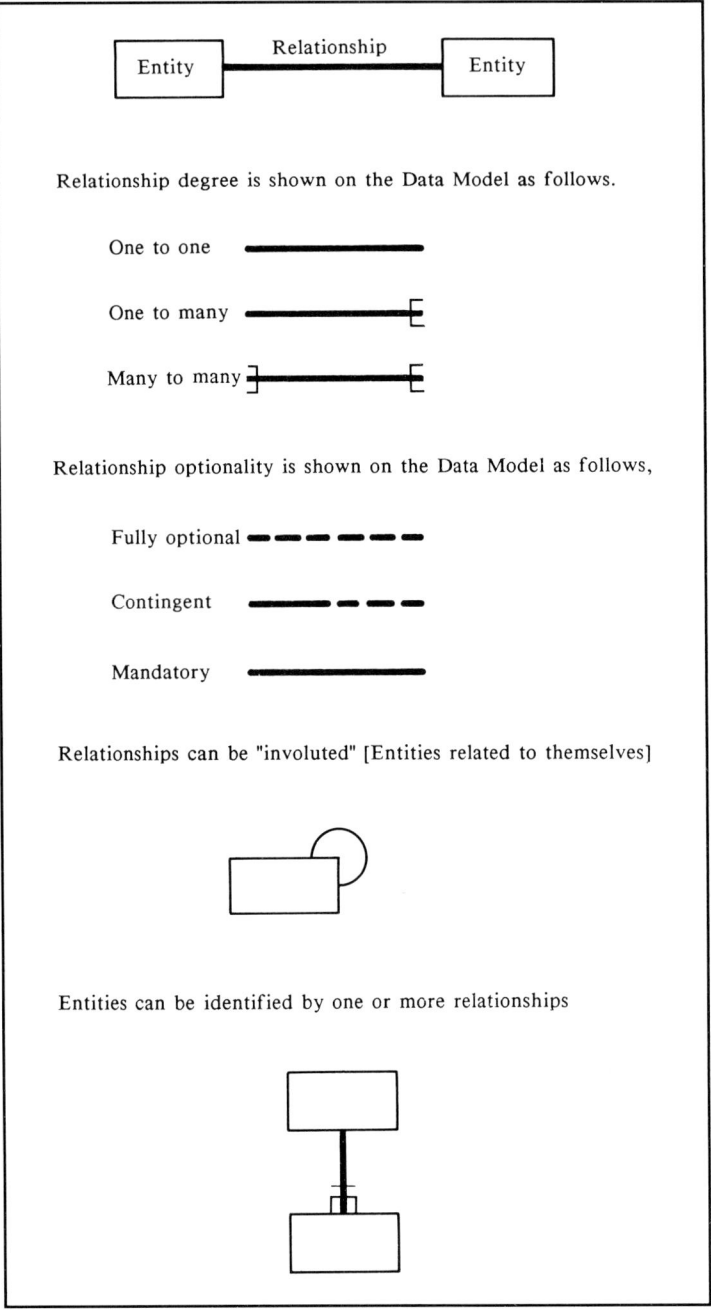

Figure 2.35

e) *An Entity occurrence must not belong to more than one Entity*
   In other words "Joe Bloggs" cannot be classified as both a Customer *and* a Supplier – you need to choose another Entity which allows Joe Bloggs to be both customer and supplier at the same time, e.g. "Business".

All Data Modelling depends on these rules.

2.7 SUMMARY

There are three main concepts used in Data Analysis – the Entity, Attribute and the Relationship.

Entities and Relationships are represented diagrammatically on a Data Model as shown in Figures 2.35 and 2.36.

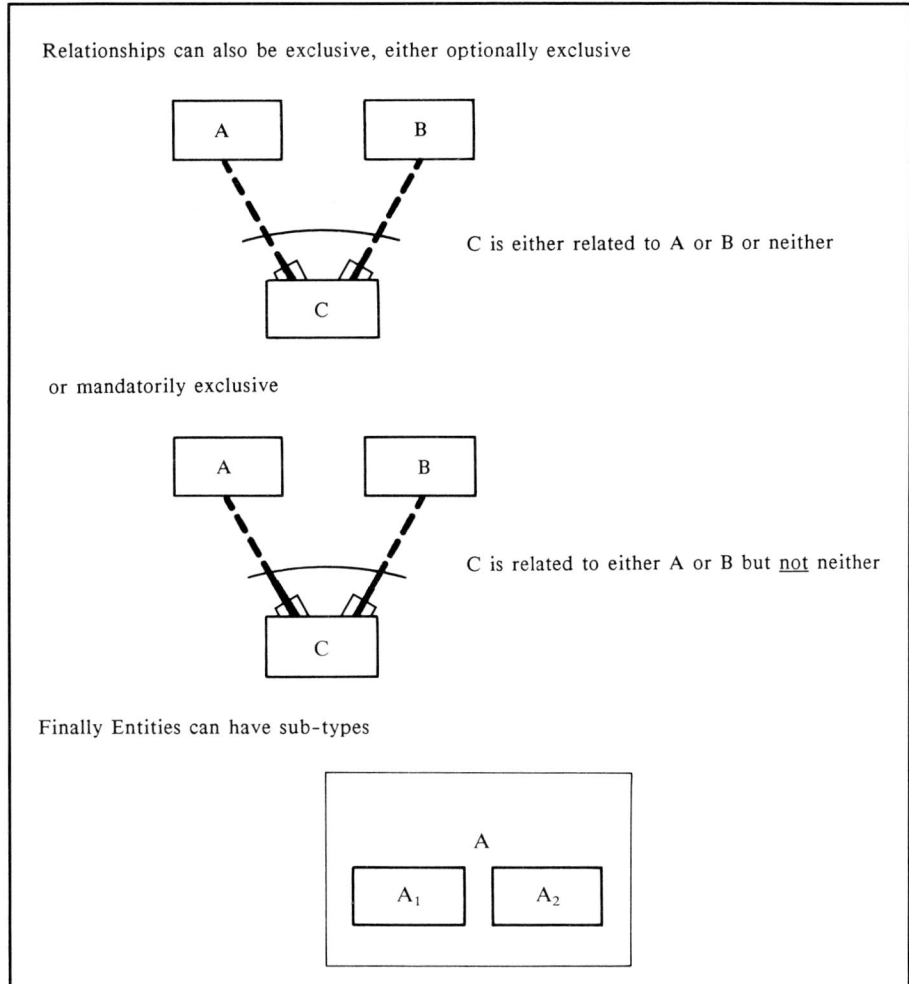

Figure 2.36

3 How to do Data Analysis

3.1 INTRODUCTION

This chapter shows you how to get the Data Analysis deliverables – the Data Model and all the related information from a number of well defined "inputs".

These inputs are those you would expect to get from the collection task (interviews, observation, meetings, study of existing documentation).

They fall into four main types:-

* Real world abstractions/classes
* Real world occurrences/things
* Design abstractions/classes
* Design occurrences/things

Real World Abstractions and Real World Occurrences

When a user talks about his existing system or we read policy documents, explanatory books or similar sorts of business type literature we often find that the business is being described in 'conceptual' terms and at either the abstract or 'occurrence' levels.

The difference between abstract and occurrence is the difference between classes of things and the things themselves. For example:

> "We take orders from customers quite regularly for products in our product range. We can get orders which specify many products. We have a standard price for the product. . . ."

That paragraph describes *classes* of thing – orders, products, customers – which are *potentially* Entities. But until we have done the analysis we don't know for sure.

"Joe Smith sent in Order No. 19654 recently which was for 16 cases of our Whizzo Gooey Bars, 20 cases of our Chocopopso Bars and 10 cases of our Whippy Flakes".

These are occurrences – the things themselves as opposed to their types.

When we do fact finding we often find that classes and things are mixed up in sentences. A user, for instance, often finds it helpful to give examples of what he means while he is explaining things to us. It is common for the examples to be clearer and more revealing than the classes he is attempting to explain,

Example
> Most of our products are priced, but some aren't. Orders always use the current price, but other prices are quite useful – for example John Smith's Order No. 19254 asked for Gooey Choc Bars, but the order came in after we'd upped the price from 10p to 12p and as we'd agreed a price of 10p with him we charged him the 10p.

If you look at this, the user's example contradicts his first statement – not all orders use the current price; some use a previously agreed price and there is probably a class of thing called an "Agreement" which records this.

When we do Data Analysis, we use both types of input – classes and things – and separate them for the purposes of analysis.

Design Abstractions and Occurrences

If we examine computer system specifications for record layouts, or look at listings and forms, we are looking at the "Design Abstractions". A Design Abstraction is simply the means by which the information needed manifests itself in the system design.

Look for   record layouts
           forms (input, output or master file)
           listing layouts
           screen layouts

The abstractions are simply the "templates": the record layouts and forms themselves.

If time is limited, for Data Analysis purposes concentrate on master record layouts and forms.

36 *A Simple Introduction to Data and Activity Analysis*

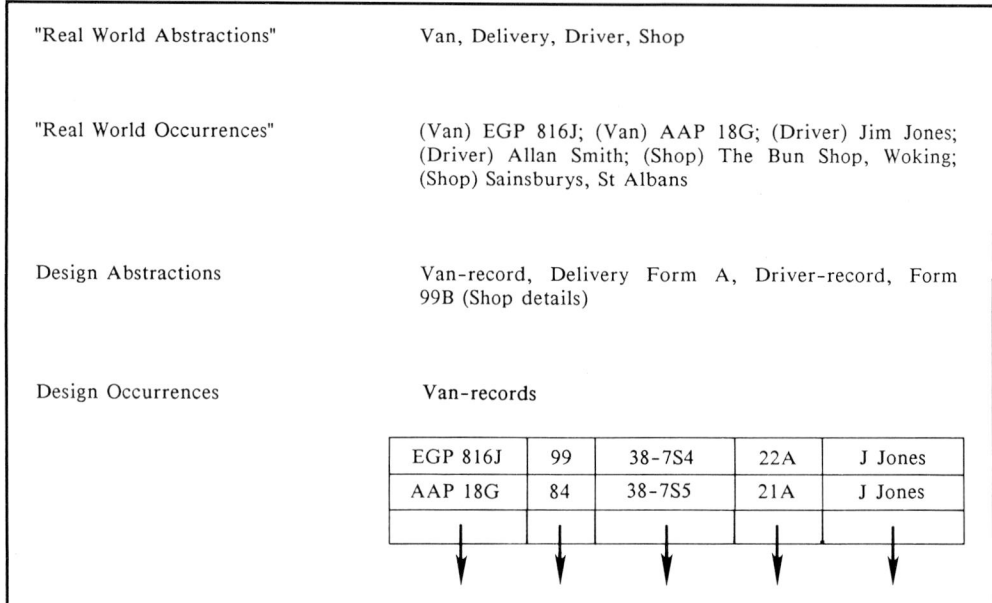

Figure 3.1 An example showing the difference betweeen each type of input

Design Occurrences are the forms filled in with real data or a print of the contents of a number of records showing the value of the items in each actual record.

Figure 3.1 is an example summarising the difference between each type of input.

All are *valid and legitimate* types of input.

By analysing them, you will get a picture of what the *existing* system looks like (warts and all!).

Because there are four types of input, there are four methods of Data Analysis.

Figure 3.2 summarises these four methods. Our "raw data" is of the four types mentioned, but we only have the one common output, a Data Model. Hence each method gives us the Data Model.

The advantages and disadvantages of each method are related more to the advantages and disadvantages of the types of input rather than the methods themselves. We will see this during the explanation of each method.

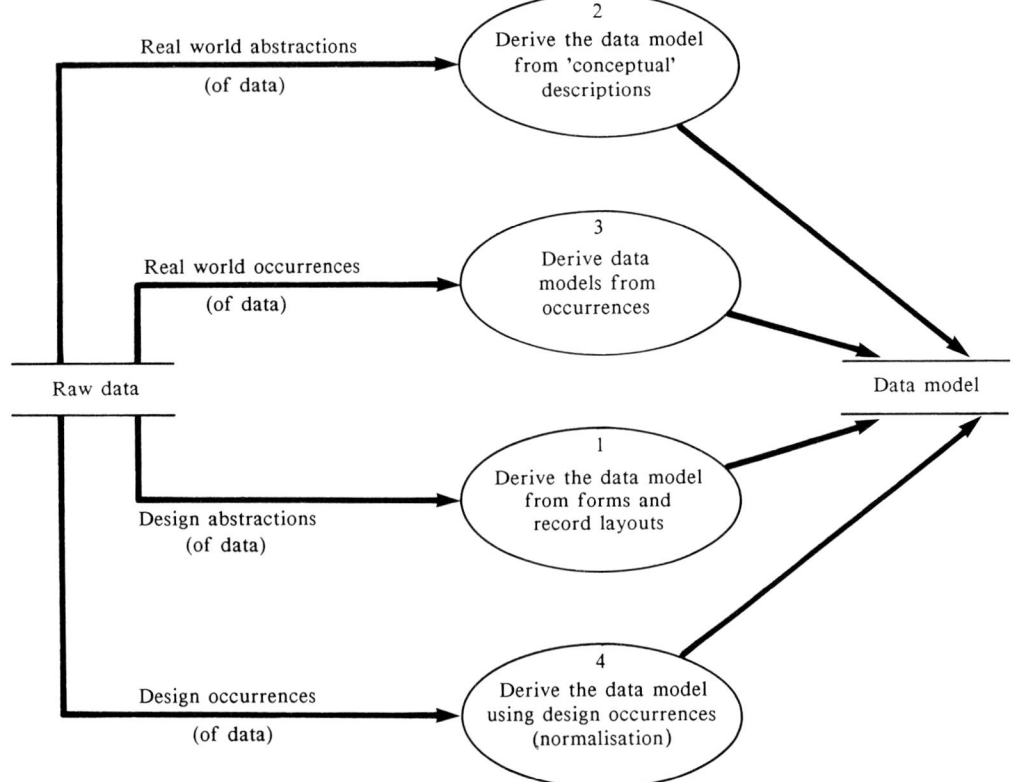

Figure 3.2 Summary of the four methods of data analysis

3.2 ANALYSIS
As we have seen in the introduction, there are four methods of Data Analysis:

* Deriving the Data Model from Design Abstractions – such as forms and record layouts.
* Deriving the Data Model from Conceptual Descriptions (interview notes etc.)
* Deriving the Data Model from Conceptual Occurrences
* Deriving the Data Model from Design Occurrences – this is the well known method of "normalisation".

Throughout the rest of this chapter and the book itself, I will be using one example to demonstrate the methods. It is based on "Course Administration", and is about the activities and data needed by a training firm to organise and run its courses.

You will be able to see how a Data Model, and subsequently the activity models, are built up using this example.

3.2.1 Using Forms and Record Layouts
On the following pages you will find four examples of forms and record layouts (Figures 3.3, 3.8, 3.14 and 3.19), which I will use to demonstrate the basic steps to follow when analysing forms and record layouts.

I will show you how to derive a Data Model from each form, but I will not attempt to merge them as we go along. The merging process will be described later as a separate step.

SCHEDULES OF COURSES FOR YEAR: ......

COURSE NO: .... COURSE NAME: ....
NO OF SESSIONS: ....

Public/ In-house	Start Date	End Date	Lecturers	Hotel/Location

Figure 3.3 Example 1 – Form 1

38 *A Simple Introduction to Data and Activity Analysis*

The basic steps in analysing a form or record layout are fairly simple, but need attention to detail and careful thought to be done well. Although they bear some resemblance to the steps of "normalisation" the emphasis is on building the Data Model as you go along.

1. List out the Data Items on the form and indicate where one group of data items is repeated with respect to another. Where a single data item is in the *plural* (e.g. Hotels, Courses) assume this data item is also repeated.
   Ignore words which are 'design' oriented or dependent e.g. schedule, report, listing, form, print, date of print etc.
2. Split the repeating from the non-repeating groups.
   Draw a line between the group of data items in the non-repeating group and the repeating group and add the "many" trident symbol to the repeating group end.
   Do this for as many times as there are repeating groups within repeating groups.
3. Pick out or choose a name for the thing which is being described by all the data items.
   Names are not always obvious. This often requires some thought. If you can't find a "real world" name give it a name corresponding to any obvious important data items or groups of items.
4. Check each data item. Is it describing the class of thing you have given the name to?
   Ask "of what", "where" and "when".
   Could it describe anything else, any other hidden class of thing in the list of data items?
   If it can, remove these data items from the set they are in. Name the new set and create a one to one Relationship from the new set to the old.
5. Draw the Data Model separately and list the potential Attributes. Do not duplicate Entities if they appear more than once. Merge the Relationships together.

Form 1 – Schedule of Courses for Year (see Figure 3.3)
Step 1. There are two repeating groups – one is a group of data items as shown with the lecturer data item also repeating, as we can see from the "s". We assume until verified that it is the lecturer's name which is the data item. See Figure 3.4.
Step 2. The data items are split, and one to many Relationships are created. See Figure 3.5.
Step 3. Course is an obvious choice for the first group of items, but the second group poses a problem. What is being described? The start and end date give the clue. The course is a type of course e.g. Basic Systems, so the group of four data items describe an actual giving of the course. See Figure 3.6.

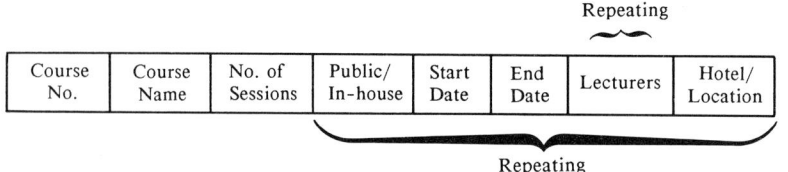

Figure 3.4 Example 1 – Step 1

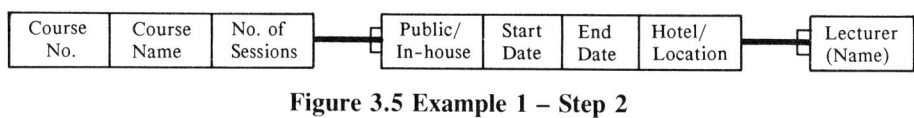

Figure 3.5 Example 1 – Step 2

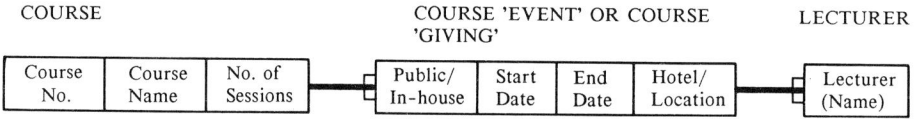

Figure 3.6 Example 1 – Step 3

Step 4. Course number is the identifier of the course, course name describes the course and the number of sessions is the number of sessions in the course. Public/In-house describes whether the course event is a public or in-house one. Start date is of the course event, end date is of the course event, Hotel/Location is the location of the course event. Hence no change is needed.
Step 5. The model from Form 1 is shown in Figure 3.7.

Form 2 – Lecturer's Student List (see Figure 3.8)
Step 1. The block headed 'students' is repeated with respect to the top block. The block headed 'been on one of our courses before?' also repeats – notice the plural names. See Figure 3.9.

How to do Data Analysis 39

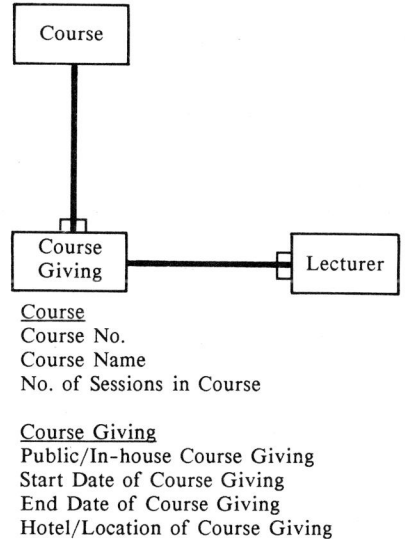

Course
Course No.
Course Name
No. of Sessions in Course

Course Giving
Public/In-house Course Giving
Start Date of Course Giving
End Date of Course Giving
Hotel/Location of Course Giving

Lecturer
Name of Lecturer

Figure 3.7 Example 1 – Step 5

LECTURER'S STUDENT LIST

Course No: ....   Course Name: ....

Start Date: ....   End Date: ....

STUDENTS

Name	Job Title	Description of Experience	Been on one of our Courses before?	
			Course Names	Start Dates of Course

Figure 3.8 Example 2 – Form 2

40 *A Simple Introduction to Data and Activity Analysis*

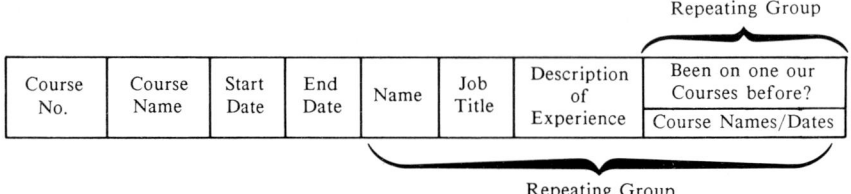

Figure 3.9 Example 2 – Step 1

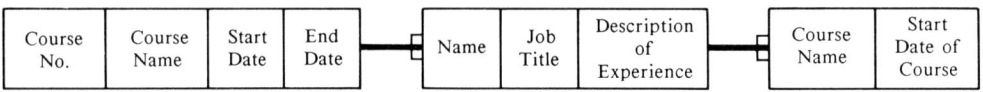

Figure 3.10 Example 2 – Step 2

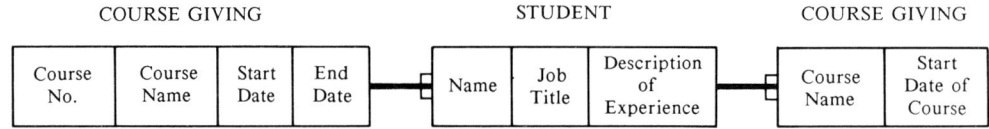

Figure 3.11 Example 2 – Step 3

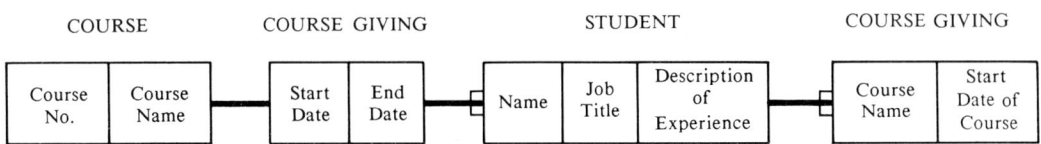

Figure 3.12 Example 2 – Step 4

Step 2. See Figure 3.10.
Step 3. At first sight the first Entity could be assumed to be a 'course' but start date and end date show this not to be true. Again, for the third Entity, the start date of the course gives us the clue that it is the course giving not course itself which is being described. See Figure 3.11.
Step 4. Course name and course number describe a course not the course giving. They are taken out and a one-to-one Relationship created. See Figure 3.12.
Step 5. The model from Form 2 is shown in Figure 3.13.

Notice how the Course Giving Entity has not been duplicated, but placed once in the Data Model. Instead the Relationships have been merged into one many-to-many Relationship.

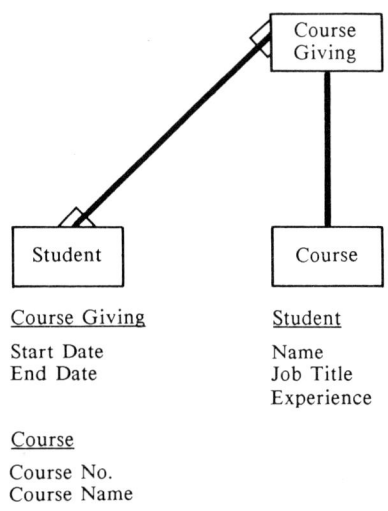

Course Giving
Start Date
End Date

Student
Name
Job Title
Experience

Course
Course No.
Course Name

Figure 3.13 Example 2 – Step 5

How to do Data Analysis 41

Form 3 – Hotel Booking Request (see Figure 3.14)
Step 1. It is not obvious from the names what the 'To' and 'Address' refer to until the title of the form is examined. This would have had to be verified in a real project. See Figure 3.15.
Step 2. See Figure 3.16.
Step 3. See Figure 3.17.
Step 4. No data item in any table can be grouped with any others (even though by now we would suspect the 'course' item). Hence there is no change – each potential Attribute describes the Entity. See Figure 3.18.

```
┌─────────────────────────────────────────────────────────────┐
│                   HOTEL BOOKING REQUEST                     │
│                                                             │
│   To:        ...........                                    │
│   Address:   ...........                                    │
│              ...........                                    │
│              ...........                                    │
│                                                             │
│   Please would you book us one of the rooms shown in your hotel for the courses
│   and dates shown:-                                         │
│                                                             │
│     Course              Start Date           End Date       │
└─────────────────────────────────────────────────────────────┘
```

Figure 3.14 Example 3 – Form 3

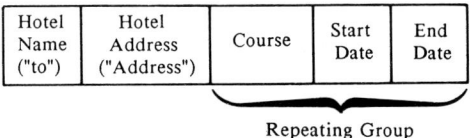

Figure 3.15 Example 3 – Step 1

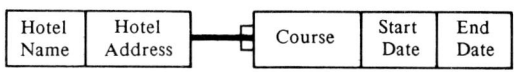

Figure 3.16 Example 3 – Step 2

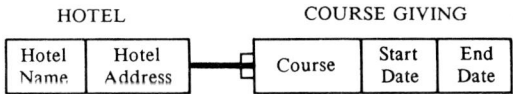

Figure 3.17 Example 3 – Step 3

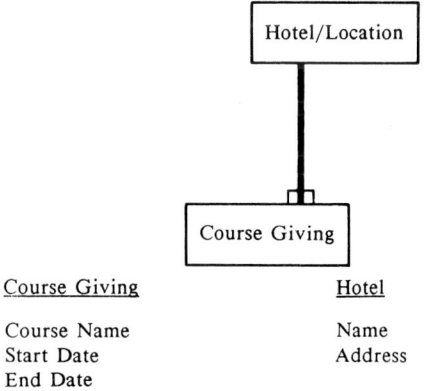

Figure 3.18 Example 3 – Step 5

42 *A Simple Introduction to Data and Activity Analysis*

Form 4 - Record Layout (see Figure 3.19)
Step 1. No repeating groups here. Repeating groups in record layouts usually have OCCURS X TIMES (or equivalent) in the layout. See Figure 3.20.
Step 2. No change.
Step 3. This seems the most obvious name – especially bearing in mind the name of the record. See Figure 3.21.
Step 4. Date of invoice describes the invoice, as does invoice no. The amount charged is the amount charged on the invoice, the currency is the currency of payment, the date payable is the date the invoice is payable. Course name, start date and end date, however all describe the course giving. No. of students is slightly less obvious. It could be no. of students on invoice or no. of students on course giving. The latter seems more probable, but you would have to check this. The company name describes the company, the account number is that of the company, the address is the company's. See Figure 3.22.

The Model from Form 4 is shown in Figure 3.23.

Record: Invoice Record   Name: INVC-REC   Length: ....

Level	Name	Name in Record	Picture	Occurs	Depending On	Comments
03	Date of Invoice	INVC-DAT	PIC 9(6) C-3	-	-	
03	Invoice Number	INVC-NO	PIC 9(4)	-	-	KEY
03	Amount Charged	INVC-AMT	PIC 9(7) V99	-	-	
03	Currency	INVC-CURR	PIC 99 C-3	-	-	
03	Date Payable	INVC-DATP	PIC 9(6) C-3	-	-	
03	Course-Name	INVC-C-N	PIC X (50)	-	-	
03	Start-Date	INVC-S-D	PIC 9(6) C-3	-	-	
03	End-Date	INVC-E-D	PIC 9(6) C-3	-	-	
03	Company Name	INVC-COMP-NO	PIC X (60)	-	-	
03	Account-No	INVC-ACCT-NM	PIC 9(3)	-	-	
03	Address	INVC-ADDR	PIC X (160)	-	-	
03	No. of Students	INVC-STUD	PIC 99	-	-	

Figure 3.19 Example 4 – Form 4

Date of Invoice	Invoice No.	Amount Charged	Currency	Date Payable	Course Name	Start Date	End Date	Company Name	Account No.	Address	No. of Students

Figure 3.20 Example 4 – Step 1

INVOICE

Date of Invoice	Invoice No.	Amount Charged	Currency	Date Payable	Course Name	Start Date	End Date	Company Name	Account No.	Address	No. of Students

Figure 3.21 Example 4 – Step 3

How to do Data Analysis 43

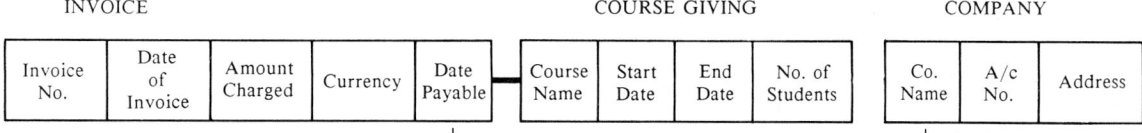

Figure 3.22 Example 4 – Step 4

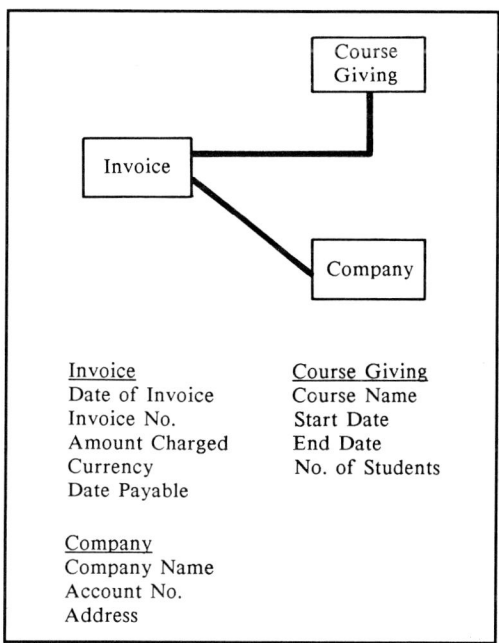

Figure 3.23 Example 4 – Step 5

Summary of Method

The disadvantages and advantages of using forms and record layouts are shown in Figure 3.24. Remember that forms and record layouts provide an easily accessible detailed source of data on the *existing* system.

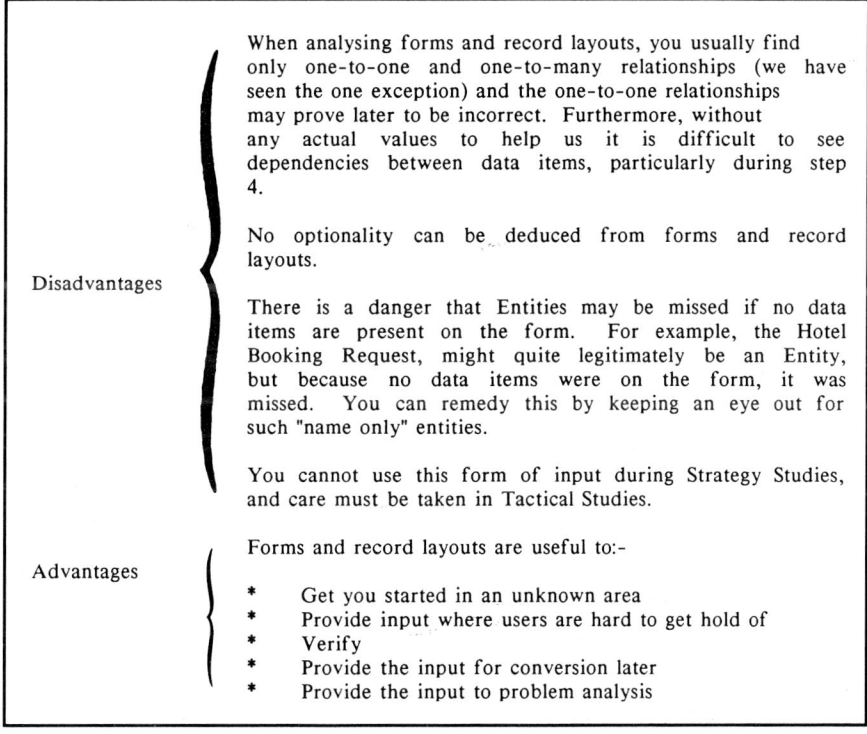

Figure 3.24 Analysing forms and record layouts

3.2.2 Using Conceptual Descriptions

The type of input we are using at this stage is derived from "real world abstractions": descriptions of our business system, free from any discussion of the 'mechanisms' of design and at the level of a "class" – a type of thing.

We usually obtain this sort of input from users themselves, either verbally or from something they have written in text form.

The method of analysis is not easy, so be warned.

In my series on Analysis, I have tried to provide many more pointers on what to do with text, in a much more 'formalised' way. I have simplified these steps for this book, but any analysis of natural language is bound to have its problems.

In the end, some measure of common sense is still required.

The following steps help to show the main stages in producing a Data Model from unstructured text.

If you want to practise, try analysing newspaper or magazine articles. It is surprising how much information they often contain, but also how much duplication, opinion and, in some cases inconsistency!

As an example, here is an imaginary interview with a user who deals with Course Administration, the Training Administrator.

The example will be dealt with in two parts. The first shows you how the steps can be used to pull out a "trial Model".

The second part shows you how you can use this Model to derive the *questions* you need to ask the user to fill in the detail you don't know.

STEP 1

Reduce the Text to Factual Sentences

Remove filler words, unsubstantiated opinion and 'link' type words e.g. however and but.
Replace any 'its', 'hes', 'shes' and 'theys' by the word it replaces.
Reduce any long sentences to simple ones of, roughly, the noun-verb-noun form.
Leave in any 'mays', 'somes' or indications of numbers.
Where a series of complex sentences seems to imply something simpler, use your common sense to weed out the simpler sentence implied – be careful, however, not to lose or distort any meaning when doing this.

STEP 2

Remove any single occurrence

Remove any sentences of the form
  "Object, verb, class" or
  "Class, verb, object".

but leave the class in place as a stand-alone word,

  e.g. John likes all Books
     The children like Mary

Any sentences dealing with the things themselves are handled using a different method.
Any sentences dealing with *activity*, create an Attribute representing the activity,

  e.g. Orders are cancelled
     Attribute = Date cancelled
         or Cancelled Signal values 'Y' or 'N'

It is possible that Attributes are also hidden in the text. These are known from the sentence and the words themselves. Ask yourself if the word describes a 'property' of the object noun?

  e.g.– Appointments have a *time* and *date*   Appointment date
                                Appointment time
     – Doctors have a *name*   Doctor name
     – Doctors have a *date of birth*   Doctor date of birth

   Ask also if ownership is implied
   e.g. The doctor's date of birth
       The doctor's name

How to do Data Analysis 45

STEP 3

Draw a Data Model for each Sentence (Figures 3.26 and 3.27)

Pick out the nouns in the sentences and the verbs (if any exist).
Deduce from the text whether many or one is implied.
Create Entities from the nouns and draw boxes round them
Create Relationships from the verbs
Where many is implied (a number of, or plural nouns) put a trident at this end OR denotes exclusivity
If the sentence is of the form "All As are Bs" or "As are all Bs" create sub-types as shown in Figure 3.25.
Ignore any sentence of the form, A becomes B [this denotes a change of 'state' and is not put in the Model].
Ignore sentences implying the same thing.

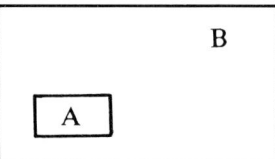

Figure 3.25

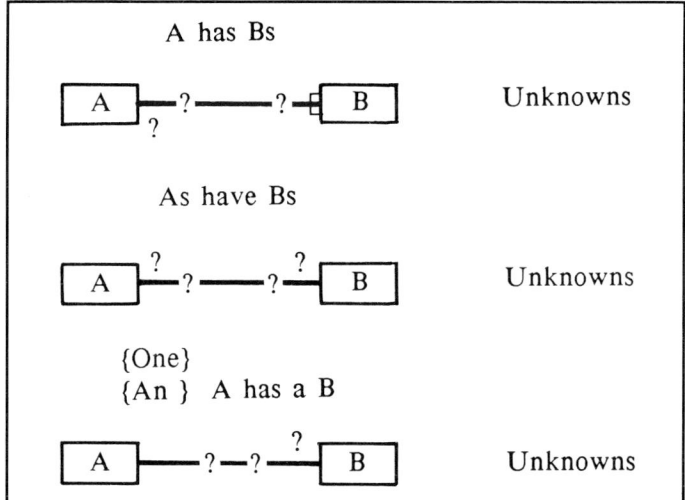

Figure 3.26

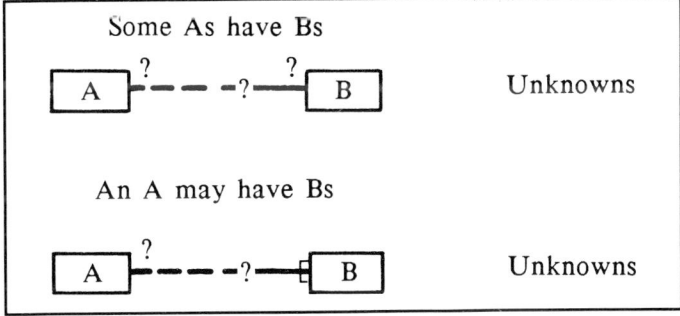

Figure 3.27

STEP 4

Combine each Model using Names to combine

Combine each Model derived from the sentences using the Entity and Relationship names
Ensure the question marks are placed on the combined Model
Where question marks are resolved by other Models, remove them.

46 *A Simple Introduction to Data and Activity Analysis*

STEP 5

See if there is any implied sequence to the activities or in the text
The verbs in the text often denote activity.

The user will very often imply a sequence to the activities by using such words as then, next and so on.

We will be seeing in the Activity Analysis how we structure this information properly. However, the sequence is essential to us in Data Modelling as it can show us where optionality can occur.

    e.g.   If A is created   { A can exist without B
           then B is created for A
           then C is created   C can exist alone
           then C is allocated to B { B can exist without C

This is shown in diagrammatic form in Figure 3.28. This can be reflected in the Model.

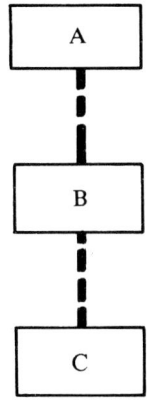

Figure 3.28

Exercise in deriving the Data Model from interview notes

Analyst: The area of your job which covers course administration. Could you tell me a bit about what happens?
User: Well, we have a number of courses which can be requested by a client or company.
Analyst: What form do these courses take?
User: Well the teachers we have, who by the way are all consultants, create new courses from scratch if a company requests a sort of course we haven't got.
Analyst: In other words, courses are created on demand.
User: Yes.
Analyst: How are the courses created?
User: Well, the sessions on the course are worked out in outline and allocated to the consultants to actually create them.
Analyst: Can a consultant be given many?
User: Oh yes, our consultants, generally speaking have created a fair number in their time.
Analyst: So there are some teachers who haven't created any sessions?
User: A few – not many though.
Analyst: Do you always have to create new sessions for a new course?
User: Now then, let me think, no we do re-use some.
Analyst: You mean you take them as they are and slot them in without alteration?
User: Yes we do.
Analyst: Do you alter any?
User: Yes, but we have to regard those as new sessions even though they may have started off the same. Very often as time goes on they diverge more and more and they end up being very different. There's no value in recognising that they were once the same.
Analyst: Tell me about your course brochure – I know you have one – what does that show?
User: Well it has a little bit of information on all our teachers and which courses they teach. It's funny how a face can sometimes sell a course!
Analyst: What else?
User: Well a description of the courses themselves of course.
Analyst: What sort of thing.

User: Well, the prices for them in different currencies and sometimes, if we think that people need to go on the courses in a set sequence, then we give that as well – you know the sort of thing – Information Analysis is our foundation course, then you can go on Systems Design and Database Design. Simple stuff really.

Analyst: That was most helpful. Thank you for your time. May I come back and just verify I've understood correctly?

User: Sure, bye bye.

SAMPLE SOLUTION

Step 1
1. Company 'X' has a number of courses
2. Courses are requested by a client or company
3. Company 'X' has teachers
4. Teachers are all consultants
5. Teachers create courses
6. Company requests course (sort of course = course)
7. Sessions are on a course
8. [Sessions are worked out in outline]
9. Sessions are allocated to consultants
10. Consultants create sessions
11. Consultants can create many sessions
12. Some teachers have not created any sessions
13. {New sessions are not always created for a new course
    {Some sessions are re-used by a new course
    Implies: Sessions can be used for more than one course
14. {Some sessions may be altered for a new course
    {Altered sessions become new sessions
    Implies: that if a session is altered it becomes a new session.
    This has no effect on the Model, only the definition of a session.
15. Company X has a course brochure
16. Course brochure has teachers (details)
17. Course brochure has [teachers teach courses]
18. Course brochure has course (descriptions) – description is a loose term for some of its attributes
19. Course has course prices in currency
20. Courses have sequence

Step 2
1. Courses
2. Courses are requested by a client or company
3. Teachers
4. Teachers are all consultants
5. Teachers create courses
6. Company requests course
7. Sessions are on a course
8. [converted to Attribute-session worked out in outline – Y/N]
9. Sessions are allocated to consultants
10. Consultants create sessions
11. Consultants can create many sessions
12. Some teachers have not created any sessions
13. Sessions can be used for more than one course
14. –
15. –
16. Teachers
17. Teachers teach courses
18. Course (descriptions)
19. Course has course prices in currency
20. Courses have sequence

Step 3
Please see Figures 3.29, 3.30 and 3.31.

48 *A Simple Introduction to Data and Activity Analysis*

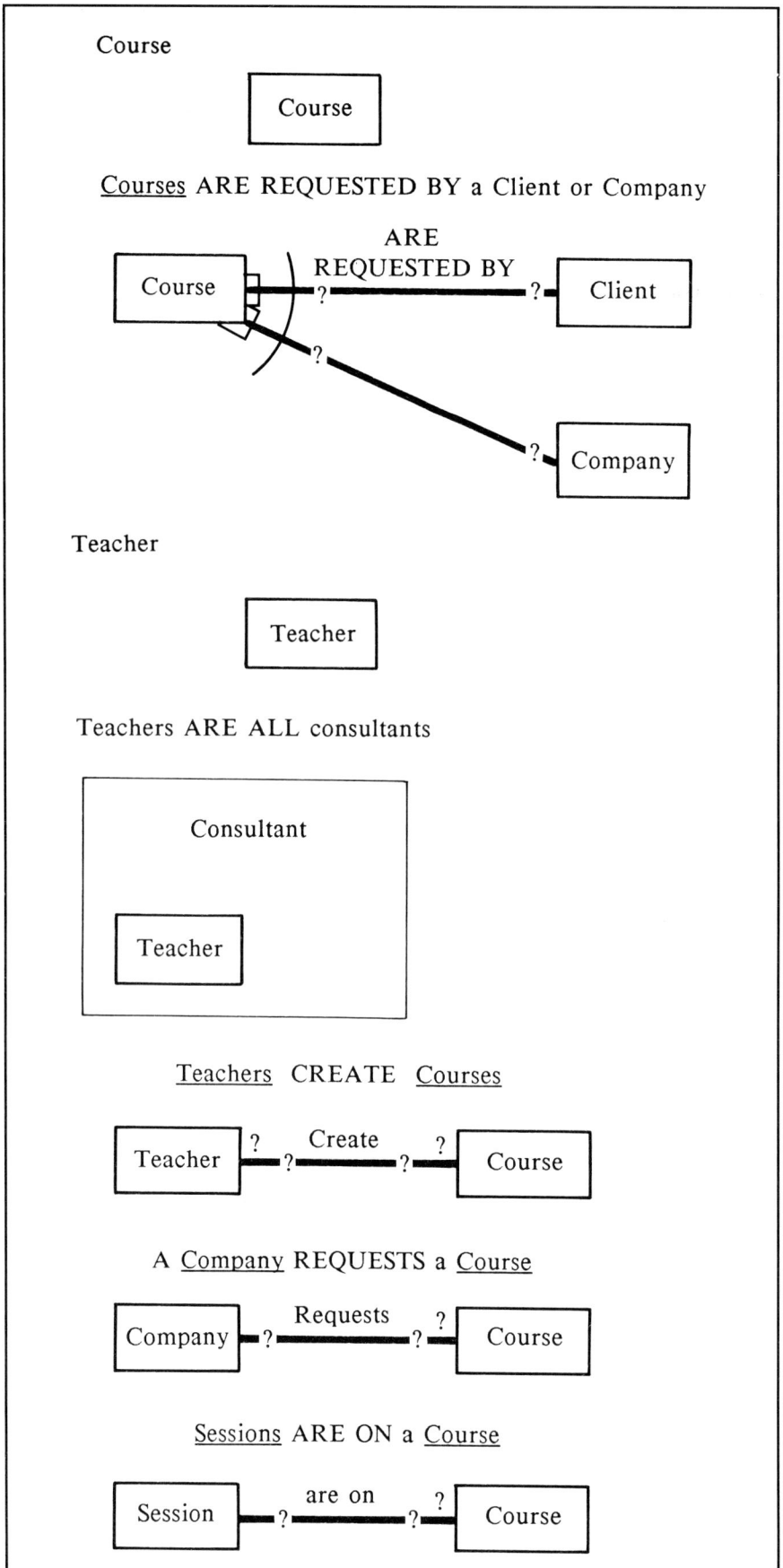

Figure 3.29

9.   Sessions are allocated to Consultants

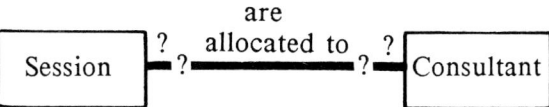

10. +11.   Consultants <u>create</u> sessions/Consultants <u>can create</u> many sessions

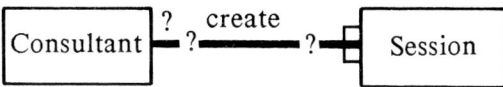

12.   Some teachers have not created any sessions
         N.B. If some teachers have not created sessions then by implication some consultants won't have either.

13.   Sessions can be used for more than one course

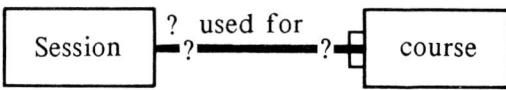

16.   Teacher

17.   Teachers teach courses

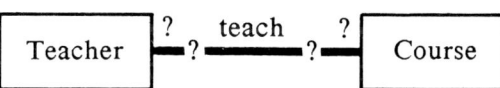

Figure 3.30

50 A Simple Introduction to Data and Activity Analysis

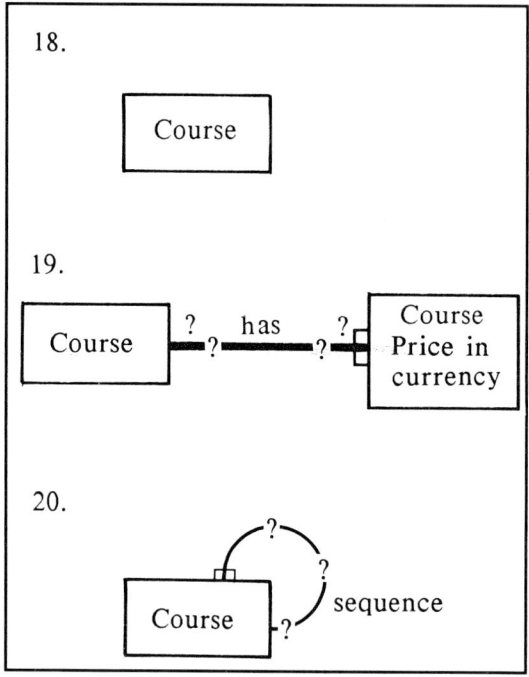

Figure 3.31

Step 4
This is shown in Figure 3.32.

Step 5
See Figures 3.33 and 3.34.

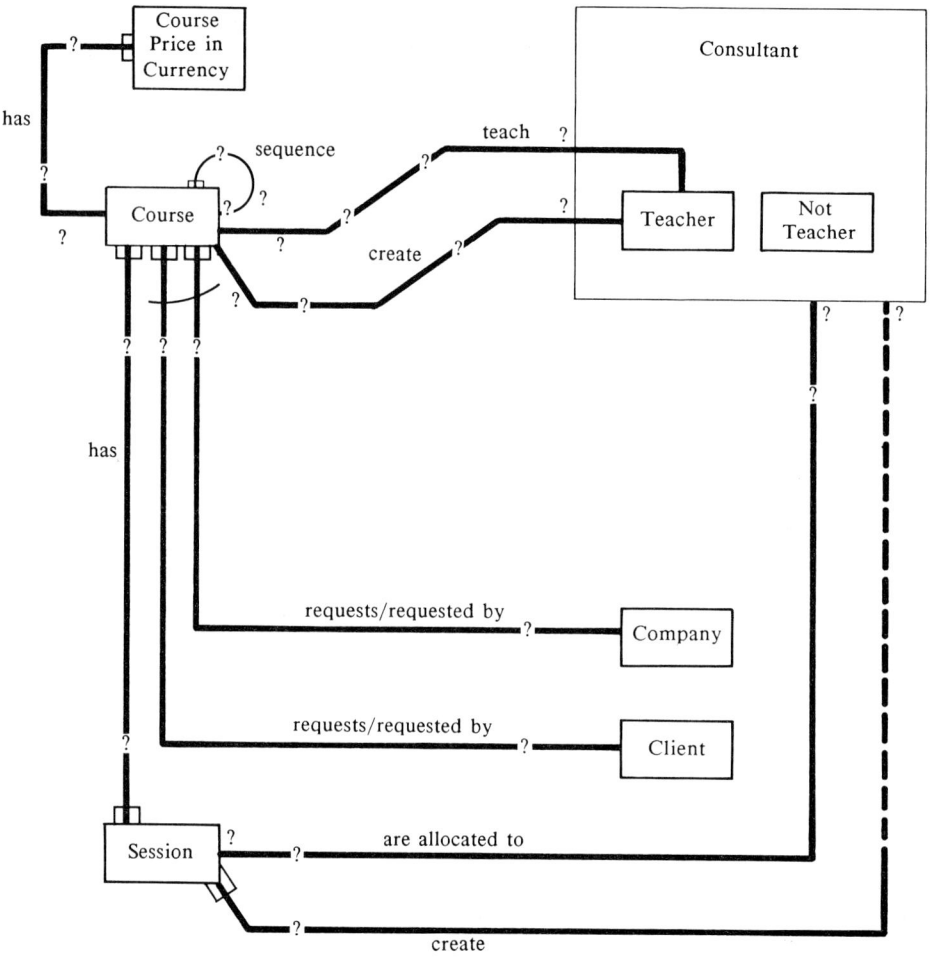

Figure 3.32

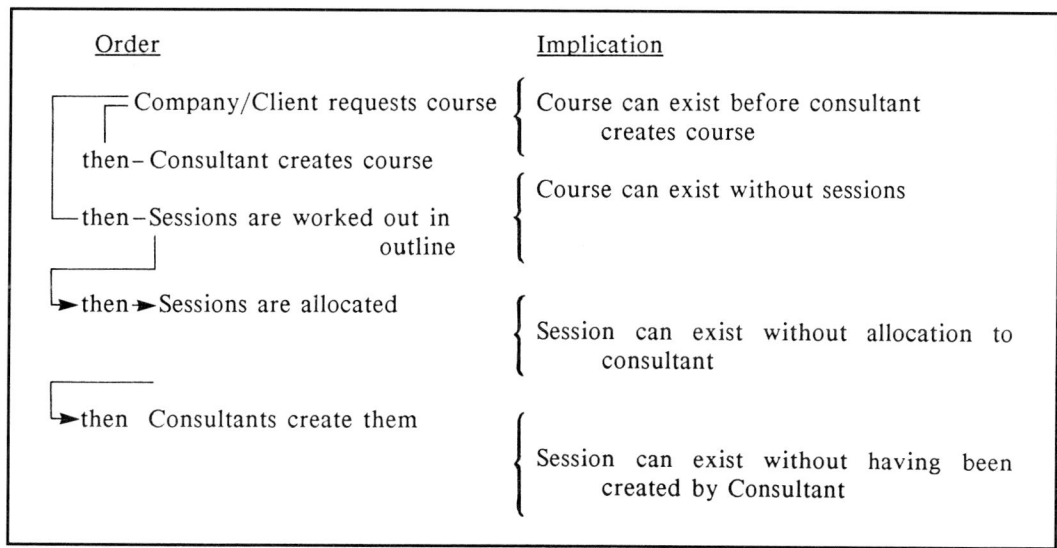

Figure 3.33

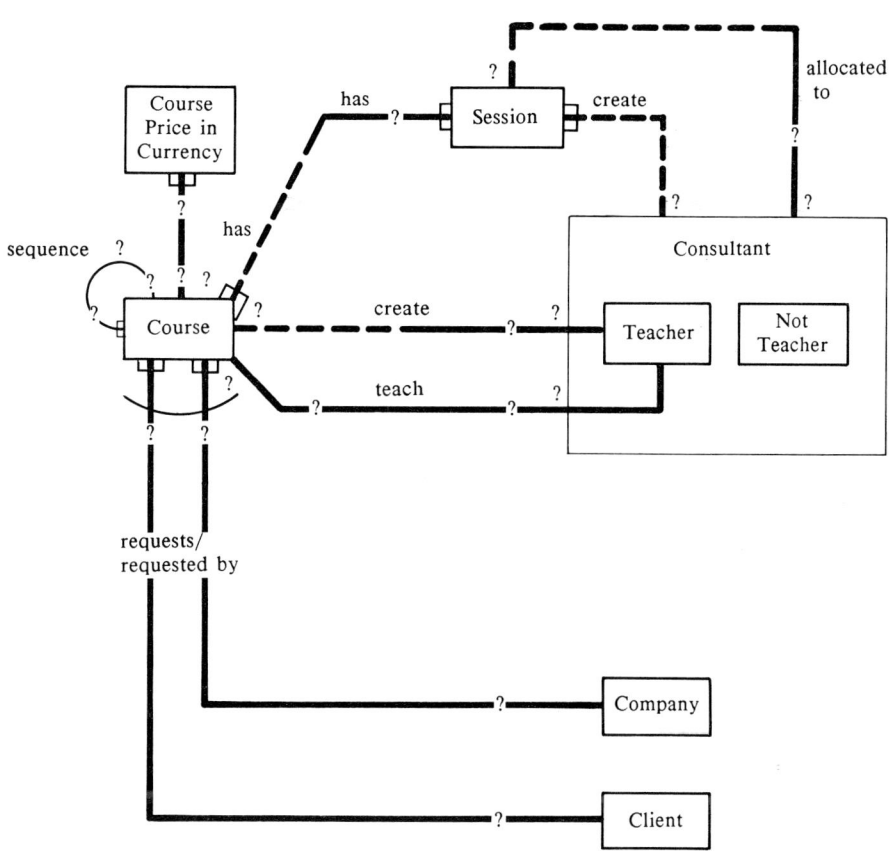

Figure 3.34

The next step we can show is the questions which we produce to fill in the missing details on the Model.

Using the Data Model in Step 5, all we have to do is draw up a list as follows: I have put the answers a user might have given by the side and you can see the effect on the Model on the next page.

QUESTION	ANSWER
1. Are all courses priced?	NO
2. Is the course price applicable to more than one course?	NO
3. Can the course price exist without a course?	NO
4. Can a session be created independently of courses?	NO

52 A Simple Introduction to Data and Activity Analysis

5. Are all courses sequenced?	NO
6. Is the sequence always one followed by many or one preceded by many?	THE FORMER
7. Can a session be created by more than one consultant?	NO
8. Can a session be allocated to more than one consultant?	NO
9. Have all consultants been allocated sessions at one time or another?	NO
10. Can a consultant have been allocated many sessions?	IN TIME, YES
11. Have all consultants created a course at one time or another?	NO
12. Will consultants have created many courses?	YES
13. Can a course be created by many consultants?	YES
14. Can a company exist without having requested a course? What about a Client?	YES A COMPANY BECOMES A CLIENT WHEN IT REQUESTS A COURSE
15. Is it possible for courses to exist without having been requested?	NO
16. Can a teacher teach many courses?	YES
17. Do all teachers teach?	YES
18. Are all courses taught?	SOME NOT, NOT WHEN THEY'RE BEING CREATED
19. Can a course have more than one teacher?	YES

The final Model after questions is shown in Figure 3.35.

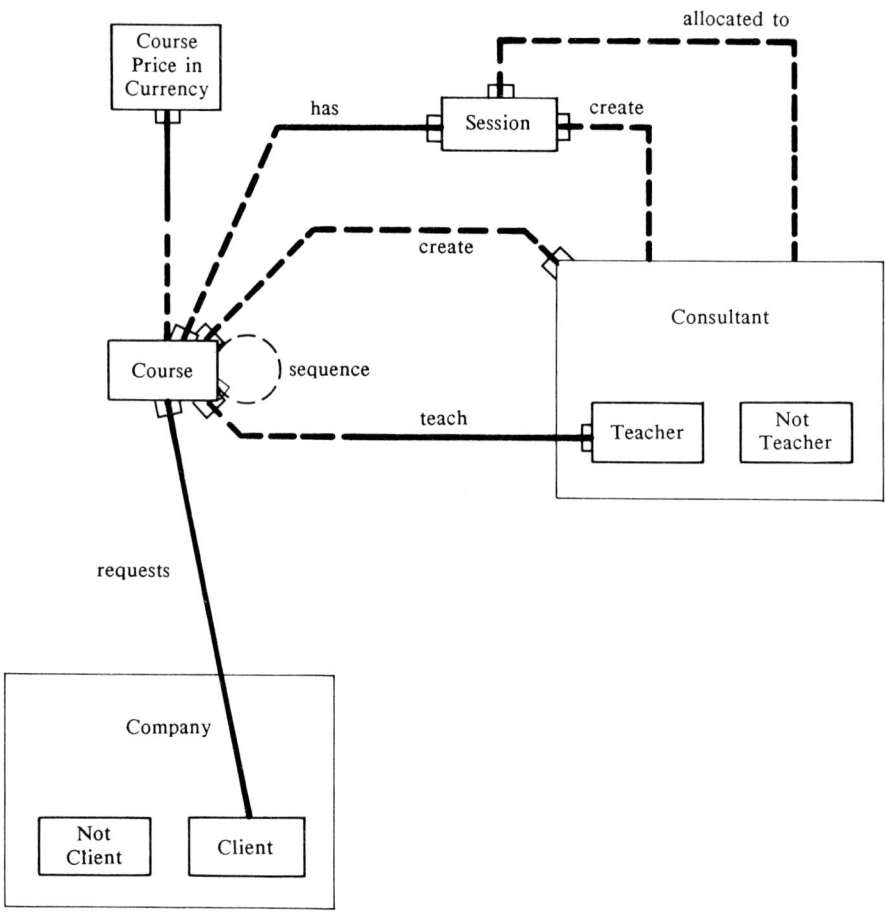

Figure 3.35 Final Model after Questions

Summary

Analysing text is the most difficult method of analysis but, assuming your user is easily available it is the quickest way of building a Data Model. You therefore have to balance the risks of incorrect analysis against the speed.

You do run the risk, when using a person as your source of input, that his forgetfulness will also cause errors.

If you use this method you must make sure every fact is verified, either by using the output from a different method to cross check or by going back to your user.

3.2.3 Using Occurrences

I find real-world occurrences the most fascinating input to be analysed. It may be because this method of analysis is very new, but I also think it is because, of all the methods, it offers the greatest potential for automated support.

Real-world occurrences are the things themselves and the Relationships between the things rather than the classes.

The method depends on a form of progressive structuring of the sentences containing the things until short factual statements are produced. Then, using a diagram called a semantic network, you can generalise the facts to produce the Data Model.

Real-world occurrences can give us good, reliable information about other deliverables as well, deliverables such as "relationship degree" (see the earlier list) which show *how many* of one type of thing are related to another,

e.g. Orders contain 10 order lines.

Real-world occurrences can be obtained using various methods of collection, such as observation, interviewing, study of factual documents.

I have spent some interesting hours poring over newspapers, extracting the facts and building Data Models. The exercise proved the more interesting because it unearthed a lot of anomalies and contradictions, much as it did when I used the method for analysing classes.

Again, using our Course Administration Area example, I will outline the main steps in producing a Data Model from occurrences.

This is one area where my four books on Analysis provide considerably more detail and a lot more pointers on what to do with certain types of sentence or language construction.

This does not mean, however, that you won't be able to use the method described here; it simply means you will need to apply more common sense and judgement, and invent these rules yourself.

Below is a description which could have been obtained by observation of the Course Administration area.

CASE STUDY
Of the Feasibility Study Course, Prototyping Course and Information Analysis Course only two have actual courses planned or given. The Feasibility Study Course was given on 3.3.87; it was requested by Piggymon of Line House, Vienna. The Information Analysis Course will be given on 1.6.87 and 3.9.87 and was given on 8.8.86. The course to be given on 3.9.87 is to be held at The Hotel Splendid Vista, Brightside, Sheffield and was requested by Piggymon. The course held on 8.8.86 was requested by ABC Tubes and was held at their 5 Acacia Avenue, Geneva premises.

ABC Tubes' other premises at 9 High Street, Letchworth and 10 Green Street, Wapping have not been used by us.

The 1.6.87 course was also requested by ABC Tubes and held at their 5 Acacia Avenue premises. On this course were two of ABC Tubes Employees, Amby Dextrus and Jerry Atrick, along with To Kyo, Sydney Harbour-Bridge and Minnie Appolis, all from the Loob Company of Holland in Hash Street, Amsterdam. Minnie Appolis has also been on a course given on 3.3.87. (Feasibility Study).

Invoice 8897 has been sent for 8.8.86 to ABC Tubes and another invoice 8898 has been sent to the High and Dry Whisky Distillers Company of Glen Fiddick, the Glen, Scotland for the 50 employees they sent.

An invoice 8397 has been prepared for the 1.6.87 course which will go to ABC Tubes and another, 8399, which will go to the Loob Company of Holland.

The steps are as follows:

Step 1. Reduce the Text to Factual Sentences
- Remove filler words, unsubstantiated opinion and 'link' type words, e.g. however, and, but.
- Replace any 'it's, 'he's, 'we's, 'she's and things by the actual thing itself.
- Where a number of things are mentioned but not by name give each of them an arbitrary identifier, e.g. We have two hospitals (We) have hospital 1, hospital-2.
- Reduce all long sentences to simple sentences of the form
  noun-verb-noun   e.g. John Smith visits Hospital-1

54 *A Simple Introduction to Data and Activity Analysis*

or   noun-verb-list of nouns   e.g. Nurse Richards treats Patient-1, Patient-2, Patient-3
or   list of nouns-verb-noun   e.g. Doctor Harris, Doctor Jones and Dr. Allan are treating Mrs. Smith

- Where several complex sentences seem to imply something simpler use your common sense to weed out the simpler sentence implied – be careful, however, when doing this.
- Do not lose occurrences of things even if they are not involved in any factual sentences.
- Remove any sentences of the form
  {Object verb class}
  {Class verb Object}
  but leave the object in place.

Step 2
This is illustrated in Figure 3.36.

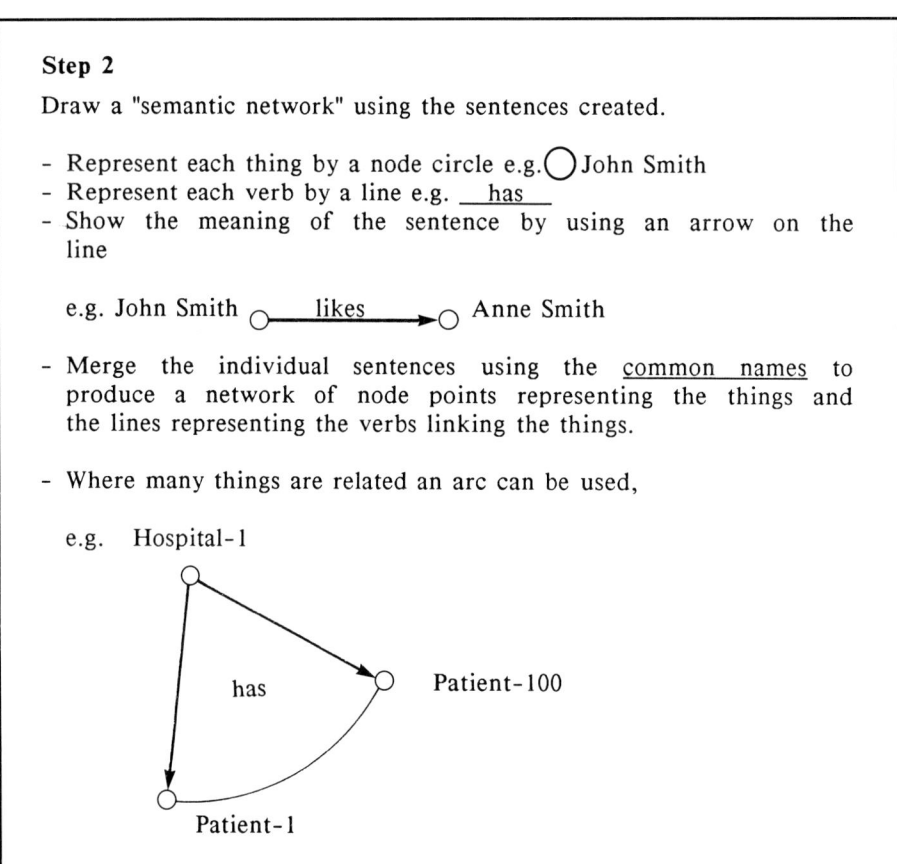

Figure 3.36

Step 3. Classify the Occurrences
- Using the Entity occurrences first see what classes of thing are in the picture. Use the names to help you and patterns of similar relationship. You can also use the original sentences if this helps.
- Combine the individual relationships to produce types as follows:
- Use the name to combine, be aware of synonym names and the active/passive voice expressing the same relationship,
  e.g. {are premises of}
       {has premises at}
  Ignore the tenses for the purposes of classification, e.g. has been given, will be given, but be sure to write all the tenses on the relationship line. They will be resolved later.

The following degree is known from the occurrences as shown in Figures 3.37, 3.38, 3.39 and 3.40.

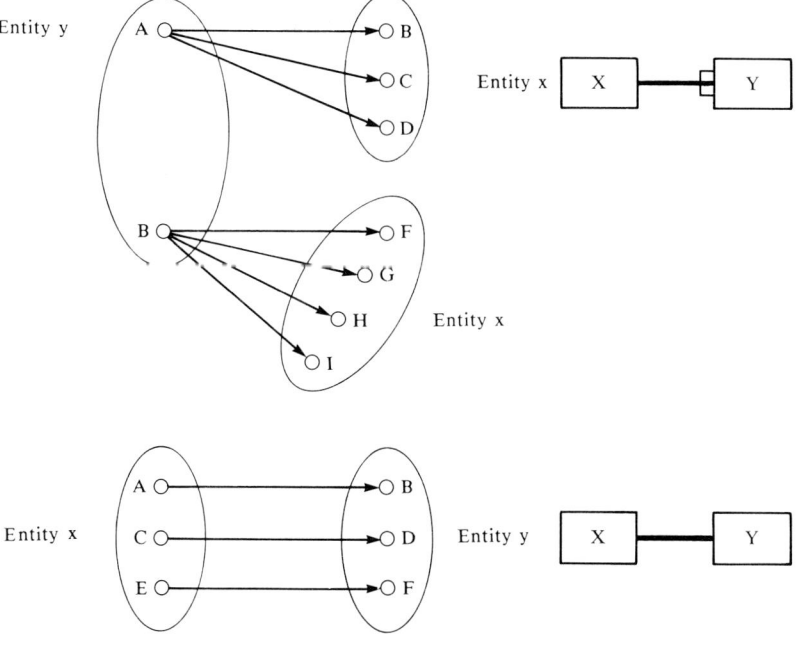

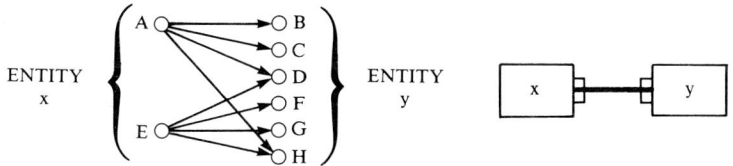

Figure 3.37

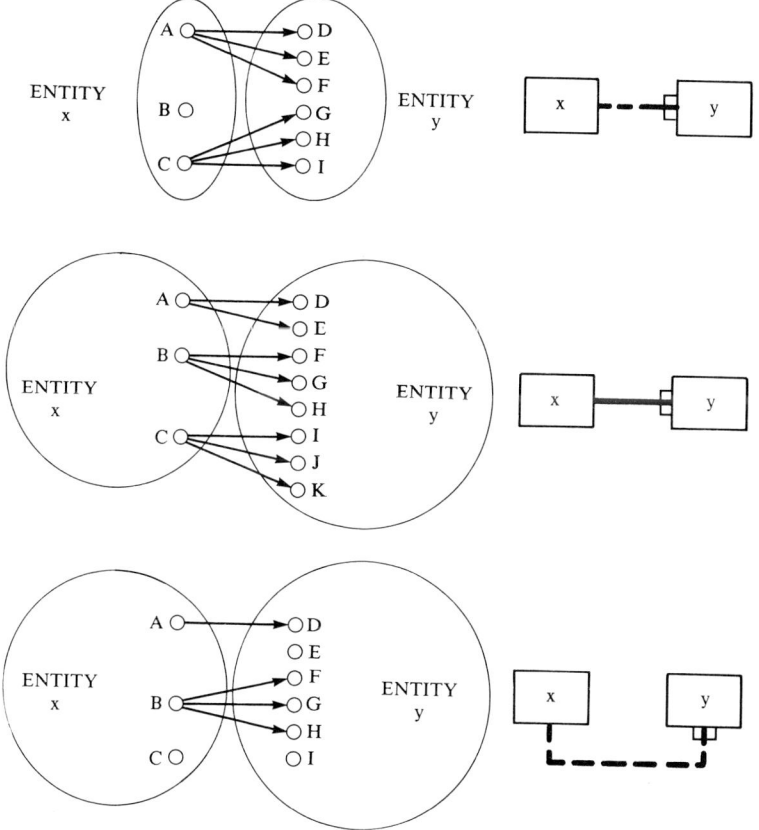

Figure 3.38

56 *A Simple Introduction to Data and Activity Analysis*

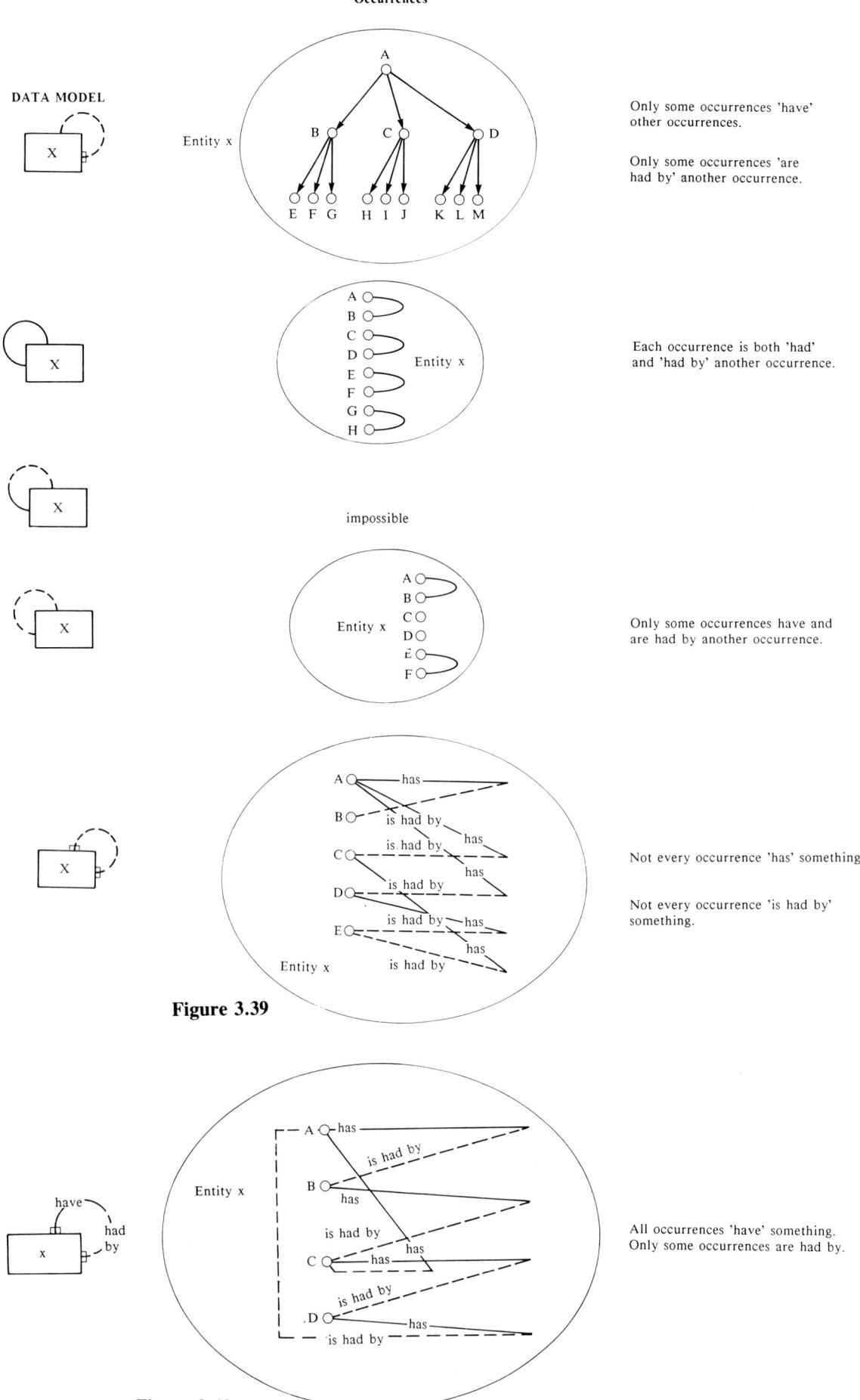

Figure 3.39

Figure 3.40

How to do Data Analysis   57

Step 4
Create an Attribute classifying the Attribute values which identified each Entity occurrence. An example is shown in Figure 3.41.

Results after Step 1
The results after Step 1 are shown in Figure 3.42.

Results after Step 2
The results after Step 2 are shown in Figure 3.43.

Results after Step 3
The conclusions after Step 3 are shown in Figure 3.44. The Data Model resulting after Step 3 is shown in Figure 3.45.

Results after Step 4
See Figure 3.46.

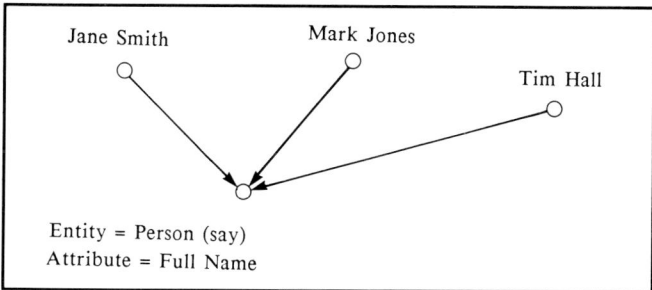

Figure 3.41

Results after Step 1

Of the Feasibility study Course, Prototyping   ⎧ Introductory sentence
Course and Information Analysis Course only two ⎨ amplified in next
have actual Courses planned or given   ⎩ sentences
Prototyping Course (occurrence saved from sentence above)
Feasibility Study Course was given on 3.3.87
Feasibility Study Course of 3.3.87 was requested by Piggymon
Piggymon is at Line House, Vienna
Information Analysis Course will be given on [1.6.87, 3.9.87]
Information Analysis Course was given on 8.8.86
Information Analysis Course on 3.9.87 is to be held at Hotel Splendid Vista, Brightside, Sheffield
Information Analysis Course on 3.9.87 was requested by ABC Tubes
Information Analysis Course on 3.9.87 was held at 5 Acacia Avenue Geneva
5 Acacia Avenue Geneva are the premises of ABC Tubes
ABC Tubes has premises at [9 High Street, Letchworth], [10 Green Street, Wapping]
Information Analysis Course of 1.6.87 was requested by ABC Tubes
Information Analysis Course of 1.6.87 was held at 5 Acacia Avenue
Information Analysis Course of 1.6.87 had on it [Amby Dextrus, Jerry Atrick, To Kyo, Sydney Harbour-Bridge, Minnie Appolis]
[Amby Dextrus, Jerry Atrick] are employees of ABC Tubes
[To Kyo, Sidney Harbour-Bridge, Minnie Appolis] are employees of Loob Company
Loob Company has premises at Hash Street, Amsterdam, Holland
Minnie Appolis was on Feasibility Study Course of 3.3.87
Invoice 8897 was for Information Analysis Course 8.8.86
Invoice 8897 has been sent to ABC Tubes
Invoice 8898 has been sent to High and Dry Whisky Distillers Co.
High and Dry Whisky Distillers Co. have premises at Glen Fiddick, The Glen Scotland
Invoice 8898 was for Information Analysis Course 8.8.86
Information Analysis Course 8.8.86 had [Employee 1 to Employee 50]
[Employee 1 to Employee 50] are employees of High and Dry Whisky Distillers Co.
Invoice 8397 is for Information Analysis Course of 1.6.87
Invoice 8397 will go to ABC Tubes
Invoice 8399 will go to Loob Company (of Holland)
Invoice 8399 is for Information Analysis Course of 1.6.87

Figure 3.42

58 *A Simple Introduction to Data and Activity Analysis*

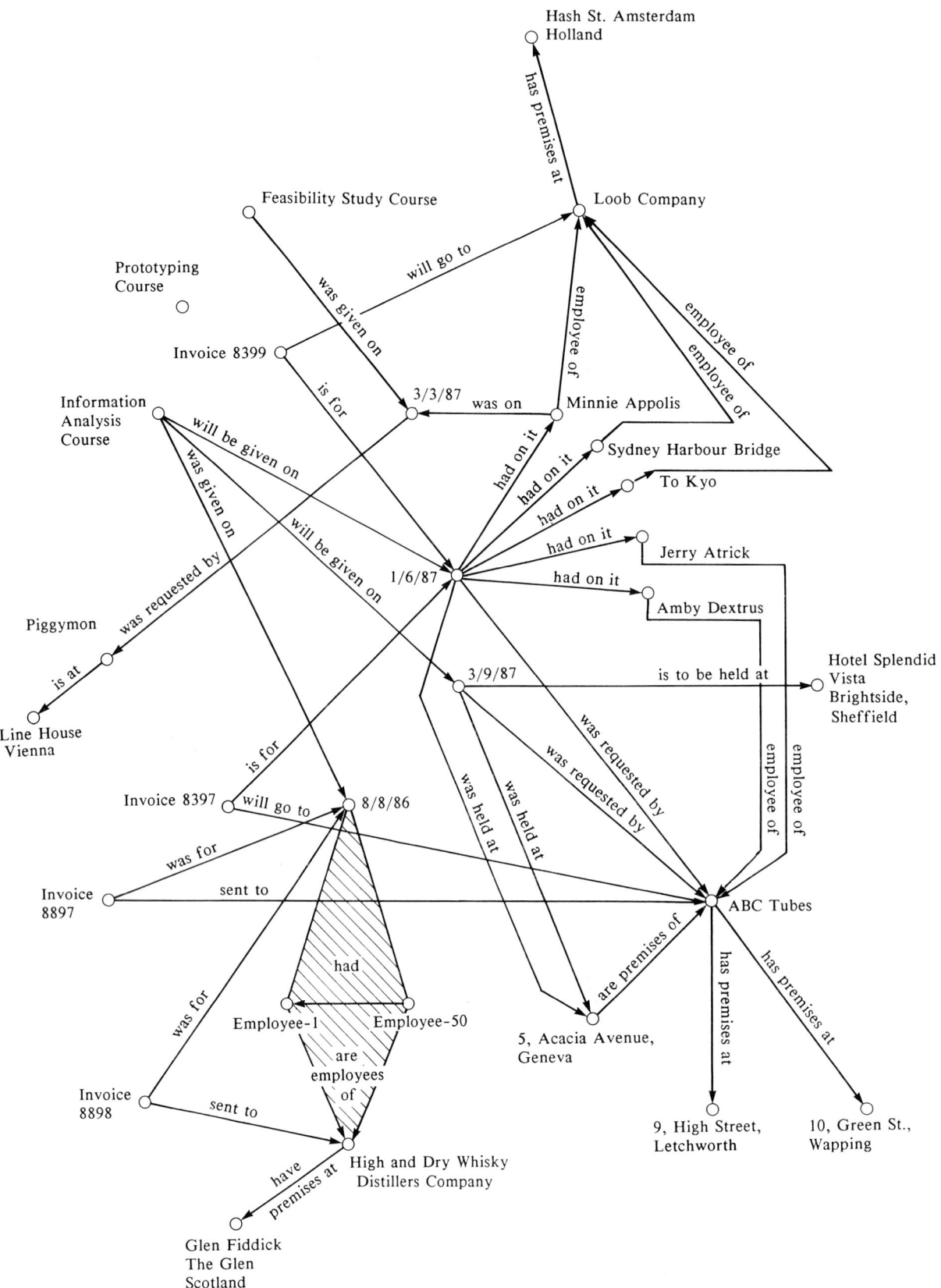

Figure 3.43 Results after Step 2

How to do Data Analysis 59

> There are some courses (Prototyping) having no Course Givings.
> All Course Givings were for a Course and only one course
> Courses can have more than one Giving (Information Analysis, 1.6.87, 8.8.87, 3.9.87)
> All Students had been on course givings and could have been on more than one (Minnie Appolis on 3.3.87 and 1.6.87)
> Course Givings had more than one student on them
> Not all Course givings had Students (3.9.87)
> All Students were employed by the one Company
> A Company could have more than one employee
> Some companies had no employees (Piggymon)
> Only some Companies had requested Course Givings (Piggymon, ABC Tubes)
> Companies could request more than one Course Giving (ABC Tubes)
> Not all Course Givings were requested (8.8.86)
> Course Givings were requested by only one company
> All Companies had company Locations
> All Company Locations were those of one company
> Companies could have more than one Location (ABC Tubes)
> Only some Companies had been sent an Invoice (Loob Company, ABC Tubes, High and Dry Whisky Distillers)
> Some Companies could have received more than one Invoice (ABC Tubes)
> All Invoices had been sent to or were to go to one Company
> All Invoices were for one Course Giving
> Some Course Givings had no Invoice (3.3.87, 3.9.87)
> Some Course Givings had more than one Invoice (8.8.86)
> The (only) hotel had one Course Giving (3.9.87)
> A Course Giving was either at one Hotel or one Company Location
> A company location could have had more than one Course Giving (5 Acacia Avenue, Geneva)
> Not all Course Givings had a Location (3.3.87, 8.8.86)
> Only some Company Locations had had Course Givings (5 Acacia Avenue, Geneva)

Figure 3.44 Conclusions after Step 3

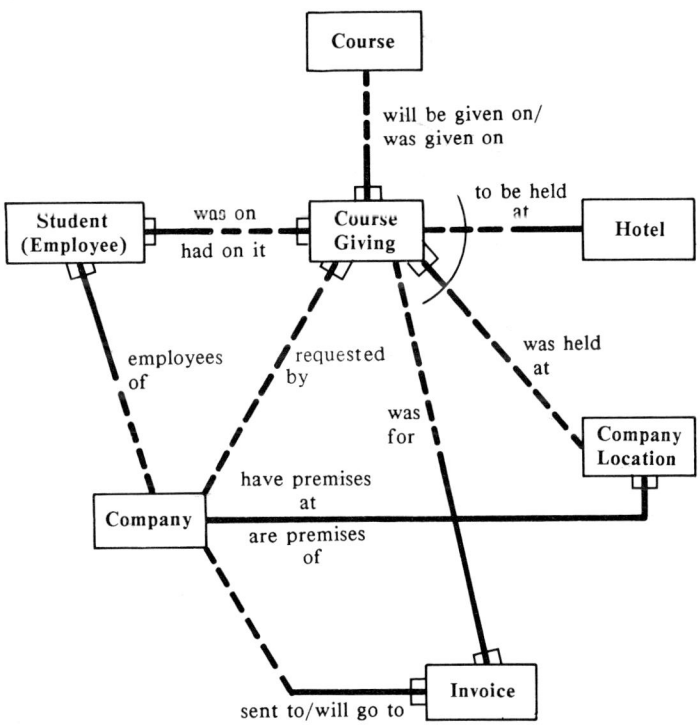

Figure 3.45 The Data Model after Step 3

> Course   Company
>
> Name of course   Name of company
>
> Invoice   Student
>
> Invoice number   Student (full) name
>
> Hotel   Company location
>
> Hotel name   Address
>
> Hotel address
>
> Course giving
>
> Start date

Figure 3.46 Results after Step 4

Summary
The advantages of 'real-world' occurrences are that they give a complete and accurate picture of things and can be used to derive many other deliverables. They are less reliant on user memory and the user is often more accurate when asked to give examples.

They tend to be less 'error prone' than some of the other methods.

The disadvantages with the occurrences is that the classification process is somewhat tedious and laborious (automation would help here). A good representative sample needs to be obtained, so that inaccuracies are not introduced – for example one hotel is not enough to base any Data Model on.

The semantic network can also get quite complex, although this could be solved by a mixture of partitioning classes into manageable study areas, and automating and manipulating the drawing of networks. I have been told that a company or university in Israel has already done this.

A final disadvantage is that this method is obviously not suitable for use during a Strategy Study and is only of use in a limited way during a Tactical Study as a check.

3.2.4 Using Design Occurrences

Whenever you analyse a listing or a form which has actual values on it you can use 'normalisation' to derive a Data Model.

I don't intend to go into any of the theory or the 'whys' and 'wherefores' of the method, whole books have been written on this subject. Instead, I will treat it as simply as possible, concentrating on the main steps.

The method does have its attractions, but also quite a few disadvantages and we will see this as we go along.

You can use the design 'occurrences' – the values, to get information about the 'Relationship degree' (see last method) and valid values, but it can be less reliable than that obtained from real word input, primarily because the design itself may be poor, placing unnecessary restrictions on what is required, duplicating data and creating a distorted view.

All you need to get input for normalisation is to collect a good sample of the forms, records and listings used in the system. You can also use screens, if the existing system is an online computer one.

Where time is short, however, concentrate on the main inputs and outputs and main forms and records.

In order to demonstrate the steps I am going to assume that we have collected a form which has actual values on it. The form is about our example Course Administration Area.

The steps will be explained so that the "solution" is kept with the description of what to do.

STEP 1
The first step is to take the box or column headings and lay them out in simple table form with the

headings across the top of the page and the values below the headings in rows. Repeating blocks of values should be listed against the set of values for which they repeat.

Examples 1 and 2
See Figures 3.47 and 3.48.

Example – Course Administration
In our example of the Lecturer's Schedule, the schedule is laid out in this way for us, having column headings and repeating values. (Figure 3.49.)

The Form

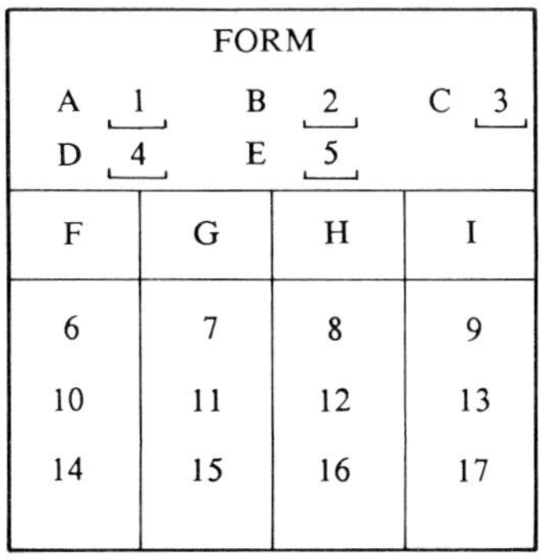

The table which results

A	B	C	D	E	F	G	H	I
1	2	3	4	5	6	7	8	9
					10	11	12	13
					14	15	16	17

Figure 3.47 Example 1

The Form

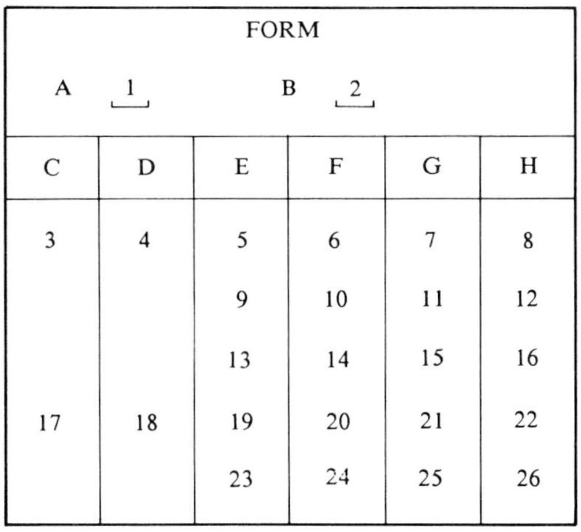

The table which results

A	B	C	D	E	F	G	H
1	2	3	4	5	6	7	8
				9	10	11	12
				13	14	15	16
		17	18	19	20	21	22
				23	24	25	26

Example 2

STEP 2
Find a column heading which will uniquely identify a *full row* of values. Ideally it should be just one heading. If we can't get uniqueness using one we must combine two or more until a unique identifier is found.

In our example, there are six full rows of values.

Looking down the values in the column headings, both the 'Name' and the 'Number' would give us a unique identifier.

62 *A Simple Introduction to Data and Activity Analysis*

NAME	NUMBER	DATE START	DATE END	NO. OF STUDENTS	COURSE NAME	COURSE NO.	ABBREV. NAME
Angela Angle Poise	112	5.4.86	9.4.86	15	Information Analysis	01	INFO ANAL
		6.6.86	10.6.86	10	Feasibility Study	02	FEASIBILITY
		7.7.87	11.7.87	15	Database Design	04	DB DESIGN
James Robertson	133	3.3.86	5.3.86	20	Strategy Study	03	STRATEGY
		5.4.86	9.4.86	15	Information Analysis	01	INFO ANAL
		7.7.87	11.7.87	30	Feasibility Study	02	FEASIBILITY
		1.8.87	11.8.87	20	Application Systems Design	05	APPLIC DESIGN
Martin Henry	188	6.6.86	10.6.86	10	Feasibility Study	02	FEASIBILITY
		3.3.87	7.3.87	8	Information Analysis	01	INFO ANAL
		7.7.87	11.7.87	15	Database Design	04	DB DESIGN
Pat Winters	354	–	–	–	–	–	—
John Smith	338	5.4.87	8.4.87	0	Information Analysis	01	INFO ANAL
Blank	000	6.4.87	11.4.87	0	Feasibility Study	02	FEASIBILITY

Figure 3.49 Lecturer's schedule

We will choose the number because it is shorter and probably less likely to change over time. (Although of course we don't know this just from the table itself)

Underline the Number to show it is the key of this Table.

STEP 3

Now remove the repeating groups. This may have to be done in a series of steps if several layers of repeating group occur, or could be done in one step if only one occurs.

Create a separate table for the repeating group and duplicate the key value in the new table. Choose a key for the new table in the same way as you chose a key for the original table. You may have to invent a temporary one if one does not exist. See Figure 3.50.

This step in Normalisation is called "Creating First Normal Form".

Now we will have a look at the example and examine the realities and problems we might face in real life using this method.

Over the page we have our split table. Splitting it was simple, duplicating the number in the new table was easy, but finding a new key for the table is not.

(Number + Start Date)   appear to be unique
(Number + Date End)   appear to be unique

Number + No. of Students are not
(Number + Course Name) appear to be unique
(Number + Course No.) appear to be unique
(Number + Abbrev. Name) appear to be unique

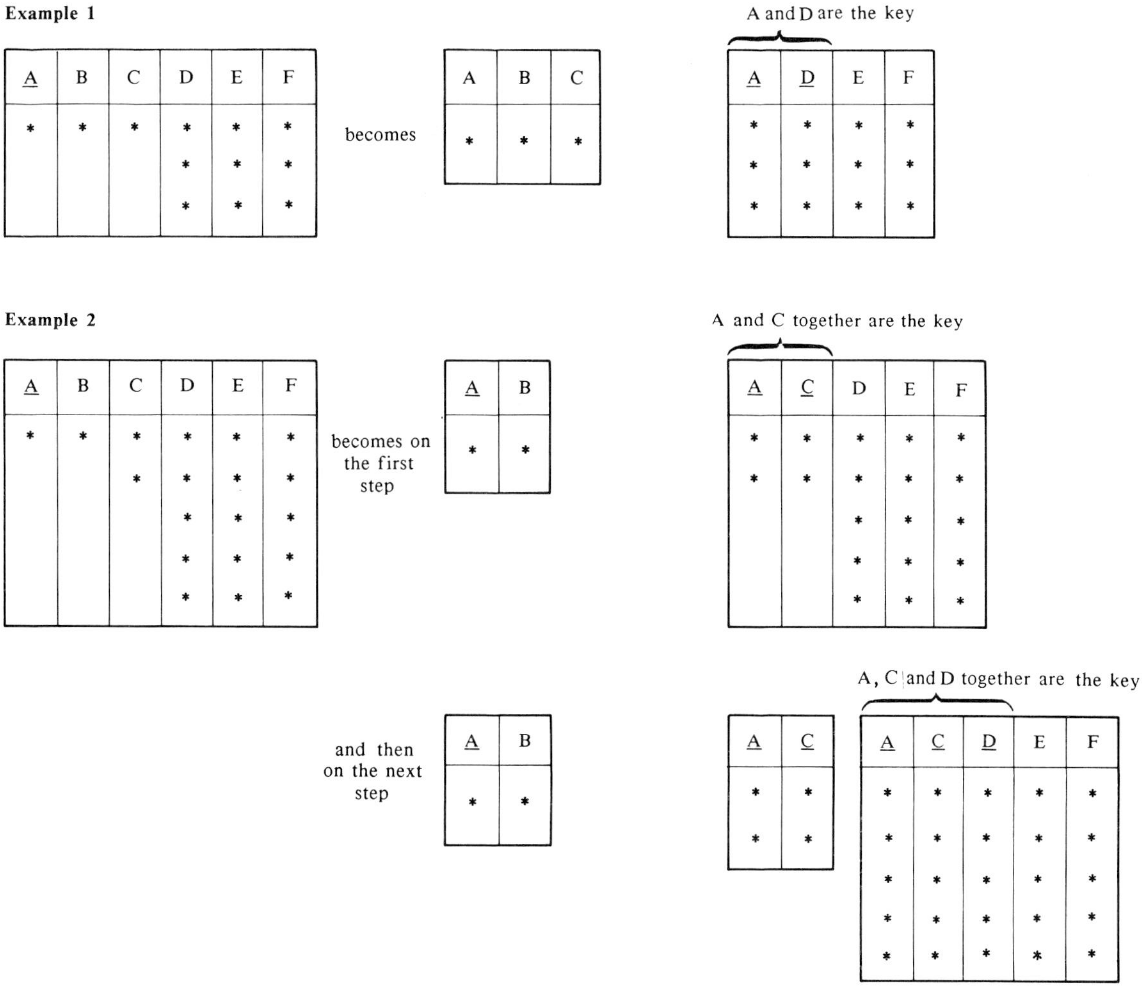

How to do Data Analysis 63

Example 1

Example 2

Figure 3.50 Examples 1 and 2 - Step 3

First Normal Form

Study Figure 3.51. We have five possible candidate keys!

Remember that we may be using this method knowing very little about the meaning of the words or the Entities and Relationships which exist – in fact we may be using the method to give us a start in a complicated area that the user doesn't seem able to explain in words.

We can rely only on the data values to help us.

What should we do?

If we are going to persist with this method we need a *bigger sample* of data values to help us decide. This will show us whether or not these candidate keys are reliable.

Without this additional data, I will pick on the *Date Start* as the second part of the key to the table. Course Name and Abbrev. Name are too long to be good keys. Either Date Start or Date End would have done. I have chosen Date Start partly because it is next to the number and also because common sense tells me that if this is a lecturer's schedule a lecturer couldn't have two identical start dates for courses.

STEP 4

(In normalisation this is called "Conversion to Second Normal Form").

Look at the keys which have been formed from a combination of column headings.

Taking each part of the key in turn, look through the non-key items and see if any items look like they depend on the part key rather than the whole key. The way to do this is to look at the data values to help you.

Let us use our example. There is only one table with a combination key and that is formed from [No. + Date Start].

Using 'Number' first, go through each row in the table. When a key data value appears on successive rows does a value appear correspondingly for another item?

The answer is 'no' for the number. Every time 112 appears, for example, date end, no. of

64 *A Simple Introduction to Data and Activity Analysis*

NAME	No.
Angela Anglepoise	112
James Robertson	133
Martin Henry	188
Pat Winters	354
John Smith	338
Blank	000

No.	DATE START	DATE END	NO. OF STUDENTS	COURSE NAME	COURSE NO.	ABBREV. NAME
112	5.4.86	9.4.86	15	Info Analysis	01	INFO ANAL
112	6.6.86	10.6.86	10	Feas. Study	02	FEASIBILITY
112	7.7.87	11.7.87	15	Database Design	04	DB DESIGN
133	3.3.86	5.3.86	20	Strat.Study	03	STRATEGY
133	5.4.86	9.4.86	15	Info Anal	01	INFO ANAL
133	7.7.87	11.7.87	30	Feas.Study	02	FEASIBILITY
133	1.8.87	11.8.87	20	Application Sys.Design	05	{ APPLIC DESIGN
188	6.6.86	10.6.86	10	Feas.Study	02	FEASIBILITY
188	3.3.87	7.3.87	8	Info Anal	01	INFO ANAL
188	7.7.87	11.7.87	15	Database Design	04	DB DESIGN
354	—	—	—	—	—	—
338	5.4.87	8.4.87	0	Info Analysis	01	INFO ANAL
000	6.4.87	11.4.87	0	Feas.Study	02	FEASIBILITY

Figure 3.51 First Normal Form

students, course name and course no. can all differ as well as abbreviated name. We need only one value to deduce that there are no dependencies here.

Date Start is, however, different.

Whenever a Date Start value appears, so does the corresponding date end value (shown overleaf). Otherwise, as you follow the values for all the other items, this is not true.

What we now do is create a new table.

We make the key of the new table the part key on which other items depend, and we remove these other items and place them in the new table. Their values go, too, but we don't duplicate anything: the set of values appears only once in the new table.

The example shows this. Figure 3.52 shows the First Normal Form, whilst Figure 3.53 shows the Second Normal Form.

NAME	No.
Angela Anglepoise	112
James Robertson	133
Martin Henry	188
Pat Winters	354
John Smith	338
Blank	000

No.	DATE START	DATE END	NO. OF STUDENTS	COURSE NAME	COURSE NO.	ABBREV. NAME
112	5.4.86	9.4.86	15	Info Analysis	01	INFO ANAL
112	6.6.86	10.6.86	10	Feas. Study	02	FEASIBILITY
112	7.7.87	11.7.87	15	Database Design	04	DB DESIGN
133	3.3.86	5.3.86	20	Strat.Study	03	STRATEGY
133	5.4.86	9.4.86	15	Info Anal	01	INFO ANAL
133	7.7.87	11.7.87	30	Feas.Study	02	FEASIBILITY
133	1.8.87	11.8.87	20	Application Sys.Design	05	{ APPLIC DESIGN
188	6.6.86	10.6.86	10	Feas.Study	02	FEASIBILITY
188	3.3.87	7.3.87	8	Info Anal	01	INFO ANAL
188	7.7.87	11.7.87	15	Database Design	04	DB DESIGN
354	—	—	—	—	—	—
338	5.4.87	8.4.87	0	Info Analysis	01	INFO ANAL
000	6.4.87	11.4.87	0	Feas.Study	02	FEASIBILITY

Figure 3.52 First Normal Form

Name	No.
Angela	112
Anglepoise	
James	133
Robertson	
Martin	188
Henry	
Pat Winters	354
John Smith	338
Blank	000

No.	Date Start	No. of Students	Course Name	Course No.	Abbrev. Name
112	5.4.86	15	Info Analysis	01	INFO ANAL
112	6.6.86	10	Feas.Study	02	FEASIBILITY
112	7.7.87	15	Db.Design	04	DB DESIGN
133	3.3.86	20	Strategy Study	03	STRATEGY
133	5.4.86	15	Info.Analysis	01	INFO ANAL
133	7.7.87	30	Feas.Study	02	FEASIBILITY
133	1.8.87	20	Application Systems Design	05	APPLIC DESIGN
188	6.6.86	10	Feas.Study	02	FEASIBILITY
188	3.3.87	8	Info.Analysis	01	INFO ANAL
188	7.7.87	15	Db Design	04	DB DESIGN
354	—	—	—	—	—
338	5.4.87	0	Info.Analysis	01	INFO ANAL
000	6.4.87	0	Feas.Study	02	FEASIBILITY

DATE START	DATE END
5.4.86	9.4.86
6.6.86	10.6.86
7.7.87	11.7.87
3.3.86	5.3.86
1.8.87	11.8.87
3.3.87	7.3.87
—	—
5.4.87	8.4.87
6.4.87	11.4.87

Figure 3.53 Second Normal Form

66 A Simple Introduction to Data and Activity Analysis

Notice that in the (Date Start, Date End) Table each row is unique, Date end no longer appears in the old composite key table, but the composite key stays the same.

Second Normal Form
See Figure 3.53.

STEP 5

In normalisation this step is called "Conversion to Third Normal Form". We now look at each table in turn.

Taking all non-key items in turn, we ask if any non-key item is dependent on another non-key item.

The values are there to help us.

In our example, every time Course No. with Value '01' appears, Course Name "Info Analysis" appears and Abbreviated Name "INFO ANAL".

We must check that this is true for *every* value in the table. See Figure 3.54.

The dependent group of items is removed from the table and a new table is created with the items in it. Again, no rows of values are duplicated as they are removed to the new table.

A key is found for the new table. This key is then placed back in the table from where the items were extracted but as a *non-key* item.

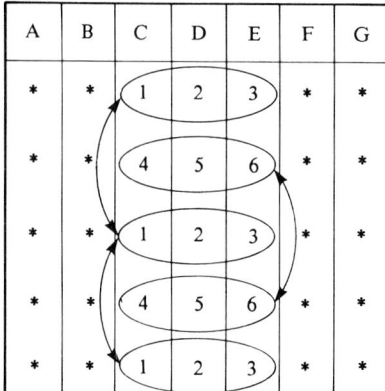

C, D and E are dependent on one another

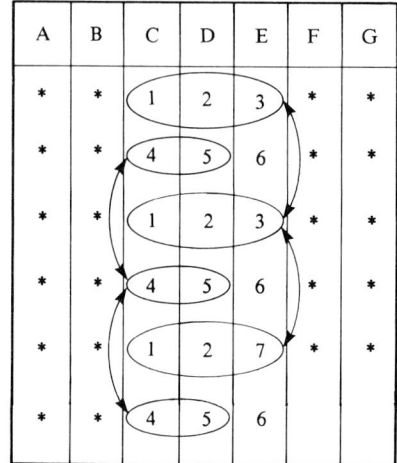

C + D may be dependent on one another, but C, D and E are not

Figure 3.54 Step 5

See Figure 3.55. Remember to repeat this process with every table. Remember also that even after one dependency is found, you may still find others in the *same* table. Keep on going until no dependencies are left.

Third Normal Form
See Figure 3.56.

In our example, we have removed Course No., Course Name and Abbreviated Name, made Course No. the key because it was the shortest, and put Course No. back in the old table as a non-key item.

How to do Data Analysis 67

A	B	C	D	E	F
*	*	1	2	3	*
*	*	4	5	6	*
*	*	1	2	3	*
*	*	1	2	3	*

before

A	B	C	F
*	*	1	*
*	*	4	*
*	*	1	*
*	*	1	*

C	D	E
1	2	3
4	5	6

after

Figure 3.55 Example

NAME	No.
Angela Anglepoise	112
James Robertson	133
Martin Henry	188
Pat Winters	354
John Smith	338
Blank	000

No.	DATE START	COURSE NO.	NO. OF STUDENTS
112	5.4.86	01	15
112	6.6.86	02	10
112	7.7.87	04	15
133	3.3.86	03	20
133	5.4.86	01	15
133	7.7.87	02	30
133	1.8.87	05	20
188	6.6.86	02	10
188	3.3.87	01	8
188	7.7.87	04	15
354	–	–	–
338	5.4.87	01	0
000	6.4.87	02	0

COURSE NO.	COURSE NAME	ABBREV. NAME
01	Info Analysis	INFO ANAL
02	Feas.Study	FEASIBILITY
03	Strategy Study	STRATEGY
04	Database Design	DBDESIGN
05	Application Systems Design	APPLIC DESIGN

DATE START	DATE END
5.4.86	9.4.86
6.6.86	10.6.86
7.7.87	11.7.87
3.3.86	5.3.86
1.8.87	11.8.87
3.3.87	7.3.87
–	–
5.4.87	8.4.87
6.4.87	11.4.87

Figure 3.56 Third Normal Form

68 *A Simple Introduction to Data and Activity Analysis*

STEP 6
Now we can convert the tables to a Data Model.

Remove the data values leaving only the column headings. Place the tables with the fewest key items at the top of the page and work progressively down the page as the number of key items increases (i.e. number of items which make up the key). For an example, see Figure 3.57.

Working from top to bottom connect the *keys* by always placing the many end at the bottom end of the line. See Figure 3.58.

Now connect up the key and non-key items. Where an item appears as a key in one table and a non-key in another, put the one end of the Relationship at the key end and the many end at the non-key end. See Figure 3.59.

Name each table. Use either the key name as a clue or look at the overall item contents of the table. Go back to the original source document and see if there are any clues. If all else fails with a composite key table, give it a name which is the combination of its "parent" tables. See Figure 3.60.

Finally, *remove* any 'foreign key' items from the tables. Now that you have the Relationship established you do not need 'foreign keys'. See Figure 3.61.

The result for the lecturer schedule example is shown over the page, first showing the tables (Figure 3.62) and then as a Data Model with a list of Attributes (Figure 3.63).

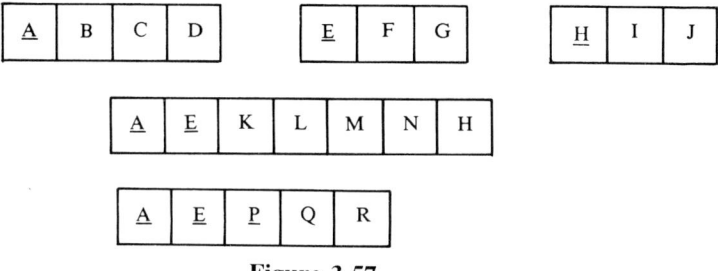

Figure 3.57

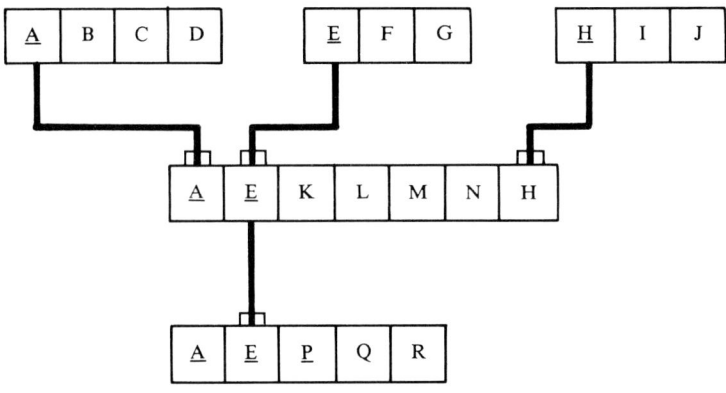

Figure 3.58

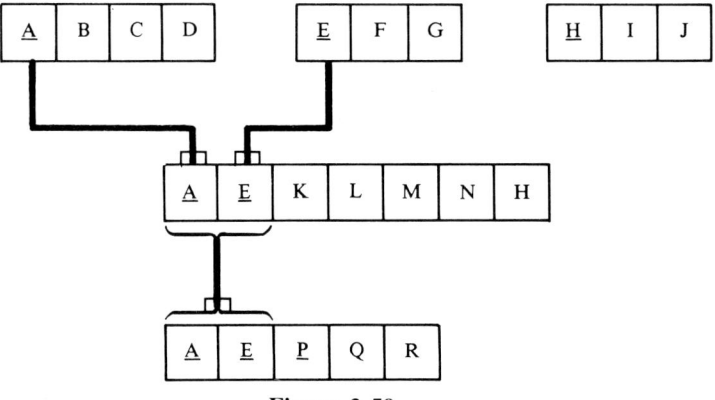

Figure 3.59

How to do Data Analysis 69

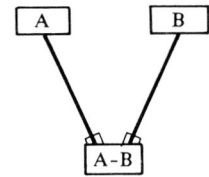

Figure 3.60

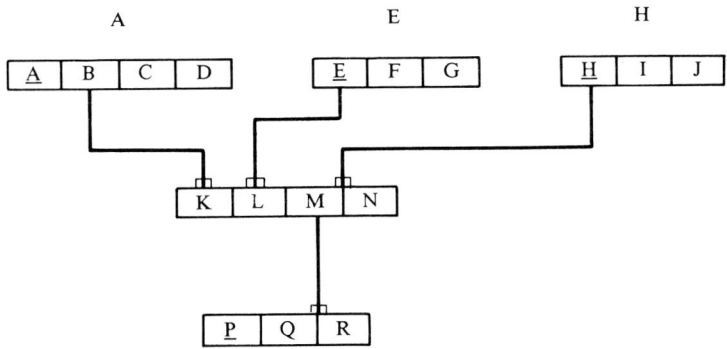

Figure 3.61

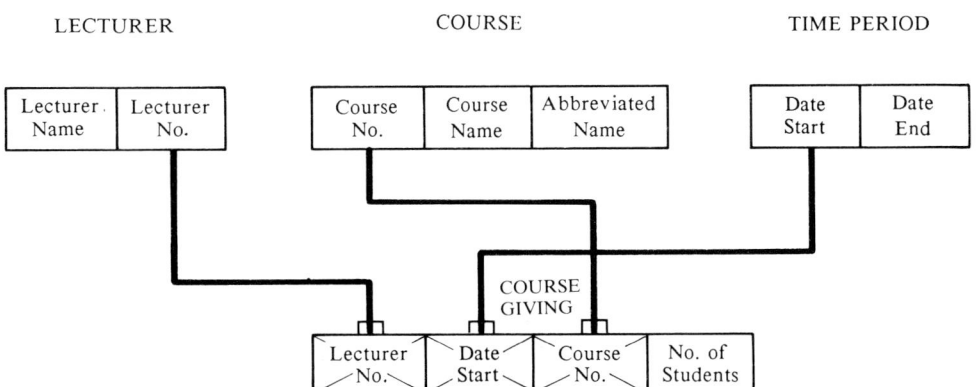

Figure 3.62 Lecturer's schedule example – tables

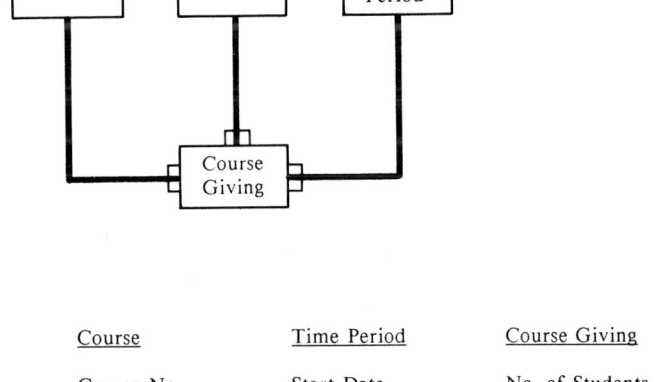

<u>Lecturer</u>	<u>Course</u>	<u>Time Period</u>	<u>Course Giving</u>
Name	Course No.	Start Date	No. of Students
No	Course Name	End Date	
	Abbreviated Name		

Figure 3.63 Lecturer's schedule example – Data Model with list of Attributes

70 A Simple Introduction to Data and Activity Analysis

STEP 7

Go back to the "Third Normal Form" table which had the data values in it.
Look through the rows of each table in turn.
Are there any 'blank' or 'null' values?
If there are we can use these to help us to determine optionality.
See Figure 3.64.
The results from the exercise undertaken in Figure 3.64 are shown on the Data Model in Figure 3.65.

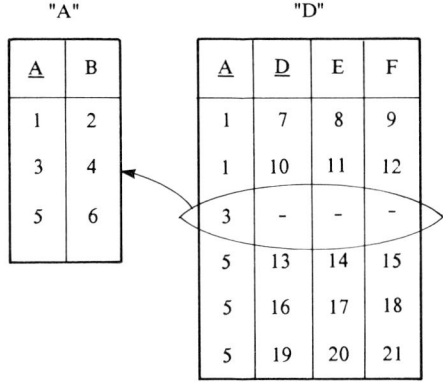

Where a line of null values appears against a part of a composite key item and the part key is the key of another table, optionality can be assumed.

Remove the line of null values from the table

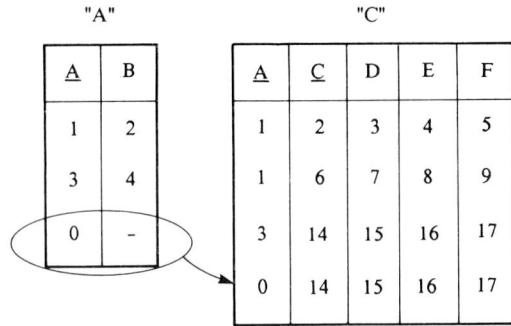

Where a zero or "null key" in one table with all null values is to be found as a part key in another, but where actual values are present, optionality can be assumed.

Remove the null valued row from the table

Figure 3.64 Lecturer's schedule example – Step 7

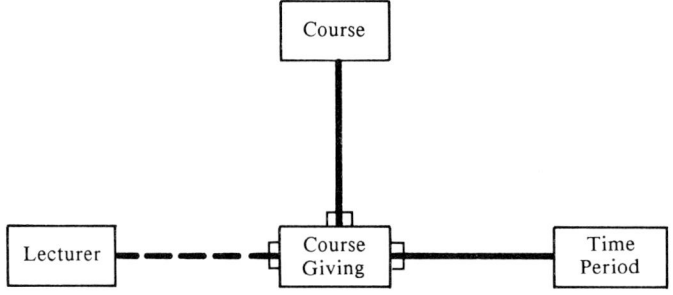

Figure 3.65 Lecturer's schedule example – Data Model

How to do Data Analysis 71

Where an item is a key item in one table and a non key item in another, and where null values appear as a *full row* in the table with the key item, and the null value key *also* appears as a non-key in the other table, then optionality can be assumed. See Figure 3.66.

Finally, see if you can deduce anything about the optionality from the items themselves. Look for zero or null values. In our example, zero appears in the number of students column. This means that some Course Givings may not have any students and we can update our Model accordingly.

The resulting Model is shown in Figure 3.67.

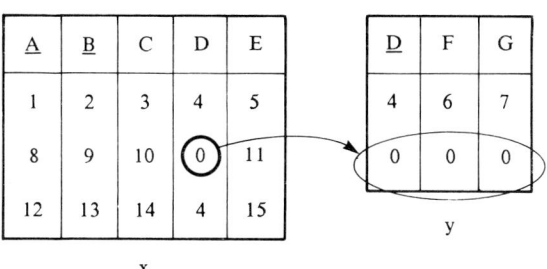

Figure 3.66 Lecturer's schedule example – Step 7 continued

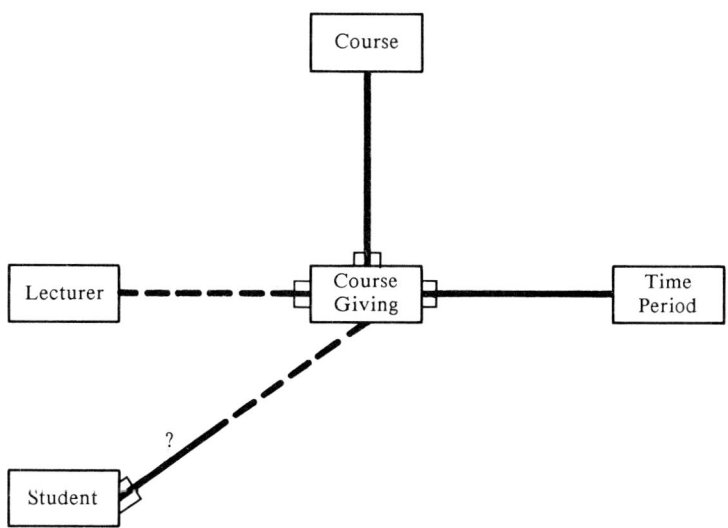

Figure 3.67 Lecturer's schedule example – Resulting Model

Summary
This method is useful for determining very complicated areas of a system, which revolve around abstract rather than concrete things.

I found it useful, for example, while analysing a pensions and payroll system's data and when looking at a banking system with almost entirely abstract concepts.

It requires very careful selection of the input used, however, as well as a good, representative sample of data to ensure that the conclusions drawn are correct.

The method cannot sensibly be used for Strategy or Feasibility/Tactical Studies. Some strange models often result from this method, which can be caused by:

* The original poor design
* The unusual 'view' of the data which the particular listing or form being analysed presents.

You cannot do anything about the former problem, but the latter can be eased by concentrating less on derived outputs, such as listings, and more on 'master' type design documents.

72 A Simple Introduction to Data and Activity Analysis

None of these methods is perfect on its own; it is their combination which can give you more powerful results. Normalisation followed by a user interview to verify the results, for example. Analysis of design abstractions followed by a meeting to verify.

You should use them all, wherever possible, to give you more reliable results.

3.3 MERGING THE MODELS

In practice, we would merge each source's Data Model into one composite Data Model as we went along. We would not do *all* the analysis and then merge. This is because once we know about an area, we have no need for more input, and by merging we keep the number of collection sessions and analysis effort to a minimum.

Merging is a simple, if not almost mechanical task.

The main thing you have to bear in mind is not to make quantum leaps in judgement. Instead, you should simply merge and identify all those conflicts of information which require further questioning.

The steps are shown in Figure 3.68.

All the Data Models which resulted from the Analysis task are shown again in Figures 3.69, 3.70, 3.71, 3.72, 3.73, 3.74 and 3.75. Then, in Figures 3.76 and 3.77, the resulting merged Data Model is shown; all the questions which arose from the conflict are listed in Figure 3.78.

3.1 Merge entities which have the same name together.

3.2 Merge relationships which have the same name together, <u>otherwise</u> keep separate on the Model.

    IF the degrees are not the same   then devise <u>questions</u> which
          optionality is different   will check these things
          exclusivity is different

3.3 Merge attributes which have common names. If the attributes have conflicting -

    codes/permitted values   then devise <u>questions</u> which
    formats   check these things
    or other properties

Figure 3.68 Steps to Merging the Models

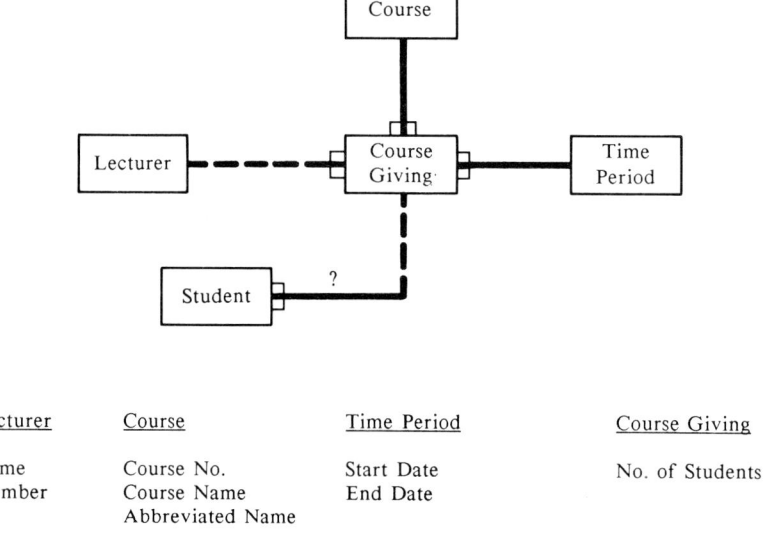

Lecturer	Course	Time Period	Course Giving
Name	Course No.	Start Date	No. of Students
Number	Course Name	End Date	
	Abbreviated Name		

Figure 3.69

How to do Data Analysis 73

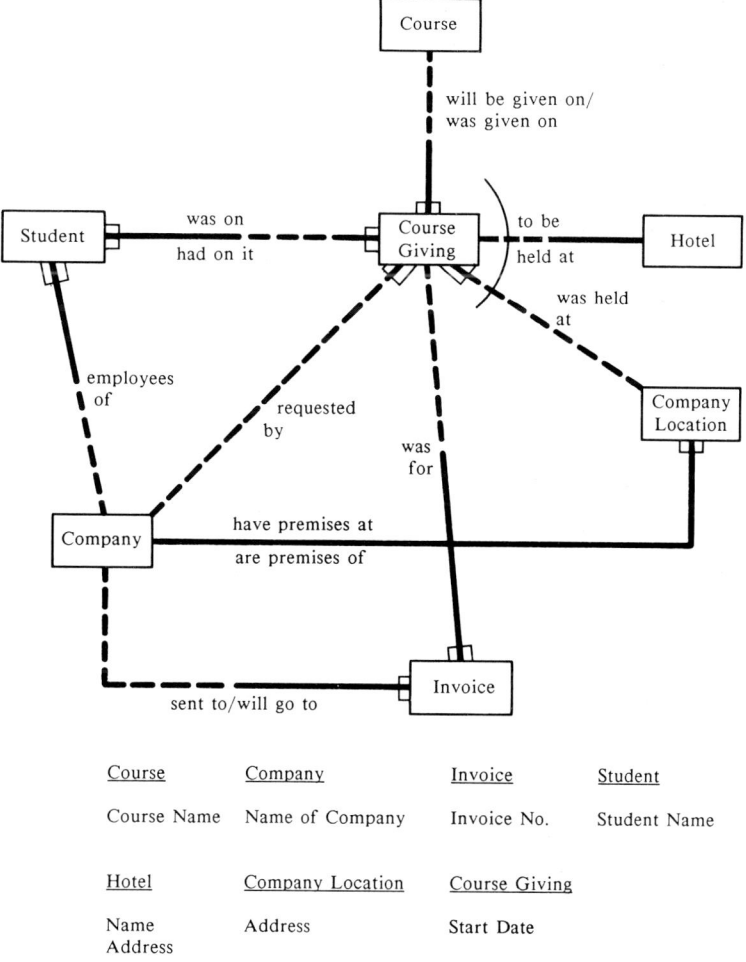

Course	Company	Invoice	Student
Course Name	Name of Company	Invoice No.	Student Name
Hotel	Company Location	Course Giving	
Name Address	Address	Start Date	

Figure 3.70

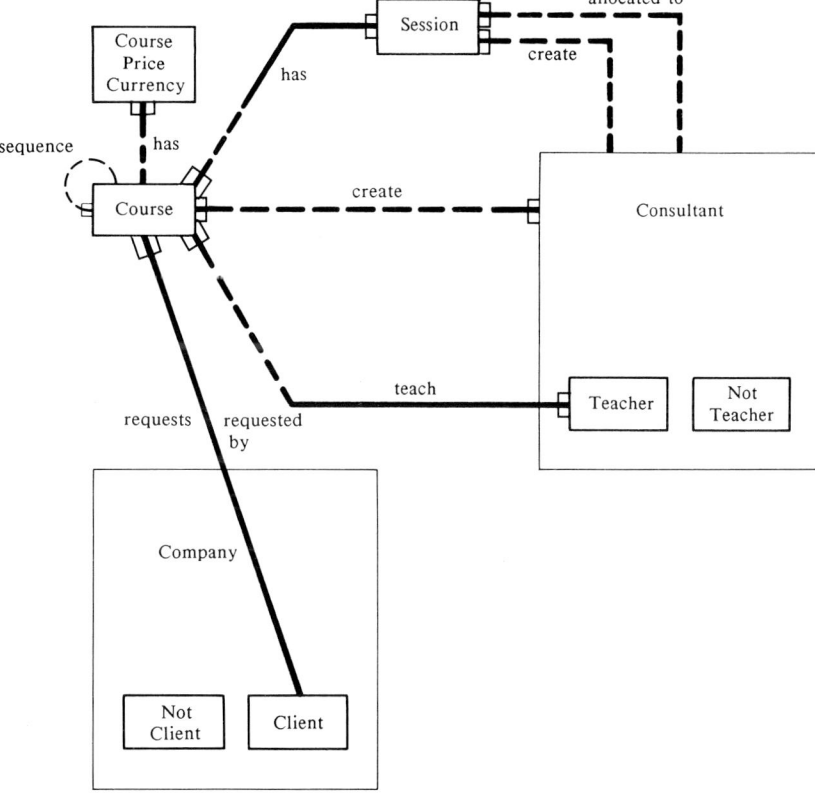

Figure 3.71

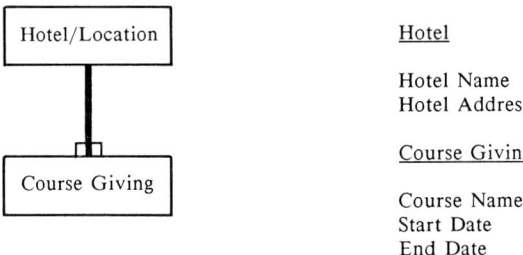

Hotel

Hotel Name
Hotel Address

Course Giving

Course Name
Start Date
End Date

Figure 3.72

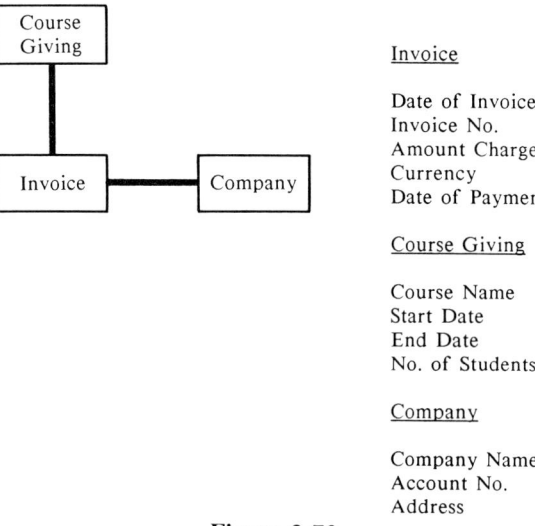

Invoice

Date of Invoice
Invoice No.
Amount Charged
Currency
Date of Payment

Course Giving

Course Name
Start Date
End Date
No. of Students

Company

Company Name
Account No.
Address

Figure 3.73

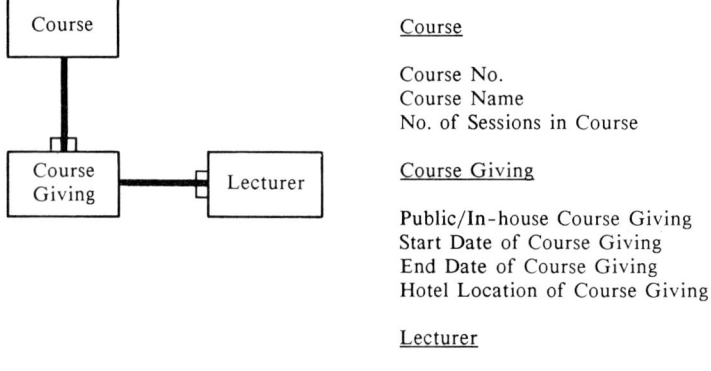

Course

Course No.
Course Name
No. of Sessions in Course

Course Giving

Public/In-house Course Giving
Start Date of Course Giving
End Date of Course Giving
Hotel Location of Course Giving

Lecturer

Name of Lecturer

Figure 3.74

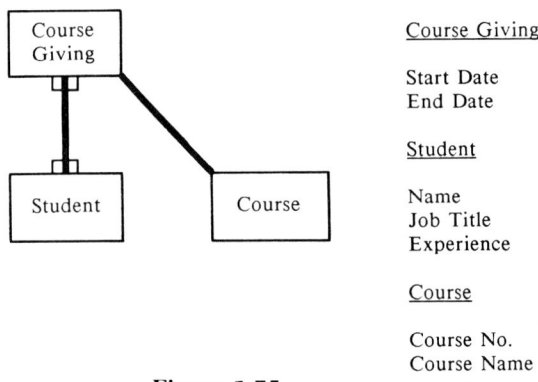

Course Giving

Start Date
End Date

Student

Name
Job Title
Experience

Course

Course No.
Course Name

Figure 3.75

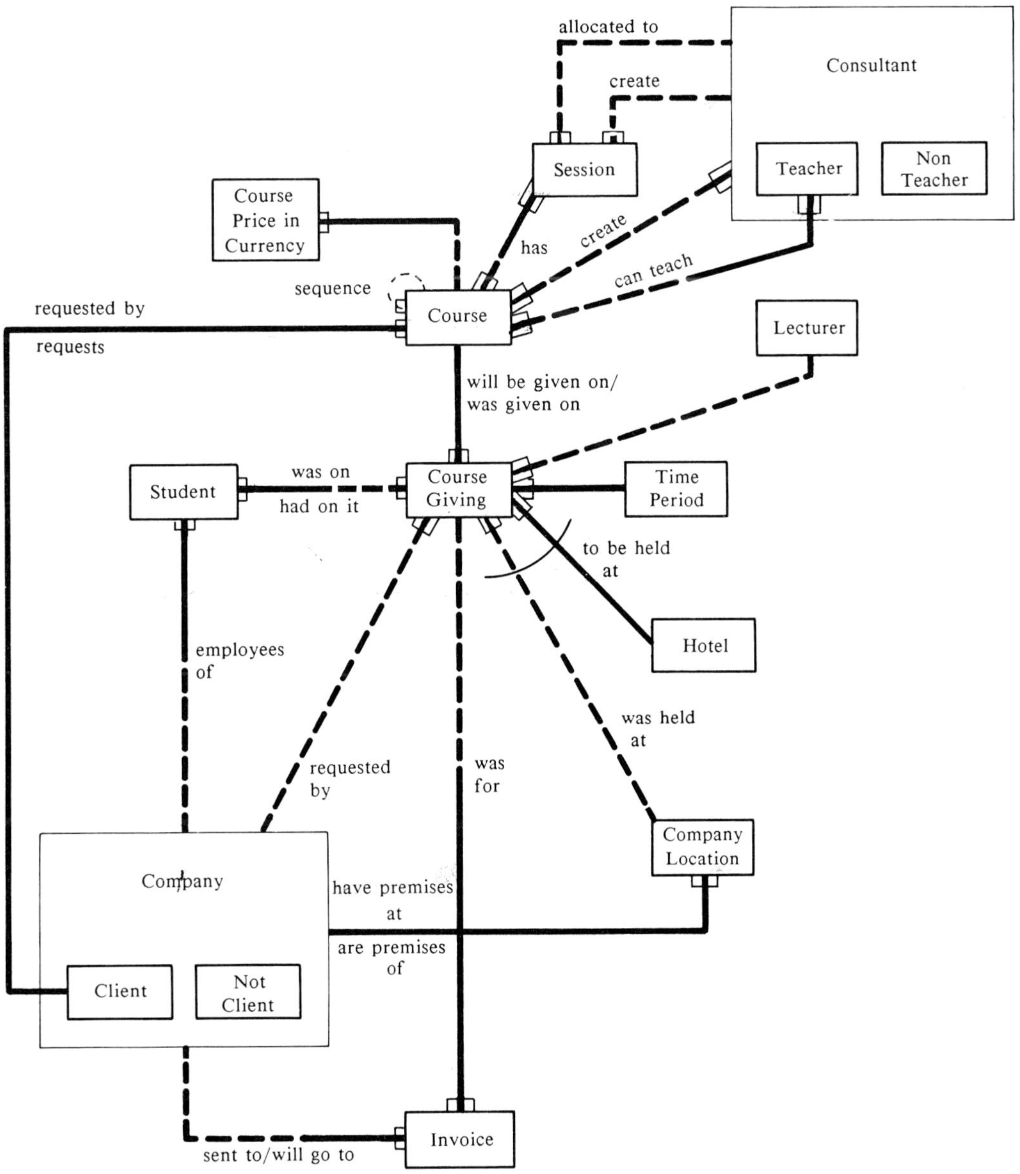

How to do Data Analysis 75

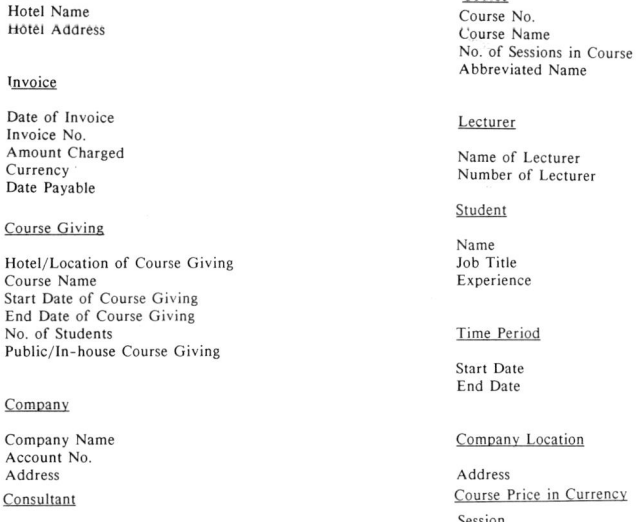

Figure 3.76 Resulting Merged Data Model

Hotel
Hotel Name
Hotel Address

Invoice

Date of Invoice
Invoice No.
Amount Charged
Currency
Date Payable

Course Giving

Hotel/Location of Course Giving
Course Name
Start Date of Course Giving
End Date of Course Giving
No. of Students
Public/In-house Course Giving

Company

Company Name
Account No.
Address

Consultant

Course
Course No.
Course Name
No. of Sessions in Course
Abbreviated Name

Lecturer

Name of Lecturer
Number of Lecturer

Student

Name
Job Title
Experience

Time Period

Start Date
End Date

Company Location

Address
Course Price in Currency
Session

Figure 3.77 Resulting Merged Data Model – List of Attributes

76 *A Simple Introduction to Data and Activity Analysis*

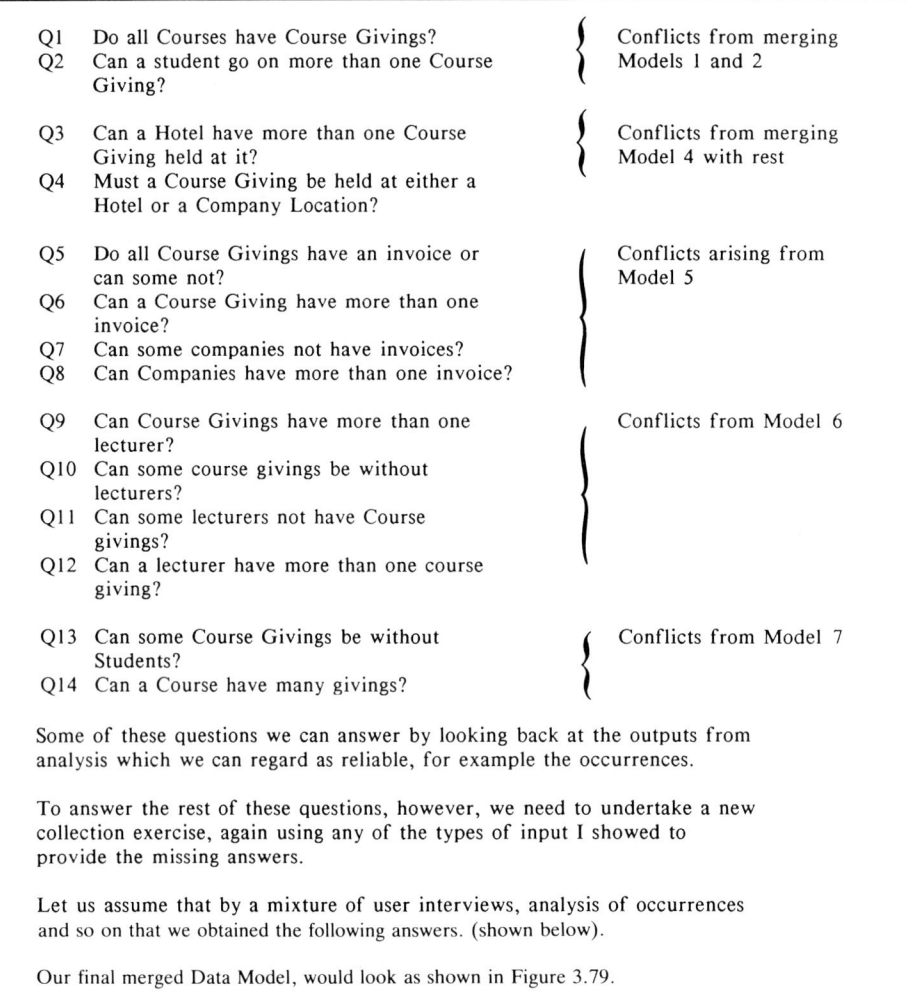

Figure 3.78 **List of Questions Which Arose From the Conflict**

The answers to these questions are as follows:

Q1 No, when courses are being created they do not
Q2 Yes
Q3 Yes
Q4 Yes, even on 'creation' a decision must have been made about where it is to be located
Q5 No, some won't yet have been invoiced
Q6 Yes (in respect of each Company with students in it)
Q7 Yes, some may have not yet received an invoice, some may have requested courses but no course givings yet
Q8 Yes, over time
Q9 Yes
Q10 When they are first created yes – during the 'planning stage'
Q11 Some may be recognised as lecturers, but not have been allocated to a course giving, so yes
Q12 Yes, over time
Q13 Yes, at the initial planning stage
Q14 Yes

The merged Model after questioning is shown in Figure 3.79.

3.4 REFINING THE DATA MODEL
The aims of this step are to look for improvements in the way the data is classified in the Data Model and to remove duplication.

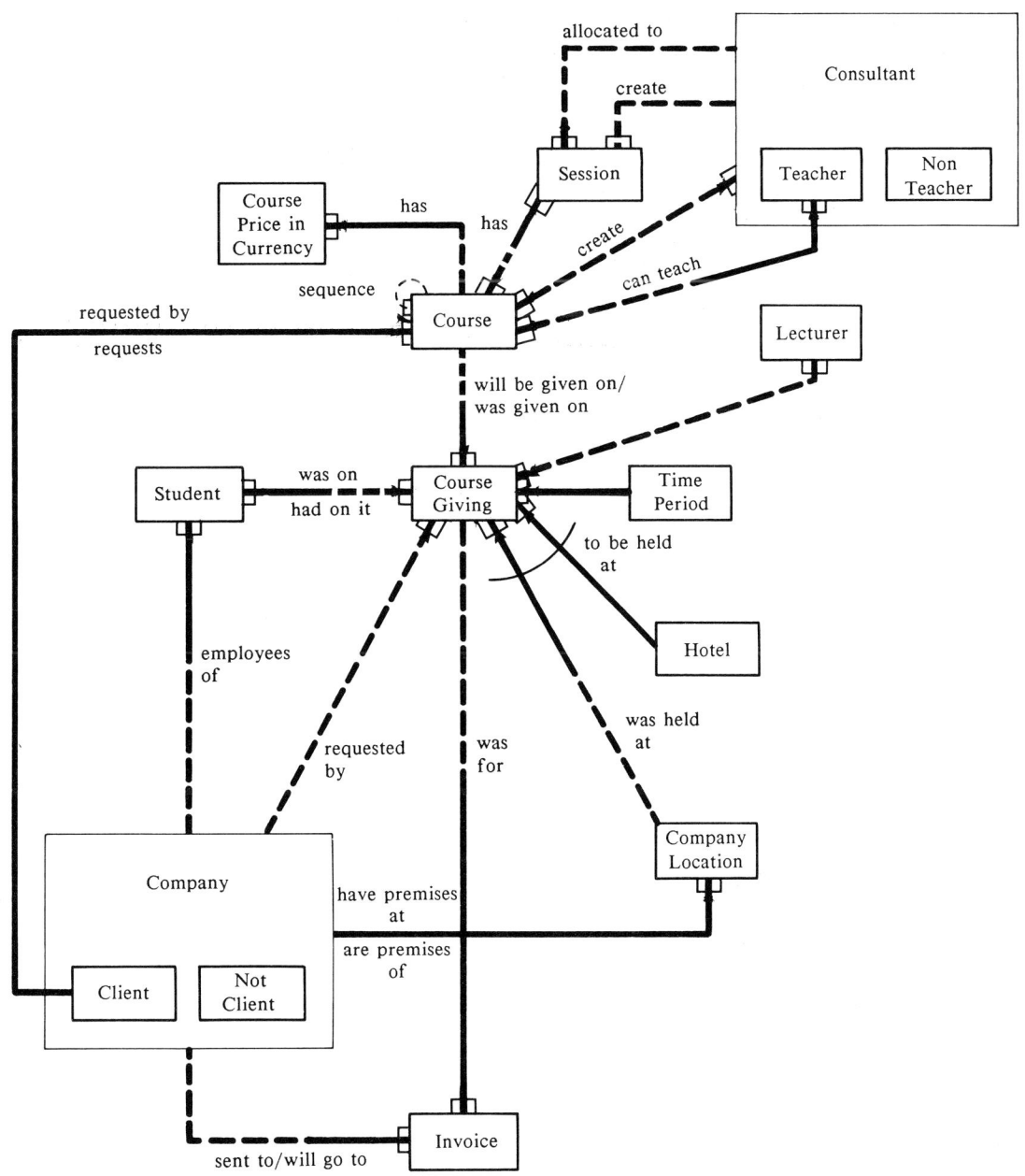

Figure 3.79 The Merged Model After Questioning

We are not looking for improvements in the *type of data*. This is something we do when we look for improvements in business practice.

The changes we make in the Data Model at this stage will make it clearer, more "robust" and ensure it contains no duplication, but it will still be the *same data*.

There are several simple steps we can follow to refine the Data Model, some of which are more powerful in their effect than others and some more prone to error. I will pinpoint the dangers as I describe each one.

Removing Synonyms

A synonym is a word which has the same *meaning* as another,

 e.g. Customer = Client
    Order = Sales Order

You must be careful that the words do have the *same* meaning and are not covering slightly different

78 *A Simple Introduction to Data and Activity Analysis*

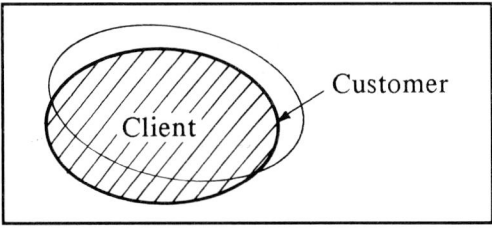

Figure 3.80

populations. For example, see Figure 3.80, in which client and customer are different because they cover slightly different populations of Entity occurrences.

You need to find out if there are any differences and what the differences are – any difference can then be added to the definition of whatever it is you are investigating.

Synonyms can exist in the merged Data Model for,

      Attributes)
      Entities)   all are possible and should be searched for
and   Relationships)

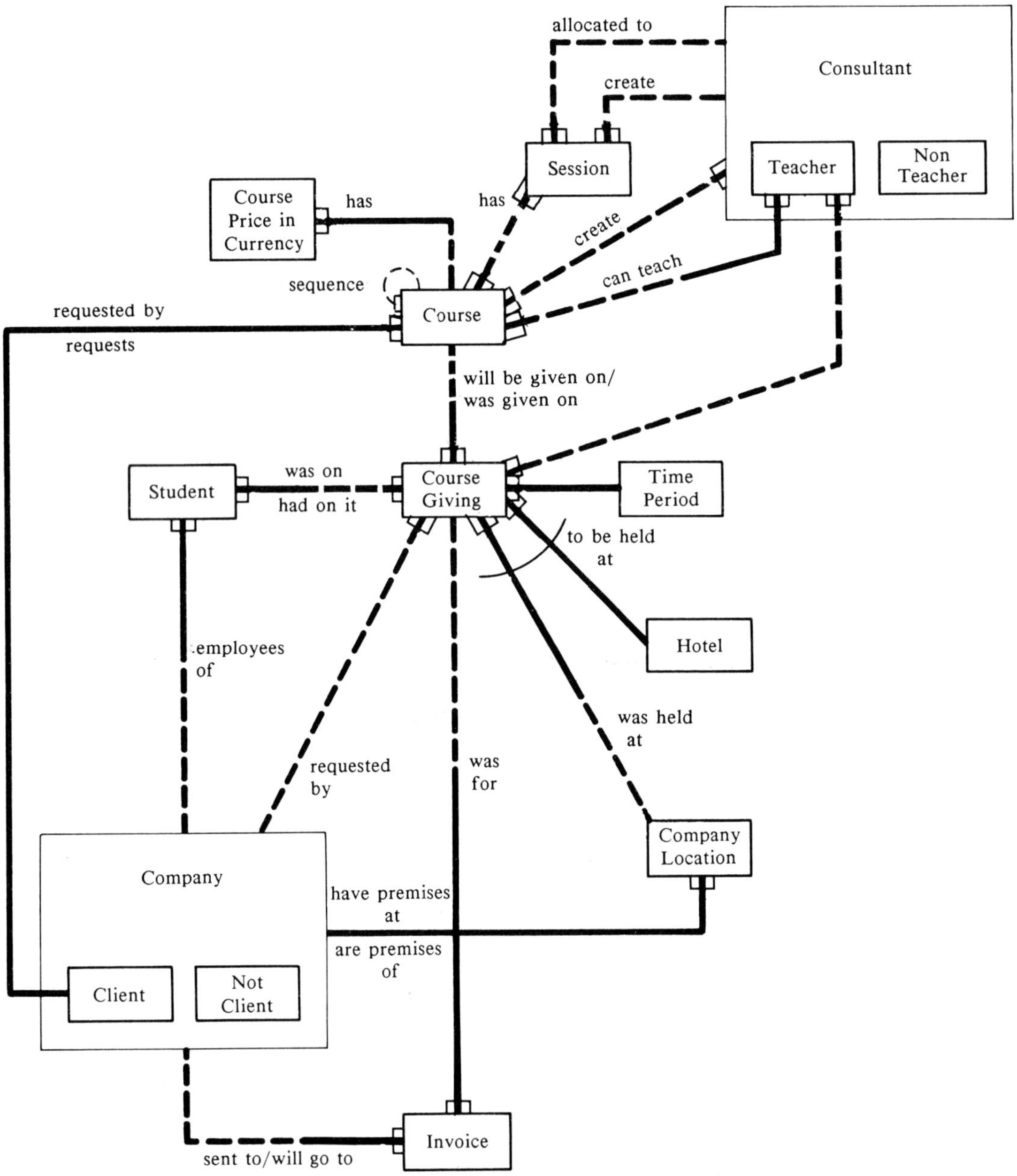

Figure 3.81 Data Model After Removal of Synonyms

If we look back to the Merged Model we obtained after questioning we find that Lecturer and Teacher are, in fact, synonyms. No Relationships are synonyms, nor Attributes.

The Entities and their Attributes are merged together. The Relationships are preserved.

The resultant Data Model is shown as Figures 3.81 and 3.82 with the teacher and lecturer Entities merged.

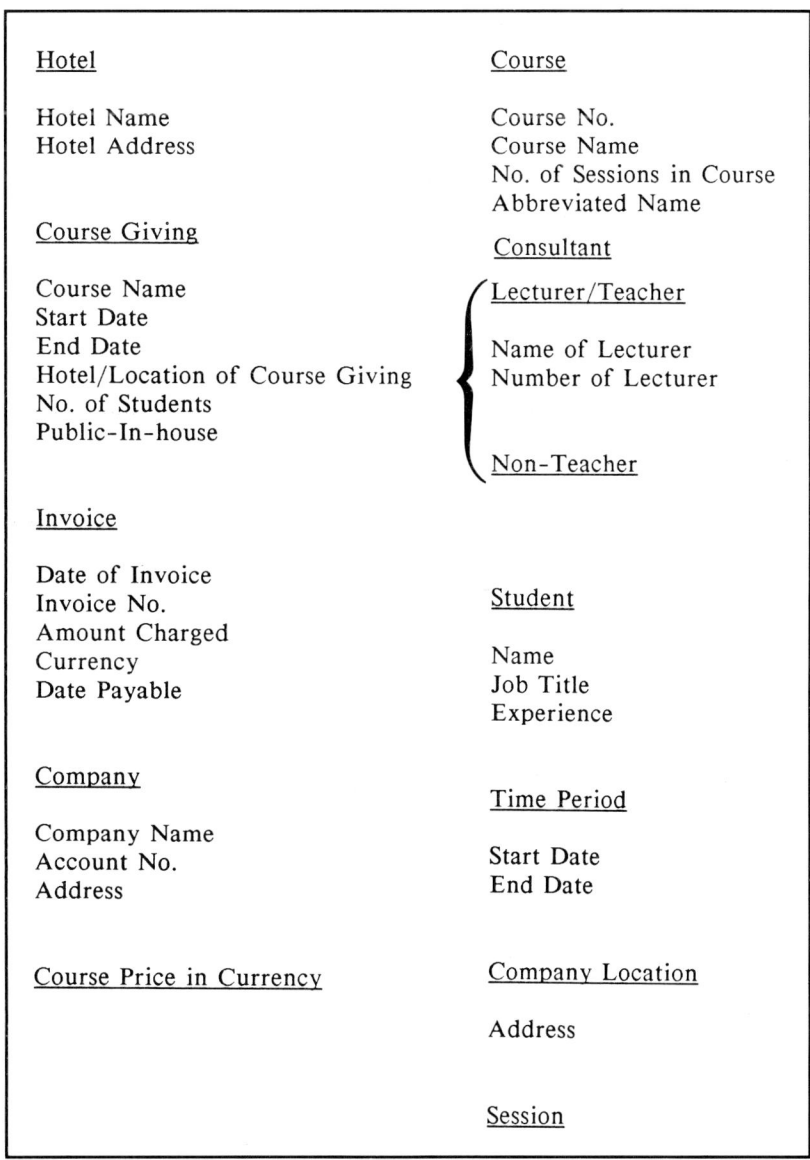

Figure 3.82 Data Model After Removal of Synonyms – List of Attributes

Check for Attribute Duplication

An Attribute can belong to only one Entity – that is the rule. Our analysis, however, and the subsequent merging of Data Models may have created a result which breaks the rule. This step aims to correct this.

There are three possible conclusions which can be drawn when Attributes are duplicated:

* An Entity is missing
* An Attribute is representing an existing or missing Relationship
* An Entity is 'false'

These three cases are demonstrated using examples on the next pages.

Case 1   An Entity is missing

In the first example (see Figure 3.83), the salesman code is duplicated in the list of Attributes of the two Entities. The salesman code does not describe either the order or the branch. In this case the salesman is treated as an Entity with Relationships to Order and Branch. We know that an Order

80 A Simple Introduction to Data and Activity Analysis

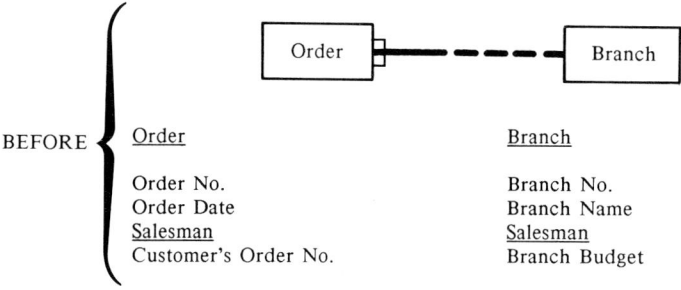

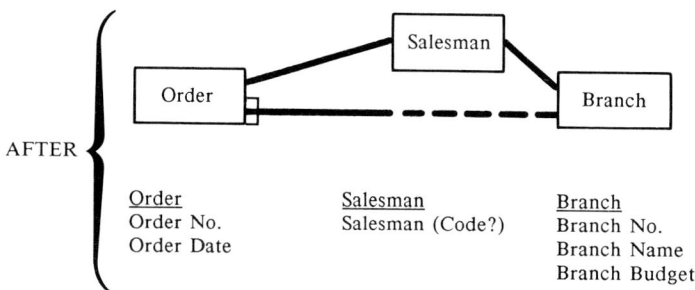

Figure 3.83 An entity is missing

can have only one salesman and a branch only have salesman. However, other facts are not known. The questions we will now need to ask are:–

- Q1 Can a salesman have more than one order?
- Q2 Do all salesmen have orders?
- Q3 Do all orders have salesmen?
- Q4 What is the Relationship between an order and a salesman? (sold, negotiated etc.)
- Q5 Can a salesman have more than one branch?
- Q6 Do all salesman have branches?
- Q7 Do all branches have salesman?
- Q8 What is the Relationship between a salesman and a branch?

Case 2 An Attribute is representing an existing or missing Relationship

In this example (Figure 3.84), the customer no. is quite clearly describing a customer. The customer no. within the order Entity has been falsely included and is actually 'duplicating' the Relationship. In other words, we know which customer placed the order from the Relationship – we have no need of the Attribute as well.

If there had been no Relationship between customer and order, we could have concluded that a Relationship was missing and would have had to devise questions about it as follows:–

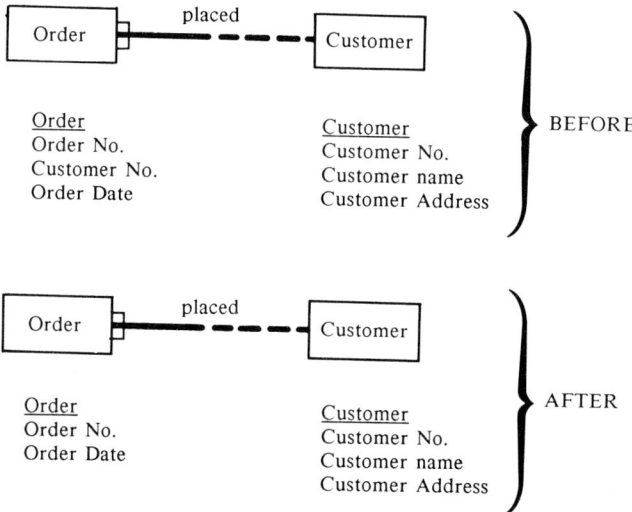

Figure 3.84 An attribute is representing an existing or missing relationship

Q1 Can a customer have more than one order?
Q2 Do all customers have orders?
Q3 Do all orders have customers?
Q4 What is the Relationship between customer and order?

Case 3   An entity is "false"

It may be quite true that the same value range applies to a large number of cars, as in Figure 3.85, but the Entity 'value range' is a meaningless type of Entity in business terms. It is coincidence, rather than business rule, which has led us to believe that it has some special importance. It should be removed. See Figure 3.86.

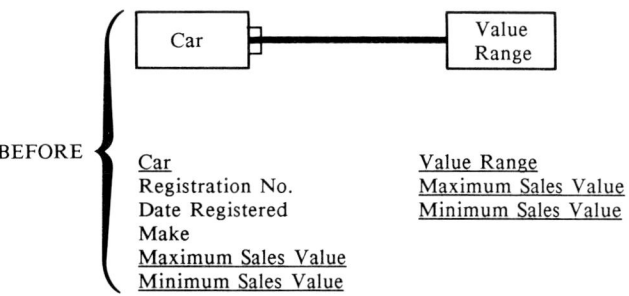

Figure 3.85 An entity is false

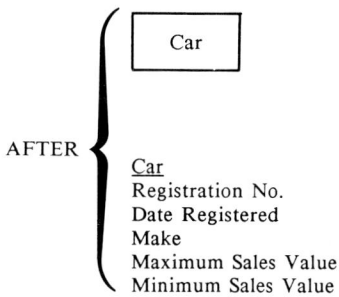

Figure 3.86

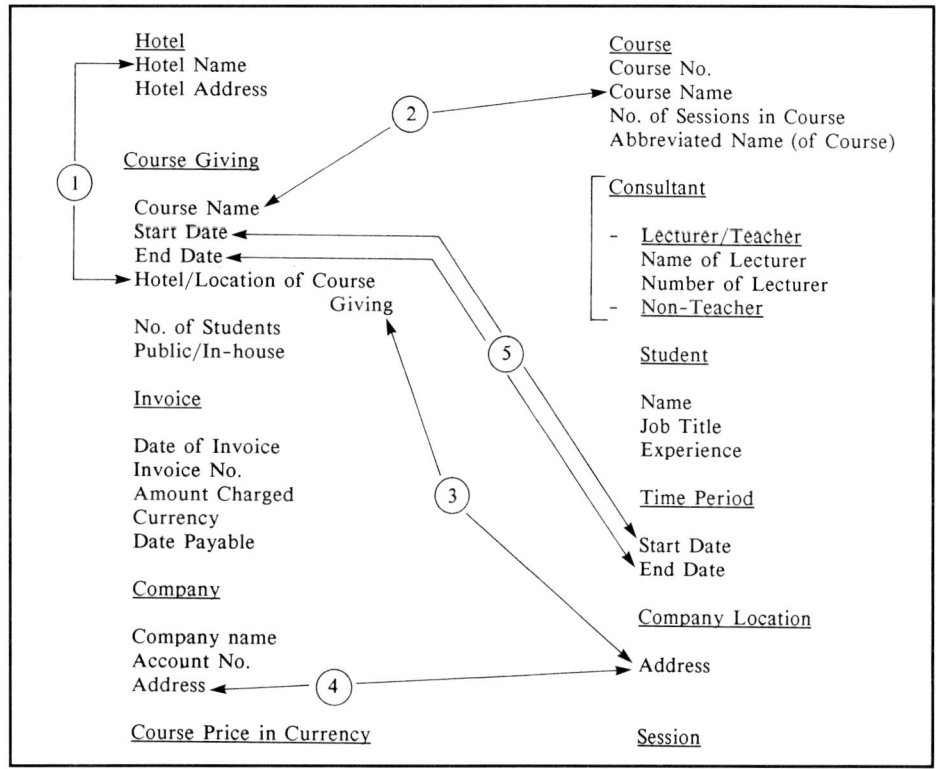

82 A Simple Introduction to Data and Activity Analysis

Using these three rules we will apply them to the list of Attributes shown in Figure 3.82. The results are shown in Figure 3.87.

1. The hotel name is duplicated. It correctly describes the hotel. The Relationship between hotel and Course Giving already exists, so does not need creating – we remove the hotel name from the Course Giving's List of Attributes.
2. Course name correctly describes a course. The Relationship between course and Course Giving already exists, so does not need creating. We remove the course name from the Course Giving's List of Attributes.
3. Location of Course Giving. Location = company location. The Relationship already exists so does not need creating. Remove location from the Course Giving's List of Attributes.

Notice that the Hotel/Location of Course Giving Attribute – now removed – confirms that a Course Giving is either given in a hotel or a company location. If it had been both, two Attributes would have been present.

4. Company address = company location address. The Relationship between company and company location already exists, so there is no need to create it. Remove address from the company Attribute list.
5. Start Date and End Date (Time Period) = Start Date and End Date (Course Giving). Time Period is a false Entity and needs to be removed.

The Data Model after this Step is shown as Figure 3.88 and 3.89.

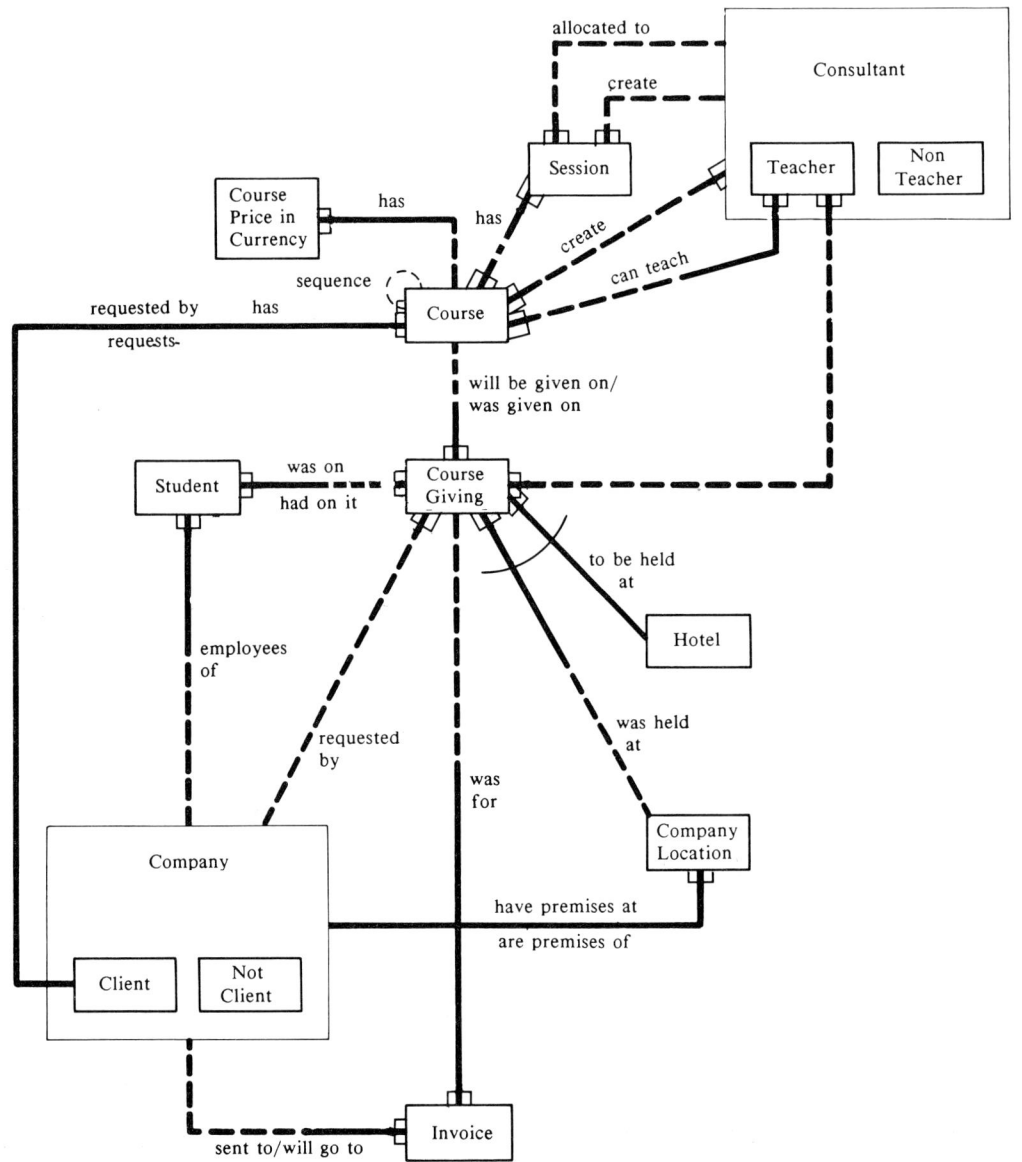

Figure 3.88 Data model after three rules applied

How to do Data Analysis 83

<pre>
Hotel   Session

Hotel Name
Hotel Address

Course Giving   Course Price in Currency

Start Date
End Date
No. of Students
Public/In-house

Invoice

Invoice Number
Date of Invoice
Amount Charged
Currency
Date Payable

Company

Company Name
Account No.

Course

Course No.
Course Name
No. of Sessions in Course
Abbreviated Name

Consultant

 - Lecturer/Teacher

    Name of Lecturer
    Number of Lecturer

 - Non-Teacher

Student

Name
Job Title
Experience

Company Location

Address
</pre>

Figure 3.89 Data model after three rules applied – list of attributes

Generalisation – Entities

When we decide what our classes of data are going to be in the Data Model, we base it very much on the view our sources have of the business. Sometimes this view is quite narrow and we may have a Data Model with hundreds of Entities on it, all containing small populations which might be better regarded as sub-types of larger, more general classes.

Generalisation is at the same time one of the most powerful and one of the most error-prone refinement processes.

We are saying that, as far as the business is concerned, there are business rules which apply for the larger class as a whole as well as perhaps the sub-types.

We can generalise from two different "inputs". In Activity Analysis, the activities will show us if

84 *A Simple Introduction to Data and Activity Analysis*

general rules exist for more general classes of things. We can, however, use the Data Model itself and the following two pages show how two general pointers can be used to produce more general Models.

There is real value in having a generalised Model. It is easier to change activities and add populations. It is simpler to read and it shows up patterns of Data and Business Activity which can prove invaluable in deciding strategy and understanding business priorities.

Don't, however, try to combine Entities the business itself does not recognise, just because similar patterns seem to exist. Use your common sense, context and an understanding of the business activities to help you.

Looking for Patterns
In Figure 3.90, there is a repeating pattern. B + F, C + G, D + H, and E + I not only look the same but have the same Relationship. You need to ask whether the Data Model in Figure 3.91 is a more valid and generalised picture.

Exclusivity Case
Where a Data Model contains exclusivity (for an example, see Figure 3.92), then the exclusive Relationship, where there are a large number all relating to a group of Entities, can be replaced using sub-types, as shown in Figure 3.93, and a more generalised Entity.

Another example of the exclusive case is shown in Figure 3.94 using our 'Course Administration'

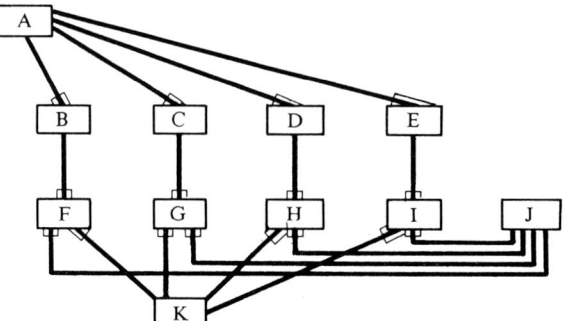

Figure 3.90 Looking for patterns

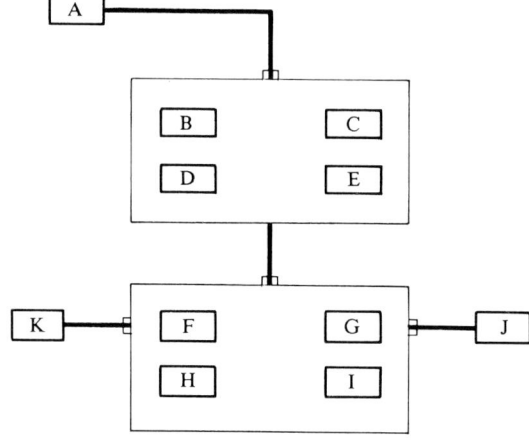

Figure 3.91

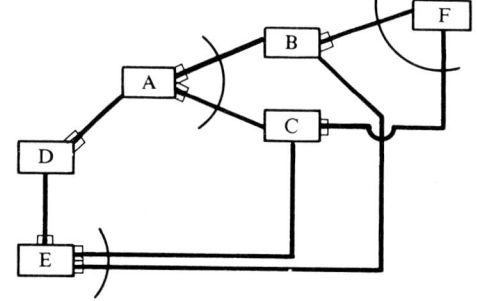

Figure 3.92 Data model containing exclusivity

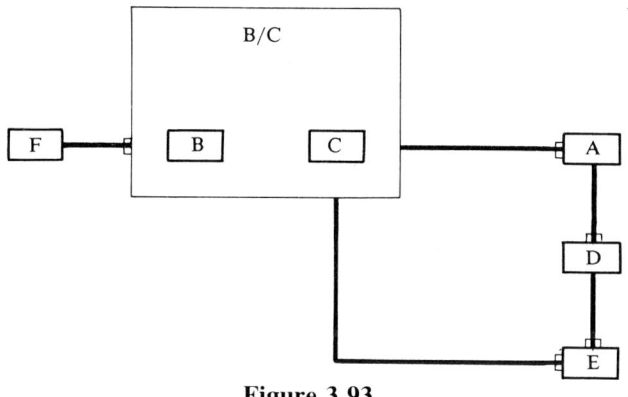

Figure 3.93

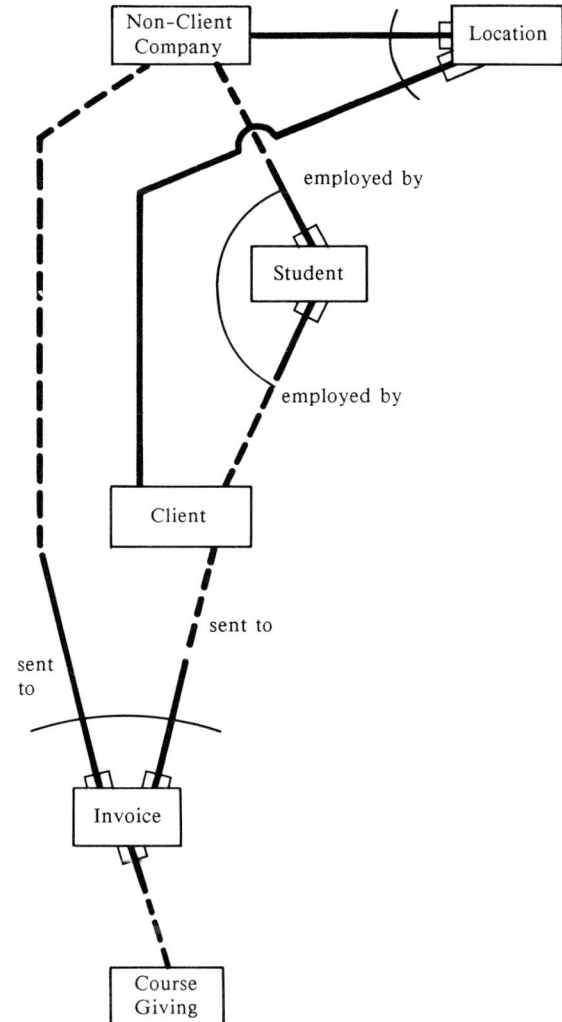

Figure 3.94 Example of the exclusive case

system. In this example, the assumption has been made that we have obtained input from another source which views the data in a less general way than we do.

By generalising, we can see that we have ended up with a sub-set of the Data Model we already have. See Figure 3.95.

Generalising – Relationships

Relationships are expressed using verbs. These verbs show which events and activities affected the entities,

    e.g.   Customer places Order
            Teacher creates Course

86 *A Simple Introduction to Data and Activity Analysis*

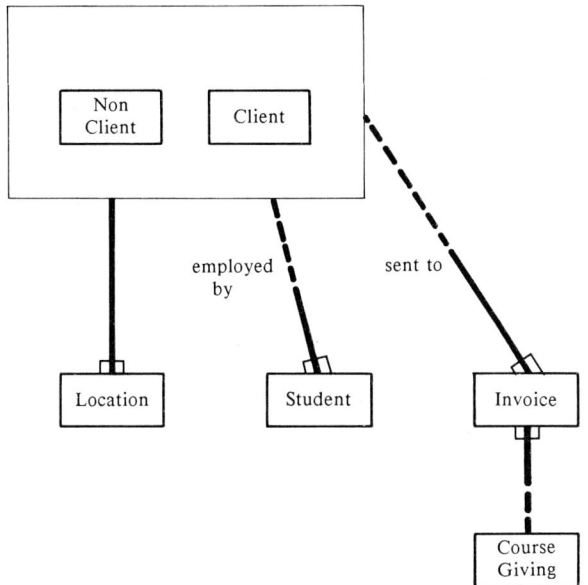

Figure 3.95 A sub-set of the Data Model we already have

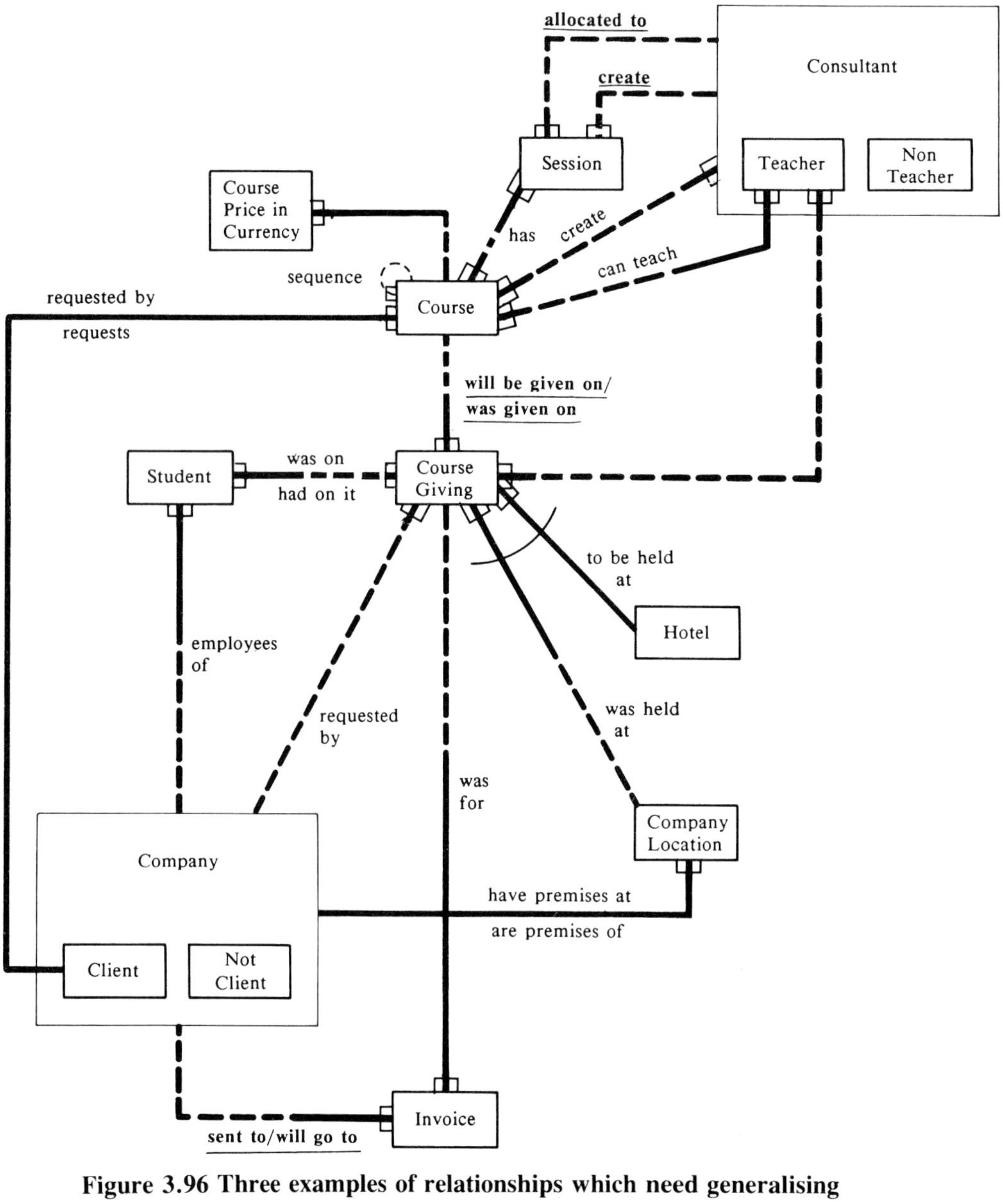

Figure 3.96 Three examples of relationships which need generalising

How to do Data Analysis 87

There will be many events and activities in the system which will need to be recorded as having happened using the Data Model.

As a general rule we must aim to record events and activities using Attributes, not Relationships. This is because an Attribute can more precisely describe *when* something happened, e.g. Event = Person Born, Attribute = Date of Birth, and because a Data Model which uses Relationships to show every event and activity becomes almost unreadable.

There are two cases where Relationships will need to be generalised:

  (i) The Relationship shows change of tense from past to present to future; and
 (ii) Many Relationships between the same two Entities simply describe different events or activities affecting those two Entities.

I will demonstrate what action is taken in these two circumstances using the Course Administration Data Model we have obtained from the previous step.

There are three examples of Relationships which need generalising.

They are shown in bold and underlined on the Data Model in Figure 3.96.

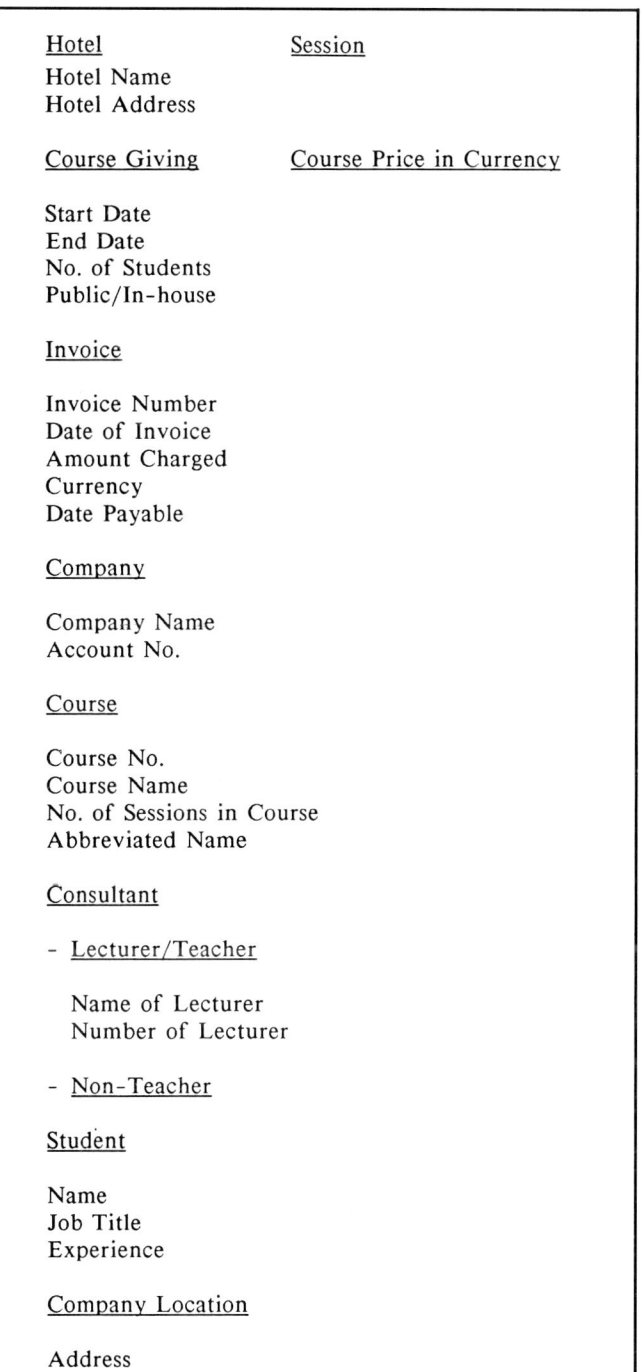

Figure 3.97 Data Model before generalisation of verbs – list of attributes

88 *A Simple Introduction to Data and Activity Analysis*

The two Relationships 'allocated to' and 'create' are an example of many Relationships between the same two Entities describing different activities affecting the entities.

The Relationships 'will be given on', 'was given on' and 'sent to/will go to' show change of tense.

Change of Tense
  * Replace the name by a more general purpose name which does not imply these changes. In many cases the verb "has" is perfectly adequate.
  * Create an Attribute which enables you to deduce whether something will happen, is happening, or has happened. Usually this is a *Date* related Attribute, but may also involve *time*..
  * Give the Attribute a name which reflects the original verb,
    e.g. Date Given
          Date Sent
  * Allocate the Attribute to the many end of a 1:N Relationship.
  * Where many-to-many Relationships exist, create a special in-between Entity and allocate the Attribute to this.

Many Relationships
  * Combine all the Relationships into one Relationship. Give this Relationship a general purpose name. 'Has' is normally adequate.
  * Where the activities or events expressed by the original Relationships are *mutually exclusive and* a record is not required of when each event or activity took place, create an Attribute having code values which represent each mutually exclusive event or activity.

If the Relationships are one-to-many, place the Attribute at the *many* end of the Relationship (see Figure 3.98 below).

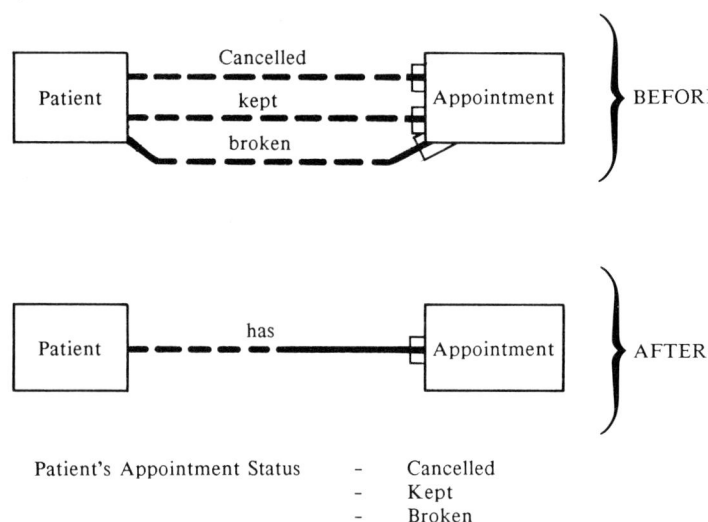

Figure 3.98 Creation of special in-between entity – examples

If the Relationships are many to many, create a special 'in-between' Entity (as shown in Figure 3.99), and allocate the Attribute to that.

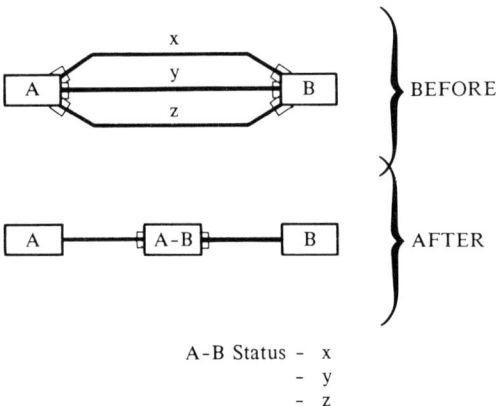

Figure 3.99 Model showing creation of special in-between entities

* Where the activities or events expressed by the original Relationships are not mutually exclusive or a record is required of when things happened, create one Attribute for each original Relationship. (It will usually be a date Attribute, or possibly time). Give each Attribute a name which reflects the original verb.

If the Relationships are one to many, place each Attribute at the *many* end of the Relationship.

If the Relationships are many to many, create a special 'in-between' Entity and allocate them to that. For an example, see Figure 3.100.

In the Course Administration Data Model, the result is shown in Figures 3.101 and 3.102. The Data Model has been simplified and the list of Attributes changed.

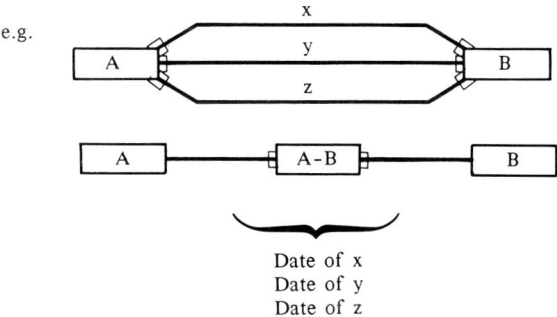

Figure 3.100 Creation of one attribute for each original relationship

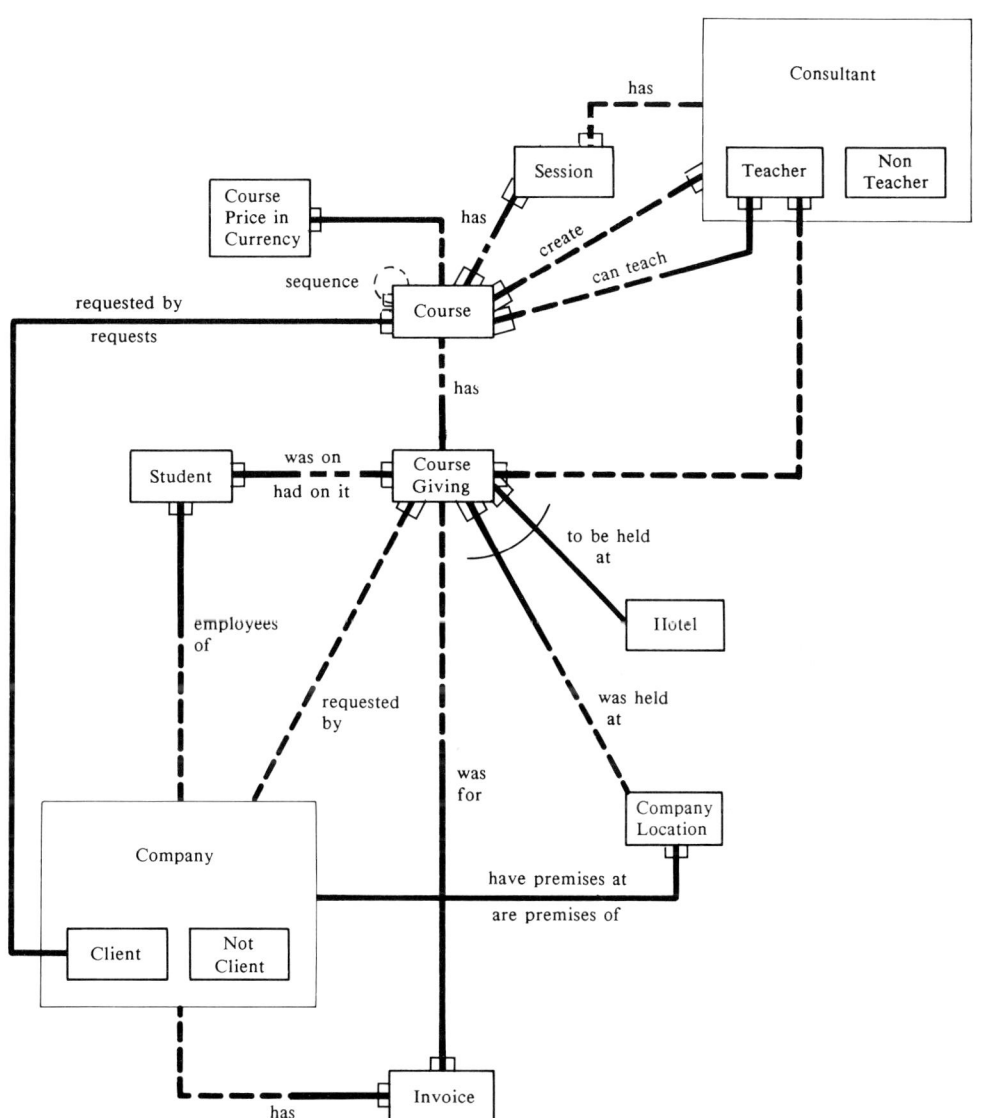

Figure 3.101 Course Administration Data Model

90   *A Simple Introduction to Data and Activity Analysis*

<u>Hotel</u>   <u>Session</u>

Hotel Name   Date Allocated to Consultant
Hotel Address   Date Session created

<u>Course Giving</u>   <u>Course Price in Currency</u>

Start Date
End Date
No. of Students
Public/In-house

<u>Invoice</u>

Invoice Number
Date of Invoice
Amount Charged
Currency
Date Payable
Date sent

<u>Company</u>

Company Name
Account No.

<u>Course</u>

Course No.
Course Name
No. of Sessions in Course
Abbreviated Name

<u>Consultant</u>

- <u>Lecturer/Teacher</u>

    Name of Lecturer
    Number of Lecturer

- <u>Non-Teacher</u>

<u>Student</u>

Name
Job Title
Experience

<u>Company Location</u>

Address

Figure 3.102 Course Administration Data Model – List of Attributes

Session now has two Attributes,

          Date allocated   (to Consultant)
and   Date Session created (by Consultant)

Course Giving already had 'start date' as an Attribute, so there is no need to create an additional one. The start date will show when the course giving was given and whether it is to be given.

The Date Invoice sent Attribute has been added to the list of the Invoice's Attributes. This will show when the invoice was sent or whether it has still to be sent – a 'null' value (zero say) means 'still to be sent'.

Removing Redundancy

A redundant Relationship is one which provides the same information as two or more other Relationships.

We want to remove redundant Relationships at this stage to keep the Data Model both simple and easy to understand, but more important, to ensure effort is not wasted by the activities in keeping duplicate information up to date.

If we can *derive* Relationship information from other Relationship information, we have no need to keep redundant Relationships.

We can't determine whether a Relationship is redundant simply by looking at a Data Model. The only way we really know is by using the *occurrences*.

This is where real-world occurrences play a vital and unique role in simplifying and improving the Data Model.

Redundancy should be suspected and checked when the following patterns of Data Model occur; all involve "closed loops". See Figure 3.103.

In the Data Model produced after the last step, we have a Relationship which might be redundant in the group. See Figure 3.104.

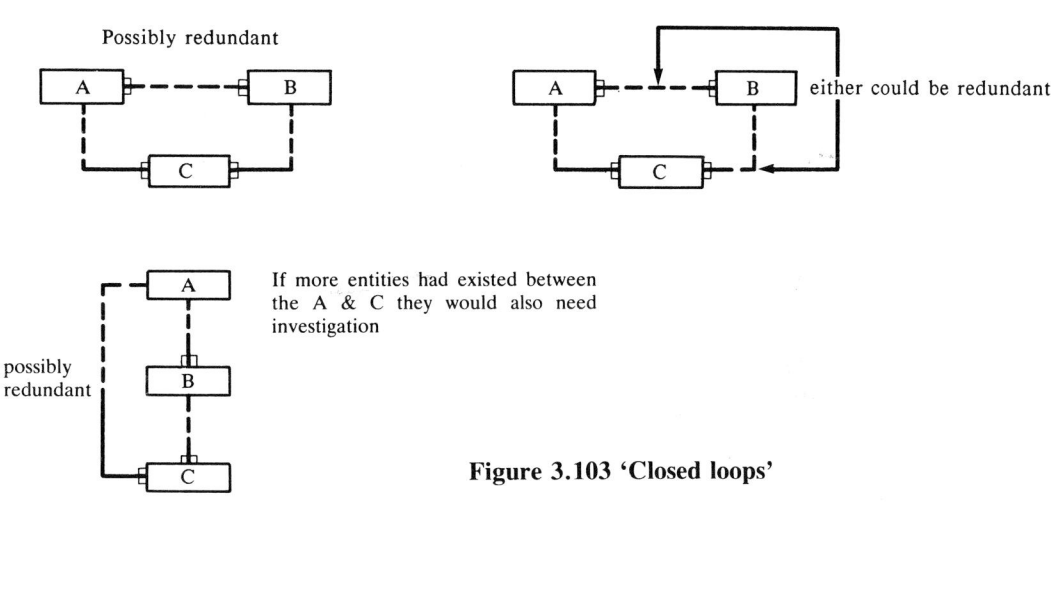

Figure 3.103 'Closed loops'

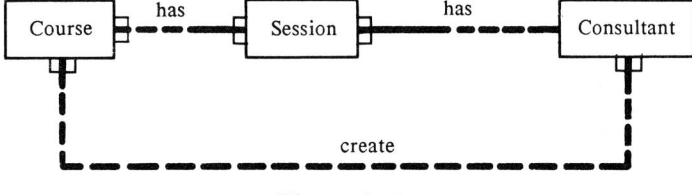

Figure 3.104

Is it true that the teachers who have created the course are the same teachers who created the sessions in the course?

I will now assume that I have collected a good sample of data on our real world occurrences to help me. Using the analysis techniques already described for real world occurrences, the data is structured and a semantic network built of the occurrences. I collect only data on the Relationships I want to check.

The result is shown in Figure 3.105.

Because Anne Mason created "Session 1", and Session 1 is used for the Strategy Study and Feasibility Study Courses, Anne Mason is deemed to have helped in creating these courses. Similarly, Alan Smith created Session 2, used by the Feasibility Study Course and so is deemed to have helped in creating the Feasibility Study Course. Finally, John Mills created session 6 which is used on the Information Analysis, Feasibility Study and Strategy Study Courses. Hence John Mills is deemed to have helped in the creation of these courses.

The conclusion is that the "Consultant created Course" Relationship is redundant and we can remove it from the Data Model. The new Data Model after removing redundancy is shown in Figures 3.106 and 3.107.

92 *A Simple Introduction to Data and Activity Analysis*

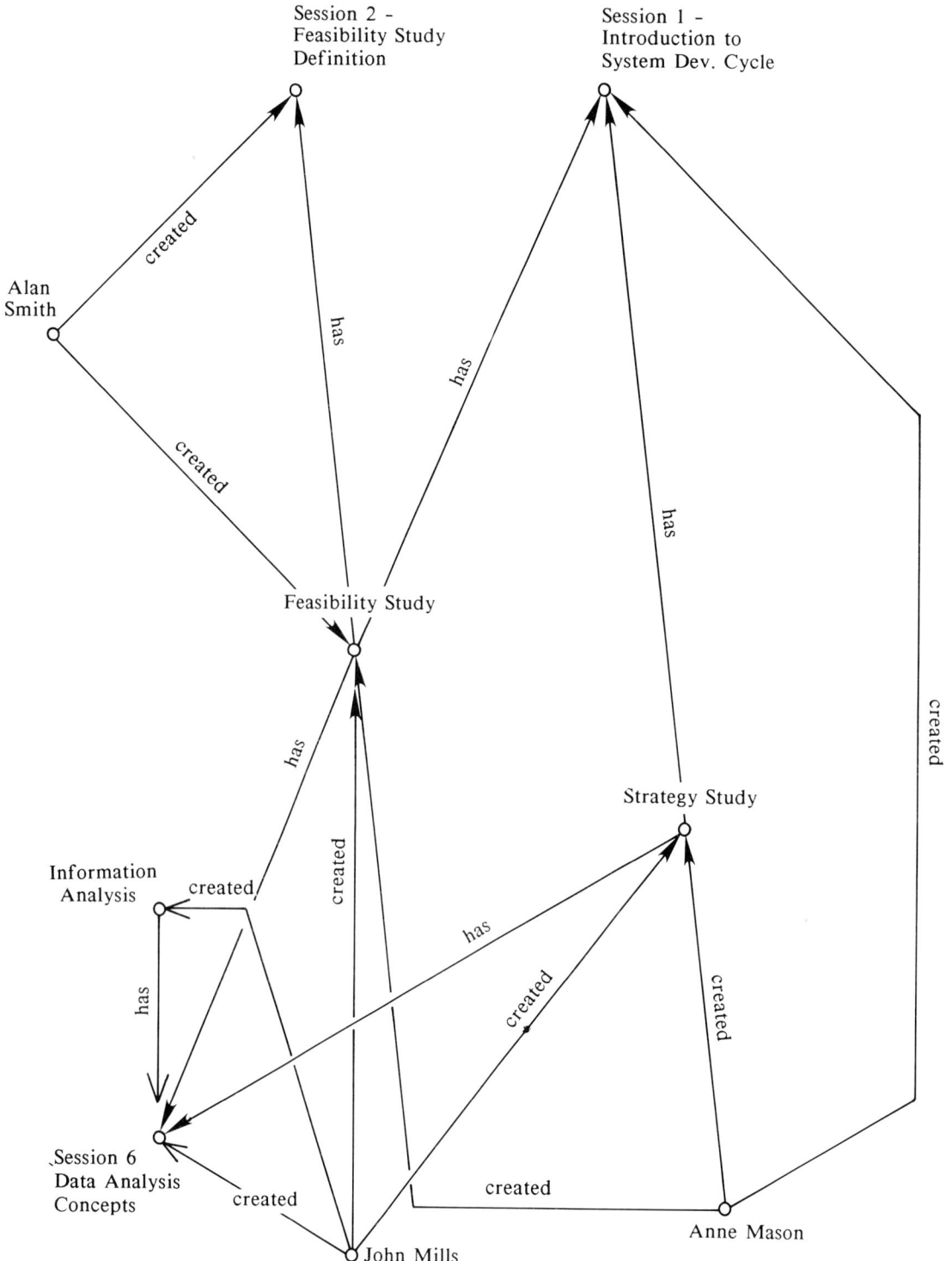

Figure 3.105 Semantic Network

Resolving Many to Many Relationships
A many-to-many Relationship is not incorrect, but it needs to be investigated. Very often many to many Relationships conceal the fact that other important Entities exist which have not yet been identified. This is especially true when you find "Closed Loops", as in Figure 3.108.

This Data Model is missing many vital Entities which would result from the removal of the many-to-many Relationships shown – Entities such as Flight and Ticket.

Ask your users if any Entities exist "in between" the two involved in a many-to-many Relationship or the Entities involved in a 'closed loop' like that shown in Figure 3.108.

The Entity should not be false, just invented for the purpose of resolving the many-to-many. It should be one which is recognised by the business and/or about which Attributes can be kept.

How to do Data Analysis 93

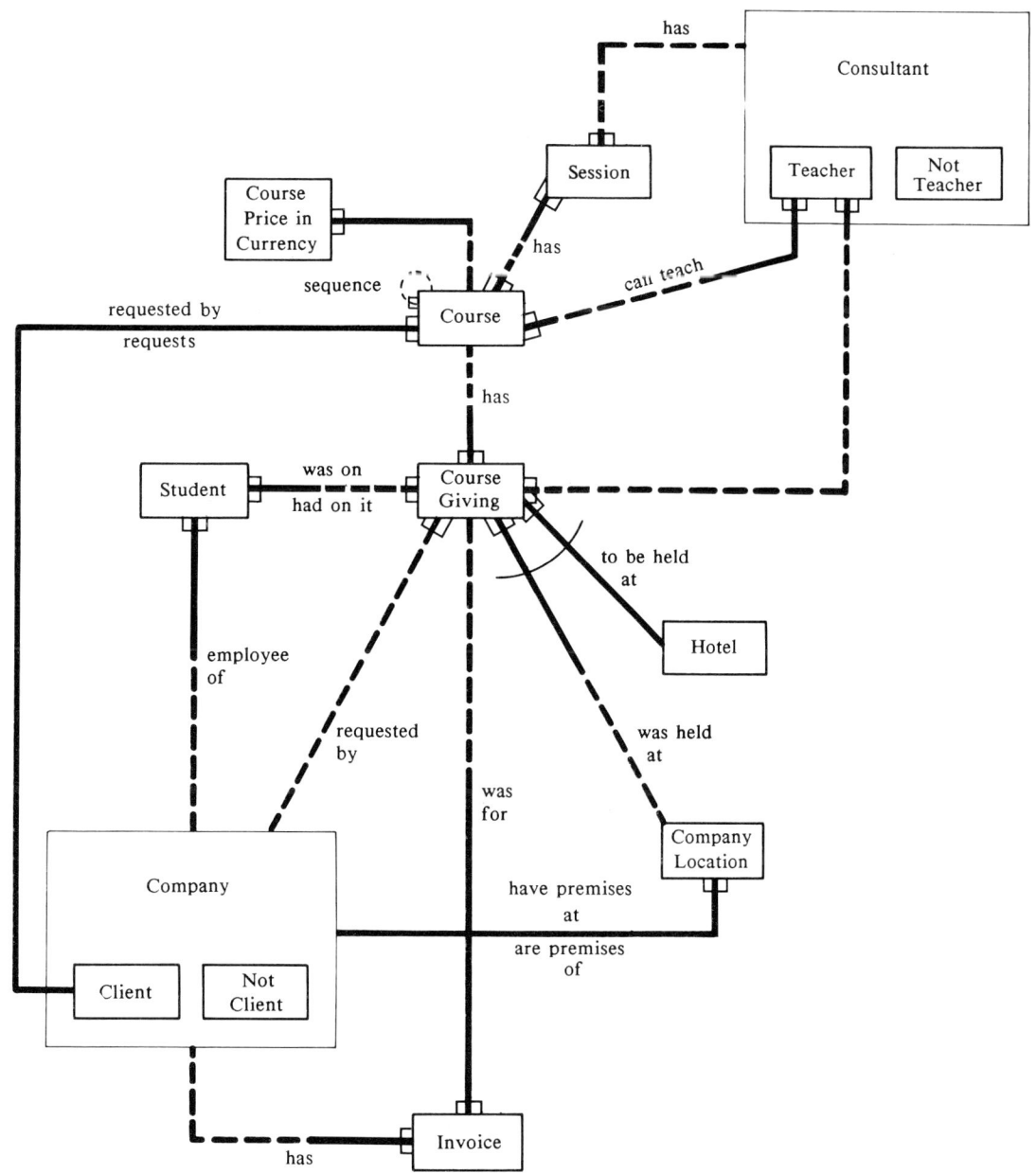

Figure 3.106 New Data Model after Removal of Redundancy

Many-to-many Relationships in the simple case are replaced as shown in Figure 3.109.

Very often, when you discover these "in-between" (often called intersection) Entities, you find that many Attributes you could not allocate before actually describe this Entity. An example is shown in Figure 3.110.

In the Course Administration Model we have several many-to-many Relationships:

Teacher can teach	Course
Teacher has	Course Givings
Student was on	Course Giving
Course has	Sessions

Let us now assume that the list of Attributes shown in Figure 3.111 were discovered during interview sessions with the user. They are all Attributes which serve a purpose during the user's activities. At this point we have not identified which Entity they describe.

I will now go through the list and use it to help me decide whether the many-to-many Relationships need to be replaced by an "intersection Entity". The action taken, the reason why and the resulting amended Model are shown on the following pages.

94 *A Simple Introduction to Data and Activity Analysis*

<u>Hotel</u>

Hotel Name
Hotel Address

<u>Course Giving</u>

Start Date
End Date
No. of Students
Public/In-house

<u>Invoice</u>

Invoice Number
Date of Invoice
Amount Charged
Currency
Date Payable
Date sent

<u>Company</u>

Company Name
Account No.

<u>Course</u>

Course No.
Course Name
No. of Sessions in Course
Abbreviated Name

<u>Consultant</u>

- <u>Lecturer/Teacher</u>

    Name of Lecturer
    Number of Lecturer

- <u>Non-Teacher</u>

<u>Student</u>

Name
Job Title
Experience

<u>Company Location</u>

Address

<u>Session</u>

Date Allocated to Consultant
Date Session created

<u>Course Price in Currency</u>

Figure 3.107 New Data Model – List of Attributes

e.g.

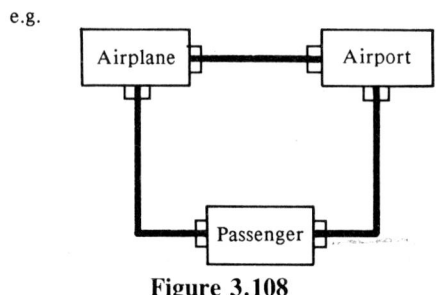

Figure 3.108

How to do Data Analysis 95

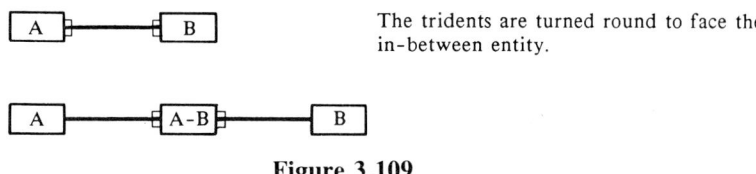

Figure 3.109

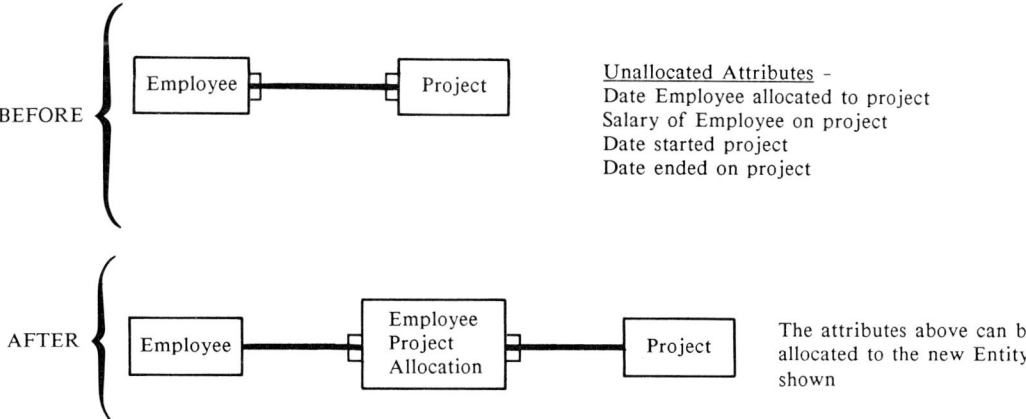

Figure 3.110

1.	Description of teacher's teaching and consultancy experience (text [CV]).
2.	Course suitable for description (shows market aimed at)
3.	No. of slides in session
4.	Length of session on course
5.	Length of session average/mean time
6.	Full description of course for brochure
7.	Company number
8.	Date material last updated
9.	Hotel telephone number and extension
10.	Workshop/seminar or conference?
11.	Is this the address to be invoiced?
12.	Price per person
13.	Number of days
14.	Room cost per night in currency
15.	Overall marks given by students
16.	Out of
17.	Price in-house
18.	Sequence of Session on Course
19.	Hotel Code
20.	Manuals to be taken or sent for this course?

Figure 3.111 List of Attributes discovered during interview sessions

RESULT

1. Describes the teacher.
2. Describes the course.
3. Describes the session
4. Describes the in-between Entity "Course Session" as it specifically relates to the length of that session on that course. The new Entity is created on the Data Model.
5. Describes the session.
6. Describes the course.
7. Describes the company.
8. Not clear from the name what it describes. It could be a session or the course itself. Here we would have to ask to clarify. Let us assume the answer is the course.
9. Describes the hotel. The extension number does not, as a hotel could have many extensions. This is probably the extension of the booking clerk for rooms. We need to verify this with the user. [I will assume it is].
10. Describes the type of course.
11. Describes the company location – is this the invoice address?
12. Price per person is not clear. It could be an Attribute of the invoice or course price. It would need to be investigated. I will assume it is the price charged per person for a course in that currency.
13. Number of days is also not clear. It could be the number of days for a course, the number of days of a session, the number of days a teacher taught on the course giving and so on and so on. We need to ask. I will assume it is the number of days of the Course.
14. Actually describes a hotel room type in currency – a missing Entity. I will assume that the user wants only one value per Hotel in one currency, and it is to be a "representative" cost of a room (to give delegates an idea of how much it will cost them to stay there).
15. Again not clear. This could be the marks given to a lecturer on the course giving by a student – a missing Entity – or the marks given to a lecturer on the course giving, a missing intersection Entity. The Models would then be as shown in Figures 3.112 and 3.113.

It could be many others also. Investigation is needed. I will assume that overall marks given by students (and the plural will help us in real projects to pinpoint likely Entities) means the overall marks given to the Course Giving by the students (as a total).

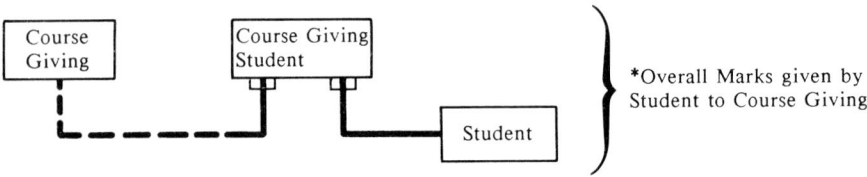

Figure 3.112

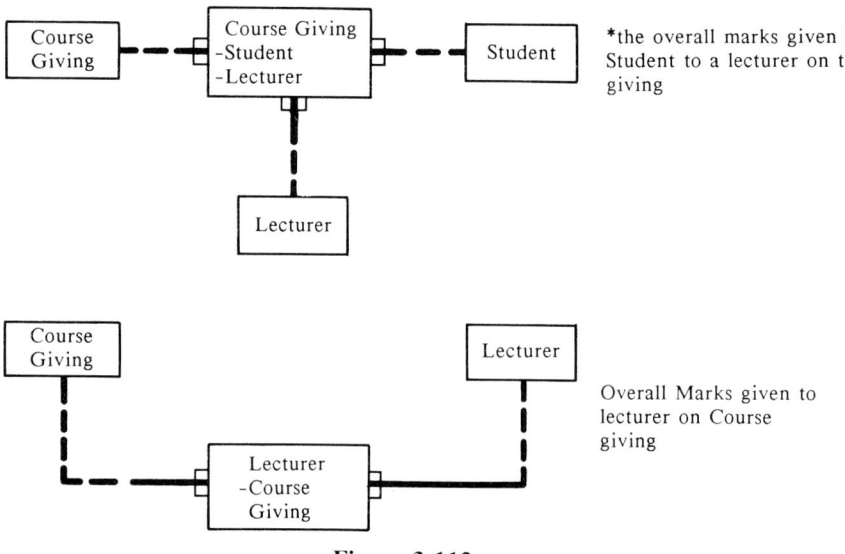

Figure 3.113

How to do Data Analysis 97

16. Not clear. Is this overall marks out of a possible total? As the total marks is dependent on the number of students attending, the 'out of' figure describes the course giving.
17. The same argument as in 12 applies. I will assume it describes the course price and is the price in currency if the course is held in-house.
18. Describes the session-course Entity.
19. Describes the hotel.
20. Not clear. Would need to be investigated. Probably means course giving rather than course, i.e. are the manuals for the course giving to be taken to the course location or sent to the course location beforehand?

The Data Model after the Previous Step is shown in Figure 3.114. Figure 3.117 shows the list of attributes from this and the next step

Conclusions

Some many-to-many Relationships remain, as no useful Attributes were found which described the 'intersection' Entity.

One was replaced – the course has session Relationship.

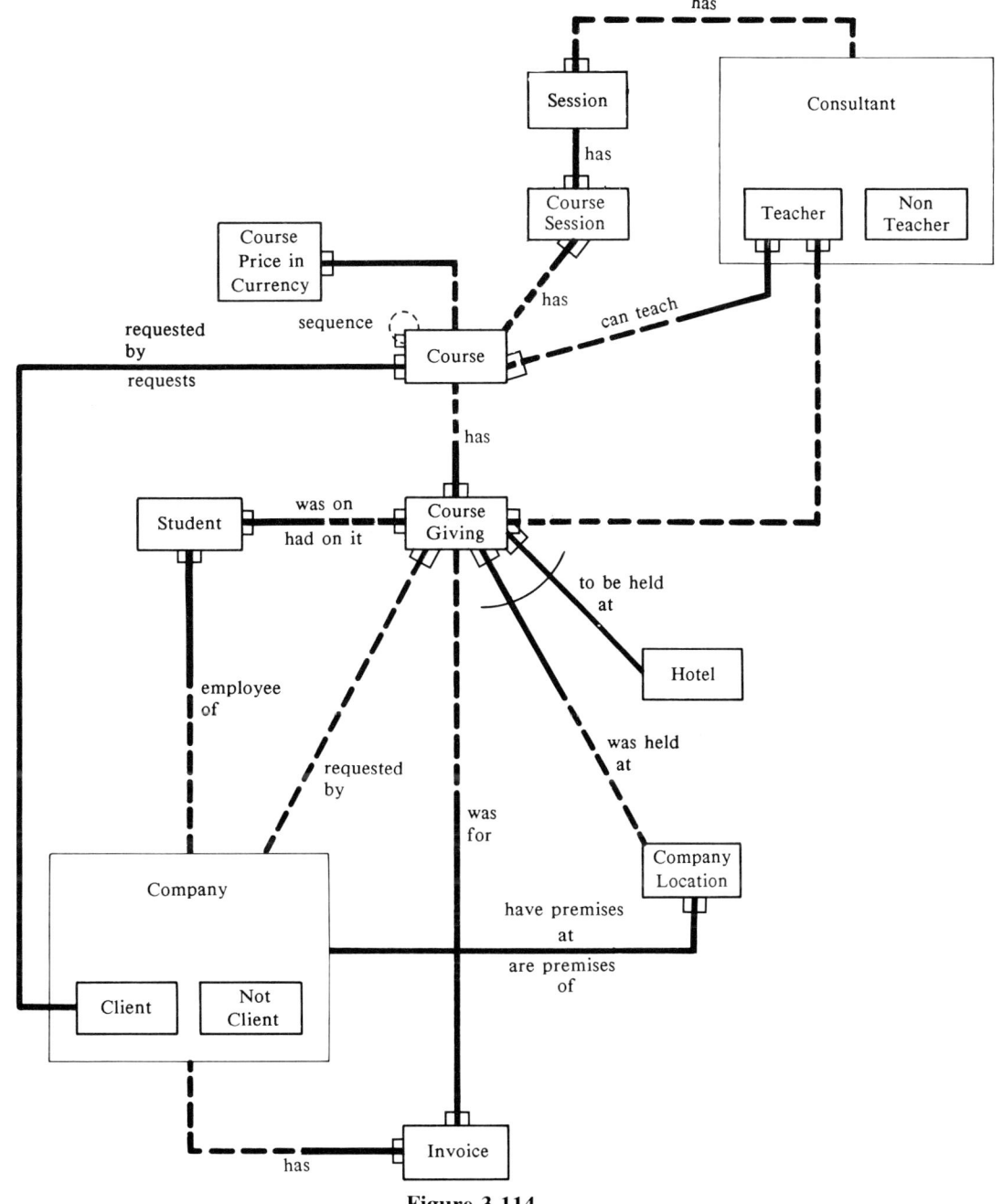

Figure 3.114

98 *A Simple Introduction to Data and Activity Analysis*

Investigating one-to-one Relationships

In the same way that many-to-many Relationships are not wrong but need investigating, one-to-one Relationships also need to be examined.

There are three possible cases you should search for:

* The Entities are synonyms to one another or one is a sub-type of the other. This is all the more obvious is the Relationship is named "is".
* One Entity is an Attribute of the other.
* The degree is not correct.

The examples shown in Figures 3.115 and 3.116 (with the Attributes shown in Figure 3.117) should help to demonstrate this since there are no one-to-one Relationships in our example Data Model.

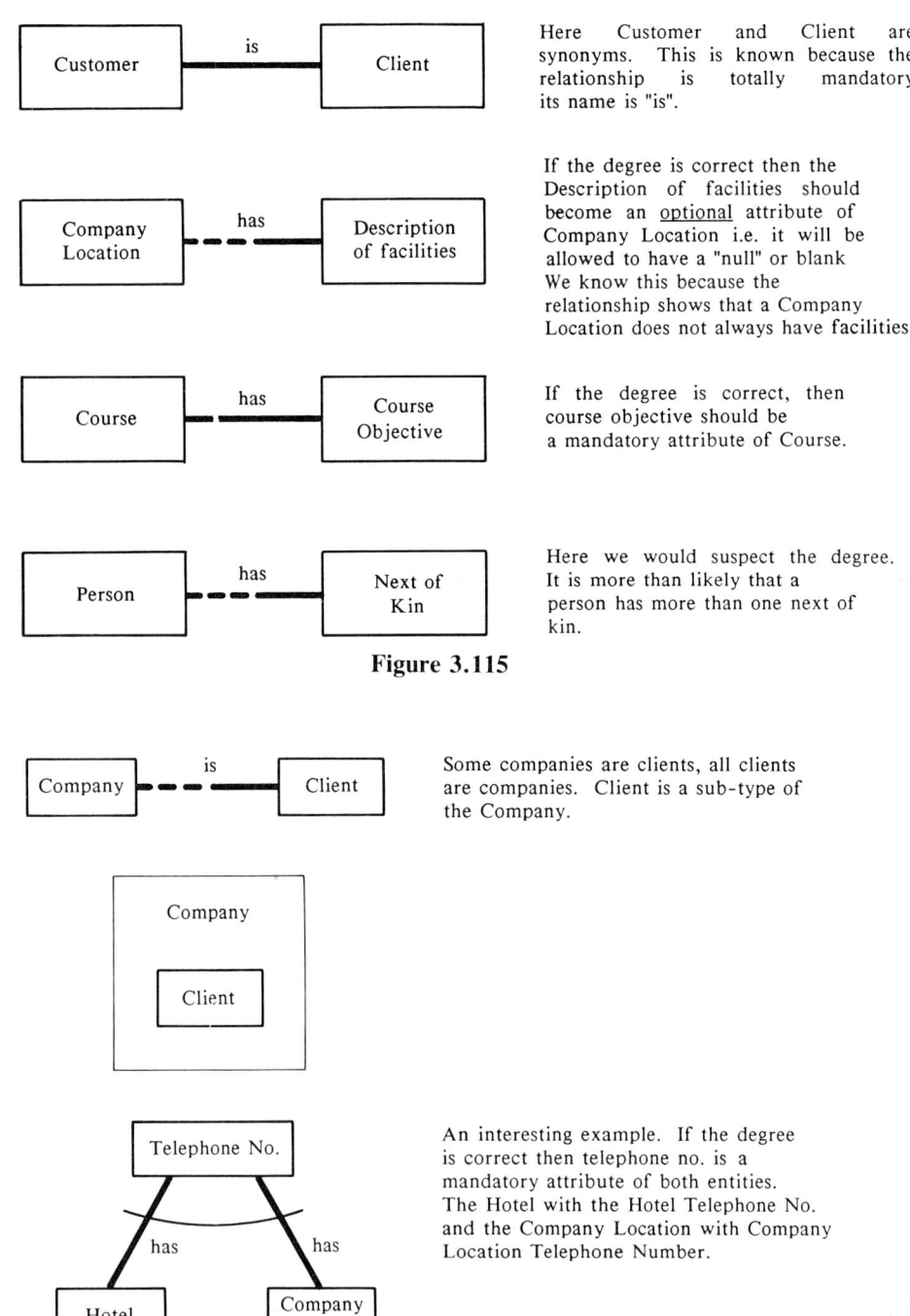

Here Customer and Client are synonyms. This is known because the relationship is totally mandatory - its name is "is".

If the degree is correct then the Description of facilities should become an <u>optional</u> attribute of Company Location i.e. it will be allowed to have a "null" or blank We know this because the relationship shows that a Company Location does not always have facilities.

If the degree is correct, then course objective should be a mandatory attribute of Course.

Here we would suspect the degree. It is more than likely that a person has more than one next of kin.

Figure 3.115

Some companies are clients, all clients are companies. Client is a sub-type of the Company.

An interesting example. If the degree is correct then telephone no. is a mandatory attribute of both entities. The Hotel with the Hotel Telephone No. and the Company Location with Company Location Telephone Number.

I have incorporated the additional attributes mentioned here into the overall list.

Figure 3.116

How to do Data Analysis 99

List of Attributes

Hotel

Hotel Name
Hotel Address
Hotel Tel. No.
Extension No. of Booking Clerk
Representative room cost per
    night in currency
Currency of room cost
Hotel Code

Course Giving

Start Date
End Date
No. of Students
Public/In-house
Overall Marks given
Out of a possible for
    this giving of
Manuals taken or sent?

Invoice

Invoice Number
Date of Invoice
Amount Charged
Currency
Date Payable
Date sent

Company

Company Name
Account No.
Company Number

Course

Course No.
Course Name
No. of Sessions in Course
Abbreviated Name
Course suitable for
Full description of the course
    for the brochure
Date last updated
Type of Course (W, S, C)
No. of days of course
Course Objective

Session

Date Allocated to Consultant
Date Session created
No. of Slides in Session
Length of Session average/mean
    time

Course Price in Currency

Price per person
Price in-house

Company Location

Address
Invoice Address?
Description of Facilities
Telephone number

Course-Session

Length of Session on Course
Sequence of Session on Course

Student

Name
Job Title
Experience

Consultant

- Lecturer/Teacher

Name of Lecturer
Number of Lecturer
Description of teaching and
    consultancy experience

- Non-Teacher

Figure 3.117

Remove 'code only' Entities

Once you have completed a thorough Data Analysis of the system in the scope, *and only then*, you need to see whether you have any entities in your Model which have either only one Attribute, the name, or one Attribute, a code.

During Analysis, your Data Model should contain *all* candidate Entities even if they do have only one Attribute. Once your analysis is complete, however, single Attribute Entities are normally removed from the Data Model.

They are replaced by the Attributes of other Entities in the way shown in Figure 3.118.

If B is a single Attribute Entity, the B Attribute becomes two Attributes describing A and C and each is given an appropriate name. This usually incorporates the original Relationship name, e.g. Currency Invoice is in.

The reason for removing these Entities is to ensure that the Data Model is not full of what are effectively 'validation tables'. These are usually better held as part of a Data Dictionary/CASE or similar system, and used for validation as part of the DBMS validation checks.

As no examples exist in the Course Administration Data Model, the following will serve to demonstrate. I will add the results to the Course Administration Data Model. (See Figure 3.119)

Figure 3.118

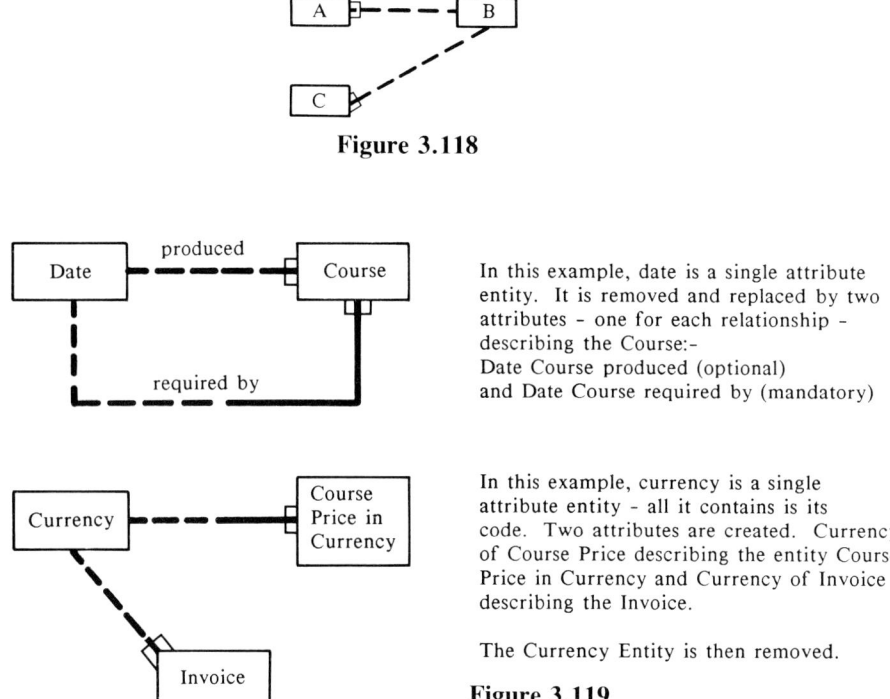

Figure 3.119

Figure 3.120 provides another example.

As in the first example, two Attributes are created and date is removed:
  Provisional start date of Course Giving
  Provisional end date of Course Giving

In this latter example, we now need to be precise about what 'start date' and 'end date' mean in the list of Attributes. Are they the same as the provisional date? I have assumed that investigation has shown them to be different and that there are two sets of dates – final start and end dates, and provisional start and end dates.

The final Model and list of Attributes is shown in the Summary.

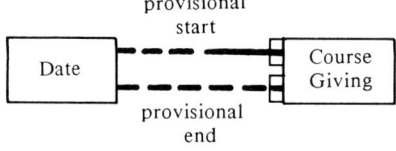

Figure 3.120

Degree Verification

It is always worth asking the user, for each Relationship, whether a 1:N or 1:1 Relationship would be more useful as an M:N Relationship. The reason is that the raw input obtained for use in analysis is often what is termed a 'snapshot' view. In other words, it portrays only the current state of things rather than the long term historical perspective. Historical data – data which reflects and records the changes of things over time – is often not only useful and interesting, but essential to the workings of many systems. A payroll system could not operate unless a history of past tax, insurance and pay was kept. Accounting information is historical over quarters, years, months and weeks.

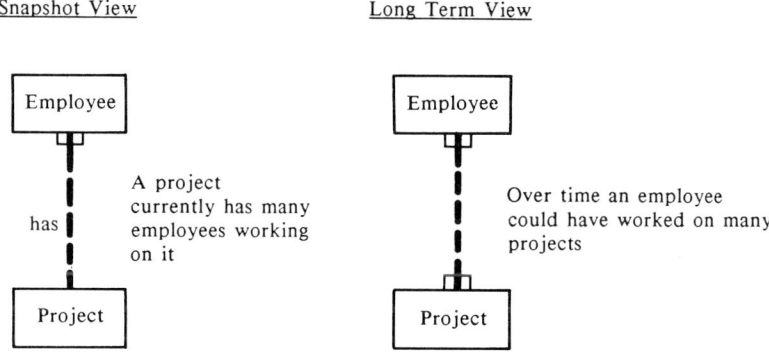

Figure 3.121

The one simple question: "Could A have many B's *over time*?" and the follow on question, "Is this important in the system?" will make a big difference in whether your Data Model is right or not.

For an example, see Figure 3.121.

3.5 SUMMARY

The Data Model and List of Attributes overleaf shows the final outcome from all the stages we have been through, from first analysing the raw data, merging the results, then finally refining the results.

The Data Model shown is still at a fairly incomplete stage. Many of the additional deliverables I showed in Chapter 2, for example, have not yet been identified. The steps I have described, however, do go a long way towards providing you with the main building blocks.

The main steps we have been following during this chapter were those of:

* Analysis of the raw data;
* Merging the resulting Data Models – the Data Models obtained from each source; and
* Refining the Data Models – where we do not seek to change the data, merely make it in an 'optimum' state.

When analysing the raw data, the method we used was dependent on the type of raw input available to us. Where we had 'design abstractions' (forms, record layouts and so on), we used an adaptation of the 'normalisation' method. Where we had design occurrences (forms and record layouts with actual data values in them), we used normalisation. When using real-world occurrences (actual things themselves), we drew up semantic networks to show the relationships between the things and then classified the occurrences. Deriving the Data Model from 'conceptual' abstract descriptions probably represented one of the harder forms of analysis, but in the end it was probably the quickest and most powerful.

Merging the Data Models was a simple, almost mechanical process, which we saw would help us in generating questions to fill any gaps in knowledge or resolve conflicts.

When refining the Data Models, we went through a number of simple steps all of which aimed to make the Model more flexible, robust and free of redundancy or inconsistency, but which did not aim to change the actual data being described. Thus we were aiming to refine the Data Model itself, not the system on which it was based.

Refinement involved the following steps:

>Removal of Synonyms
>Removal of duplicate Attributes
>Generalisation of Entities and Relationships
>Removal of redundant Relationships
>Investigation of many-to-many Relationships
>Investigation of one-to-one Relationships
>Removal of single Attribute Entities

and

>Degree verification

All these steps led to the Data Model shown in Figures 3.122 and 3.123.

102 *A Simple Introduction to Data and Activity Analysis*

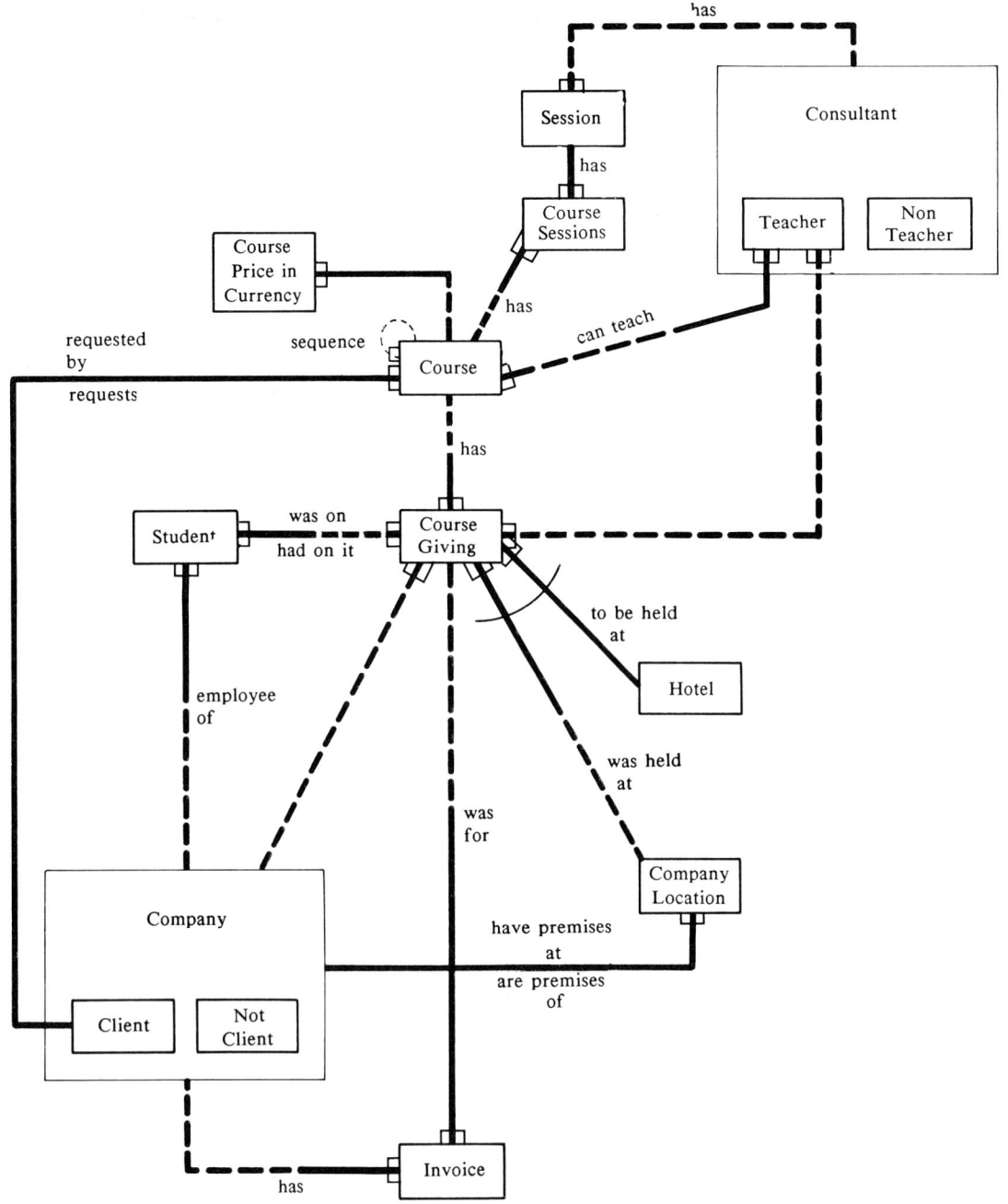

Figure 3.122

List of Attributes

Hotel

Hotel Name
Hotel Address
Hotel Tel. No.
Extension No. of Booking Clerk
Representative room cost per
    night in currency
Currency of room cost
Hotel Code

Course Giving

Provisional Start Date
(Final) Start Date
(Final) End Date
Provisional End Date
No. of Students
Public/In-house
Overall Marks given
Out of a possible for
    this giving of
Manuals taken or sent?

Invoice

Invoice Number
Date of Invoice
Amount Charged
Currency
Date Payable
Date sent

Company

Company Name
Account No.
Company Number

Course

Course No.
Course Name
No. of Sessions in Course
Abbreviated Name
Course suitable for
Full description of the course
    for the brochure
Date last updated
Type of Course (W, S, C)
No. of days of course
Course Objective
Date Produced
Date Required by

Session

Date Allocated to Consultant
Date Session created
No. of Slides in Session
Length of Session average/mean
    time

Course Price in Currency

Currency of Course Price
Price per person
Price in-house

Company Location

Address
Invoice Address?
Description of Facilities
Telephone number

Course-Session

Length of Session on Course
Sequence of Session on Course

Student

Name
Job Title
Experience

Consultant

- Lecturer/Teacher

    Name of Lecturer
    Number of Lecturer
    Description of teaching and
            consultancy experience

- Non-Teacher

Figure 3.123

4 Activity or Function Analysis

4.1 INTRODUCTION

This chapter describes the most important concepts and diagrammatic conventions used in Activity Analysis.

Activity Analysis is also often known as Function or Process Analysis.

An extremely important distinction needs to be made between Activity Analysis and the documentation of an existing system design. Activity Analysis aims to determine what is being done and what should be done, unrelated to *how* it is being done.

Hence we should not see mention of 'forms' or 'listings', programs or any other "mechanism" (or means of achieving the Activities), in any of the diagrams.

This may be one of the more difficult aspects to grasp. It is also the very aspect which gives Activity Analysis its power. If we know *what* needs to be done we can decide how it should be done far more easily.

If I know I have to –

    "Record an order"
or "Pay people"
or "Calculate the tax to be paid"

The decision on *how* can be made far more easily. I can use people and paper; computers, paper and magnetic media; I can even *change* these mechanisms and be able to control and plan the change. But the overall requirements of what I want to do remains constant and clear.

Thinking about systems at this 'conceptual' level, though admittedly hard, is also very rewarding. Many of the users I have involved in projects have themselves benefited from divorcing themselves from the mechanism of pen, paper and screen to look at what they are doing and aiming to achieve. It can be an alarming experience. It can show up illogical or pointless Activity as well as holes where Activities are missing, but it always brings benefit because it shows where improvement is needed. I have found that the major problems experienced by a business are not caused by the *means* they are using to achieve their Activities, but the Activities themselves.

More than once I have recommended fundamental change in Business Activity while recommending no change to the type of mechanism (person, computer etc.) being used to achieve it. All the benefit has been gained from doing the right thing, rather than doing the wrong thing faster!

4.2 MAIN CONCEPTS OF ACTIVITY ANALYSIS

There are five main concepts used in Activity Analysis:

* The Activity (or 'Function' or 'Process')
* The Event
* The Data Flow
* The Data Store
* The Source/Sink (Sender or Recipient)

Each one of these is more precisely a *type,* ie a *type* of Activity, a *type* of Event, a type of Data Flow as opposed to an Occurrence, but for simplicity's sake I will keep the name simple as shown. The exception to this is the Source/Sink, which can be a type of Source or Sink, eg customer, or a single Occurrence, eg Inland Revenue.

These concepts are the main deliverables from Activity Analysis. It is possible to collect additional facts about these basic concepts and a list of them will be provided later in the Chapter, much as it was in Chapter 2 when a list of additional deliverables was provided for the main concepts used in Data Analysis.

As we shall see, however, it is still possible to produce useful and powerful Activity Models with just the main building blocks and diagrammatic conventions.

Activity
An Activity is something the business either does now or wants to do or should be doing.

106   A Simple Introduction to Data and Activity Analysis

The 'does now', 'wants to do' or 'should be doing' are essential parts of the definition, because, as analysts, we are interested not only in what the current situation is, but also what it should be. Part of our job is to improve business systems and one of the prime means is not by automation, but by realignment and change of Business Activity.

An Activity is different from an Entity in that we can define it to mean any 'level' of Activity we are interested in. By this I mean that it can be a very general Activity.

For example
- Pay people
- Cure patients
- Help the aged
- Provide training services

or it can be very detailed and 'low level'

For example:
- Calculate gross pay of person
- Record temperature of patient
- Give aged person a warm drink
- Book Course Giving

The definition of the 'Activity' is deliberately worded to include all sorts of Activities, because the method we will be using of 'Activity Decomposition' enables us to break down our Activities in progressive steps from very general to very detailed, and all Activities will be included.

Activities are usually expressed using a verb, which shows what is being done, together with an object which shows what is being acted on.

Verb	*Object*
Pay	People
Cure	Patients
Help	The Aged

During design, the very detailed Activities we discover become transactions (computer or human) and then, after more design steps, programs and the tasks of a user's job.

For this reason, we are interested in all the Activities of a business irrespective of whether they are currently the Activities of a person or a machine. We need to build up a picture of how all those Activities interrelate. Only then can we decide whether who or what does something should change – from man to machine or even from machine back to man.

Don't exclude any Activities from your study – expert or non-expert, mental or physical, 'intelligent' or 'not intelligent'. Understanding the sequence in which the different types occur is essential both when improving business systems and designing good, 'user-friendly', integrated computer and human systems.

Event

An Event is something that happens to one of the things (the Entities) in our business. In other words, an Event is the Activity of something else *outside* the scope and control of the business,

  e.g.   Customer cancels order
         Employee leaves
         Car rusts
         Car breaks down

Events are other systems Activities, whether these are the personal systems of an employee, the chemical or mechanical systems of a car or the business systems of another organisation.

We will see in a later chapter that Events are fundamentally important in determining what Activities should be in place in our business.

Sources and Sinks

A Source is either a type of person or organisation outside the scope of the business which sends us data, or alternatively it is an actual person or organisation which sends us data. (See Figure 4.1.)

A Sink is either a type of person or organisation, or alternatively an actual person or organisation, to which data is sent. (See Figure 4.2.)

People, organisations, types of people and organisations are obviously not exclusively Sources or Sinks. They can act both in a receiving and sending capacity, as with the example of the supplier and Inland Revenue.

Activity or Function Analysis 107

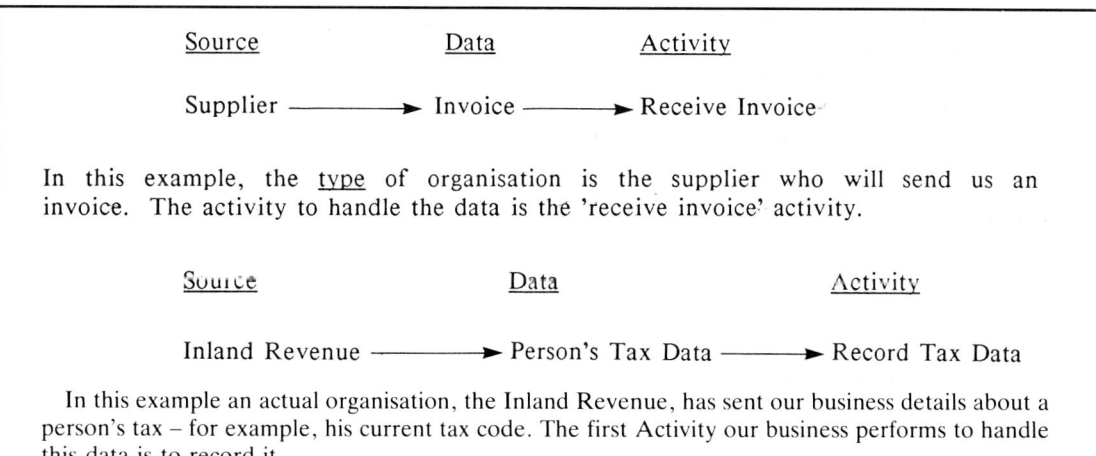

Figure 4.1 Example of a source

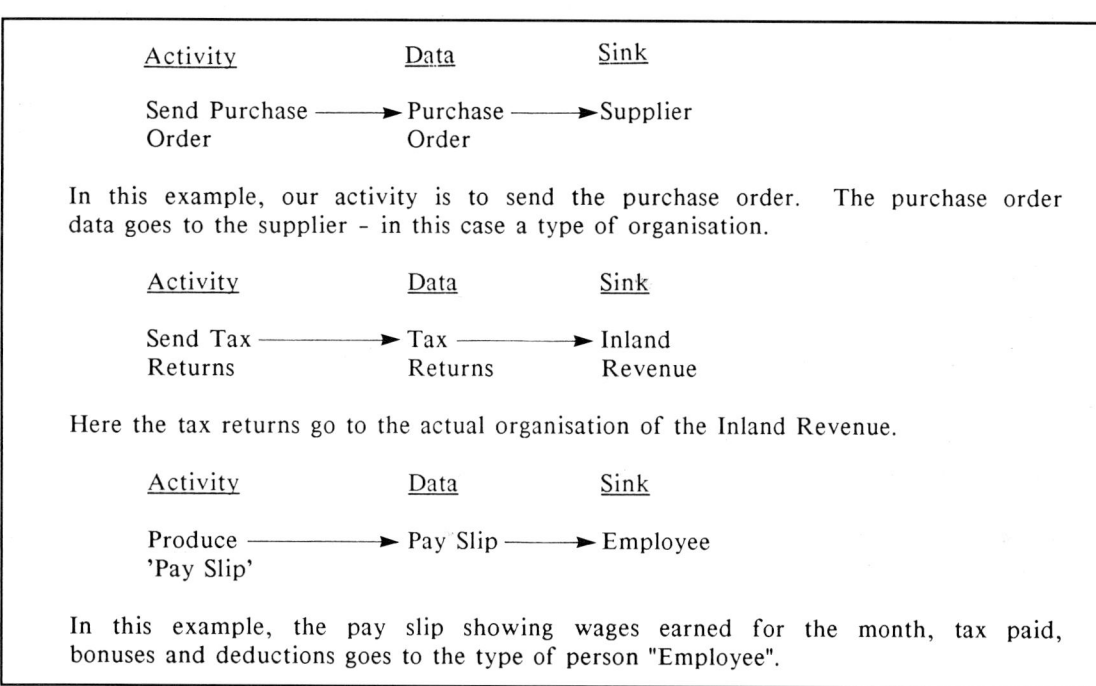

Figure 4.2 Example of a sink

Sources and Sinks are especially important in all systems because it is the Sources on whom we depend for information, and this information is often about an Event.

For example:
   When a driver has an accident he, as a Source, sends an accident claim form to his insurance company.

Furthermore, we are often under an obligation to produce information for a 'Sink'.

For example:
   Legally, we are under an Obligation to send our tax returns to the Inland Revenue.

Where no Obligation actually exists, sending data to a Sink usually has some business Objective from our point of view.

For example:
   We send an invoice to a Customer in order to trigger him into sending us payment.

Recognition of Sources and Sinks is recognition of the fact that no business or system operates as an island.

Data Flow

A Data Flow is a collection of Attributes, Entities and Relationships (plus optional messages and signals) which are related in some way.

Data Flows coming from Sources often contain collections of data about an Event, e.g. if a driver has an accident, the Data Flow will be the accident claim. Data Flows going to Sinks often contain collections of data which the Sink has specified.

e.g. The tax returns

Within our system, a Data Flow either goes to and from a Data Store (see next section), or may flow between two Activities where the data is intermediate "working" data. [We will see this more clearly later.]

In most cases, a Data Flow will be capable of being described in terms of just the concepts of Data Analysis) the Entities, Attributes and Relationships. The only exception is when it also contains a "message" or "signal" (real time systems).

A message is effectively an Attribute having only one permitted value. A signal is an Attribute probably having only two – on or off being one possibility and yes/no being the other.

Activities convert input Data Flows to output Data Flows. (See Figure 4.3.)

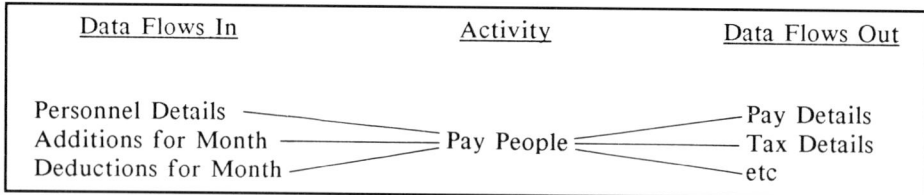

Figure 4.3 Example of activities converting input data flows to output data flows

In the example, the Activity of paying people converts the personnel details of tax code, annual salary, tax to date and so on, together with details of the additions to salary to be made that month and the deductions, and 'converts' them into the person's pay for the month (pay details) and tax to be paid (tax details).

Data Flows when implemented as part of a design system, are "carried" on all sorts of media. When two Actitivies are performed by two different people you may find the data on memos, forms, scraps of paper or even as verbal/sound flows. When two Activities are performed by a human and a machine, the Data Flow can be on listings, punched cards (in rare cases), magnetic tape, screens and so on. Data Flows between two Activities which are both 'computerised' are usually on disk, magnetic tape or in core. They may also go down the communication lines between machines.

As analysts we are interested in *what* data is needed not how it is to be transported. The difficult and imaginative job of deciding how is part of the *design* task.

Data Store

A Data Store is "a permanent or temporary store for a Data Flow or part of a Data Flow".

This is the definition which you will find in most books on analysis. It is much more helpful, and certainly more useful and revealing, to think of a Data Store as an Entity or at any rate a group of related Entities on the Data Model.

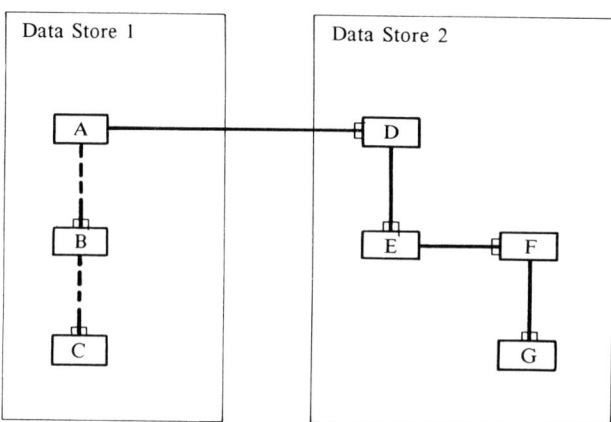

Figure 4.4

Whether the Data Store is one-for-one with an Entity or whether it is a grouping very much depends on how detailed your analysis is. At the detailed levels it will be one-for-one, at less detailed levels – say during a Tactical Study – it will be a grouping.

You should always be able to relate your Data Stores to the Data Model and, ideally, the groups of data in your Data Model which fall within a Data Store should be *different*. (See Figure 4.4.)

e.g.   *Activity*   *Data Flow*   *Data Store*
      Pay people   Pay details   Pay + tax in month
                   Tax details

In the example, the Activity 'pay people' produces two Data Flows, the pay, and tax in the month, which are 'stored' for subsequent use in a Data Store. The corresponding Data Model shows a one-for-one mapping between the Entity 'pay and tax in the month' and the Data Store 'pay and tax in month'. (See Figure 4.5.)

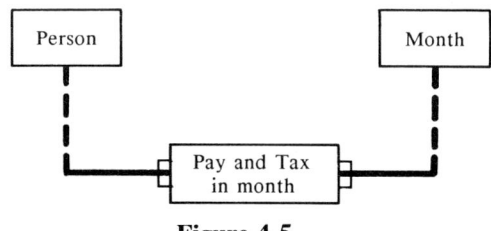

Figure 4.5

In this example, 'person' would also be a separate Data Store, as would 'month'.

It should be clear that the 'Data Stores' are the link between the Data Model and Activity Models we will be producing.

The Activities will use, update and record data in 'Data Stores'. In other words they will use, update and record data from and in the Data Model.

This tie up between the two is *essential* and fundamentally important.

This one simple concept differentiates the modern methods of analysis with the old-fashioned and out-dated 1970s and early 1980s methods and, as such, is a major and important step forward. It may seem so obvious to a newcomer that he may be unable to see why I'm making all this fuss. After all, programs have always updated files, and Activities are like programs and the Data Model is like a set of shared files.

To many early method pioneers, however, this fact was not so obvious. Their backgrounds were either in database design – where Data Models took on special importance – or in system design, where Activity Models were the all important thing.

The link between the two families of methods was very late in developing and there are still many methods being used today where the link is still weak or non-existent.

The examples in Chapter 5 will help to show how powerful this tie up is in producing a consistent and correct system.

Summary
In summary we have five basic concepts:

    *   The Activity   – something the business does, wants to do or should be doing;
    *   The Event   – an Activity external to/not that of the business;
    *   Source/Sink   – A person or organisation, or *type* of person or organisation who sends and/or receives data to or from the business;
    *   Data Flow   – A related collection of Entities, Attributes, Relationships and sometimes messages and signals; and
    *   Data Store   – An Entity or a Group of Related Entities (together with their Attributes and Relationships).

4.3 DIAGRAMMATIC REPRESENTATION

There are two diagrams we use to represent our basic concepts and how they interact. They are:

    *   The Data Flow Diagram

and

    *   The Activity Decomposition Diagram

The two are complementary, providing different views of the same factual information. We will start with the Activity Decomposition Diagram.

Activity Decomposition Diagram

One of the best ways of analysing the Activities of a business is to work from the broad, generalised Activities of a business and gradually go into more and more detail. This method is called Activity Decomposition, and is practised and recommended by virtually every methods consultancy – DCE, LBMS, JMA with Information Engineering, De Marco, Gane and Sarson, the CCTA with SSADM and so on. Not all consultancies, however, use the Activity Decomposition Diagram – LBMS, SSADM, De Marco and Gane and Sarson, for example, do not.

In practice, without this method of analysing Activities, Strategy and Feasibility Studies would be impossible, as the method guarantees a smooth follow on between stages – strategy to feasibility/tactical and on to detailed requirements. It allows Activities to be described in a very general way, giving you the broad overall view you need during Strategy Studies, and at a slightly more detailed level – giving you the less general but not absolutely specific view you need during a Tactical Study. It subsequently allows you to go into absolute detail, giving you the complete precision you need to do a good, sound design.

The advantage of 'top-down' Decomposition of Activities is that it is a progressive step-by-step method. It is far easier to work like this than delve immediately into the detail, where it can be easy to get lost when hundreds of low level Activities exist. Furthermore, the method lends itself well to planning and partitioning tasks.

During planning, Activities can be filtered out when little benefit would accrue from further study, leaving sub-sets worthy of further study. This means that effort can be concentrated into areas where it is most needed. These sub-sets can then be allocated to different teams, and the Activities within them to different team members – a nice simple way of allocating work.

It is also a method which gives the analyst a clear understanding of the 'context' of a study: how an Activity fits into the business as a whole and what the analyst has been given to look at overall. An analyst can be told the scope of any project he is working on by being told the one or more high-level Activities he is being asked to analyse.

Top-down methods also score heavily over bottom-up (delving into the detail) methods when the subject of business change is considered. It is quite possible that large areas of a business, and hence a considerable number of detailed Activities of a business, require fundamental change. This can even extend to the removal of many Activities which no longer serve any useful purpose.

Top-down methods save effort by highlighting the required changes as they are discovered at the general level. Using 'bottom-up' methods, hundreds of detailed Activities could have been investigated and recorded without the realisation that they are no longer required and so all the effort of analysis will have been wasted.

The final plus is that Activity Decomposition enables you to identify Common Activities. Common Activities can be anything from the extremely low level of Activity such as the 'validation of date' to a slightly less detailed Activity such as 'record customer details' to an even more generalised Activity such as 'monitor expenditure'. Once identified as common, they need to be analysed only once, saving effort not only in analysis, but of course further down the line, during design and programming.

Recognition of Common Activities which are very general has also resulted, during one study I worked on, in a fairly major reorganisation for the users to cut out duplicate effort, saving the company thousands of pounds.

By the very nature of Activity Decomposition, therefore, we can use the method at all stages of the Systems Development Cycle where Business Analysis is undertaken.

Figure 4.6 gives an indication of the types of Activity you might find during each stage.

During a Strategy Study you might start with the overall purpose of the business – its main Activity. In the example, this is "help the Aged". After a number of levels of Decomposition (and there is no set rule here on how many), you will have identified all the very general Activities – Activities like "provide transport services". Other examples might have been "provide meals" or "provide accommodation".

During the Feasibility/Tactical Study the Activities are still fairly general but are a little more precise and "active" as to what is being done and to what. The example of "hire buses" shows this. Again, the number of levels of Decomposition will vary considerably depending on the original scope and size of business.

During the Detailed Requirements Study the detailed Activities like those shown will be identified. Within this study we will eventually identify the *Elementary Activities* and their primitives. They have a special importance during design and a chapter of this book is devoted to them and their description. A full definition is also provided in that chapter.

You can show the breakdown of the Activities in many ways, all of which are perfectly acceptable and valid.

Figure 4.8 provides an example within the course administration context. Course handling has

Activity or Function Analysis 111

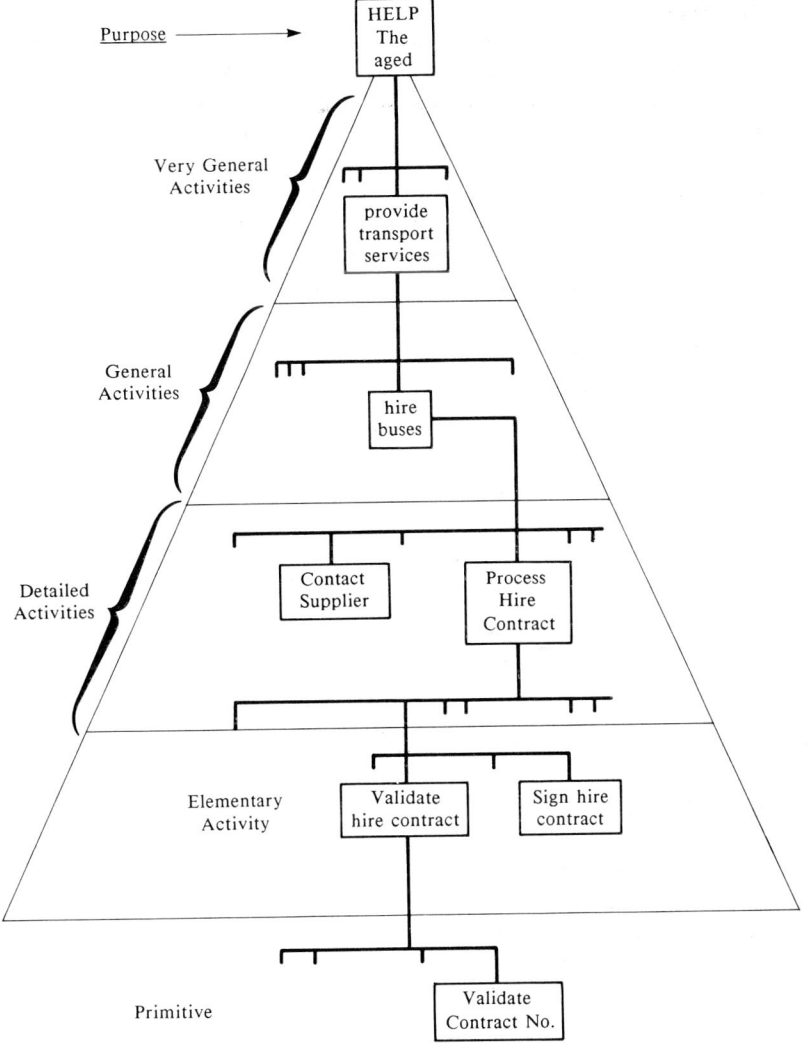

Figure 4.6 Types of activity

Events are represented by an arrow. ⟶

The decomposition is represented by the hierarchy of boxes.

In this particular example, activities filtered out at a planning stage are shown by using a solid line at the bottom of the box thus:

These are activities which have been excluded from further study because it was judged that no benefit would accrue.

If we find activities we <u>can't</u> decompose further because they are incapable of being precisely defined we can use the diagrammatic convention.

Many 'expert' activities and decision activities still fall within this category.

Figure 4.7 Diagrammatic Conventions used in Figure 4.8

112 *A Simple Introduction to Data and Activity Analysis*

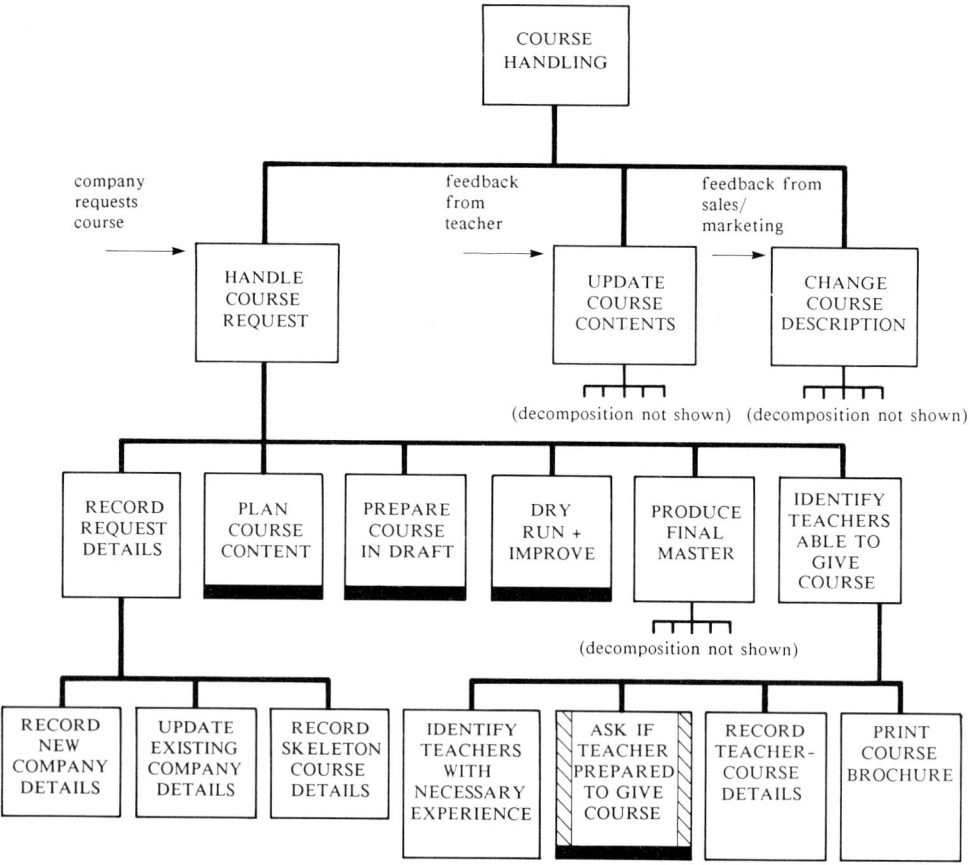

Figure 4.8

EVENT	ACTIVITIES
	<u>Course Handling</u>

Company requests course	- Handle Course request
	    - Record request details
	        - Record New Company details
	        - Update Existing Company details
	        - Record Skeleton Course details
	
	- Plan Course Content
	
	- Prepare Course in Draft
	
	- Dry run and Improve
	
	- Produce Final Master
	    -
	    -
	    -
	
	- Identify Teachers able to Give Course
	    - Identify Teachers with necessary experience
	    - Ask if Teacher prepared to give course
	    - Record Teacher/Course details
	    - Print Course Brochure

Feedback from Teacher	- Update Course Contents
	    -
	    -
	    -

Feedback from Sales/Marketing	- Change Course Description

Figure 4.9

been broken down into the Activities of handling the course request, updating the course contents and changing the course description. Shown on this diagram are the *Events* which have triggered these Activities the Event "company requests course" results in the Activity "handle course request". This, when broken down, consists of a number of more detailed Activities, all geared towards handling this Event.

Figure 4.9 has turned the diagram in Figure 4.8 on to its side to show the same information as a list.

Some users prefer lists; some like hierarchies. It doesn't really matter.

The triggering Event in this example is shown in a separate column.

The Activity Decomposition Diagram, whether shown as a list or a diagram with boxes, has one important characteristic – it is not an *hierarchy* of levels, but a *network*. The reason is because it should show "Common Activities". (See Figure 4.10.)

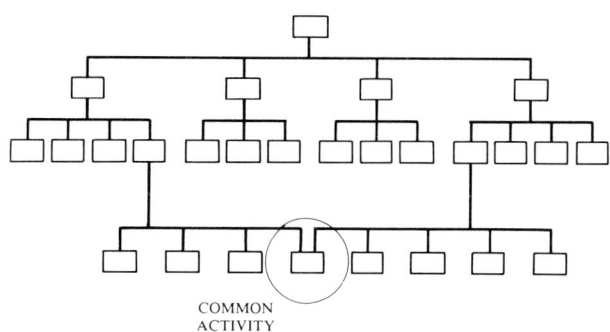

Figure 4.10

A Common Activity is one which is used to achieve more than one 'purpose' or higher level Activity. If we think about it in our own context, we should be able to see that, as people, we perform the same Activities quite often, but more often than not to achieve different purposes. I may "boil water" at one point in order to "make tea", but at another time in order to "make coffee". I may "fill a bowl with water" in order to "wash the dishes" at one time and at another to "clean vegetables" – the same Activities to achieve different ends.

We show this on the Activity Decomposition Diagram either by joining up the 'legs' or, where it is not possible, by using a common number. Once discovered, Common Activities obviously need be decomposed only once. There is obvious benefit, therefore, in doing a perpetual search for commonality to save effort, both in analysis and later in design.

Data Flow Diagram

Data Flow Diagrams show how Activities depend on one another for their information.

In a Data Flow Diagram, all the concepts introduced earlier are shown. A summary of the diagrammatic conventions and their meaning is shown in Figures 4.11 and 4.12.

You will undoubtedly find that diagrammatic conventions differ from company to company. Some companies use ovals for Sources and Sinks and rectangles for Activities. Some companies use a sort of upended test tube ⊂___ to represent a Data Store.

Differences like this don't matter at all. I have chosen this particular set of conventions because we tend to use these in DCE, but I have used numerous other ones where a firm I am helping has chosen to use other ones.

There is a fundamental link between the Activity Decomposition Diagram and the Data Flow Diagram which is summarised in Figure 4.13.

A Data Flow Diagram is drawn for each 'leg' in the Activity Decomposition. In the example, the overall Activity 'A' is shown as the top box in the Activity Decomposition Diagram and a sort of 'context' bubble showing main inputs and outputs in the corresponding Data Flow Diagram. A is then decomposed into A1, A2, A3 and A4 on the Activity Decomposition Diagram. The corresponding Data Flow Diagram has those same Activities, but shows the additional concepts of the Sources and Sinks (S1, S2, S3 and S4) together with the Data Flows (DF1, DF2, DF3 and DF4) and Data Stores (D1, D2, D3, D4). Notice how the Data Flows going into the context bubble A are preserved at the next level down.

114 *A Simple Introduction to Data and Activity Analysis*

The symbol ⊘ is compatible with the convention used on the activity decomposition diagram for an activity which <u>cannot</u> be decomposed because, for example, it is an expert or difficult decision making activity.

The symbol ⌽ is also compatible with the convention used on the activity decomposition diagram for an activity filtered out at the planning stage because no benefit would have accrued from further study.

The symbol ⊚ denotes an activity within the business but outside the scope of the project.

The symbol ◌ denotes an activity within the scope of the project but outside the scope of this particular 'leg' of the decomposition. The scope of the 'leg' of the decomposition is shown by the box surrounding the activities. It follows that the following symbols will always be found <u>outside</u> this box.

▭   Source/Sink

◯   'External' Activity

▽   Event trigger

◌   Activity outside leg

Figure 4.11

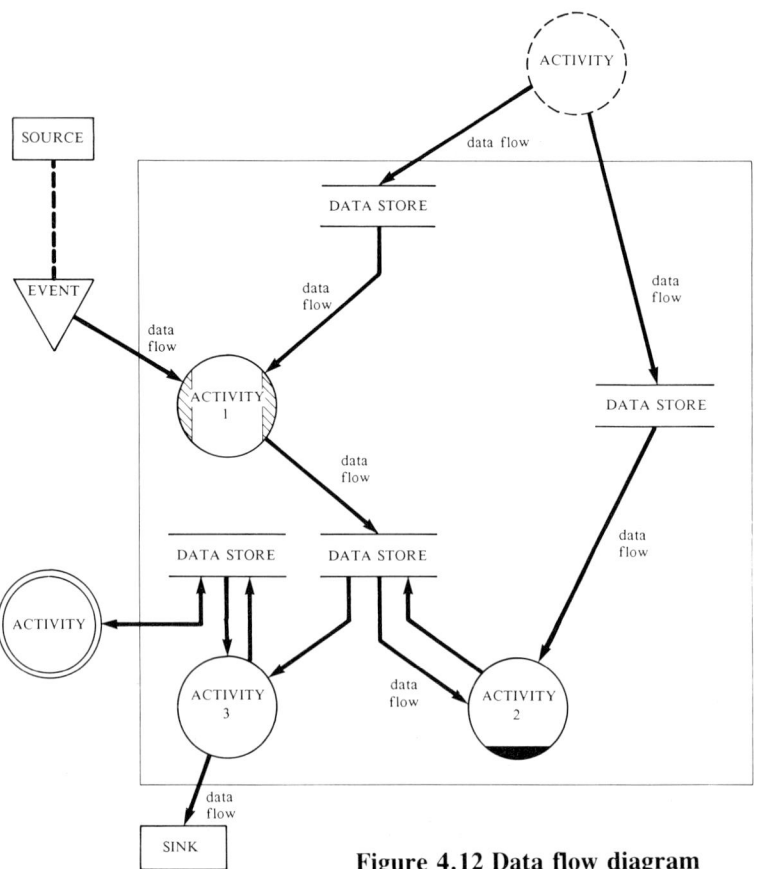

Figure 4.12 Data flow diagram

Activity or Function Analysis 115

A3 is then decomposed into Activities A31, A32 and A33. Notice how the Common Activity A31 is shown on the diagram (Figure 4.13).

The corresponding Data Flow Diagram has those same Activities. If we look at the level above again, for a moment, we see that A3 uses Data Store D2, inputs DF2 from S2, outputs DF3 to S3 and inputs data from D4.

At the next level down these facts are preserved. Data Store D2 is used, but has been broken down into more detail – D22 and D21. D4 is used, DF2 from S2 is used by A31/A12 and DF3 going to S3 is output by A33. The links with the Activities in the other legs are preserved using the "dotted" bubble. At this level of Decomposition, a Data Store D5 has been identified which is unique to that particular leg.

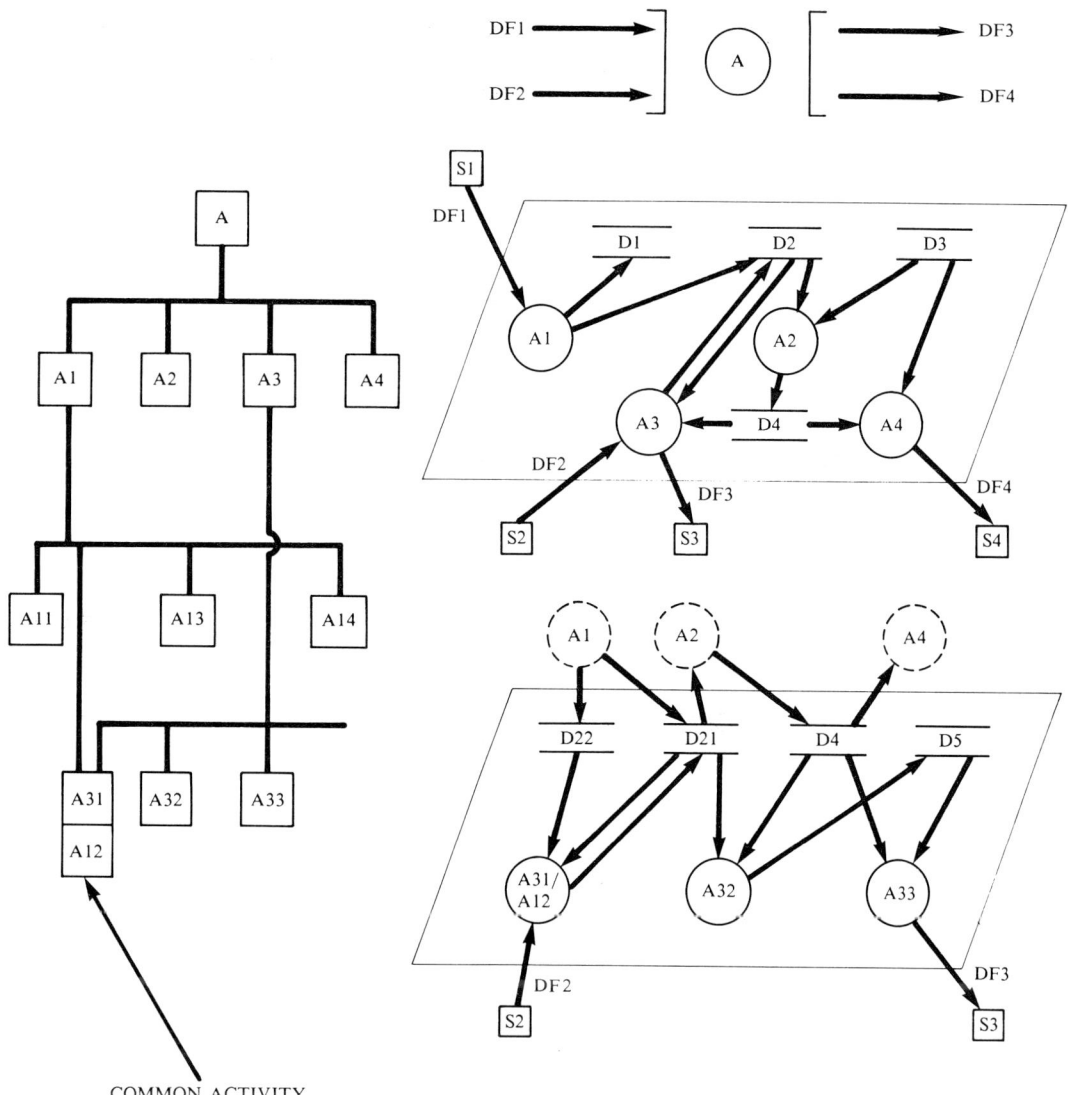

Figure 4.13

During the Decomposition, we decompose Activities and data – Data Stores and Data Flows. We may in very extreme circumstances also decompose Sources and Sinks.

Two examples follow which should be compared with the Activity Decomposition example shown earlier. You should be able to see the correspondence between the two and how the diagrams complement one another.

The Data Flow Diagram (Figures 4.14 and 4.15) shows data usage and the Activity Decomposition (Figure 4.18) gives an overall picture of 'where you are'.

116 *A Simple Introduction to Data and Activity Analysis*

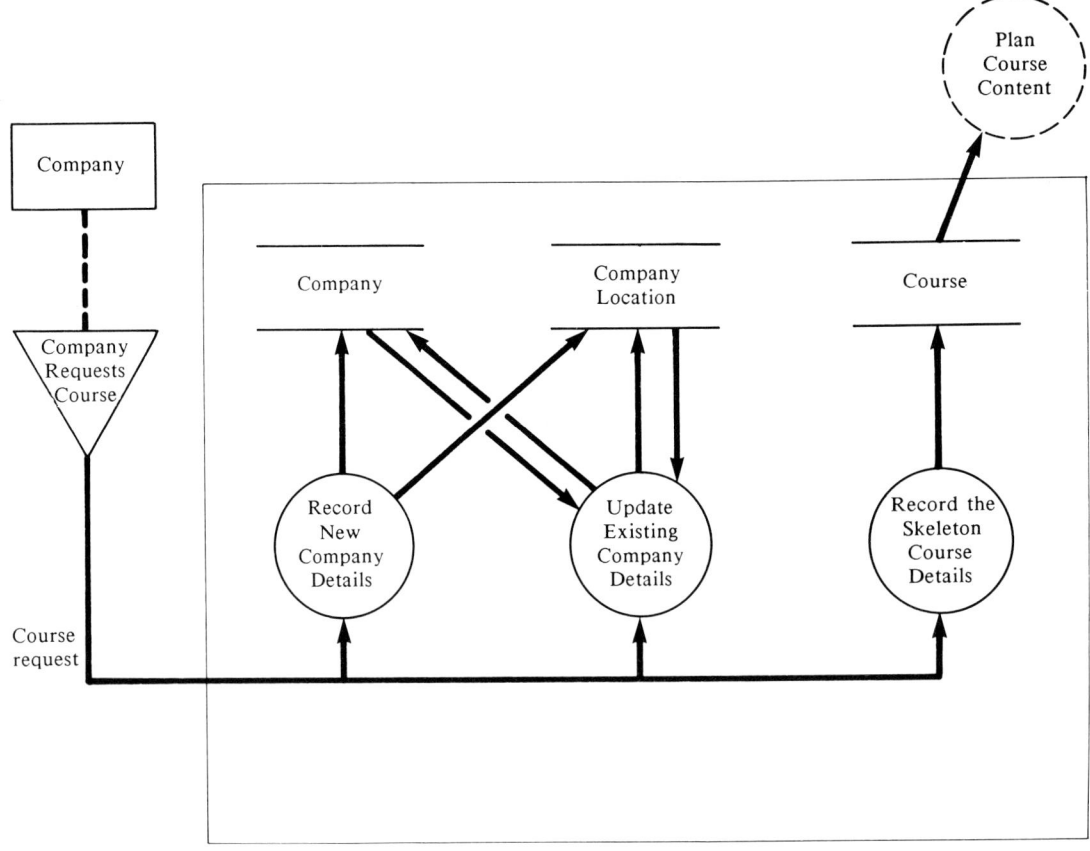

Figure 4.14 Record request details

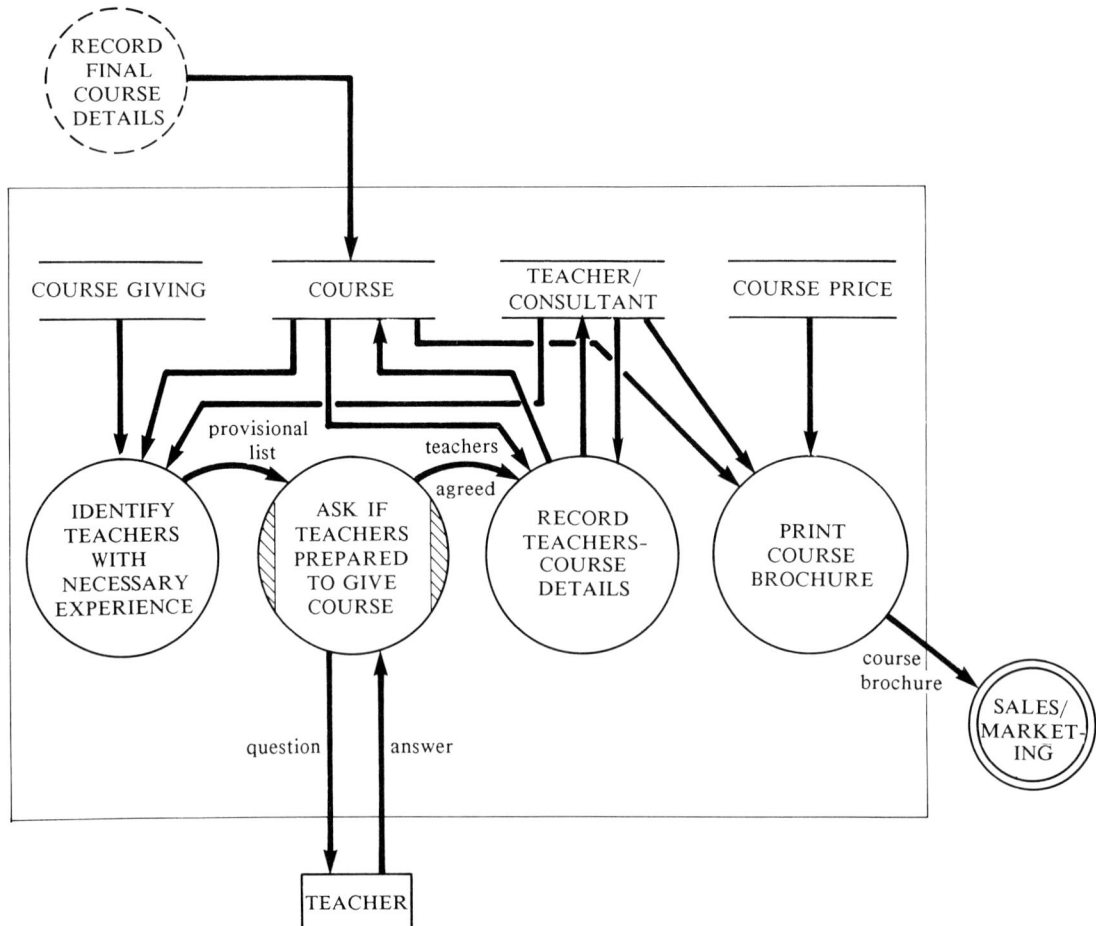

Figure 4.15 Identify teachers able to give course

Activity or Function Analysis 117

The examples also show the tie up between Data Store and our Course Data Model. Look back to the Data Model shown at the end of Chapter 3 (Figure 3.122 on page 102) and you will be able to see a direct correspondence between the Data Stores and the Entities on the Data Model.

It is essential that you always cross-relate the Data Model and Data Flow Diagrams and that they are consistent. In practice – particularly when all the different methods of analysis are used – the Data Model can become more detailed than the corresponding Data Flow Diagrams while a project is underway. In other words, the Data Analysis methods provide you with detailed information on the data needed more quickly than the Activity Analysis methods.

What you will then find is that your 'Data Stores' contain sub-sets of your Data Model.

This is shown in Figure 4.16. Source x sends us Data Flow R which is acted on by Activity M. Data Flow 'R' is stored in a Data Store and the data is known as 'R', simply because this is all we know about the data from the Activity Analysis. In fact, data R maps onto a collection of Entities in the Data Model we have already obtained from Data Analysis. Data R is, in fact, Entities A, B and C, the Relationships A-B and B-C and the Attributes of the Entities shown.

[Some analyst workbench products are particularly good at enabling you to record this].

When analysing an existing design, in practice, we do both Data and Activity Analysis. This is because we need to analyse the input forms and output listings or reports to determine the contents of a Data Flow. We use Data Analysis techniques to determine these contents. Each Data Flow,

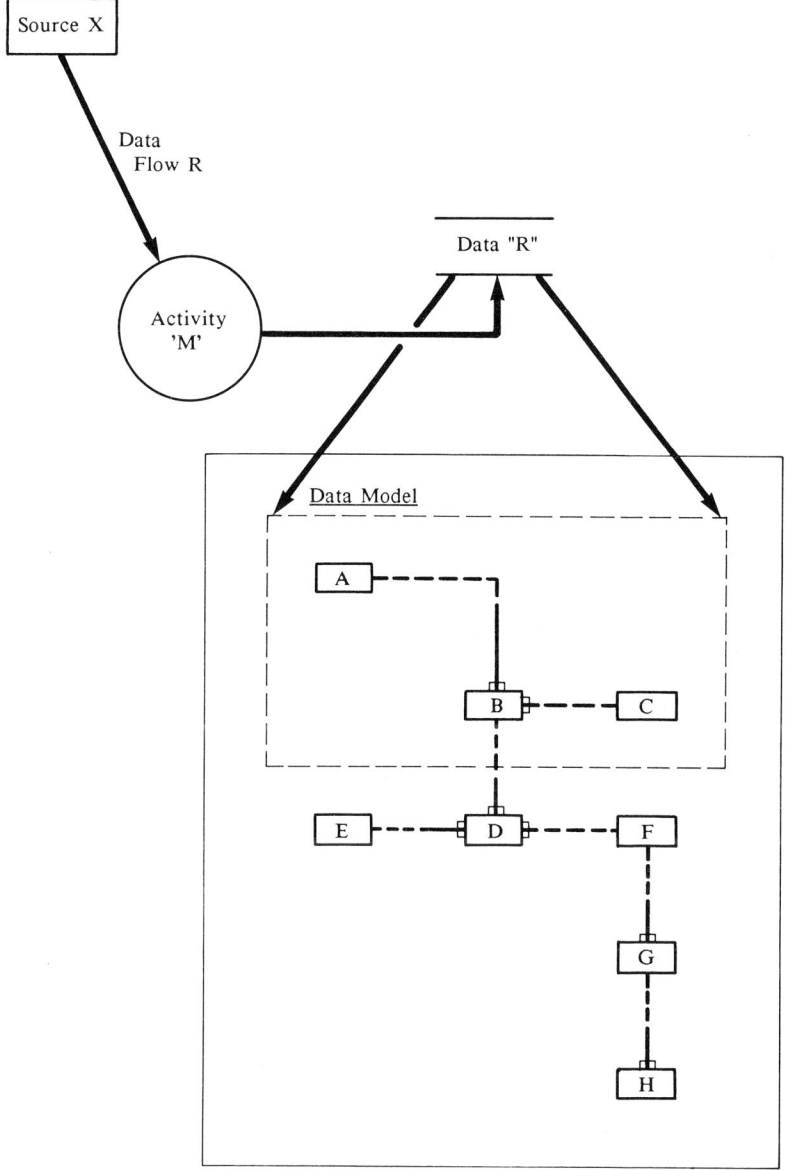

Figure 4.16

118 *A Simple Introduction to Data and Activity Analysis*

once found, is analysed using either normalisation or the method for analysing Design Data Abstractions. What we obtain are sub-sets of the Data Model (if you look back at Chapter 3 you will see this). The sub-set shows the contents of a Data Flow.

Figure 4.17 shows this. The existing design has Source X sending a Form 'P' which is handled by transaction 'Y'. When we analyse the existing design to determine what the corresponding Data Flow Diagram is we find that Source X sends Data Flow P which is handled by an Activity I have

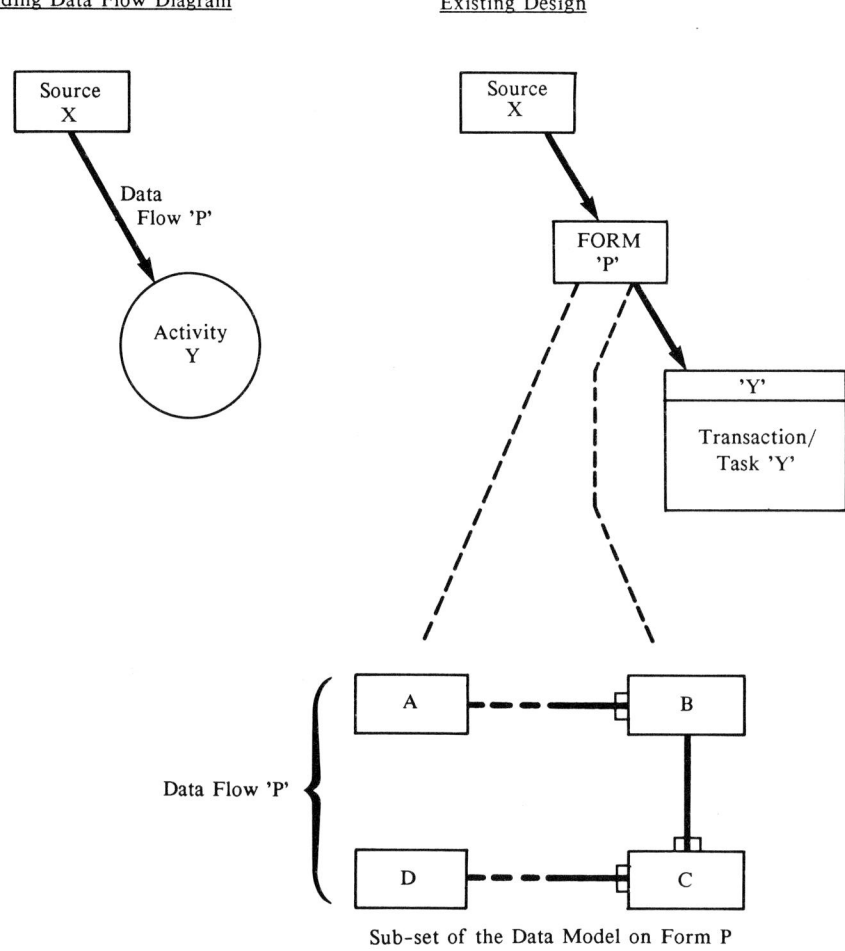

Figure 4.17

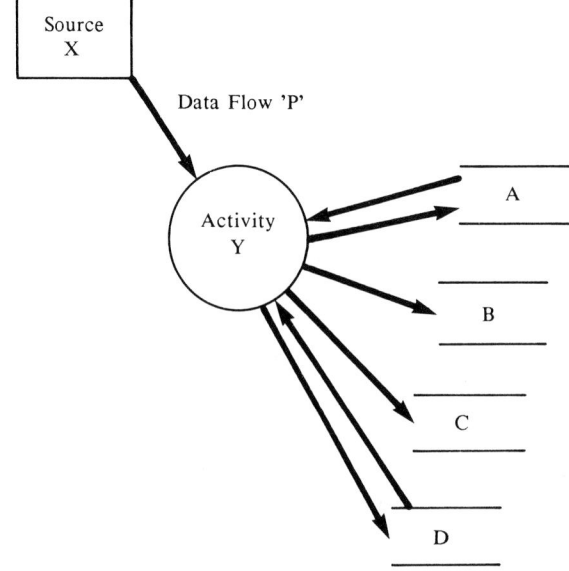

Figure 4.18

called 'Y' [in reality, its name would be different as it would show what was happening rather than how it was being done].

Form 'P' is then analysed using the Data Analysis Method of "analysing the existing Design Abstractions". We find that the Data Model sub-set obtained is as shown with Entities A, B, C and D and a set of Attributes (which I haven't shown) which will also be a sub-set of all the Attributes in the Data Model.

This sub-set Data Model defines the contents of Data Flow P.

It is more than likely that Activity Y will store or update the contents of Data Flow 'P', in which case our final Data Flow Diagram will look as shown in Figure 4.18. I have assumed that A and D will be used and updated and B and C are stored. [I make this assumption because my Data Model shows that A and D can exist before B and C exist]

When drawing your Data Flow Diagrams two guidelines may help.

* First, you need not show Data Stores which are, as it were, 'internal' to a bubble (or in other words are not used by any other Activities external to the Decomposition of the bubbles) at the higher level. This is demonstrated in Figure 4.19. Here, Data Stores V and U are used by Activities B1, B2 and B3 – the sub-activities of B – but are not used by any Activities at the level above (level 1). As a consequence they don't appear in level 1.
* Second, to help maintain the context of a lower level diagram within its higher level Decomposition, use the dotted circles to act as a 'popper' or press stud. Again, Figure 4.19 shows this. The level 2 diagram is the Decomposition of Activity B. B has an input from Activity A, an output to Data Store X which is used by C and E, an output to Activity D, an input from Data Store Y which is updated by E, and an input from Z also updated by E. All this is shown on the level 2 diagram.

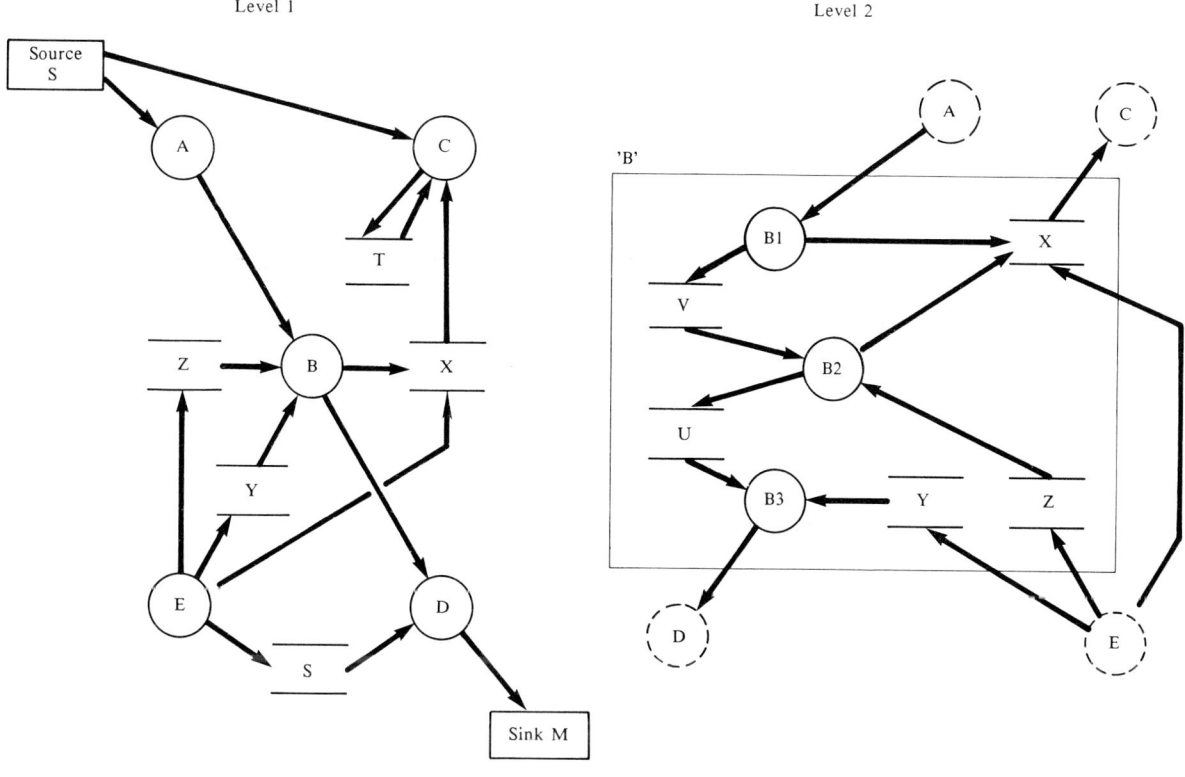

Figure 4.19

Conditions, Repetition and Sequence

Data Flow Diagrams do not show sequence, selection or repetition of Activities with respect to others. Although sequence can be roughly shown by, say, ordering the Activities in a left to right sequence across the page, it is still not explicit.

Adding extra diagram conventions to the Data Flow Diagrams to show these things makes the diagram in practice look dreadfully messy and complex. Instead it is easier to use the Activity Decomposition to show sequence, repetition and conditions.

Conditions

Where an Activity is actioned only if some condition applies, the condition can be written above the

120   *A Simple Introduction to Data and Activity Analysis*

box as shown in Figure 4.20. This same figure also shows what we can do if we have chosen to use a list rather than a Decomposition.

Some examples are shown in Figures 4.21, 4.22 and 4.23. These use the Activity Decomposition example shown earlier. In Figure 4.21, new company details need to be recorded only if the course request is from a new company, and the existing company details need to be updated only if they are out of date. The skeleton course details are always recorded.

Where only one Activity is conditional, write the *if* along the line.

In Figure 4.22, the convention used to show that a group of Activities is dependent upon the one condition is shown.

Teachers with the necessary experience are always identified. Only if a suitable teacher can be found, however, are the teachers asked and the fact they are willing to teach a course recorded.

Once the details are recorded the course brochure can be printed to show the course and the teacher who will give it.

Figure 4.23 again uses the course example to show how to handle the multiple ifs. When firming up Course Giving details, the details of students going on the course are obtained and recorded, and the provisional Course Giving confirmed with the requestee. Only if the requestee does confirm,

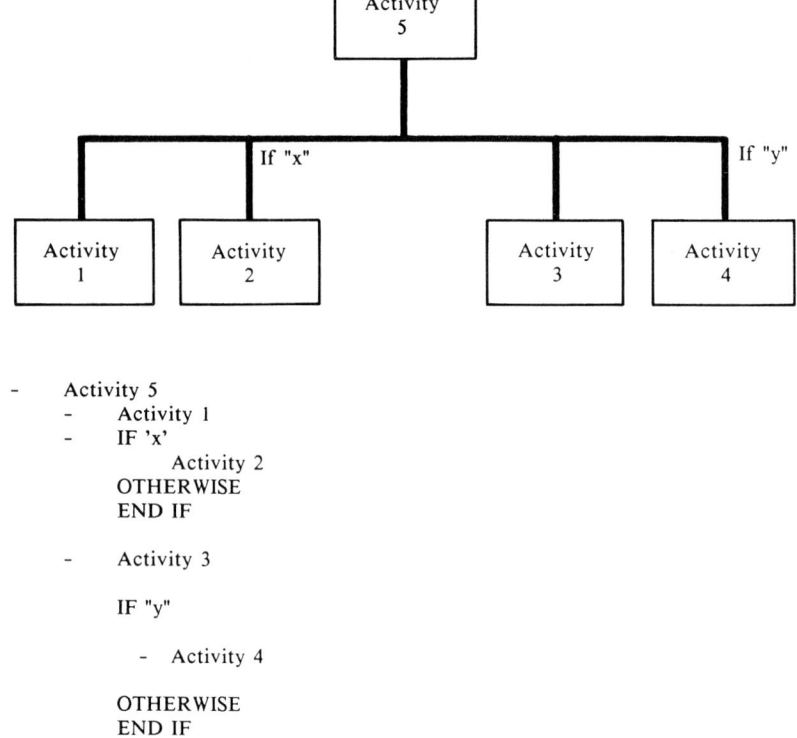

Figure 4.20

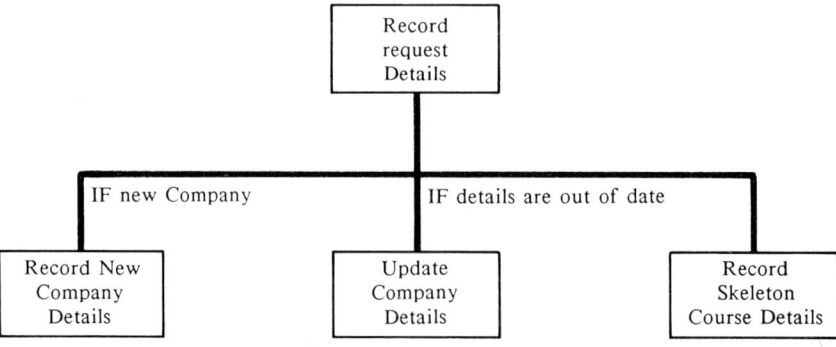

Figure 4.21 Adapting the activity decomposition to clearly show conditional activities. (Where only one activity is conditional, write the IF along the line)

Activity or Function Analysis 121

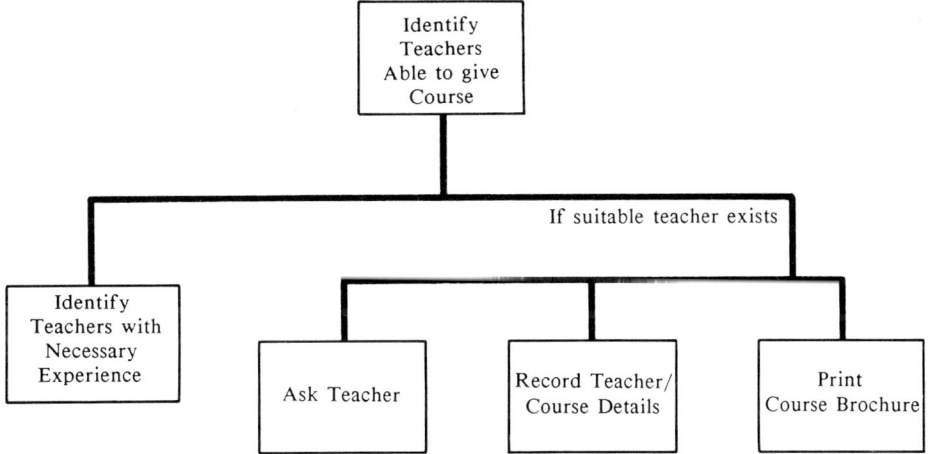

Figure 4.22 Conditional activities. (Where a group of activities is dependent upon the same condition write it as shown)

however, is the teacher's course schedule – showing what Course Givings are scheduled for the year – updated. Teachers then have to be found for the confirmed course giving and any other outstanding Course Givings of this course type. The first step is to identify all those teachers capable of giving that type of course. Only if teachers exist can their availability be checked, and from those available one or more selected and provisionally booked to that Course Giving and any other outstanding Course Givings of that type.

In the examples shown, I have put the 'positive' condition each time – if confirmed, if teacher exists and so on. In practice the *negative* condition must also be investigated.

What happens if the provisional Course Giving is not confirmed? What happens if there are no teachers capable of giving the course? What happens if no teachers capable of giving the course are available on the date the Course Giving is booked for?

Very often the negative condition is one of no Activity, but in the examples above Activity would have been required to deal with these *exception* conditions.

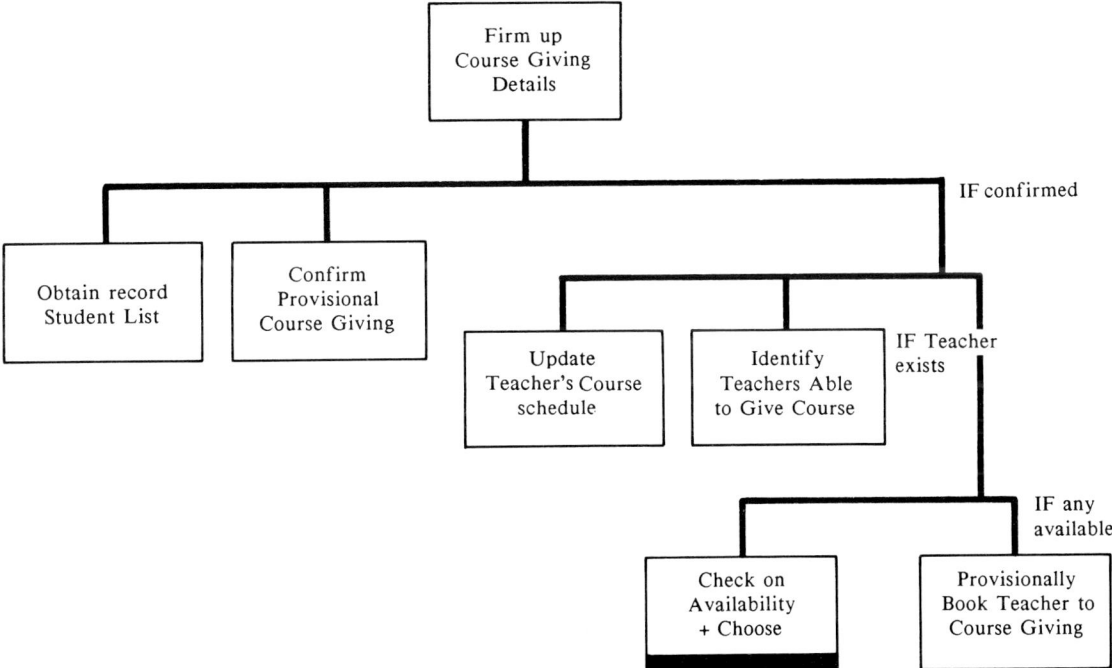

Figure 4.23 Adapting the activity decomposition to clearly show conditional activities. (IFs within IFs are allowed)

122 *A Simple Introduction to Data and Activity Analysis*

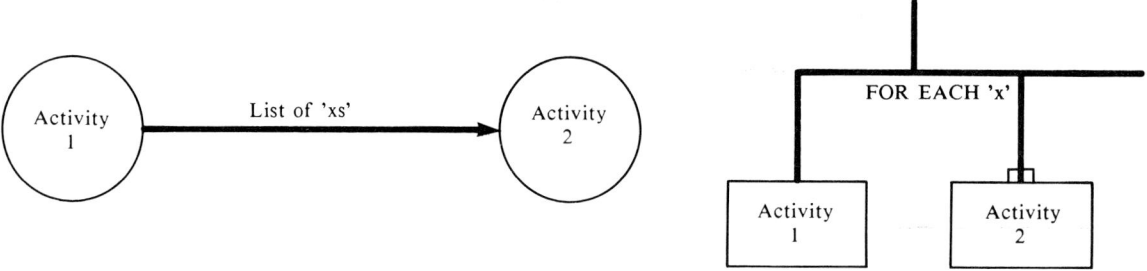

Figure 4.24

Repetition

When any chain of Activities is actioned some may be repeated with respect to the others. There are a number of alternative diagrammatic conventions you can use to show repetition, and some of them are shown in Figure 4.25. They all express the same thing; it is merely a question of individual preference which one you choose.

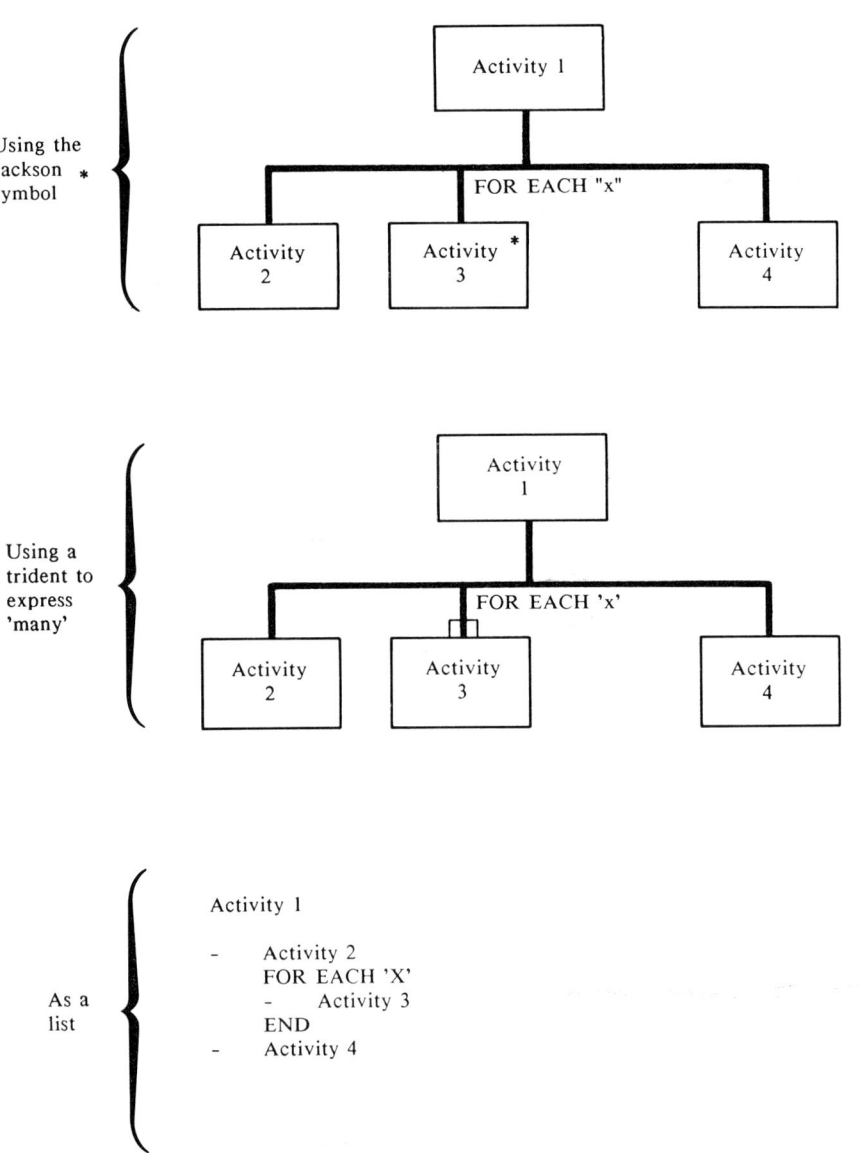

Figure 4.25 Repetition and the Alternative Conventions

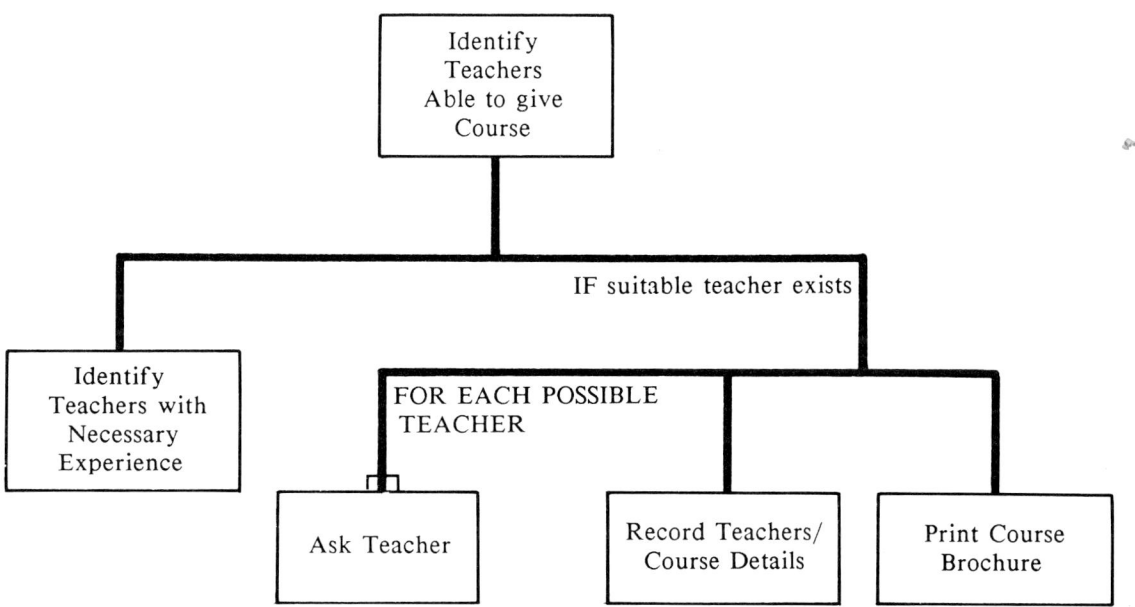

Figure 4.26 The example adapted to show repetition

It is often fairly clear from a Data Flow Diagram where repetition needs to occur, because the Data Flow contents show that the output of one Activity is a list or a number of Occurrences of something. This then shows you that the next Activity must be repeated. (See Figure 4.24.)

Great care must be taken when describing the Activities to get the description consistent with the Data Flow and Activity Decomposition. If repetition is shown on the Activity Decomposition, there is no need to describe the Activity going through the same list – this only confuses. The logic of how to handle only one Occurrence of the list is all that is needed.

In Figure 4.26, the example we have been using has been adapted to show repetition. To identify the teachers able to give a course the first step is to identify all the teachers with the necessary experience (i.e. look through their CVs). A glance back to the Data Flow Diagram of this example will show you that the output Data Flow from this Activity is a "provisional list" [i.e. a provisional list of teachers]. If the list is not empty, each teacher on that list must be asked to see whether he/she is willing to give the course. This Activity yields a list of those teachers who have agreed to give the course.

The example now shows clearly what you must do to keep Activity logic and Activity Decomposition consistent. The Activity name is 'record teachers' course details'. The description (although I haven't shown it here) shows what logic is applied to record each teacher willing to give the course. The *logic itself* has the necessary repetition inbuilt, hence *there is no repetition of the Activity on the Activity Decomposition*. Finally, the course brochure is printed.

Figure 4.27 shows the second example used earlier with repetition added. To firm up the Course Giving details, the students' details need to be obtained and recorded. The provisional Course Giving then needs to be confirmed with the requestor. If confirmed, the teacher's course schedule, showing the Course Givings scheduled for the year, is updated (and distributed to the teacher). Teachers then have to be found for the Course Giving and any outstanding Course Givings. What results is a *list* of teachers able to give the course.

The Course Giving which has just been confirmed, and any other outstanding Course Givings of the same type of course, are then gone through in turn and the following repeated for each outstanding Course Giving. The list showing teachers capable of giving the course is used and the availability of each teacher on the list is checked, with a choice being made as to which teacher(s) should give that course. What results is a list containing the teachers who will give that course. Each teacher is then provisionally booked to the Course Giving.

This example is rather special for a number of reasons. First, the company has decided to deal with any other outstanding Course Givings for the same course at the same time as the one which is being firmed up. Their reason for this is that it makes the choice of teacher for each Course Giving easier. Second, the addition of the 'FOR EACH chosen teacher' has meant that the 'IF' condition is no longer needed as the (0,n) rider shows that it is possible that this Activity is not actioned.

It is most important that 'IF' conditions are considered first, however, as it ensures that the 'OTHERWISE' Activities are handled.

124 *A Simple Introduction to Data and Activity Analysis*

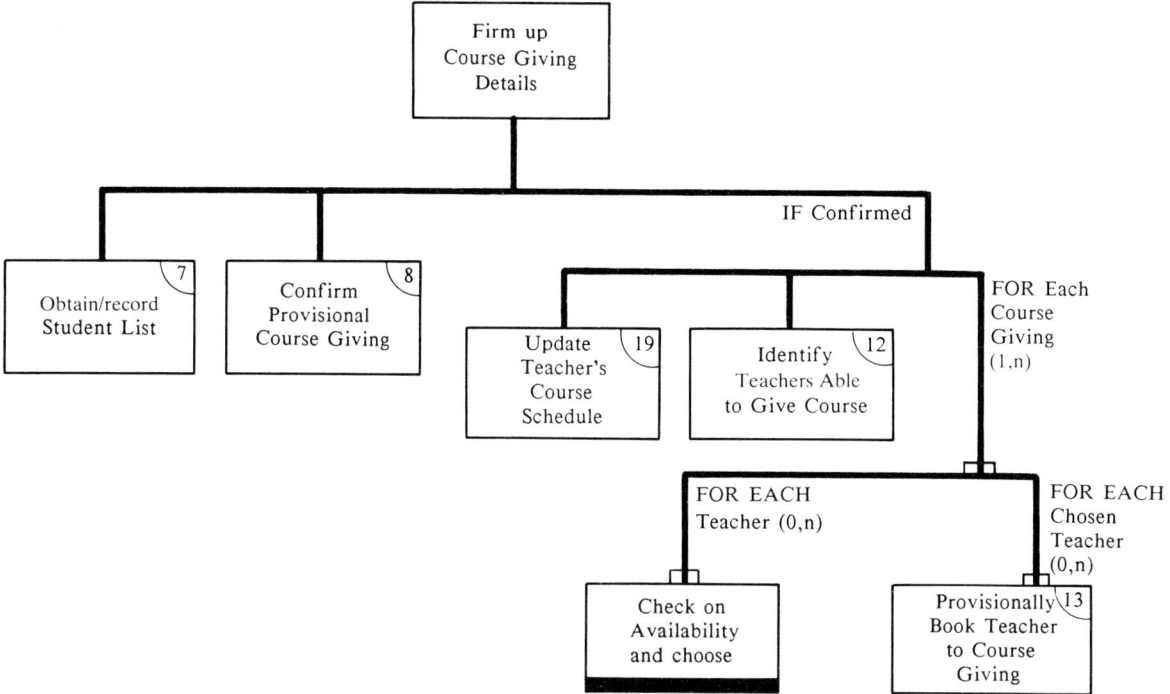

Figure 4.27 Adapting the activity decomposition to clearly show repetition/iteration of one activity with respect to others. (Activities can be repeated as a unit for the same reason)

Sequence and Parallel
Activities can occur in a set sequence or 'in parallel', in other words, not depend on one another.

The Data Flow Diagrams do show sequence and parallel Activity but not explicitly and clearly, and putting symbols on the Activity Decomposition Diagram adds considerably to understanding.

Sequence can be shown on the Activity Decomposition Diagram, as in Figure 4.28.

Where parallel Activities occur, i.e. they can be executed in parallel because they do not depend on one another, the conventions shown in Figure 4.29 can be used.

The ∥ symbol is used to denote parallel Activities. In the example, Activity 2 must be followed by Activities 3 and 4, but the 3 and 4 can occur in parallel.

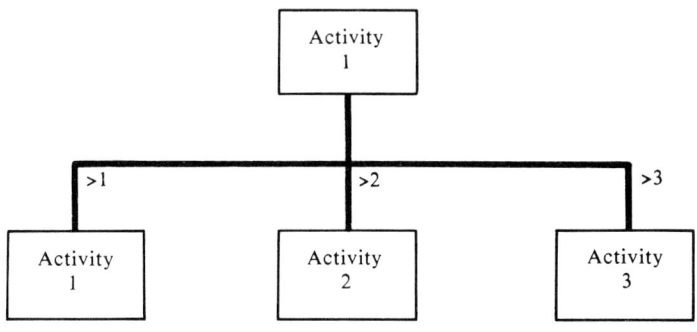

Figure 4.28 Sequence

Figure 4.30 shows an example. In order to handle a change in the Course Giving dates (requested by the client), the first step is to actually record the change of date requested. The Activities which follow can all occur in parallel. The teachers must be notified of the change in the dates of the Course Giving; the course schedule, which shows all the Course Givings planned for the year, must be updated (and sent out to each teacher) and the secretaries' work plan – which shows them what they have to do and when – must be updated.

4.4 OTHER DELIVERABLES OF ACTIVITY ANALYSIS
We saw during Data Analysis that many other useful deliverables about our concepts (types of fact) could be collected, all of them having a distinct purpose during design. This is also true of the

Activity or Function Analysis 125

deliverables of Activity Analysis, and the list which follows (Figures 4.31 – 4.37) was extracted from Book 3 of my four books, on Analysis with the Systems Development Cycle. This book defines each deliverable and explains its purpose.

The deliverables are listed under each concept heading and the relevance of a deliverable to a particular stage of study is shown.

A distinction has been made between the Activity deliverables and the Elementary Activity deliverables. This is because the characteristics of the Elementary Activity are different and it plays a very fundamental role in design. We will be seeing this in Chapter 6.

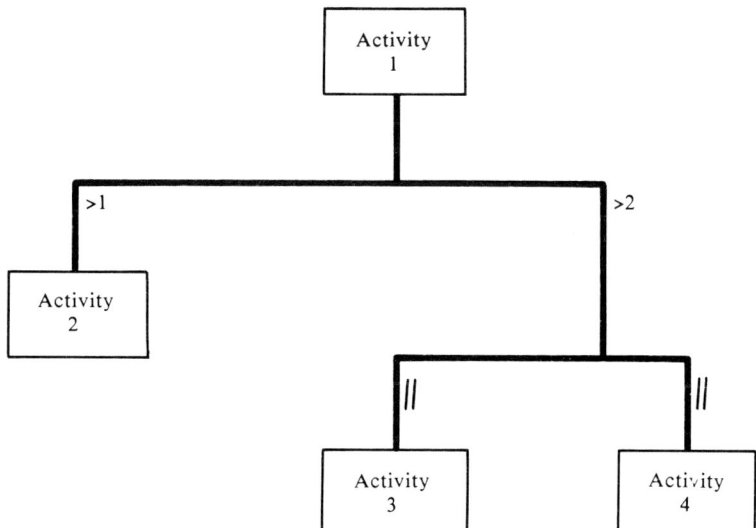

Figure 4.29 Parallel activities

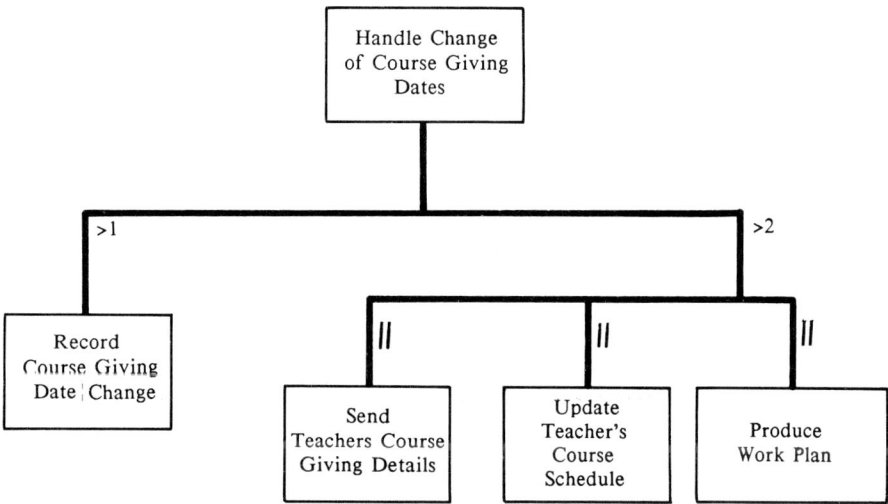

Figure 4.30 Parallel and sequence conventions

The concepts of the Elementary Activity Step (not included in the List) and the Logic Path are also applicable to Elementary Activities. The step will be described briefly as part of Chapter 6, the Logic Path will not.

Entity State is a concept included here for completeness but not described in this introductory book.

The message will be covered in chapter 6.

4.5 SUMMARY

Activity Analysis is a method of understanding what a business does now, wants to do, should be doing and the information it needs to do these things. We use five main concepts to enable us to understand the Activities of a business:

126 *A Simple Introduction to Data and Activity Analysis*

- The Activity itself
- The Event
- The Source/Sink
- The Data Store (Entity or Group of Entities)
- The Data Flow

These deliverables are represented diagrammatically using two diagrams which are complementary to one another:
- The Activity Decomposition Diagram
- The Data Flow Diagram

	Strategy	Tactical/ Feasibility	Detailed
Activity			
Responsibility			
- Analyst responsible for update or allowed to access	X	X	X
- Chief/Deputy	X	X	X
- Type of Access allowed	X	X	X
- Date last updated/looked at	X	X	X
Version	X	X	X
Names			
- Standard Name	X	X	X
- Abbreviated Name (Identifier)	X	X	X
- Other Names		X	X
Brief Description	X	X	X
Classification of extent	X	X	X
Strategic/Managerial/Operational	X	X	X
Manual/Head		X	X
Level	X	X	X
Decomposable/Not Decomposable	X	X	X
Filtered out/still active	X	X	X
Event Trigger		(X)	X
User/Activity Responsibility			
Current/Proposed		X	X
Activity Decomposition	X	X	X
- Repetition/Selection?		X	X
- Sequence		X	X

Figure 4.31 Activity Deliverables

Activity or Function Analysis 127

The Activity Decomposition Diagram shows the breakdown of Activities from very general to very detailed ones. It also shows where common Activities occur and, at more detailed levels, is used to show the sequence of Activities, where parallel Activities can take place, any conditional Activities and any Activities which are repeated.

The Data Flow Diagram shows for each 'leg' of the Activity Decomposition Diagram the dependency between Activities. It also shows what data they use – more particularly, what data in the Data Model – and how they interact with the Activities, Sources and Sinks outside the scope.

The strength of the Activity Decomposition Diagram is its ability to show all the Activities in one picture and to represent conditions, sequence etc.

Together they make up a powerful and immensely useful set of diagrams and concepts for documenting systems from a 'conceptual' point of view. They are great aids to thinking and understanding, and can (with care) be good aids to discussion with the user. I have found the list form of Activity Decomposition Diagram particularly useful in this respect.

	Strategic	Tactical/Feasibility	Detailed
Responsibility			
- Analyst responsible for update or allowed to access		X	X
- Chief/Deputy		X	X
- Type of Access allowed		X	X
- Date last updated/looked at		X	X
Names			
- Standard Name		X	X
- Abbreviated Name (Identifier)		X	X
- Other Names			X
Brief Description		X	X
Attribute Value or Value Range (used to represent event)			X
Event frequency			X
		occasionally events are applicable to the Feasibility Study	

Figure 4.32 Event deliverables

128 A Simple Introduction to Data and Activity Analysis

	Strategic	Tactical/Feasibility	Detailed
Responsibility			
- Analyst responsible for update or allowed to access	(X)	X	X
- Chief/Deputy	(X)	X	X
- Type of Access allowed	(X)	X	X
- Date last updated/looked at	(X)	X	X
Source/Sink Code		X	X
Source/Sink Name (in full)	(X)	X	X
Source/Sink Address			X
Type of Source/Sink/or Actual		X	X
Source/Sink Data Flow Usage			
- Data Flow sent/received		X	X
Source/Sink Element Usage (derived)			
- Most reliable source?			X
- Subset of population/Criteria for partitioning			X
- Source/Sink?			X
	(occasionally at a grouped level)		

Figure 4.33 Source/sink deliverables

	Strategic	Tactical/Feasibility	Detailed
- called 'Information Need' and is grouping			
Responsibility			
- Analyst responsible for update or allowed to access	(X)	X	X
- Chief/Deputy	(X)	X	X
- Type of Access allowed	(X)	X	X
- Date last updated/looked at	(X)	X	X
Version	(X)	X	X
Names	(X)	X	X
- Standard Name	(X)	X	X
- Abbreviated Name	(X)	X	X
- Other Names		X	X
Definition/Description		X	X
Data flow Decomposition (E/A/R make-up)		X	X
- Sequence of Data in Data Flow			X
Activity/Data Flow Usage		X	X
- Optionality		X	X
- Exclusivity		X	X

Figure 4.34 Data flow deliverables

Activity or Function Analysis 129

	Strategic	Tactical/Feasibility	Detailed
Responsibility			
- Analyst responsible for update or allowed to access			X
- Chief/Deputy			X
- Type of Access allowed			X
- Date last updated/looked at			X
Names			
- Standard Names			X
- Abbreviated Name			X
"Owning" Entity Type			X
Relationship state and domain value Composition			X

Figure 4.35 Entity state deliverables

	Strategic	Tactical/Feasibility	Detailed
Responsibility			
- Analyst responsible for update or allowed to access			X
- Chief/Deputy			X
- Type of Access allowed			X
- Date last updated/looked at			X
Message Identifier Code			X
Message Text			X
Language of message			X
Length of message (in characters)			X
Full description of message (causes and consequences)			X
Use - Design only - Analysis and design			X
Type - Error - Non-error			X

Figure 4.36 Message deliverables

130 *A Simple Introduction to Data and Activity Analysis*

Design Mapping	Strategic	Tactical/ Feasibility	Detailed
Mechanisms			
Sub-Types			
(i) System/Sub-system	X	X	X
(ii) Transaction Type		X	X
(iii) Computer Mechanisms			X
(a) Computer Job Type			X
(b) Program Type			X
(c) Module Type			X
(d) Sub-routine Type			X
(e) Exchange			X
(iv) Clerical Mechanisms			X
(a) Clerical Task Type			X
Responsibility			
- Designer responsible for update or allowed to access	X	X	X
- Chief/Deputy	X	X	X
- Type of Access allowed	X	X	X
- Date last updated/looked at	X	X	X
Descriptive Name of Mechanism	X	X	X
Abbreviated Name of Mechanism	X	X	X
Full Description	X	X	X
Package/In-House	X	X	X
Mechanism Decomposition (Consists of)		X	X
User/Mechanism Responsibility		X	X
Data Packet			
Name of Packet			X
Description/Classification of current mechanism			X
Packet Use			X
- Type of Use			
Designed Element Usage/Packet Composition			X
Mechanism Mapping			
System/Activity Mapping	X	X	X
- Partially covered/fully covered	X	X	X
Transaction Type/Elementary Activity Mapping		X	X
- Satisfactory/Unsatisfactory Mapping		X	X
Computer or Clerical Mechanism/Activity Mapping			X
- Satisfactory/Unsatisfactory Mapping			X

Figure 4.37 Design mapping

5 How to do Activity Analysis

5.1 INTRODUCTION

This chapter shows how to get the Activity Analysis deliverables – the Activity Models (Data Flow Diagram and Activity Decomposition Diagram) together with all the related information – from a number of well defined inputs.

These inputs, as with the Data Analysis inputs, are obtained from the collection task during interviews, meetings, observation sessions and so on.

There are three types of input, unlike Data Analysis where there are four. What is missing from the following list is the 'Design Occurrences' which are not a very helpful or useful form of input during Activity Analysis. 'Design Occurrences', when applied to Activities, would cover such things as the execution of a program or the execution of a user task.

The three useful forms of input are:

* Real World Abstractions/Classes
* Real World Occurrences/Actions
* Design Abstractions/Classes

Real World Abstractions and Real World Occurrences

A user nearly always finds it easier to talk about what he does rather than what data he uses. Similarly, most people's job descriptions, policy documents, explanatory books or similar types of business literature will often describe what is to be done, and that description is in 'conceptual' terms.

Sometimes the description is about the types of things which must be done; sometimes an example is given. When types of things to be done are described we are already seeing the system at an abstract or classified level. When examples are given we are seeing Occurrences. For example:

"The orders are received and checked to make sure they are valid and any queries are referred back to the customer. For example, J.J.A. Limited sent in Order 31954 the other day for 5,000 widgets but we don't sell widgets. The order is recorded and we check what stock we have of each of the products the customer has ordered . . ."

The example the user has given (Starting 'J.J.A. Limited' and ending 'Widgets') shows Occurrences and actually describes an Event Occurrence 'J.J.A. Ltd sent Order 31954'.

The rest of the paragraph describes what the business does at an abstract level:

It receives orders
validates orders
records orders
checks stock of products on order
and so on.

When the paragraph is unravelled we almost have our Activities and sequence. The Occurrences, however, will need to be both unravelled and classified.

Thus, any form of input which describes what the business does already in a classified way is known as 'Real World Abstraction'. You can easily recognise it because the objects of the verbs are themselves also classes,

e.g. receives **order**
checks **stock**

They may even be immediately identifiable as the Entities on our Data Model. Any form of input which describes what the business does but where the object of the verb is a thing – an Actual Occurrence – is know as 'Real World Occurrences'.

e.g. receive order 31954
validate order 31954
check widget stock

Both forms of input are useful in Activity Analysis.

131

132   A Simple Introduction to Data and Activity Analysis

Design Abstractions

Computer Systems Specifications, User Guides to Systems, and Organisation and Methods Type Procedure Guides will all be describing the means by which the business Activities are being achieved.

A Design Abstraction is simply a means by which an Activity is achieved using a mix of people and machines.

For example: Transactions, programs, online exchanges and dialogues, procedures and batch jobs are all Design Abstractions: types of mechanism which we have used to ensure an Activity is actually put into practice. We are interested in the jobs of people just as much as the work done by machines. We treat any investigation of an area of Activity in our scope without regard for whether it is done by people or machines. Both types of mechanism are equally important.

   e.g.   A user might say   "I fill in form X"
                                      "I enter it into the machine".

The machine might then "validate the form contents".

These Design Abstractions are useful input to the Activity Analysis process. We can not only find out from them what Activities are hidden within these tasks, but we can also see what problems they cause and plan **conversion** or change of mechanism from people to machine, say, or even vice versa.

Figure 5.1 demonstrates the difference between the types.

Because there are three types of input, there are three methods of Activity Analysis.

Figure 5.3 summarises these three methods. Our "raw data" is of the three types mentioned, but we have only the one common output – the Activity Models and an updated Data Model. Hence each method gives us the same common output. The presence of the updated Data Model is most important. Activity Analysis **always** effects our Data Analysis deliverables. It helps to supplement them, and it helps to verify that they are correct. We will see this in the rest of this chapter.

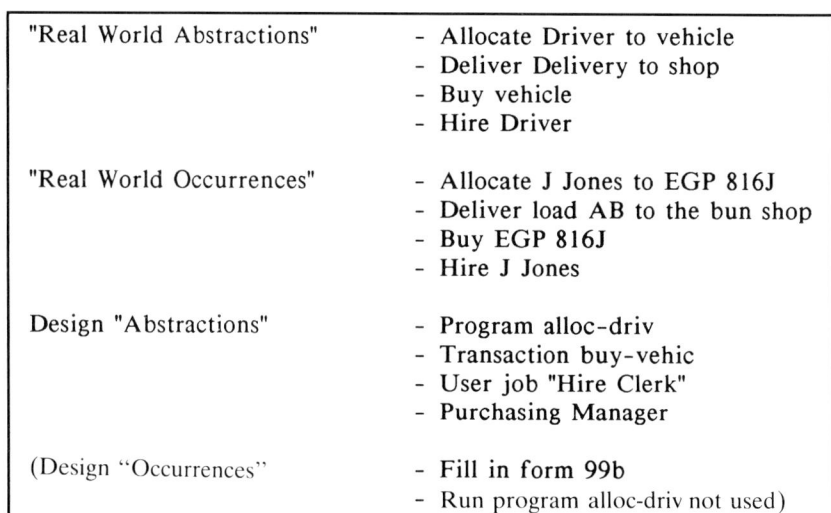

Figure 5.1 Types of input – Activities

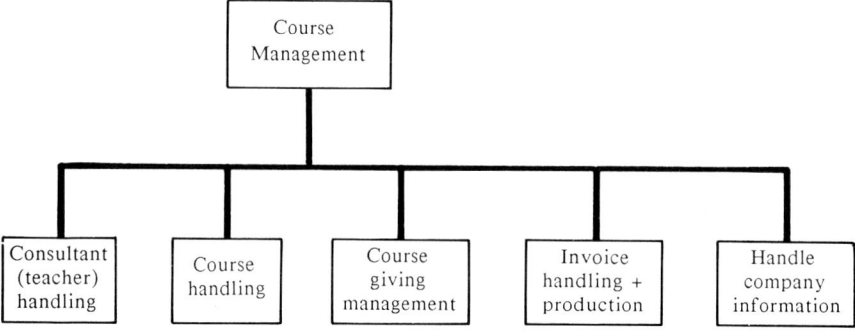

Figure 5.2 Overview of main activities in example

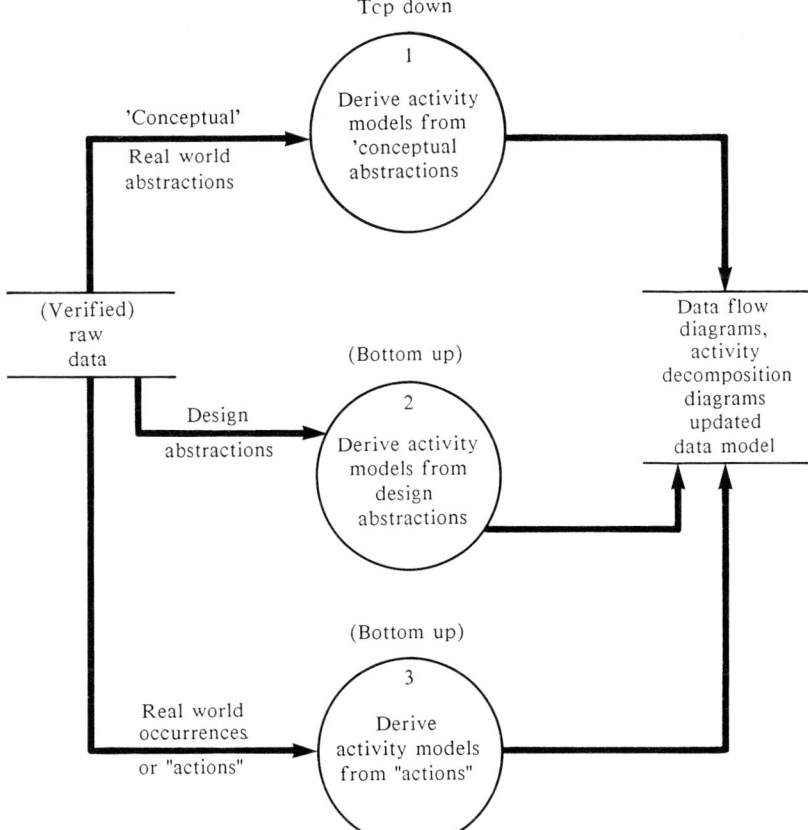

Figure 5.3 Activity Analysis – obtaining the models

5.2 ANALYSIS

As we have seen in the introduction, there are three methods of Activity Analysis.

* Deriving the Activity Models from Real World Abstractions
* Deriving the Activity Model from Design Abstractions
* Deriving the Activity Model from Real World Occurrences (which are called 'Actions' for short)

We will be seeing how each method works using the same Course Administration example I used in the Data Analysis chapter.

I will assume that some Activity Decomposition has already been done and that the scope of the system is shown by the Activity Decomposition in Figure 5.2.

Course Management (or Course Administration; they are synonymous) consists of five main Activities which are concerned with handling the consultants (teachers), the courses themselves, the actual Course Givings, the invoices and the companies who are our clients or potential clients.

I am going to assume that we have been given one 'leg' to look at in more detail and that is the 'consultant handling' Activity breakdown. Perhaps other analysts are looking at the other areas.

We will use each different form of input to help us decompose this Activity.

5.2.1 Using Real World Abstractions

On the next page you will find some interview notes which were obtained by discussing with Fred, a user, what he does when consultants go sick. Looking at Events that can happen to things is an important method of determining the Activities. First find your Event, then determine all the Activities needed to deal with it. You will have probably found 80 per cent or more of your Activities then. Some people even define the scope of their system using Events rather than Activities.

I will use the example and demonstrate the steps you follow to extract the Activity Decomposition and Data Flow Diagrams from what the user has said.

The basic steps are quite simple, but not at all mechanical. Take great care when following them.

134 A Simple Introduction to Data and Activity Analysis

Interview notes on Consultant Handling

Analyst: I know you have problems when a teacher goes sick, Fred, could you tell me what happens at the moment to handle this, once you have been informed by 'Personnel'.

Fred: Well, the teacher may be giving a course, so the first thing we have to do is make sure he's taken off any of the courses which are imminent. We give ourselves a reasonable amount of leeway here and make assumptions based on how sick the poor chap actually is.

Analyst: Then what

User: Well, we then do a scan of our teachers to find out who is able to give those sorts of courses.

Analyst: How do you do that?

User: Well we find out who are able to give the course, then whittle it down a bit by removing those who aren't free on the dates the courses are meant to be being held.

Analyst: Anything else?

User: Well it helps to have the average course marks that were obtained by the chap on past courses as it may help us to make a final choice.

Analyst: How do you make the final choice?

User: We ask them.

Analyst: Anything else?

User: Well when we're asking them we look at their marks and of those that are willing to do it, we pick out the best one.

Analyst: I see, and what is the result?

User: Well, we end up with a replacement teacher for the course the chap can't give.

Analyst: And what do you do with it?

User: (Once he has finished laughing) Do you want a polite answer?

Analyst: (patiently) Yes please.

User: Well we use it to book the teacher onto the Course Giving.

Analyst: And then?

User; We send the teacher confirmatory details about the course he's been booked on, so that he knows where to go, when it is, who his fellow teachers are and if we've got any students booked, who they are and a bit about them.

Analyst: That's all?

User: Yup, that's all.

Analyst: Thank you, Fred.

User: Not at all, bye bye.

1. Look for the triggering Event or Events.

There may be more than one mentioned, in which case you should produce a different Data Flow for each Event you find.

In the example there is only one Event.

'Teacher goes sick'.

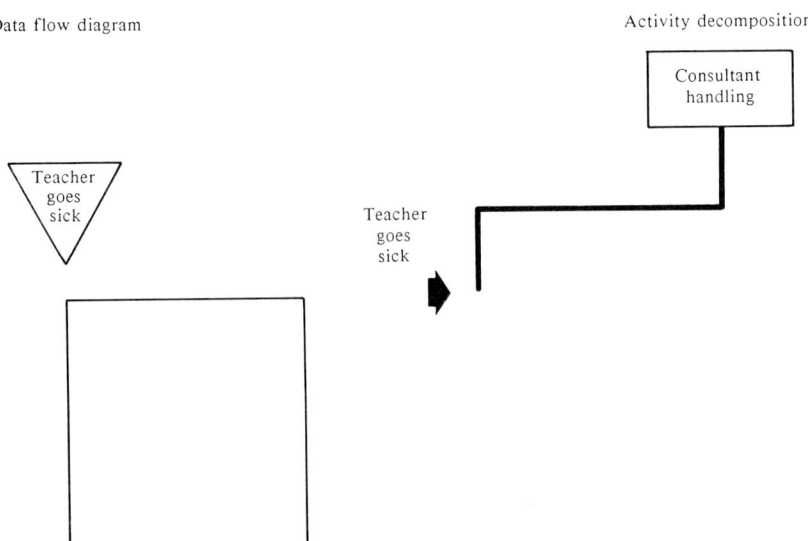

Figure 5.4 The beginnings of the Data Flow and Activity Decomposition Diagram after step 1

Draw this on the Data Flow outside the scope box and on the Activity Decomposition. See Figure 5.4.

2. Look for who or what provides the system with knowledge of the Event.

A Source could be the means by which we gain knowledge of the Event, or it could be an external Activity. In this case it is an external Activity, 'Personnel' or perhaps more correctly 'Personnel Management' (then we have the necessary verb).

Put this Source or external Activity on the Data Flow outside the scope box and connect it by the dotted line – showing that it is the Source of the Event knowledge. See Figure 5.5.

3. Now find a general name for the overall Activity needed to handle the Event. Generally speaking it is easy to invent one from the Event name by calling it "handle (Event)".

In this example, our Activity is to 'handle the consultant's sickness'. This Activity is placed in our Activity Decomposition next to the Event and becomes the title of our Data Flow Diagram. See Figure 5.6.

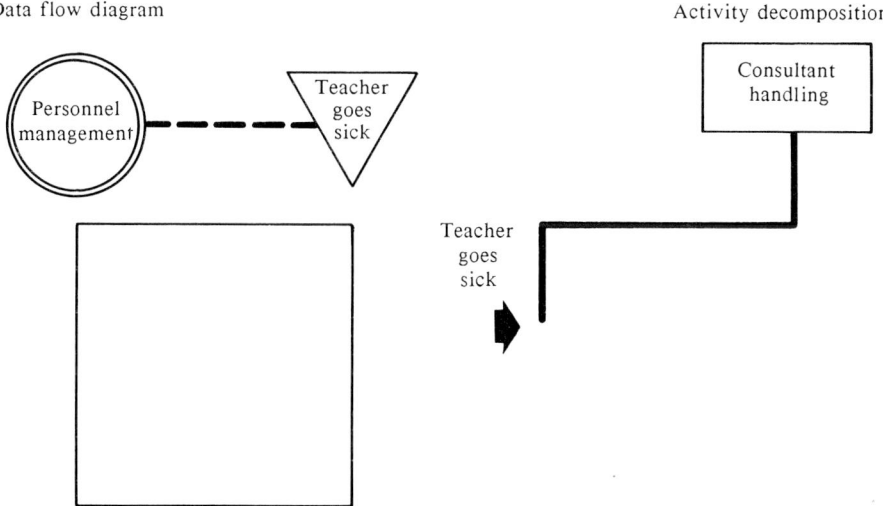

Figure 5.5 The Data Flow and Activity Decomposition after the Source or external Activity has been added

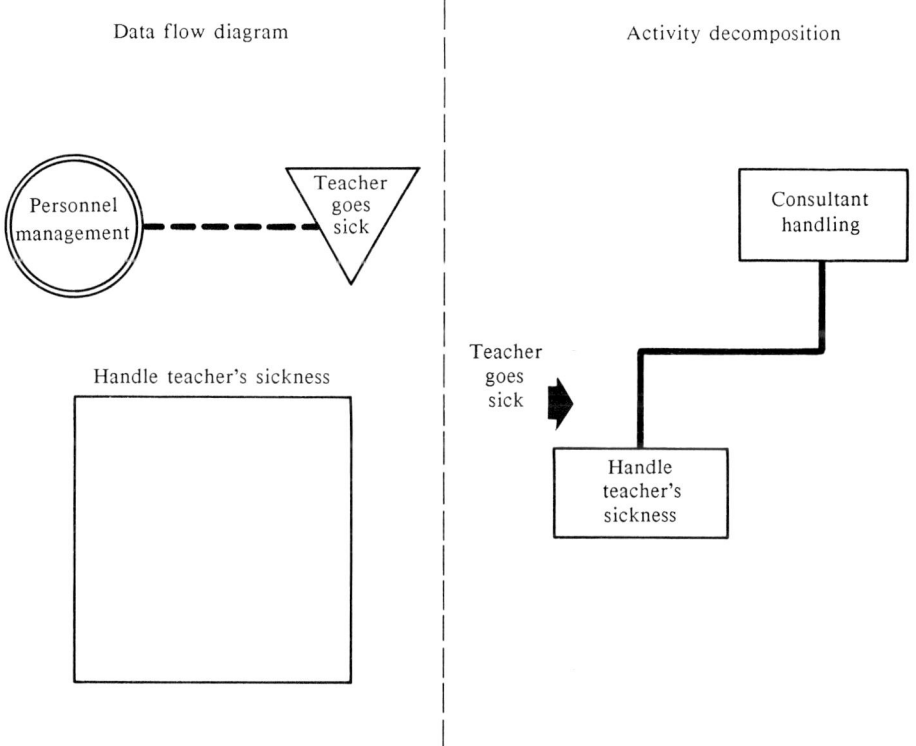

Figure 5.6 DFD and Activity Decomposition after adding main Event handling Activity

136 *A Simple Introduction to Data and Activity Analysis*

4. Now look for all the Activities which seem to be triggered by that Event.

Find a good clear short name for each Activity and place them, in the sequence in which they appear to follow, on the Activity Decomposition Diagram in a left to right order below the main Activity you've just put on the diagram.

Also place them on the Data Flow Diagram. You can also keep the sequence by using either a top to bottom or a left to right order. I will use a top to bottom order. [If you use left to right, put the Event and Source on the left of the scope box.] Where there is a definite sequence show it on the Decomposition Diagram.

Where there is no sequence – often indicated by the user saying, "While A is happening, we do B" – show that parallel Activities can happen.

Figure 5.7 shows the effect from our example. We have identified five sub-activities.

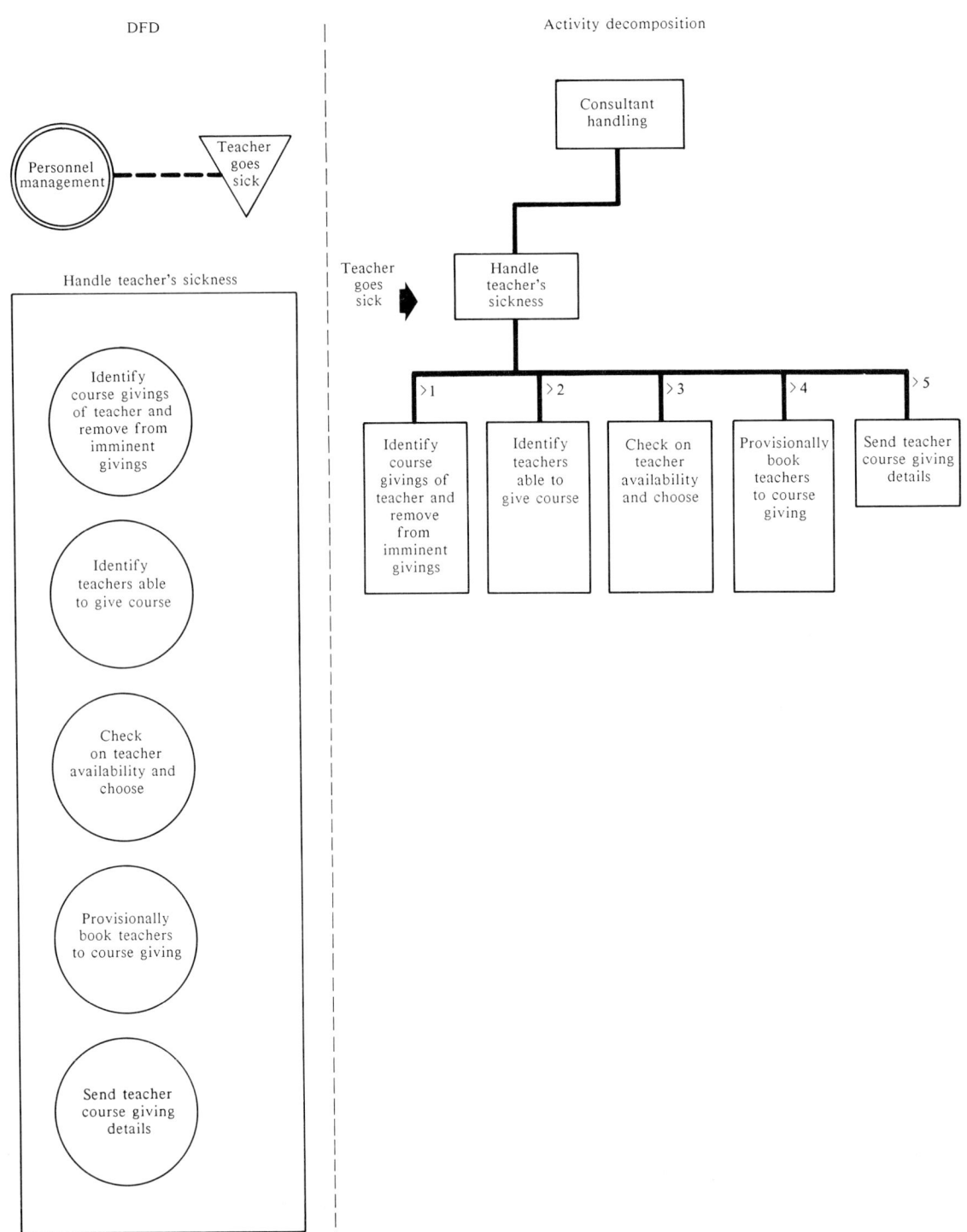

Figure 5.7 DFD and Activity Decomposition after Activity breakdown

How to do Activity Analysis 137

5. Now search for any Activities which are conditional upon something, the words **if** and **may** are initial clues here.

In our examples we see:
'The Teacher may be giving a course' hence there is the possibility that he isn't actually giving any courses. If he isn't then no subsequent Activity is needed.

There is no mention in the user's explanation of any other occasion when the Activity is dependent upon a condition. In reality we would need to check to make sure:

* Is it possible that no other teachers can give that course? What do you do then?
* Is it possible that no teacher is willing to do the course or has good enough marks? What do you do then?

I have kept the example simple, as the user expressed it.

Figure 5.8 shows the result. The IF condition has been added, and the sequence renumbered. This last step is not mandatory but often helps in understanding.

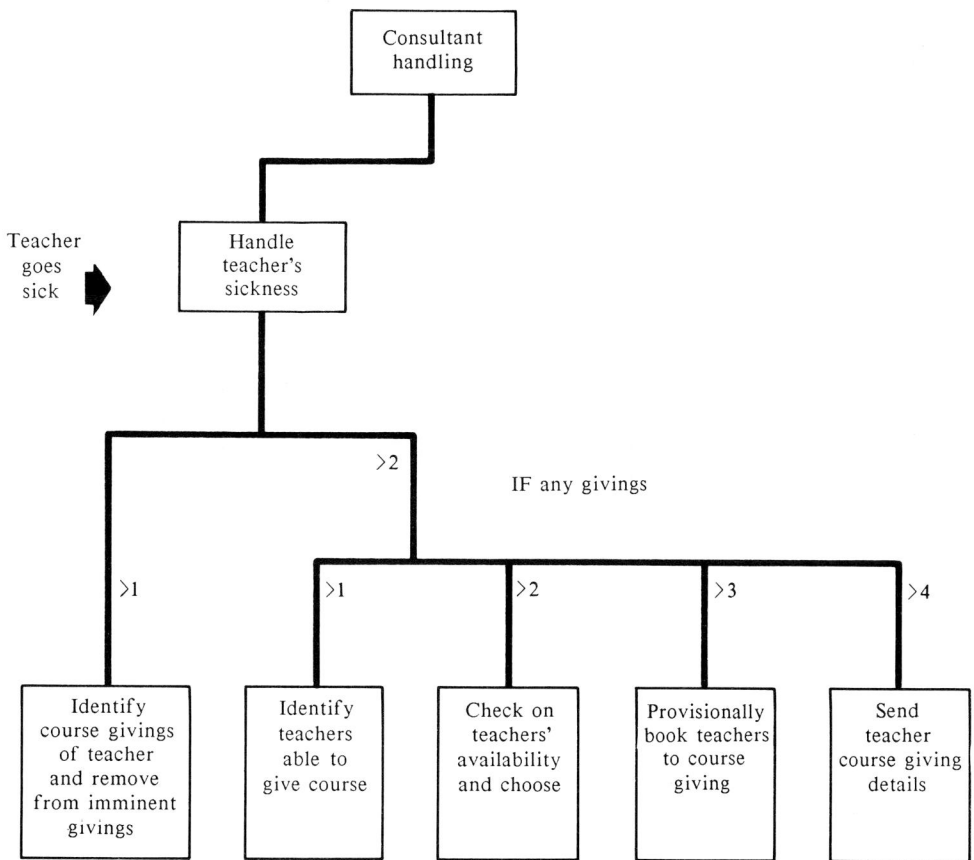

Figure 5.8 Addition of conditions to the Activity Decomposition

6. Work out from what the user has said, but also by using the names of the Activities, what Data Flows are likely to be input and output to the Activities. Describe the contents of the Data Flows using Entities, Attributes and Relationships.

In our example we must be receiving a Data Flow from the Personnel Management Activity notifying us of the sickness. I have called this 'notification of sickness' and we would need to do some more questioning to discover its contents.

In Figure 5.9 I have added this Data Flow and drawn it springing from the Event – to show which Event the Data Flow is recording.

In order to be able to 'identify the teachers able to give the course', data on which Course Givings are affected by the teacher's sickness and his removal from them must be known. I have added this Data Flow (even though the user has not stated it explicitly). We could confirm this by asking ". . . and what information do you use to . . .".

138 *A Simple Introduction to Data and Activity Analysis*

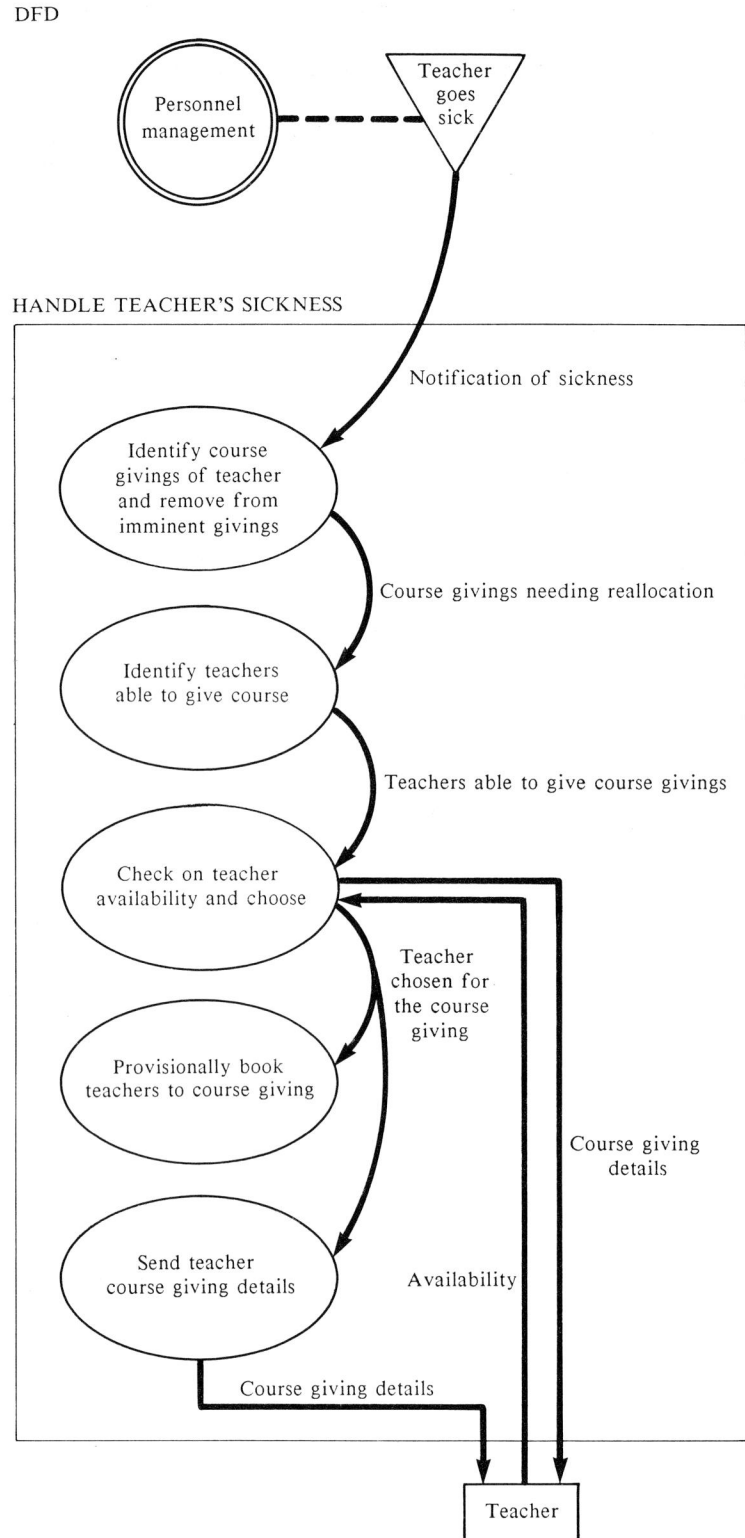

Figure 5.9 Adding Data Flows

I have called it Course Givings needing reallocation and it is probably a simple list of the form –

Course Giving 1	Course X
Course Giving 2	Course Y
Course Giving 3	Course X
Course Giving 4	Course U
Course Giving 5	Course V

The user is reasonably explicit about the data resulting from the Activity "identify teachers able to give course". He says that it is a list of teachers able to give each course (implying the Course

How to do Activity Analysis 139

Givings) meant to be held. He also gives extra details about the contents of the list mentioning 'average marks'.

We can start to build up a picture of the contents of the Data Flow.

Course Giving 1 (Course X)	Teacher A Average marks Y Teacher B Average Marks Z	Course Giving affected by teacher removal and teachers who can give course and are free on date of Course Giving
Course Giving 2 (Course Y)	Teacher A Average marks Y Teacher C Average marks P Teacher D Average marks Q	
Course Giving 3 (Course X)	Teacher E Average marks R	
Course Giving 4 (Course V)	Teacher C Average marks P Teacher D Average marks Q	
Course Giving 5 (Course V)	Teacher F Average marks S	

It may also be, from what Fred says, that teachers are listed in **mark** order so that those with high marks are asked first.

This of course would need confirming. It may be that it is in a different order – say Course Giving within teacher rather than the other way round. It is very important that we do know because the **repetition** and subsequent Activity will depend on it.

Let us assume that the above is the order used.

Fred then says that he checks on the availability of each teacher and chooses a replacement teacher for the Course Giving.

The Data Flow emerging is thus of the form,

Course Giving 1 Teacher B
(Course X)

He does not imply that a list is produced. This is most important as we will see how it affects the Activity Descriptions and the repetition.

We can call this Data Flow 'teacher chosen for the Course Giving'. (See Figure 5.9)

For the choice to be made the teacher is contacted. We know that the teacher is both a Source and a Sink. For him to make the decision a Data Flow must be sent to him, probably containing details of the Course Giving (although we don't know what details). The Data Flow which returns is either a 'yes' or 'no' answer which I have called 'Availability'.

When the user books the teacher onto the Course Giving no Data Flow results go to another Activity, but the last Activity, 'send teacher Course Giving details', does have a Data Flow. Here it is obvious Data Flow can be called 'Course Giving details', and its contents are clearly stated:

Course Giving – Dates of Course Giving
 – Location of Course Giving
 – Course
 – Lecturer(s) giving Course Giving
 – Students on course
 – (Name, title, experience)?

We could even see what sub-set of the Data Model they represent – this is shown in Figure 5.10 and

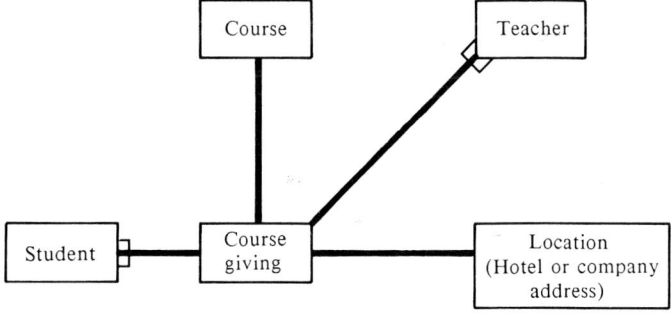

Figure 5.10 The Data Flow "Course Giving details"

represents a 'view' of the Data Model seen by that Data Flow. This view also contains a sub-set of the Attributes from the whole Data Model.

To enable us to produce this information, we must know the Course Giving so we need to show the Data Flow used for provisional booking also being used by the 'send teacher' Activity.

Finally, the 'Course Giving details' are very clearly sent to the 'teacher' Sink, so we add this to the diagram.

7. Describe each Activity.

Extract from what the user has said any description of what each Activity involves. You may replace this later either by further Decomposition or a structured description, but it is a very important intermediate deliverable.

On the following pages I have extracted a description of each Activity from the user's explanation.

Activity Descriptions and Data Flow contents must be consistent with one another. If the Data Flow has repetition so must the Activity. If it has repetition within repetition, this will be repeated in the Activity description.

Send Teacher Course Giving Details

The teachers who are due to give a certain Course Giving are sent details of the Course Giving itself.
The details are:

- A list of students and their previous experience
- The location of the course
- Details of the course giving – dates etc.
- The other teacher(s)

Provisionally Book Teacher to Course Giving

A provisional booking of the teacher to the Course Giving is made. The course is used as the start point and the Course Giving found by reference to the course.

Check Availability and Choose

A teacher able to give the Course Giving is asked if he/she would be prepared to do that particular Course Giving. (The teachers are asked in the order of merit, using details of the marks obtained on previous courses.) Verbal confirmation is given to the teacher of the Course Giving, if he is chosen.

Identify Teachers able to give Course

The courses are gone through in turn for all Course Givings requiring teachers. All the teachers able to give the course are identified and a check made that for the particular Course Giving they are not already booked for another one held at the same time.

A list of potential, suitable and free teachers is produced. When the list is produced a summary is also provided of the average marks the lecturer obtained on past courses.

Identify Course Givings of Teacher and Remove him from Imminent Givings

All the Course Givings a teacher was supposed to be giving (in the future) are listed. For each one, if the date of the Course Giving is imminent (i.e. near), the teacher is removed (disconnected) from the Course Giving, and the Course Giving, which requires reallocation, is marked.

8. Using the Activity descriptions and the contents of the Data Flows' output and input determine what data from the Data Model is used by the Activities.

If any data is **missing**, add it to the Data Model. Missing data could be an Entity, Attribute or Relationship.

Create a Data Store for every Entity used and give it the Entity's name.

If the Entity is used by the Activity, draw a Data Flow from the Data Store to the Activity. If the Entity is updated (created, modified, deleted or linked up by Relationship to other Entities) draw a Data Flow from the Activity to the Data Store.

Figure 5.12 shows our final Data Flow Diagram.

Whenever a Data Flow is actually describing a change to an Entity and the Data Flow needs to update the Data Store rather than go between Activities, change this. In the Diagram, the Data Flow "Course Givings needing reallocation" has been replaced by an update to the Course Giving Entity. The Attribute "needs reallocation?" is created, which indicates that the Course Givings require reallocation. The next Activity then selects Course Givings needing reallocation from the Data Store.

9. Now add the repetition to the Activity Decomposition Diagram.

The essential part of this step is to ensure that Activity descriptions and repetition are compatible.

In our descriptions we see mention of the phrase 'Course Giving' each time in the singular for all the Activities after the 'identify teachers able to give course'. The description of this Activity in fact

How to do Activity Analysis 141

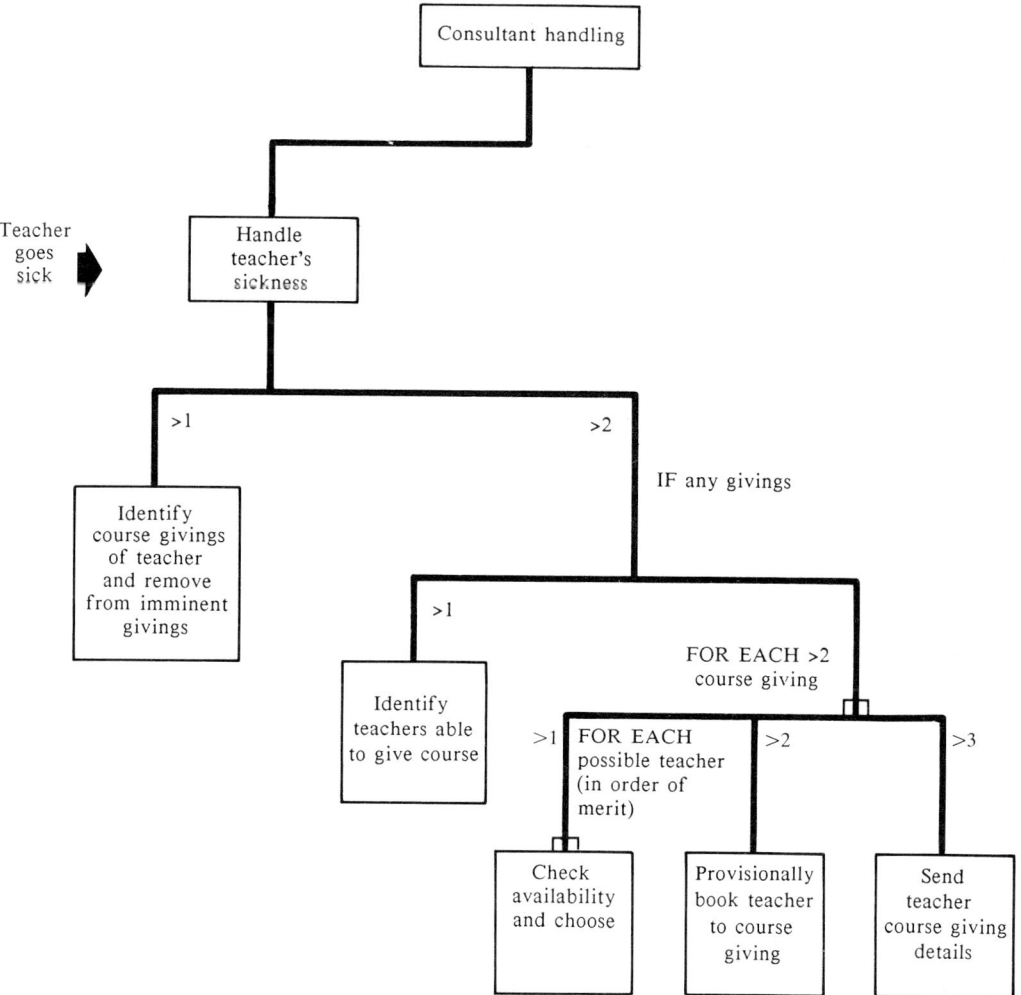

Figure 5.11 Addition of repetition to Activity Decomposition

explains that each Course Giving is gone through. The repetition implied by the Data Flow 'Course Givings needing reallocation' is thus handled from within the Activity Description and there is no need to show repetition on the Decomposition Diagram.

After this, however, we do need repetition of the group of Activities 'check on teacher availability', 'provisionally book teacher to Course Giving' and 'send teacher Course Giving details', each of which handles only one Course Giving at a time.

This group of Activities is repeated for each Course Giving and the user has implied this by using Course Giving in the singular.

This is shown in Figure 5.11.

Shown as a list rather than a diagram
Course management
    Consultant handling
        Handle teacher's sickness
        Identify Course Givings of teacher and remove from imminent givings
        IF teacher has imminent givings
        Identify teachers able to give course
            FOR each Course Giving (to be reallocated)
            FOR EACH possible teacher in order of merit
            – Check availability of teacher
            – Choose
        ENDFOR
        Provisionally book teacher to Course Giving
        Send teacher Course Giving details
        ENDFOR
    OTHERWISE
    ENDIF

142   *A Simple Introduction to Data and Activity Analysis*

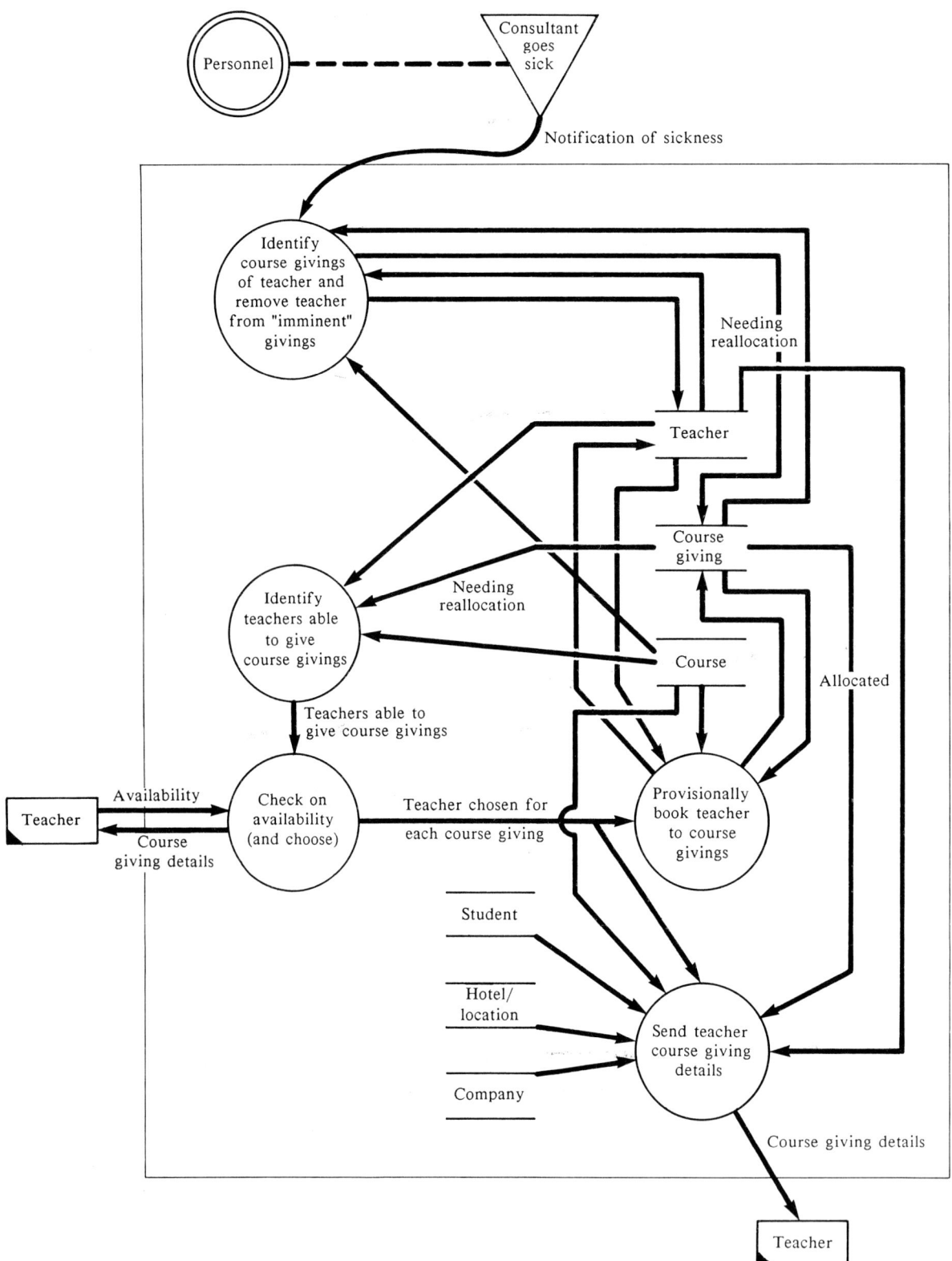

Figure 5.12   Handle consultant's sickness

We know from the Data Flow that for each Course Giving a number of teachers are candidates for selection for the Activity 'check availability and choose'. The Activity Description shows how one teacher is handled, hence repetition is needed on the Activity Decomposition Diagram.

Only one teacher results, so booking the teacher on the course and sending the details happens only once.

If you find it difficult to work out what repetition is present, use an example – a **test** to help you. (See Figure 5.13.)

How to do Activity Analysis 143

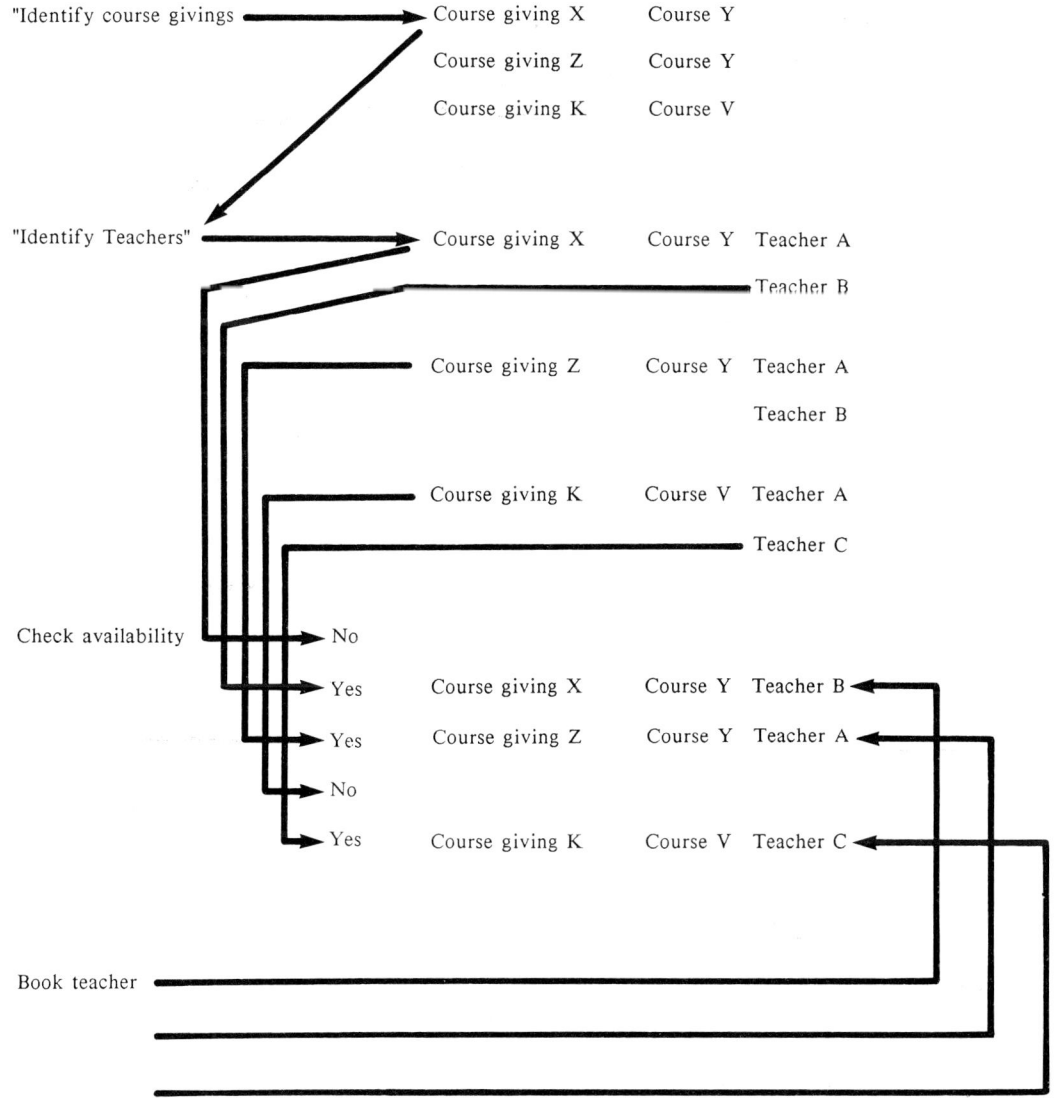

Figure 5.13

5.2.2 Using Design Abstractions

Design Abstractions can manifest themselves in Computer Systems Specifications, User Guides, Procedure Manuals – in fact, many different places.

On the following pages are two examples of the existing design of our Course Administration system. One is taken from a Computer System Specification, the other is part of one of our user's job specifications.

Using these two examples, I will show the steps you need to take to get the Data Flow Diagram and Activity Decomposition "bottom-up" from the descriptions.

(1) The first example is from the Computer System Specification.
In case the symbols are not familiar to you they are the ones which used to be used a while ago (they probably still are in some organisations) to document a computer system. (See Figure 5.14.) An example of how they are used is shown in Figure 5.15.

On the next few pages are the layouts of the forms and records mentioned in the Systems Flowchart:

* Form AB96 – New Consultant Detail Form (Figure 5.17)
* Course Master Record Layout (Figure 5.16)
* Consultant Master Record Layout (Figure 5.18)
* Course Brochure (a page from the listing) (Figure 5.19)

These are all Data Design Abstractions. We saw how they were analysed in Chapter Three. I am

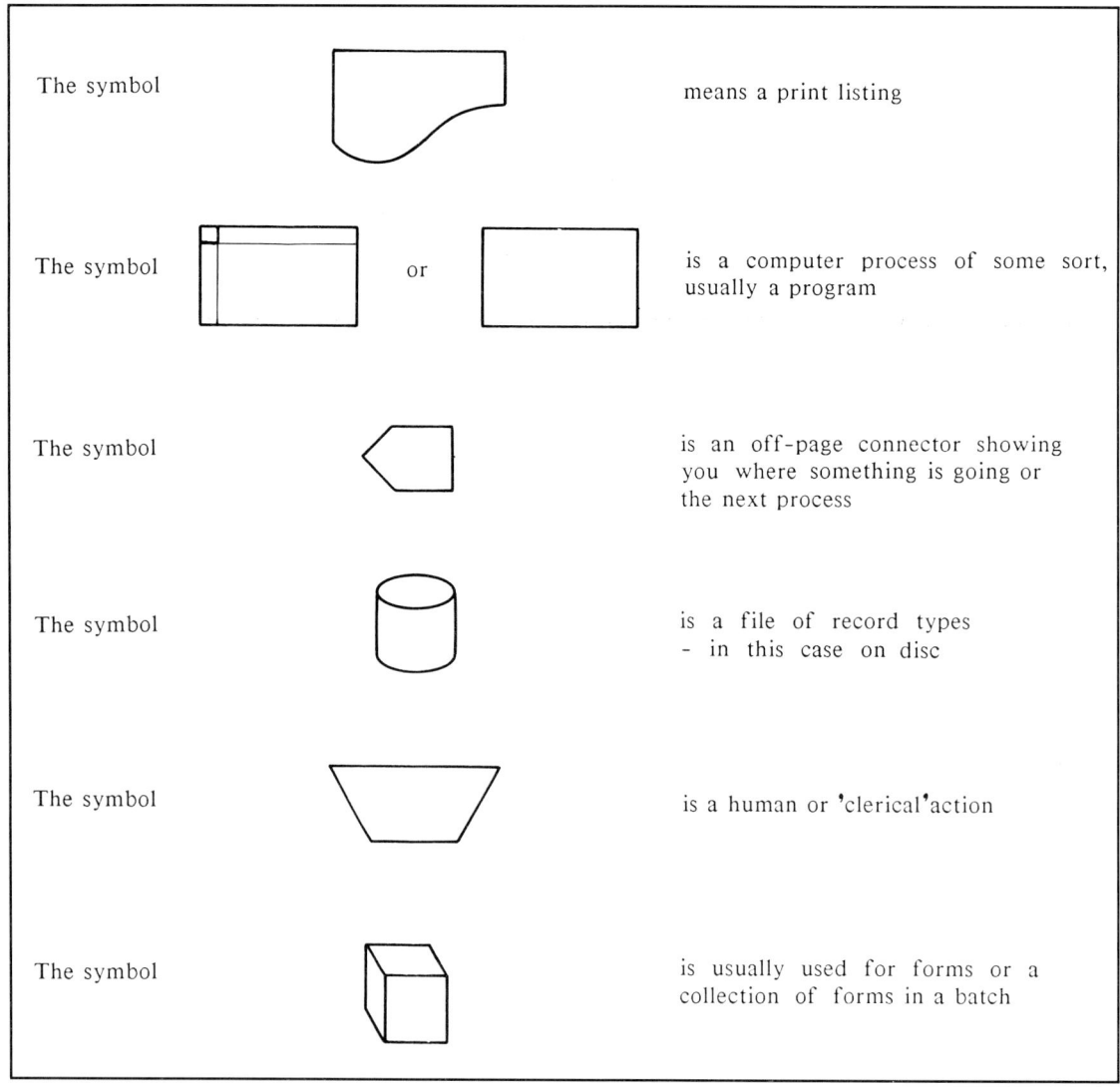

Figure 5.14

now going to assume that I have already analysed these forms, record layouts and listings and the results are as shown in Figures 5.20 to 5.23.

1. Piece together the user and the computer Actions where they have been split up into different documents.

Where a User Guide and a Computer System Specification are being used you will get only one 'view' of the system – that of the user or the computer. You need to piece these views together.

In the example, our New Consultant Details Form appears as if by magic at the start of the job. At the end it is clear that the 'Brochure Listing' goes to sales and marketing. We need to add the front end to the job to see how this sequence of processes is started.

In Figure 5.24 I have assumed that we have been able to find out this detail from the user's job description, and it has been added. I have also added what the user does with the listings. We piece together 'views' in exactly the same way, if they have also been split by user. We need all the tasks, irrespective of who or what does them.

2. Remove the following:
   * All processes which are machine-dependent – that is, they exist only because they are done by machine. Examples include:
     Sort, burst, guillotine, post by conveyor tube,
     punch to disc, decollate, deleave, stamp and so on.
   * All "error cycle" processes including error listings and confirmation listings.
   * Any batching, counting or similar tasks which have been added for control purposes.

All the above are mechanism-dependent.

How to do Activity Analysis 145

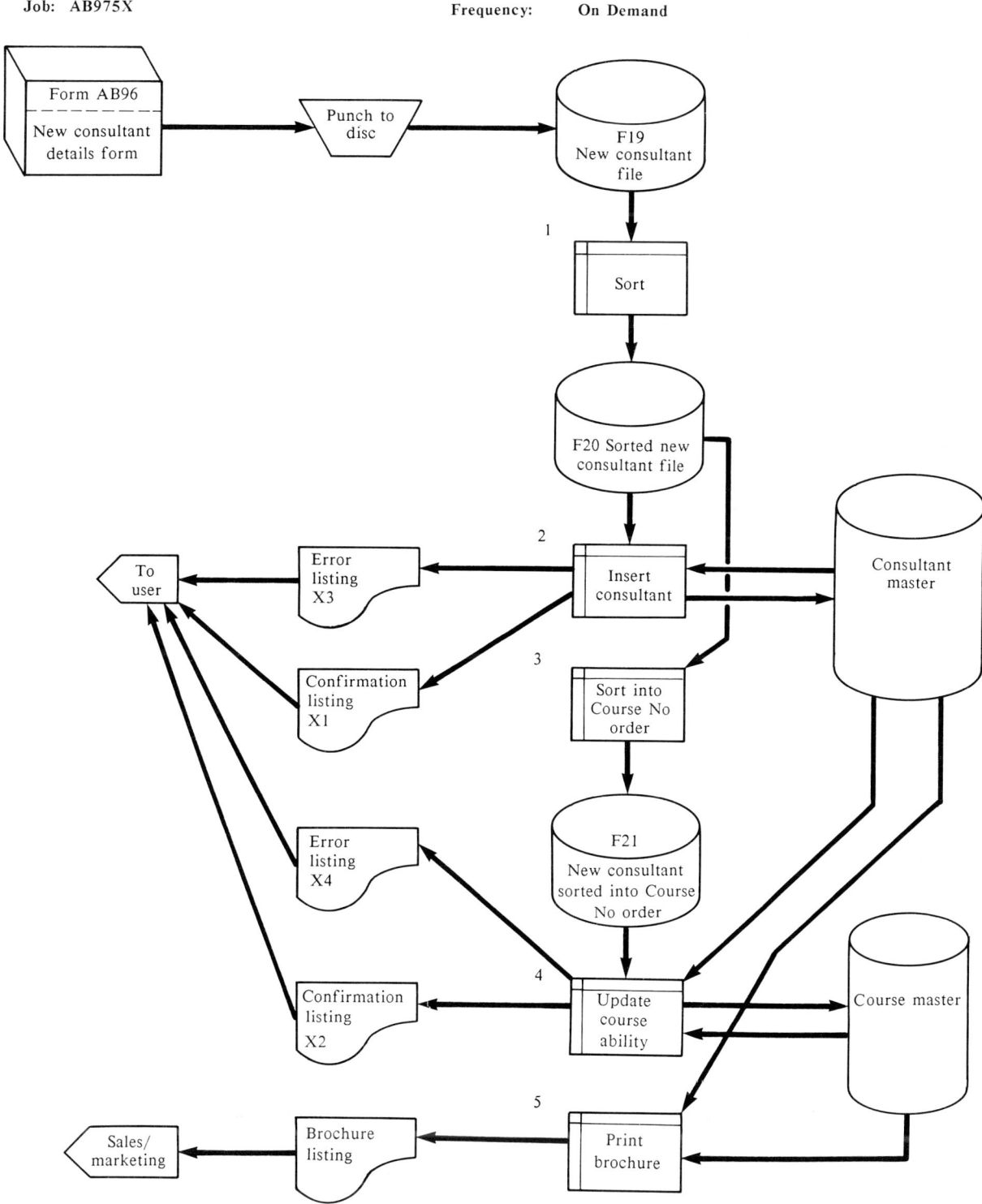

Figure 5.15 Extract from computer specification

Name of Record: COURSE MAST

Frequency:

LEVEL	NAME	PICTURE	OCCURS	DEPENDING ON	COMMENTS
03	COURSE-NO	PIC 99			
03	COURSE-NO-PRE	PIC 99			
03	COURSE-NO-DAYS	PIC 99			
03	COURSE-SUIT	PIC X(50)			
03	COURSE-TYP	PIC X			
03	COURSE-NAM	PIC X(50)			
03	COURSE-OBJ	PIC X(120)			
03	COURSE-ABBR	PIC X(10)			
03	COURSE-DESC	PIC X(120)			
03	COURSE-PRICE-1-IN	PIC 9(5)V99 C-3			
03	COURSE-PRICE-1-PUB	PIC 9(5)V99 C-3			
03	COURSE-PRICE-2-IN	PIC 9(5)V99 C-3			
03	COURSE-PRICE-2-PUB	PIC 9(5)V99 C-3			
03	COURSE-PRICE-3	PIC 9(5)V99 C-3			
03	COURSE-PRICE-3	PIC 9(5)V99 C-3			
03	ABILITY-IND	PIC 99			
03	COURSE-ABILITY		30 TIMES	ABILITY-IND	
05	TEACH-NO	PIC 999			
05	TEACH-NAM	PIC X(40)			

Figure 5.16 Course master record layout

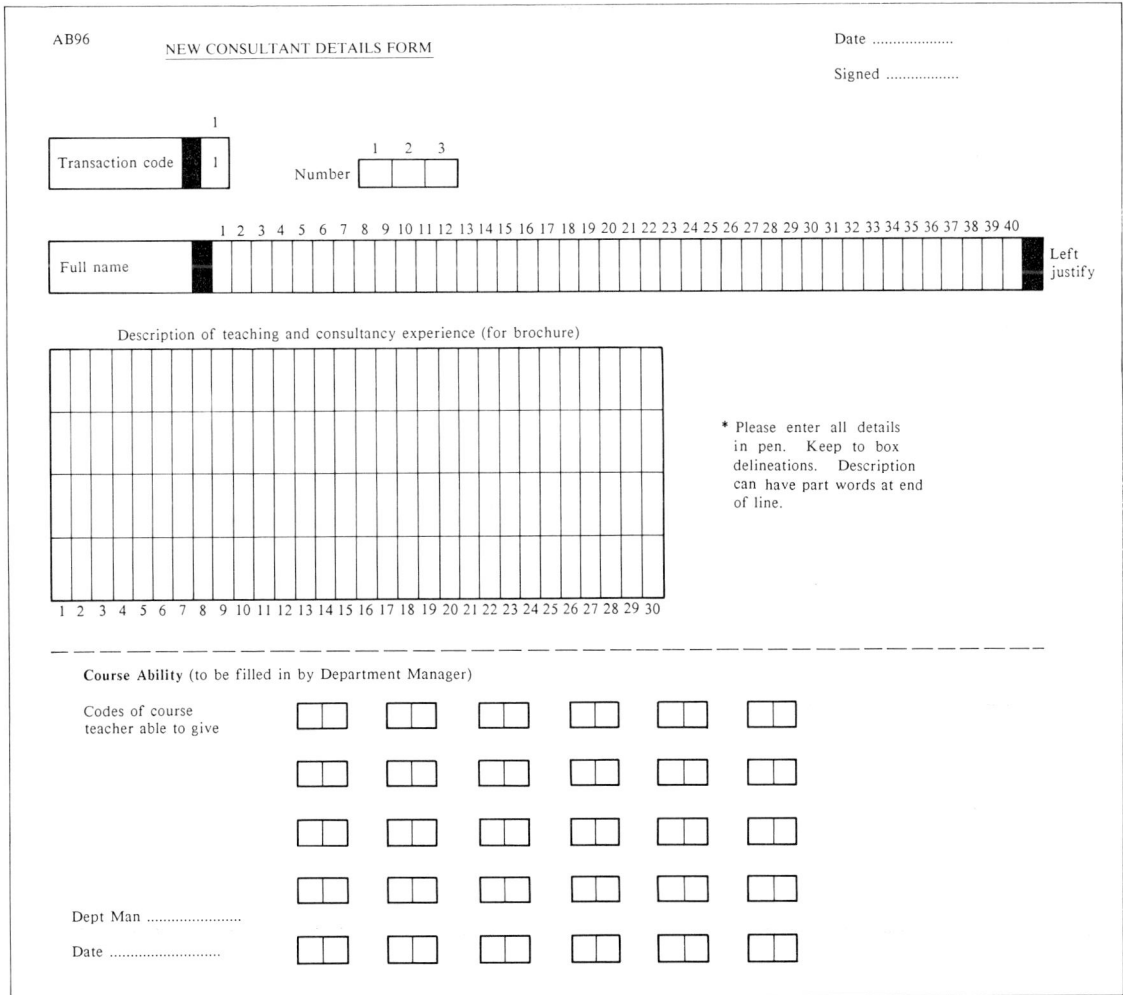

Figure 5.17 New consultant details form

Name of Record: COURSE-MAST

Level	Name	Picture	Occurs	Depending On	Comments
03	TEACH-NO	PIC 9(3)			
03	TEACH-NAM	PIC X(40)			
03	TEACH-CV-COUNT	PIC 99			
03	TEACH-CV				
03	TEACH-CV-LN	PIC X(10)	12 TIMES	TEACH-CV-COUNT	

Figure 5.18 Consultant master record layout

148 A Simple Introduction to Data and Activity Analysis

Course Name: X ———————(50)——————— X   Course Code: 99

Type: X   No of Days: 99   Course Abbreviation: X—(10)—X

Description:

Objectives:

Course suitable for:

Prerequisite Courses before you should attend this Course:

The Teachers who can give this course

Prices   Florins   £   DM

In house:

Public

Figure 5.19 Course brochure

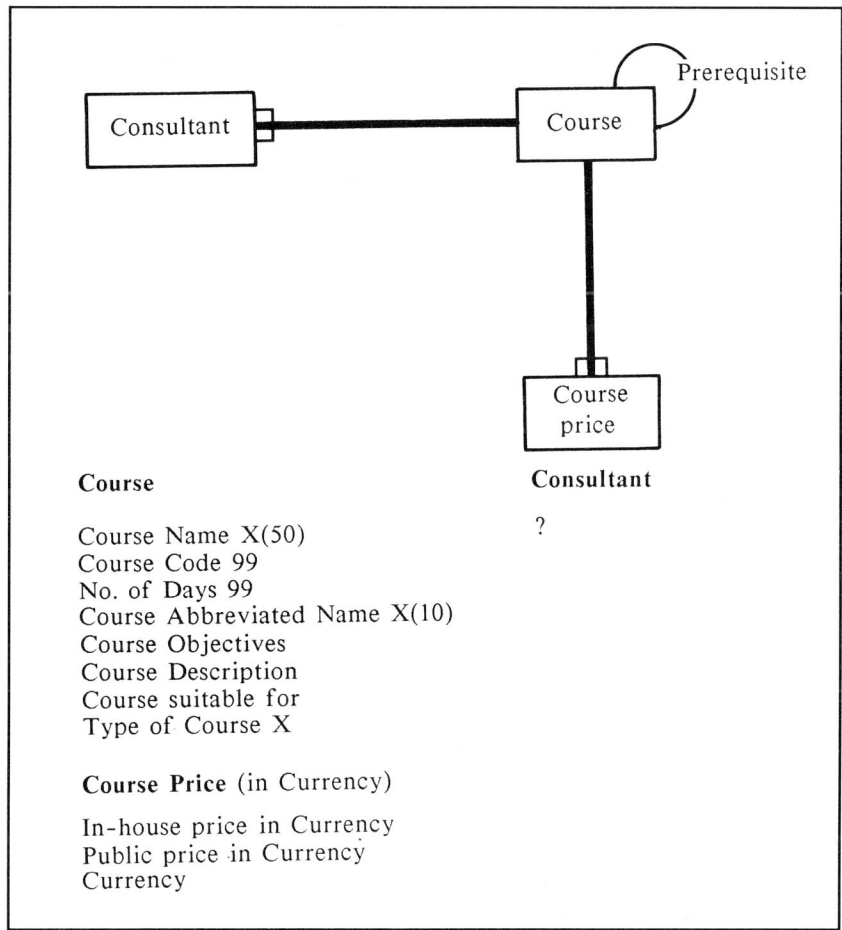

Figure 5.20 The data and model from the brochure listing

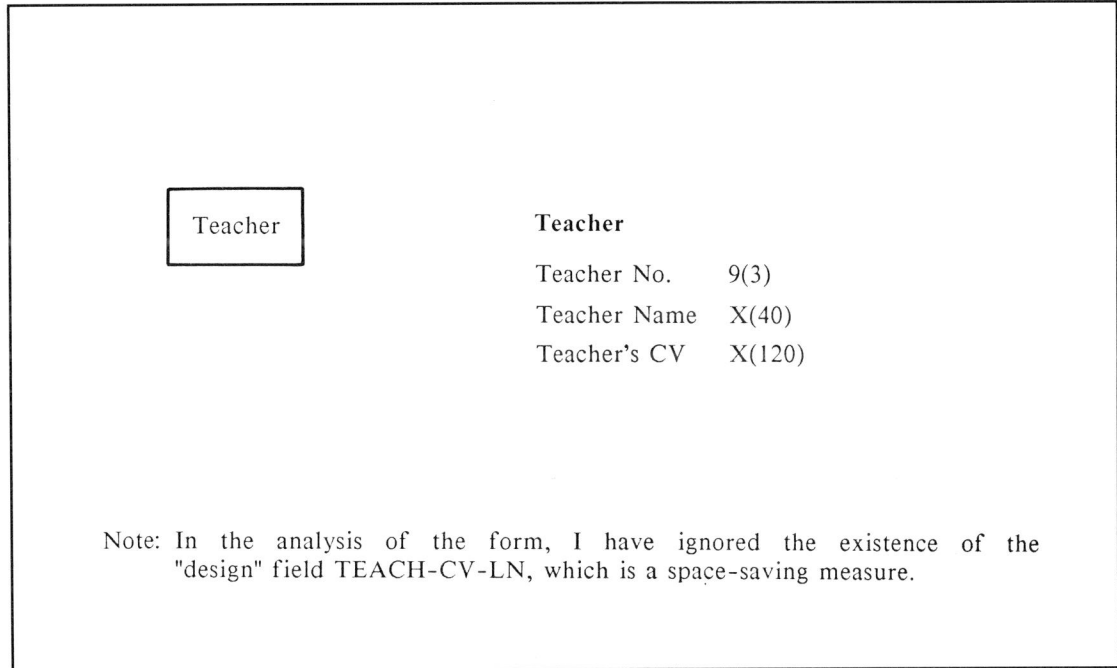

Figure 5.21 The data and model from the consultant master record layout

150 *A Simple Introduction to Data and Activity Analysis*

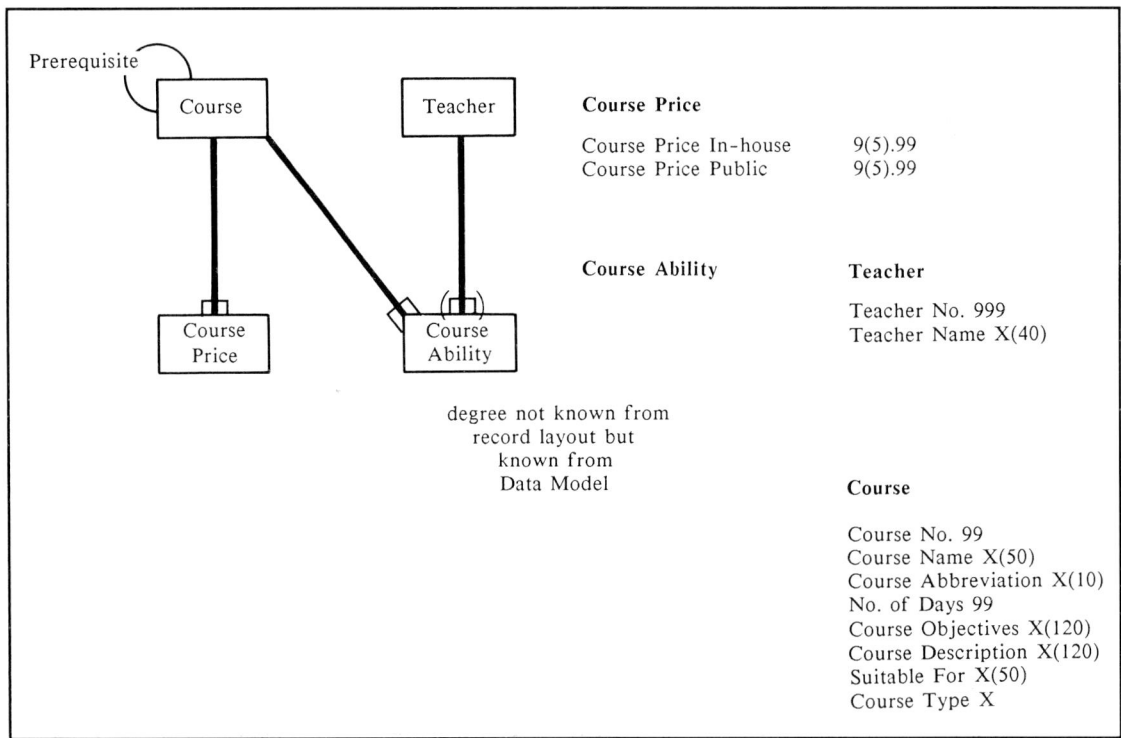

Figure 5.22 **The Data Model from the Course Master Record Layout**

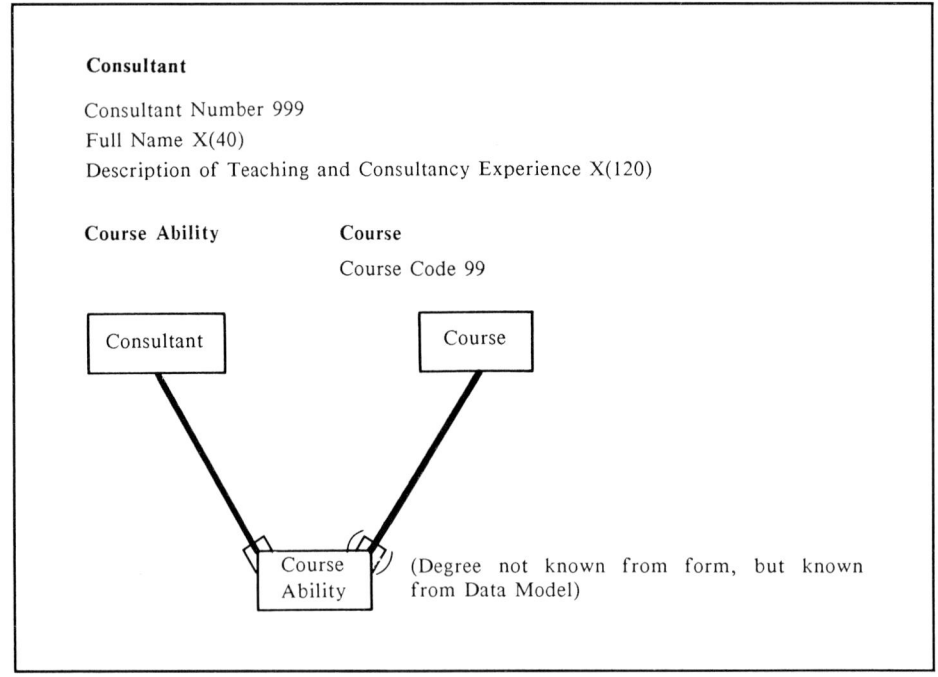

Figure 5.23 **The Data Model from form AB96**

How to do Activity Analysis 151

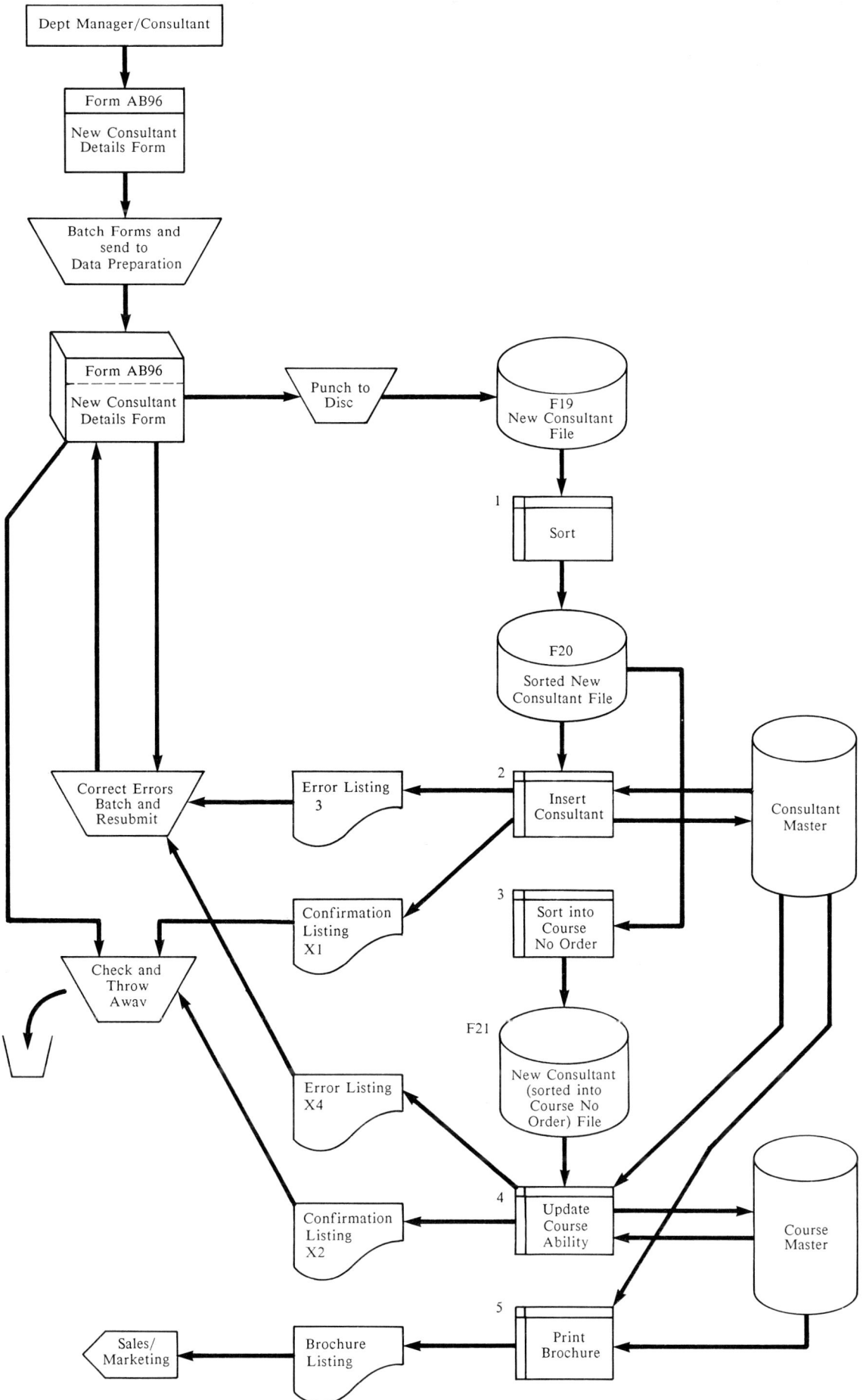

Figure 5.24 Enhanced computer system diagram

152   *A Simple Introduction to Data and Activity Analysis*

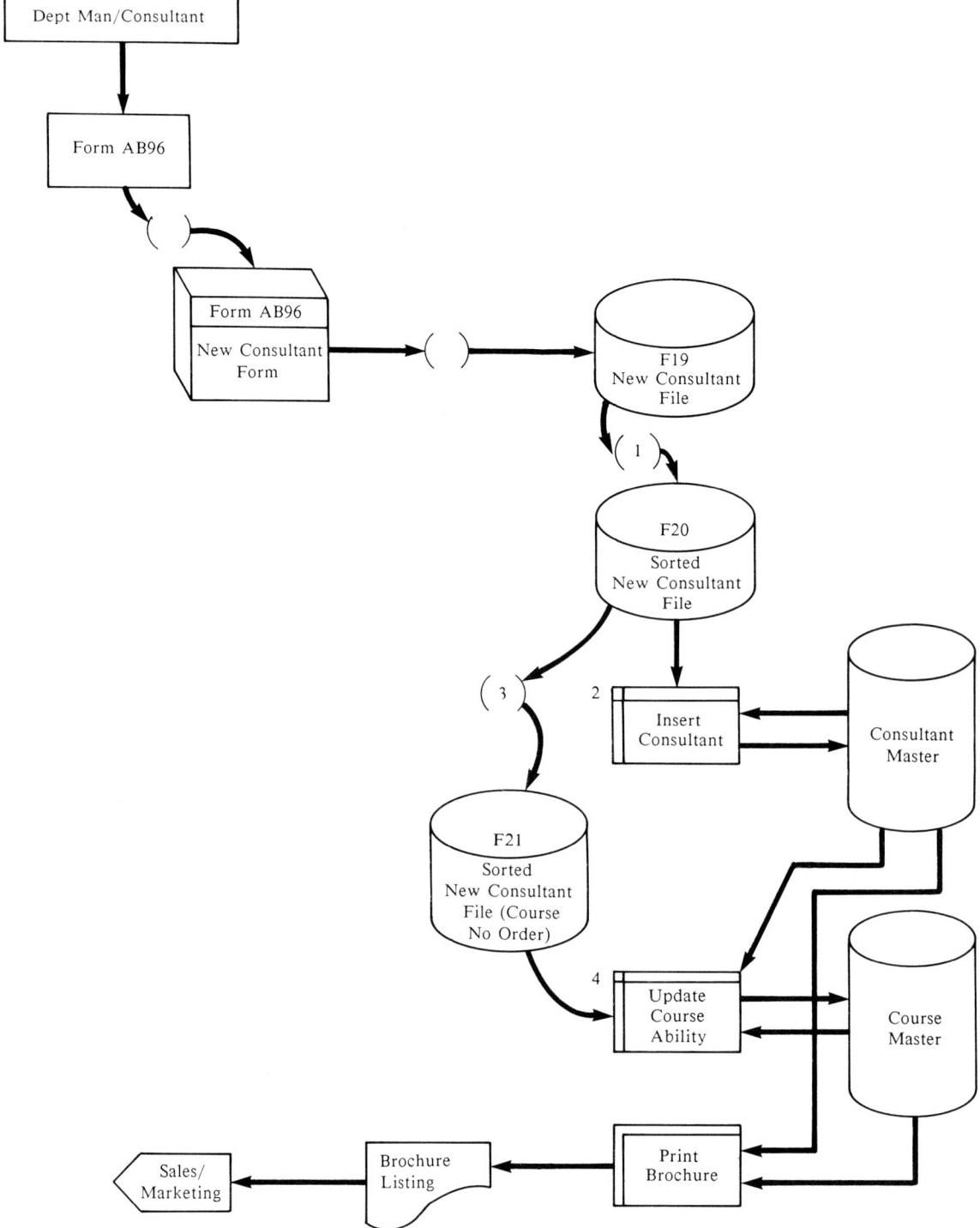

Figure 5.25 **After the mechanism dependent processes have been removed**

Any process which does not effectively change the data in any way can be removed.
In Figure 5.25 we see the result.

3. Combine all records which are the same data, but are just on different media, e.g. cards, disc, paper, and create a Data Flow.

In our example FORM AB96 (single or batched), File F19 New Consultant File, File F20 Sorted New Consultant File and File F21 Sorted New Consultant File (Course No. Order) are all identical in Data Content so are replaced by their Data Flow.

4. Replace any remaining listings, forms etc. by their equivalent Data Flow. Do not tackle master files yet. In both cases above name the Data Flow by using the results of your Data Analysis.

This has been done in Figure 5.26.

How to do Activity Analysis 153

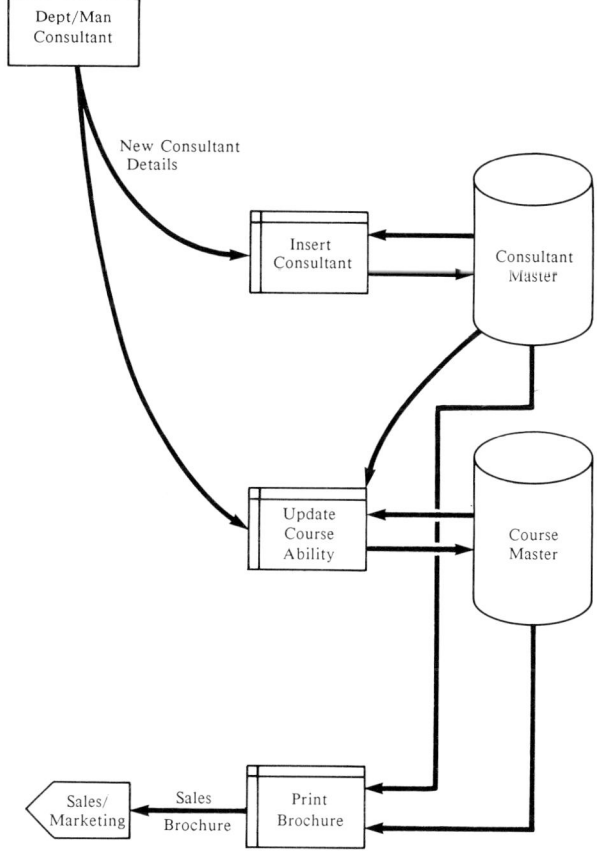

Figure 5.26 Data Flow replace forms and listings

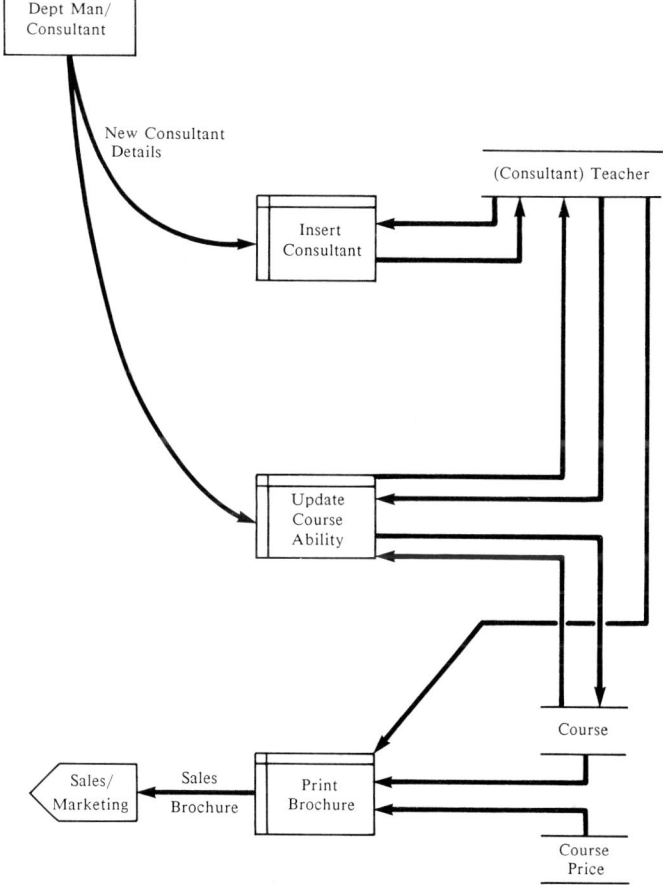

Figure 5.27 Record replaced by Entities

154 A Simple Introduction to Data and Activity Analysis

5. Replace the master records with Entities. Do this by looking at the results of your Data Analysis and replacing each file by the Entities in the Data Model obtained by analysing the file.

Look back earlier in this section and you will be able to see how I have derived the Diagram in Figure 5.27 from the Data Models I showed earlier.

Where analysis of data in a record has resulted in a Data Model of many Entities, you will need to check with user or analyst, or by looking at the specification, which **specific** bits of data are used. There is the possibility that the whole record is not used; only a subset, which covers only one or two Entities as opposed to the full number.

6. Deduce the Activities hidden by the remaining processes by asking what those processes actually **do**. You may need to go back to the specification or even analyst, designer or user here to find out.

7. Replace any remaining design symbols by asking what is being represented – a Source, Sink, external Activity, or internal Activity elsewhere on another Data Flow.

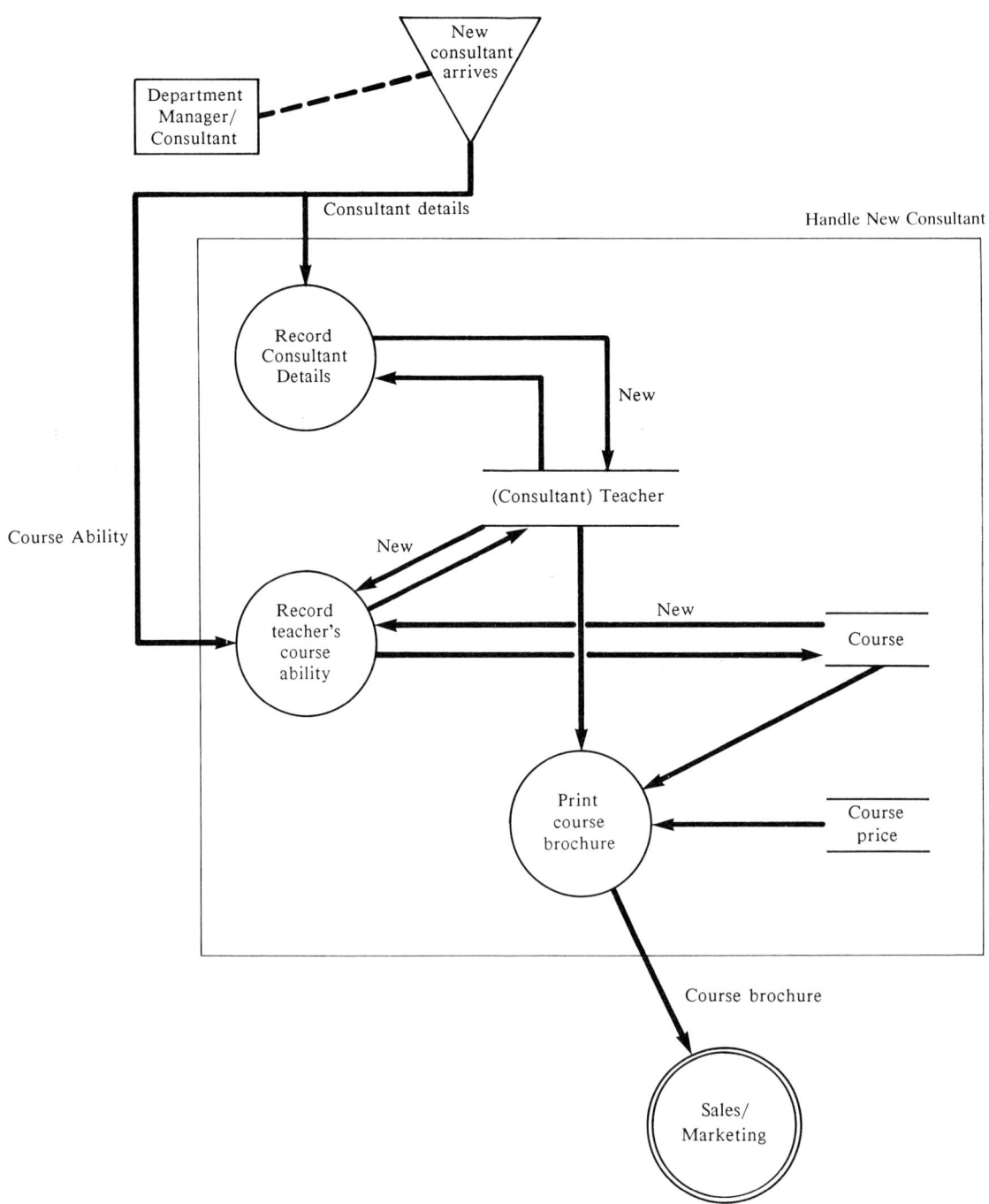

Figure 5.28 Handle new consultant

8. Determine a name for the main Activity being described, if it seems a logical grouping. Take care here as you may need to combine this with other groups or even split the group. Look again for Events this should provide the clue.

Figure 5.28 shows the result.

9. Now draw the Activity Decomposition Diagram for the Data Flow and add it to your existing one where it fits logically.

Preserve the sequence which was shown in the original job and show this on the Decomposition. See Figure 5.29.

Where data may or may not be present in a Data Flow, Activities may be conditional. The original System Flowchart may also show you this by having decision boxes in it. (See Figure 5.30.)

These will not have been removed by the analysis so far but can now be replaced and placed in the Decomposition Diagram.

Example IF 'x'

Further questioning may also be necessary. In our example, the 'course ability' part of form AB96 is optional, so the Activity which will process this is also optional and will be conditional on its being there. There is the possibility that the course brochure would not be re-printed if the consultant had

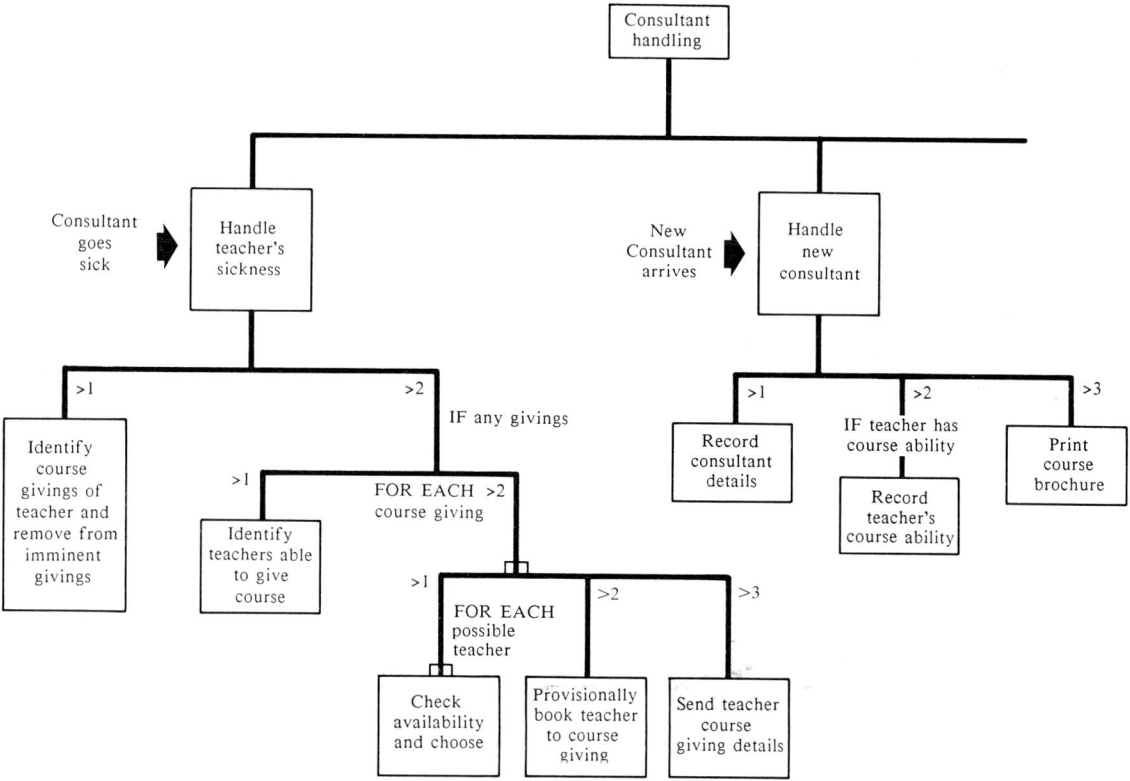

Figure 5.29 Activity Decomposition

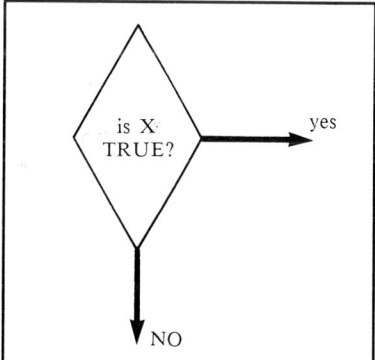

Figure 5.30

156   *A Simple Introduction to Data and Activity Analysis*

no course ability, but I have assumed that it is as there is no indication otherwise. [This may be a problem in the existing system we would need to investigate – see Chapter 6.]

   10.   Now write the descriptions for each of the Activities working from the Systems Specification and add in any repetition to the Activity Decomposition.

   You need to do this in the same way I described in the section dealing with Real World Abstractions – making sure the Activity Descriptions, Data Flows and Decomposition are all consistent.

   We have no repetition in our example, but I have included the Activity Descriptions we might have obtained for completeness' sake.

Print Course Brochure
As new courses are added, or details changed, the "course brochure" must be updated. This means a **new** brochure must be produced showing both course details and course precedence details. A list of all the teachers who can give the courses is included, and their backgrounds are added at the end of each brochure (photos are added later).

   (This brochure is used to send to clients or to take on consultancy/sales calls when an inquiry is made about a course.)

Record Consultant Details
When a new consultant joins, details about his/her previous experience, in both teaching and consultancy work, are recorded for use in selecting teachers for courses and for the course brochure. This is in addition to his/her name (which is mandatory).

Record Teacher's Course Ability
When a consultant arrives, and is able to teach, the courses which he/she is able to give are recorded.

The Second Example is from the User's Job Specification
I won't repeat the steps again; instead I will show you the result after each step and you can follow what has happened by looking back at the steps described with the first example.

   The example shown in Figure 5.31 is particularly interesting as it shows a description which has not been described using the symbols we have come to accept with computer Systems Flowcharts.

   Before we use the steps, therefore, we will need to draw a flowchart of what this user does.

   I have combined the drawing of the flowchart with Step 1 – which sought to piece together the user and computer processes. Although there are no computer processes mentioned, as the job is entirely clerical, another user has been mentioned and in the resulting flowchart shown in Figure

Task description:	Ensuring the consultant's details are kept in line with work done	Job: Training manager

-   It is up to you to trap any changes which the consultant or his department manager makes to his CV. The consultants have been informed that a copy of their updated CVs must be sent to you for information. Department Managers are similarly aware of their responsibilities in this respect. Make sure you update your Teacher records (33B).

-   From their CVs it will be clear on the form used (AX 918) if either the consultant or his department manager considers he is able to add new courses to his repertoire. Ensure that this information is recorded on your form 33B – Teacher's Course Ability Form.

-   Before filing for your information, photocopy the form and send it to the Training Administrator (who will use the form to update the course brochure in line with the changes made).

Figure 5.31

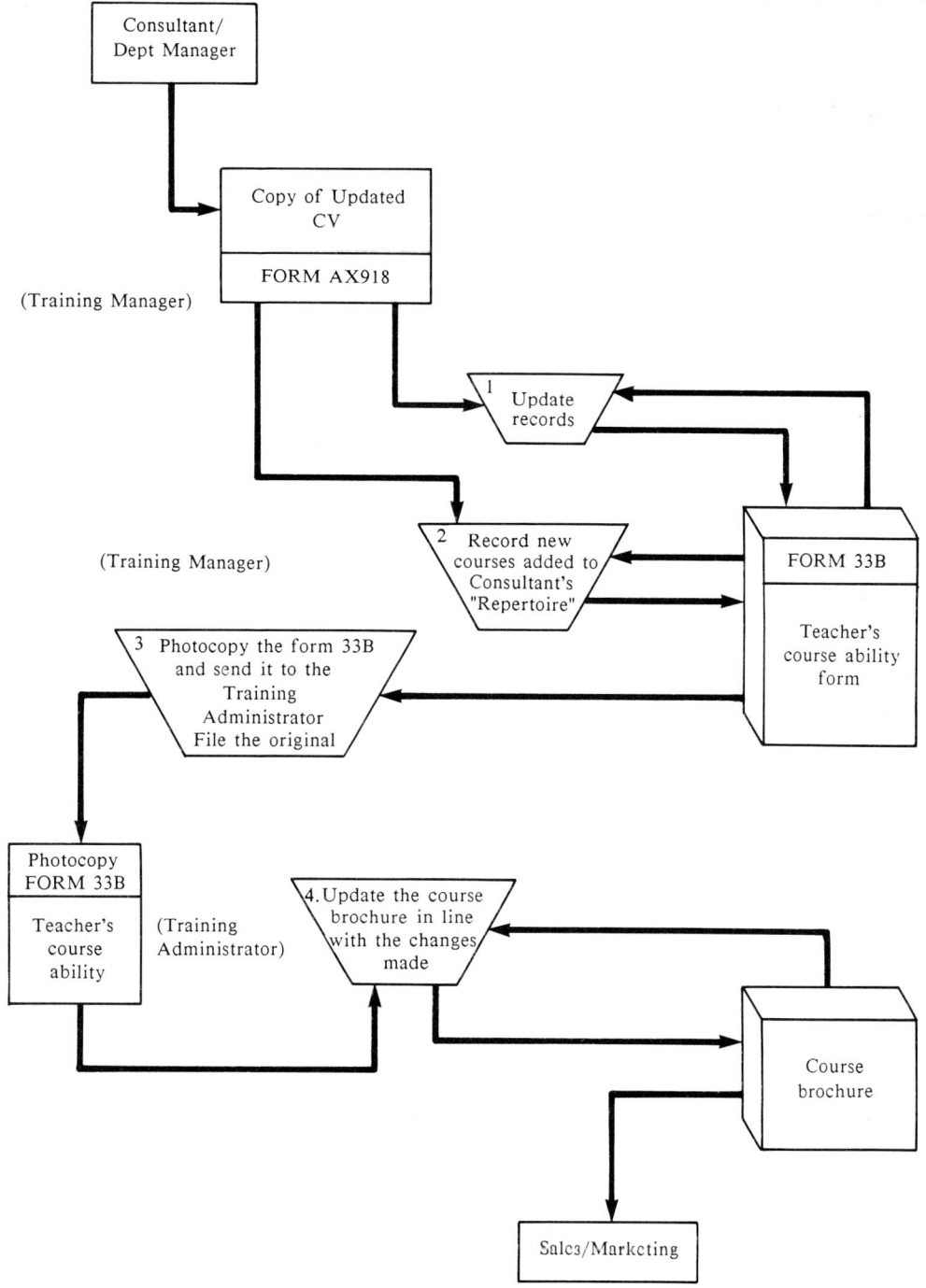

Figure 5.32 As a flowchart – ensure the consultant's details are kept in line with work done

5.32 I have completed the flow by adding his tasks. It may help to show the original responsibilities in brackets on the Diagram in case you have any questions you need to ask these users. I have assumed, as before, that the forms mentioned have been analysed using Data Analysis techniques and the results shown in Figures 5.33 to 5.36 follow the form layouts. The brochure is identical to the previous example.

Step 2
Remove processes which are machine dependent or have no effect on the data. Process 3 is in this category so we remove it. See Figure 5.37.

Step 3
Piece records together and create a Data Flow.

158   *A Simple Introduction to Data and Activity Analysis*

```
AX918                    CV

Dept Man/Consultant _____


Number


Experience








                    Dated ..........    Signed ..........


            Course codes ___.___.___.___.___.___.___
                         ___.___.___.___.___.___.___
```

Figure 5.33

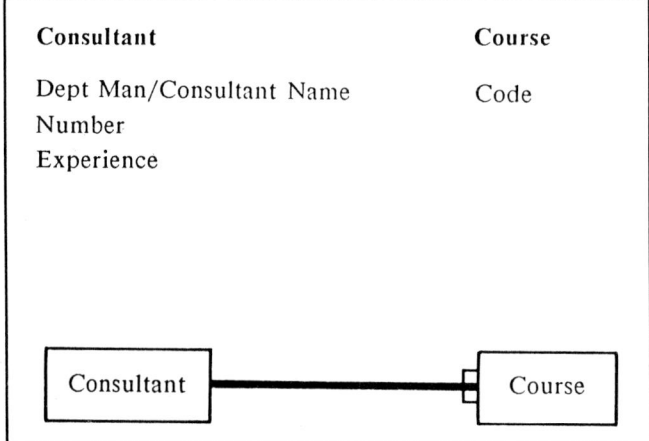

Figure 5.34   Data Model of form AX918

How to do Activity Analysis 159

33B
Teacher No: ....   Teacher Name: ....

CV/Experience

Course ability

Code	Name	Code	Name

Figure 5.35   Teacher form/course ability record

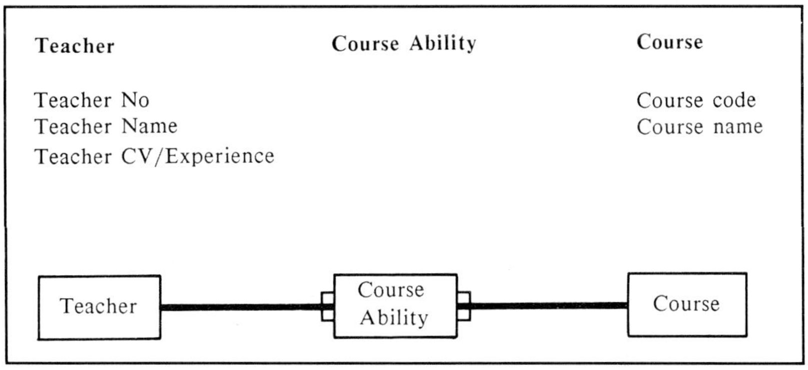

Teacher	Course Ability	Course
Teacher No Teacher Name Teacher CV/Experience		Course code Course name

Teacher —— Course Ability —— Course

Figure 5.36   The Data Model from form 33B

160 A Simple Introduction to Data and Activity Analysis

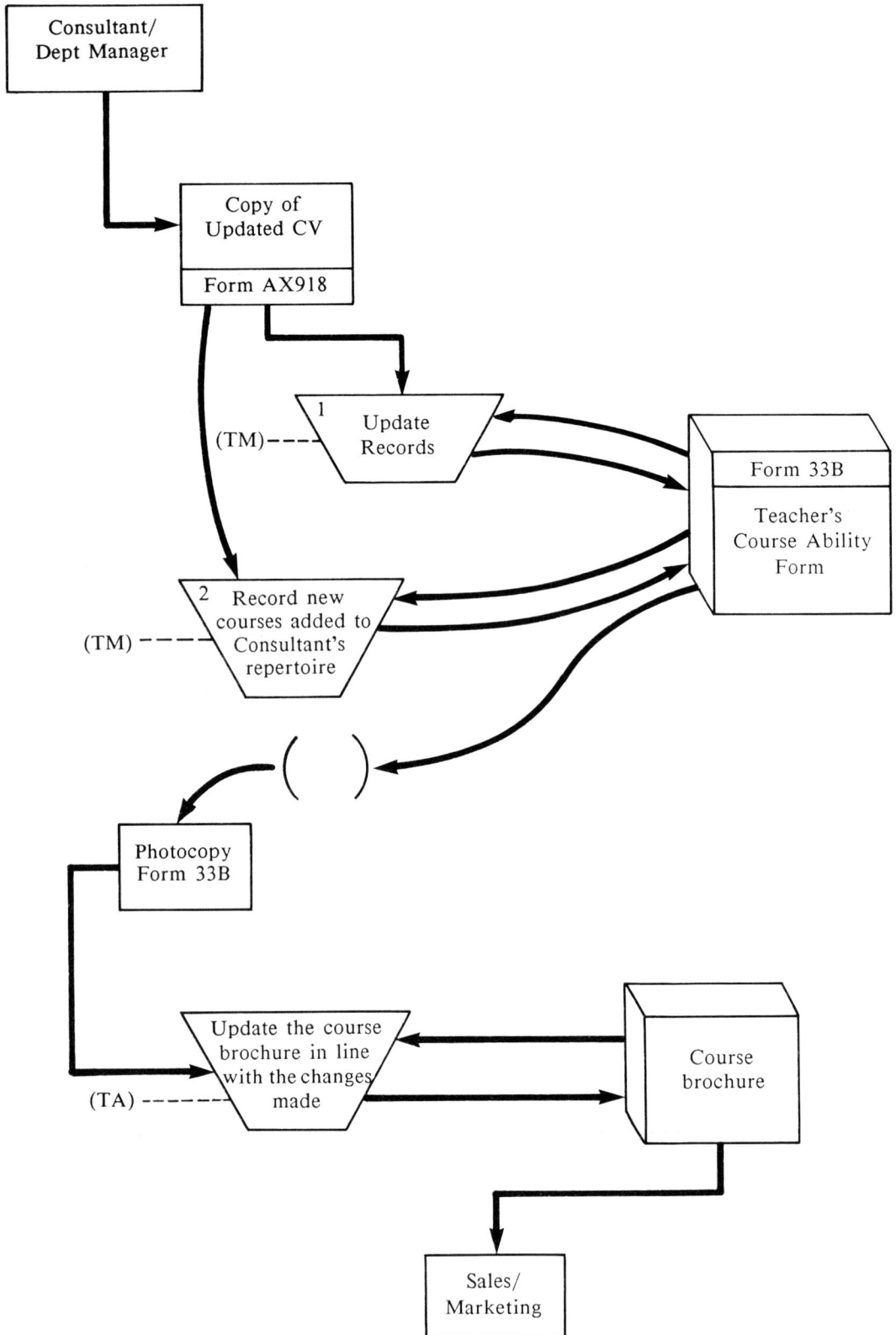

Figure 5.37 Ensure the consultant's details are kept up to date

How to do Activity Analysis 161

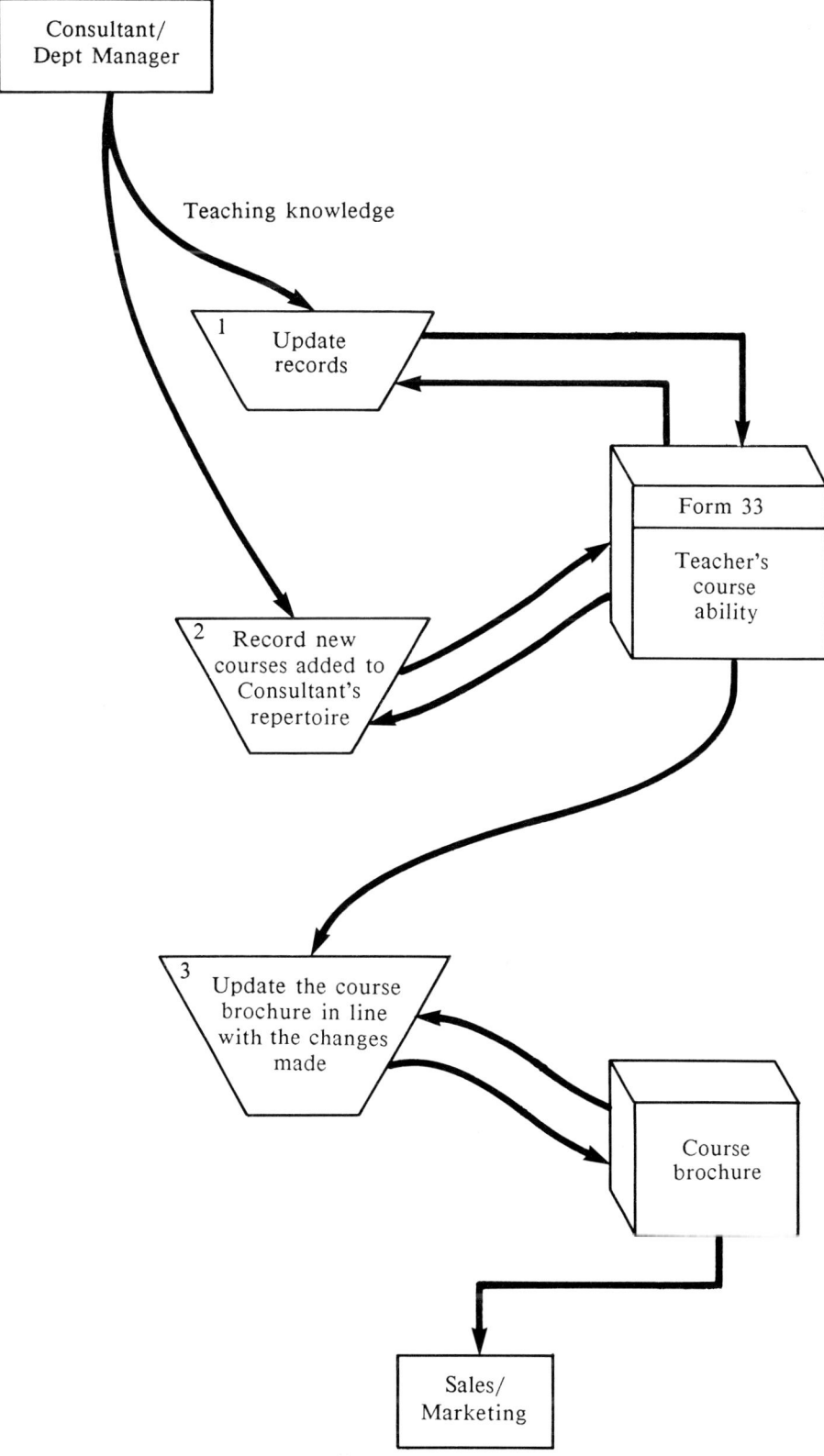

Figure 5.38

162 *A Simple Introduction to Data and Activity Analysis*

Step 4

Replace any other listings, forms etc. by an equivalent Data Flow, but do not tackle master files. The results of Steps 3 and 4 are shown in Figure 5.38.

Step 5

Replace master records by Entities – see Figure 5.39. Notice how this has changed accesses – 'Update records' updates only the teacher's CV, and 'record new courses added' updates the courses the teacher can give. Strictly speaking, Course Ability should also be present, but as it is not in the Data Model (it is an unwanted intersection Entity) I have left it out.

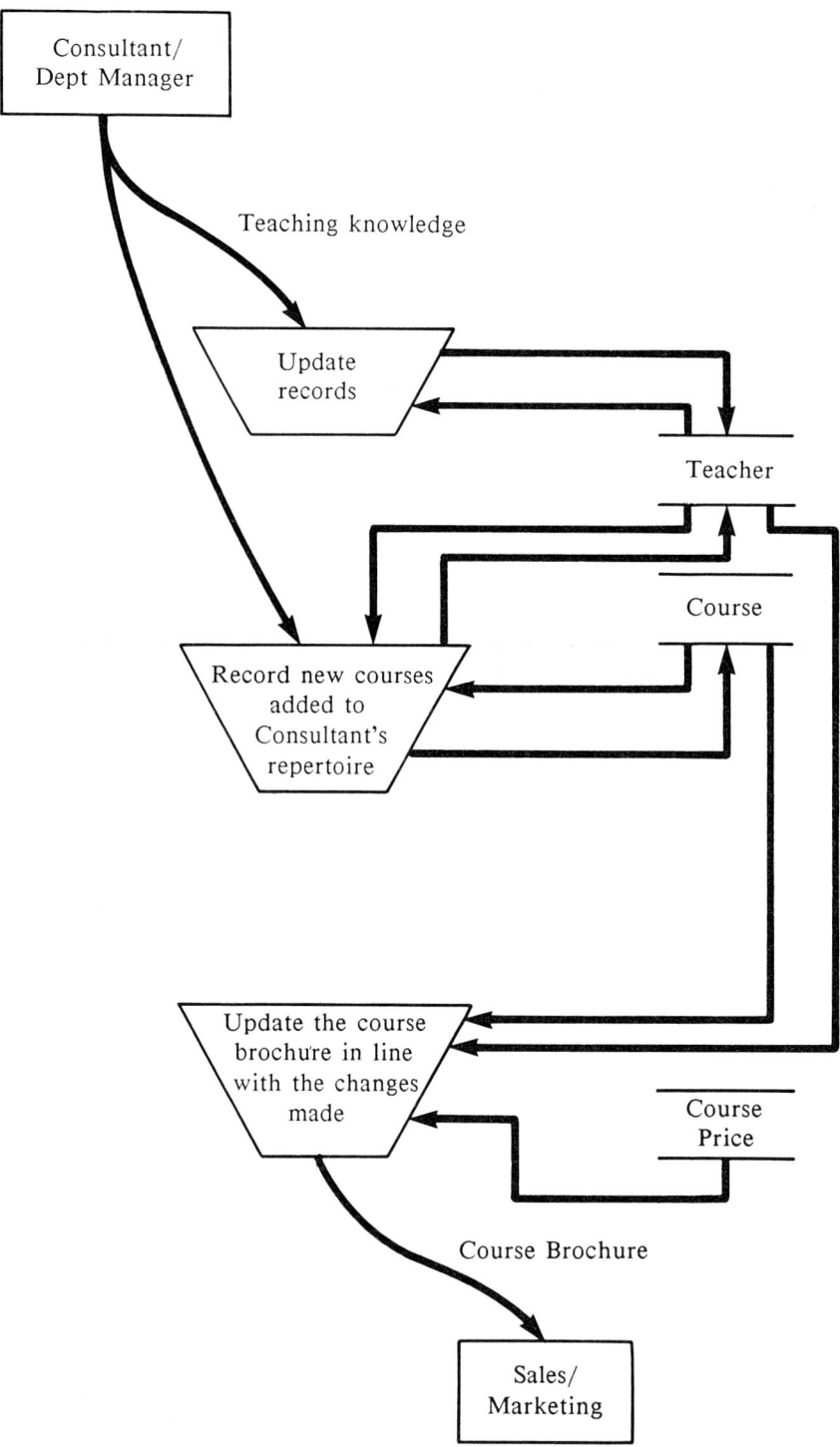

Figure 5.39 Ensure the consultant's details are kept up to date

How to do Activity Analysis 163

Step 6 Deduce the Activities
Step 7 Replace remaining symbols
Step 8 Determine main name for Activity/add in the Event trigger

See Figure 5.40

Step 9 Draw the Activity Decomposition (see Figure 5.41). We have found common Activities in our Activity Decomposition, which are indicated.

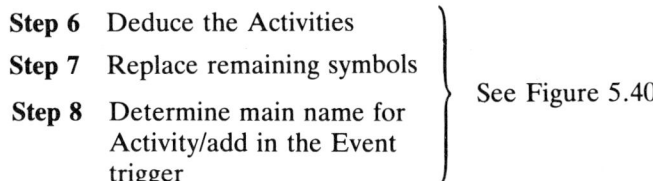

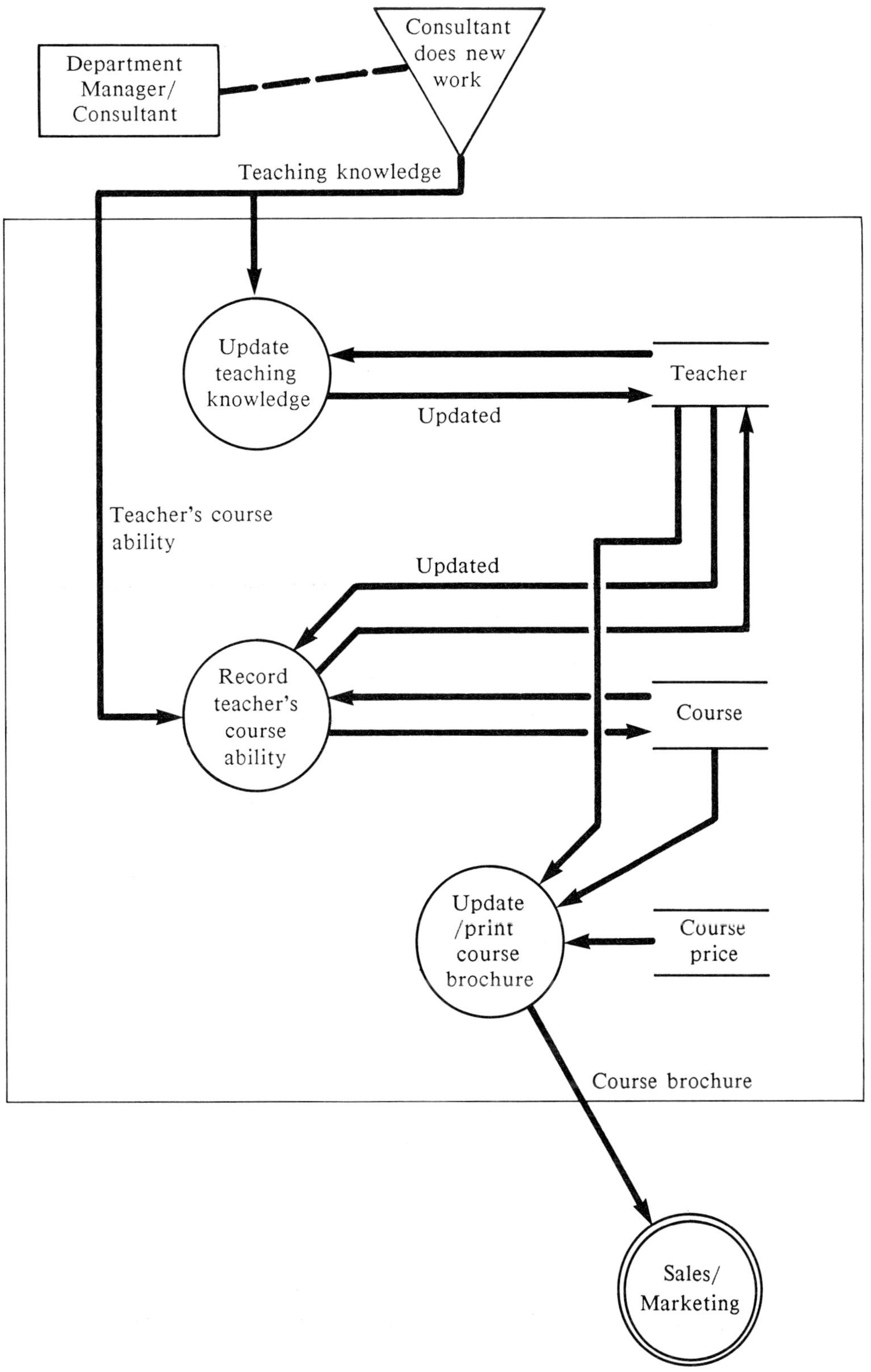

Figure 5.40 Handle consultant's new details

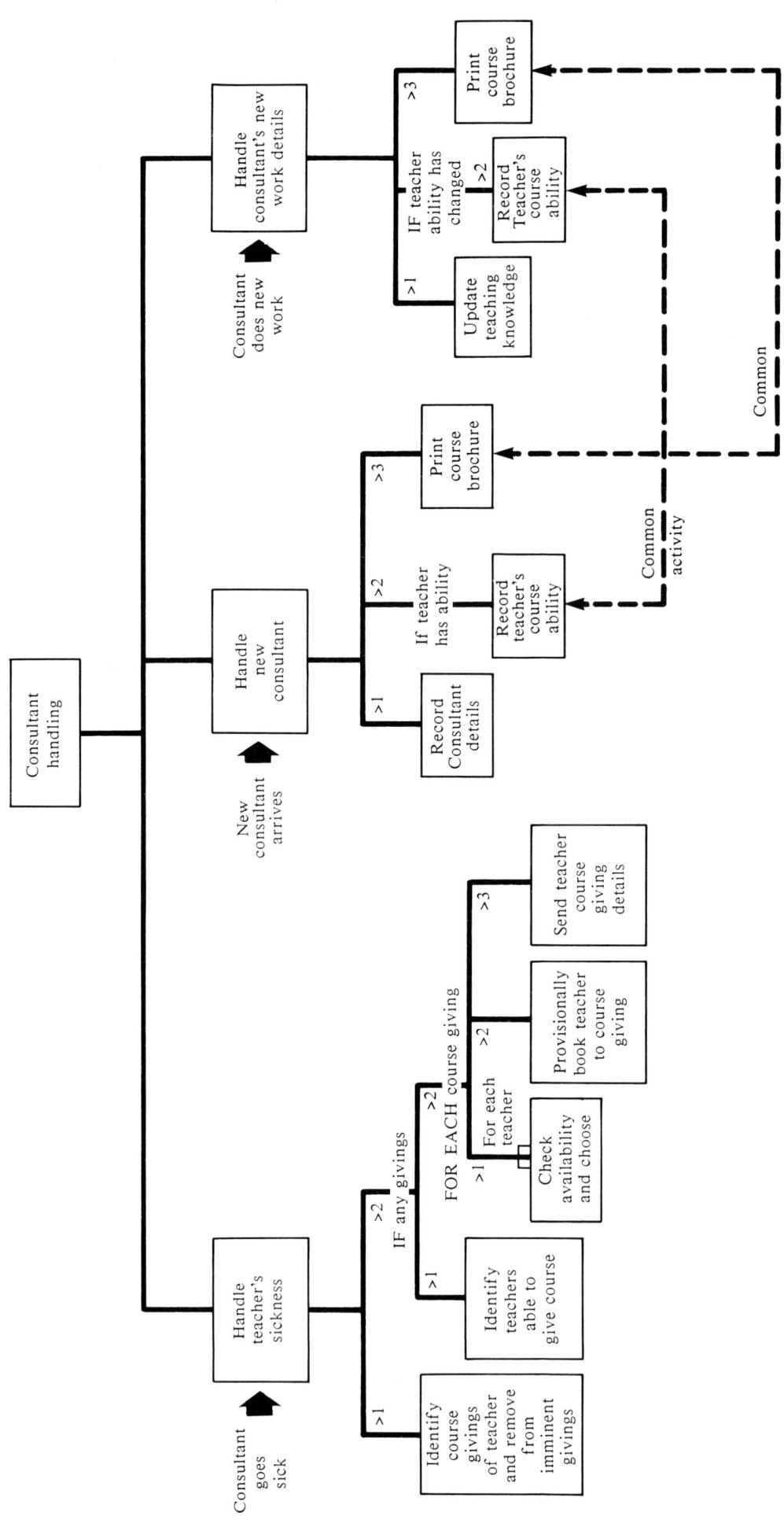

Figure 5.41 Activity Decomposition

Step 10
Activity Descriptions – we have only one new one to do because of the commonality discovered. Notice how important it is to draw the Activity Decomposition and look for commonality before you do the description. This can save you a lot of effort. The description is simple and is shown below.

Update teaching knowledge
When any teacher has done new consultancy work or gained extra teaching experience, their cv (curriculum vitae) is updated.

5.2.3 Using 'Actions' or Activity Occurrences
'Actions' are recognised by the presence of 'Entity Occurrences'. In other words, they act on Entity Occurrences. They are often difficult to obtain – perhaps the best ways being observation when we can actually 'see' a system.

    e.g.   Lorry AXB 99C arrives
              Jim Smith takes parcel 123 from Lorry AXB 99C
              Jim Smith drops parcel 123
              Parcel 123 breaks
              Jim Smith sweeps remains of parcel 123 into dustbin 'A'!

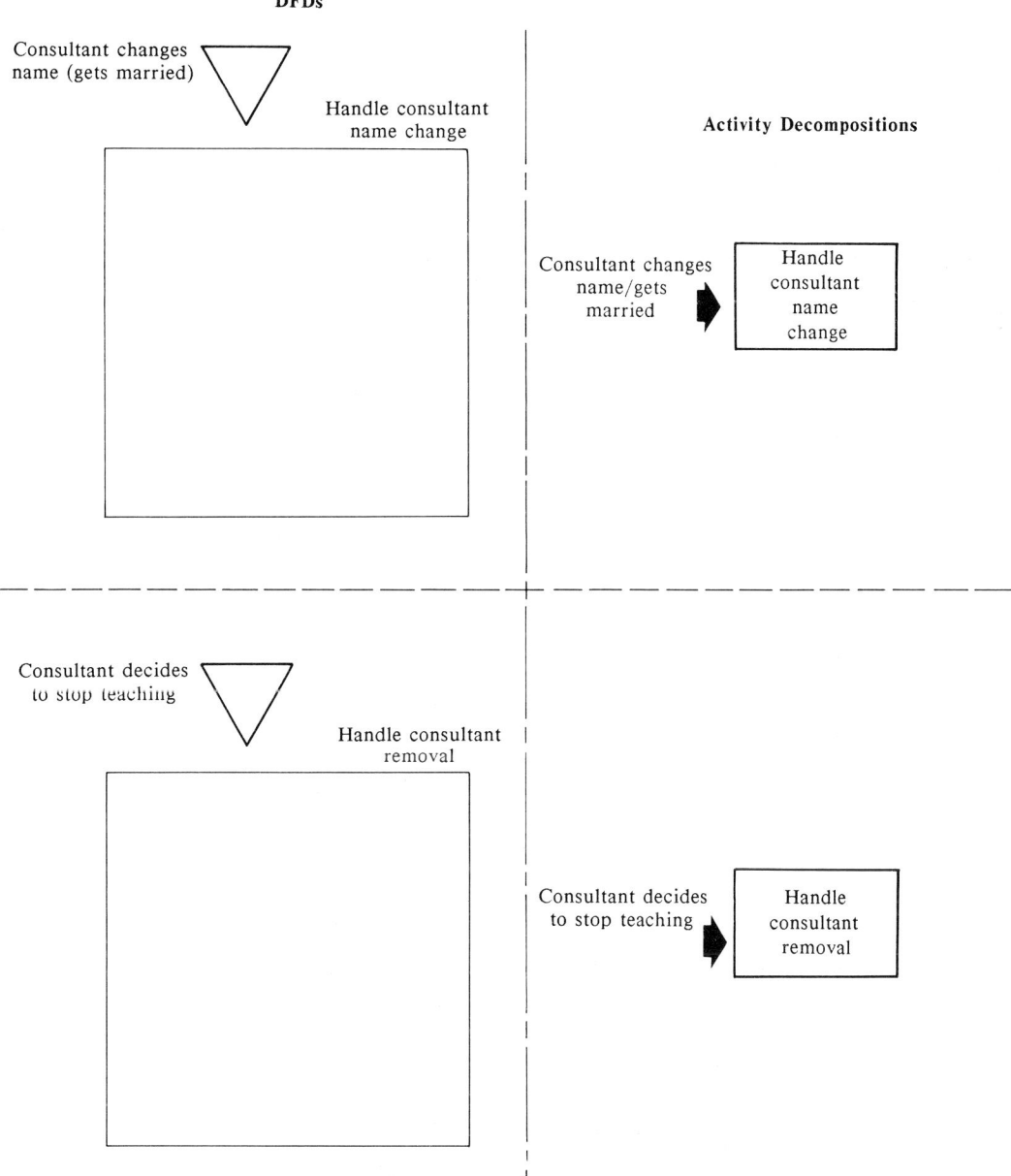

Figure 5.42 Adding Events to the diagrams from two examples

166 A Simple Introduction to Data and Activity Analysis

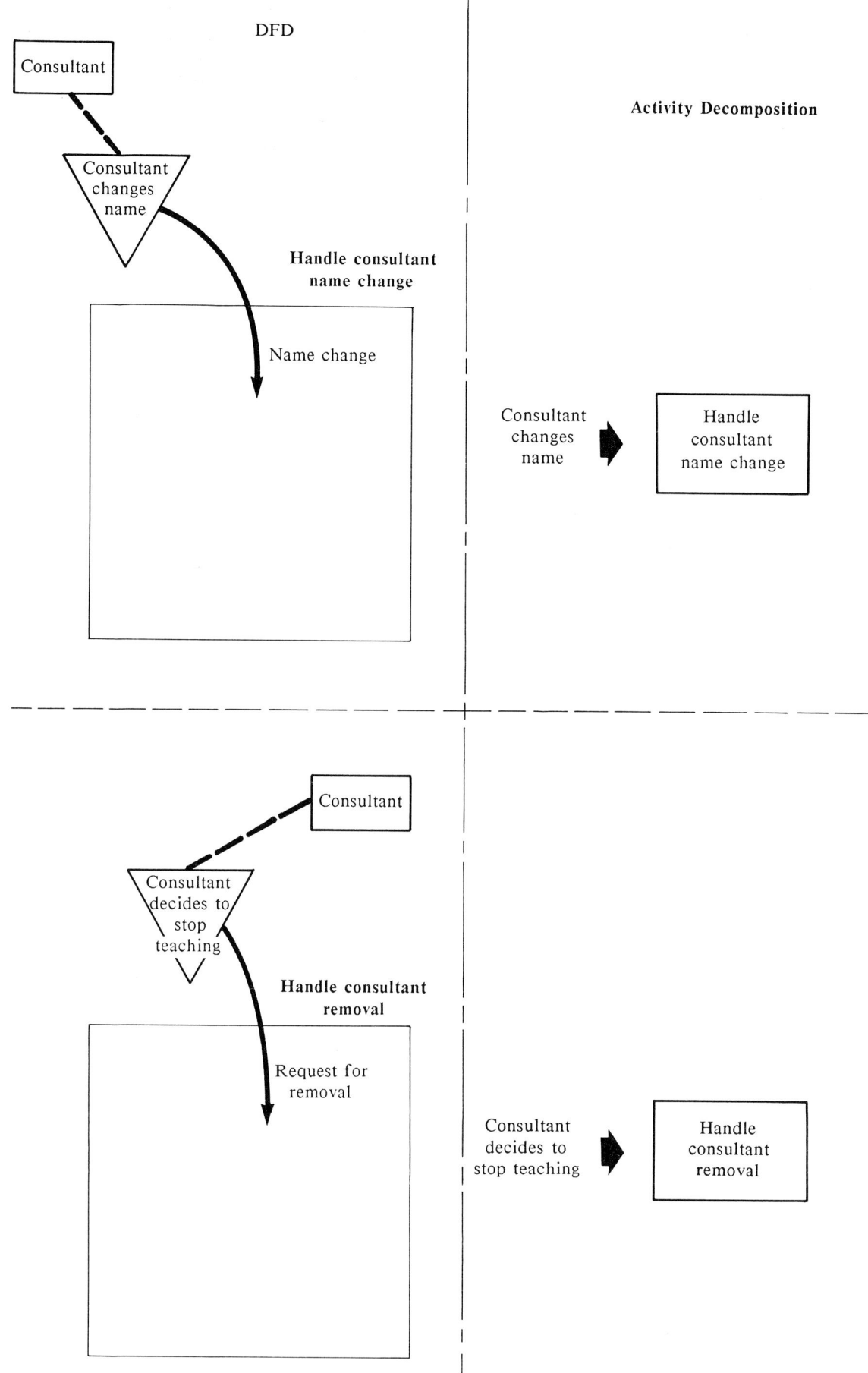

Figure 5.43 Adding Sources and Data Flows

How to do Activity Analysis 167

When we can't see a system we have to use other methods. Participation ('joining in') is one way of collecting them. If we are reliant on our user, however, we can ask him to keep a **Diary** to keep a record of every Action he performs in sequence and what made him do it (the stimulus).

In Figure 5.44 are two very simple examples which we might have obtained if our training administrator had been asked to keep a diary for us. She has also recorded the date for us, and although this is not necessary for what we are about to do, it can help us in calculating other deliverables – Event frequency and Activity frequency, for example.

The steps we follow to derive the Data Flow and Activity Decomposition Diagrams are described in the following paragraphs. I will be showing the effects on **both** examples as I go through.

Step 1
Classify the 'stimulus' (Event Occurrences) to produce Events. Draw them on the Data Flow Diagram and Activity Decomposition Diagrams. See Figure 5.42. Create a name for the overall Activity handling the Event and also add to the diagrams.

Step 2
Classify the Source of the data about the Event and the Data Flows representing the Event.
See Figure 5.43. In this case it is not 100% certain, but the Source in both cases seems to be the consultant.

User: Training Administrator		
Stimulus	Date	Action
Jenny Little got married to Samson Hugebody	1.4.87	Changed Jenny Little's name to Jenny Hugebody
	1.4.87	Changed Jenny Little's name to Jenny Hugebody on the course brochure and send the updated brochure to Sales/Marketing.
Jenny Jones decides she wants to concentrate on consultancy, not teaching	3.5.87	Removed Jenny Jones' name from being available to give: - Information Analysis - Feasibility Study - Strategy Study Changed the course brochure removing Jenny Jones' details and all references to her against the IA, FS and SS courses. Send the updated brochure to Sales/Marketing.

Figure 5.44 Diary of Actions

Step 3
Classify the Actions to produce Activities. Use the verb name to help you and the Data Occurrences to help you relate to the Entities on the model – but be careful, you may find new Entities. To be correct you can use Data Analysis techniques on the Entity Occurrences I showed you in an earlier chapter. Add the activities to both the Data Flow (in the scope box) and the Activity Decomposition (under the main Activity). Where sequence is clearly implied from the description show this on the Decomposition, similarly add in repetition and any conditional Activities.

Step 4
Classify the Sinks and add in the Data Flows going to the Sinks, see Figure 5.45.
In the example the Sink needs no classification. It is already classified.

168 *A Simple Introduction to Data and Activity Analysis*

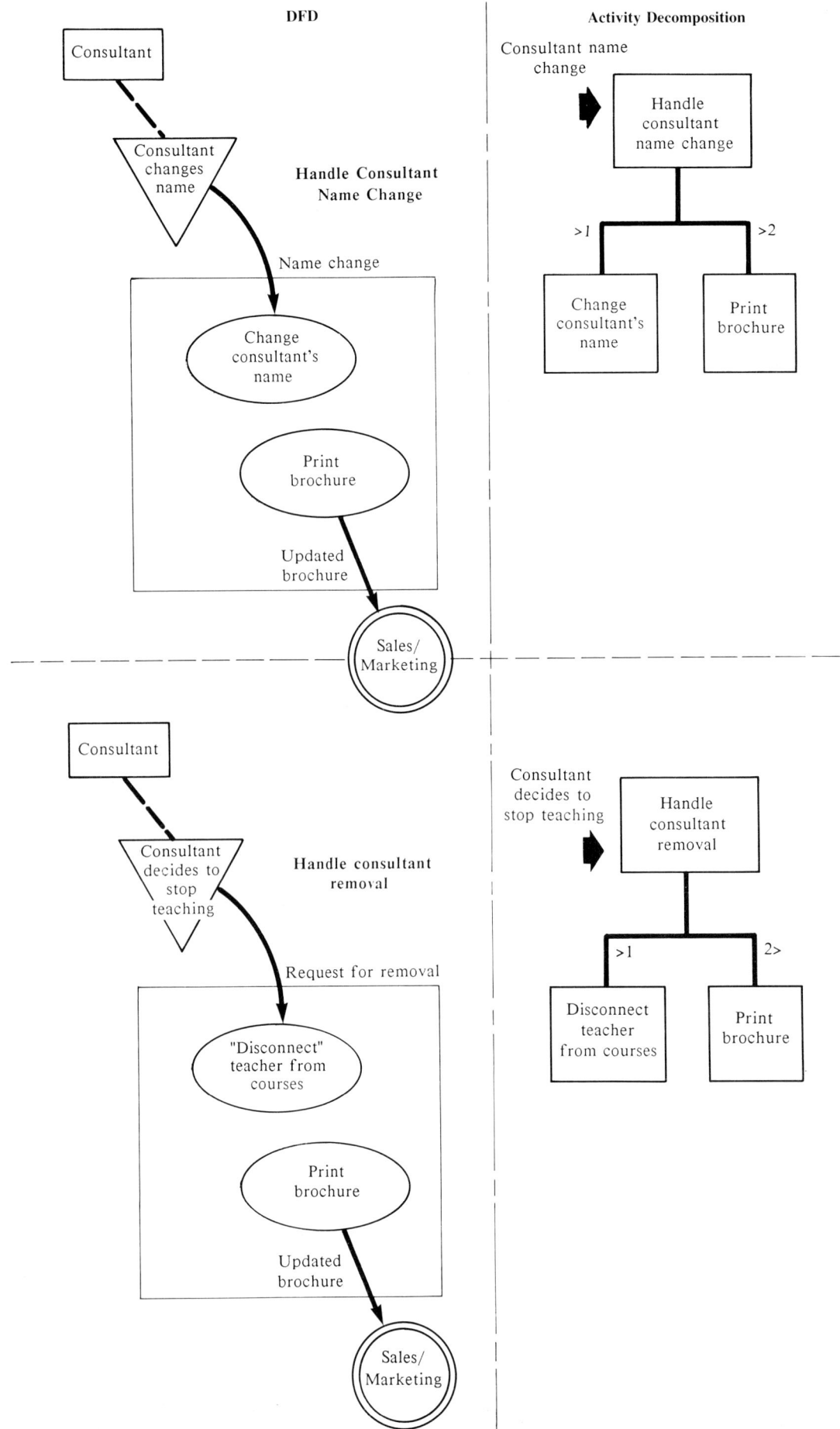

Figure 5.45 Adding Activities

Step 5
The Data Analysis you have done on the Data Occurrences in this example are:

Jenny Little
Jenny Hugebody } Teacher
Jenny Jones

Information Analysis
Feasibility Study } Course
Strategy Study

and should show the Entities and Attributes and Relationships being used. Add these to the Data Flow Diagram. See Figures 5.46 and 5.47.

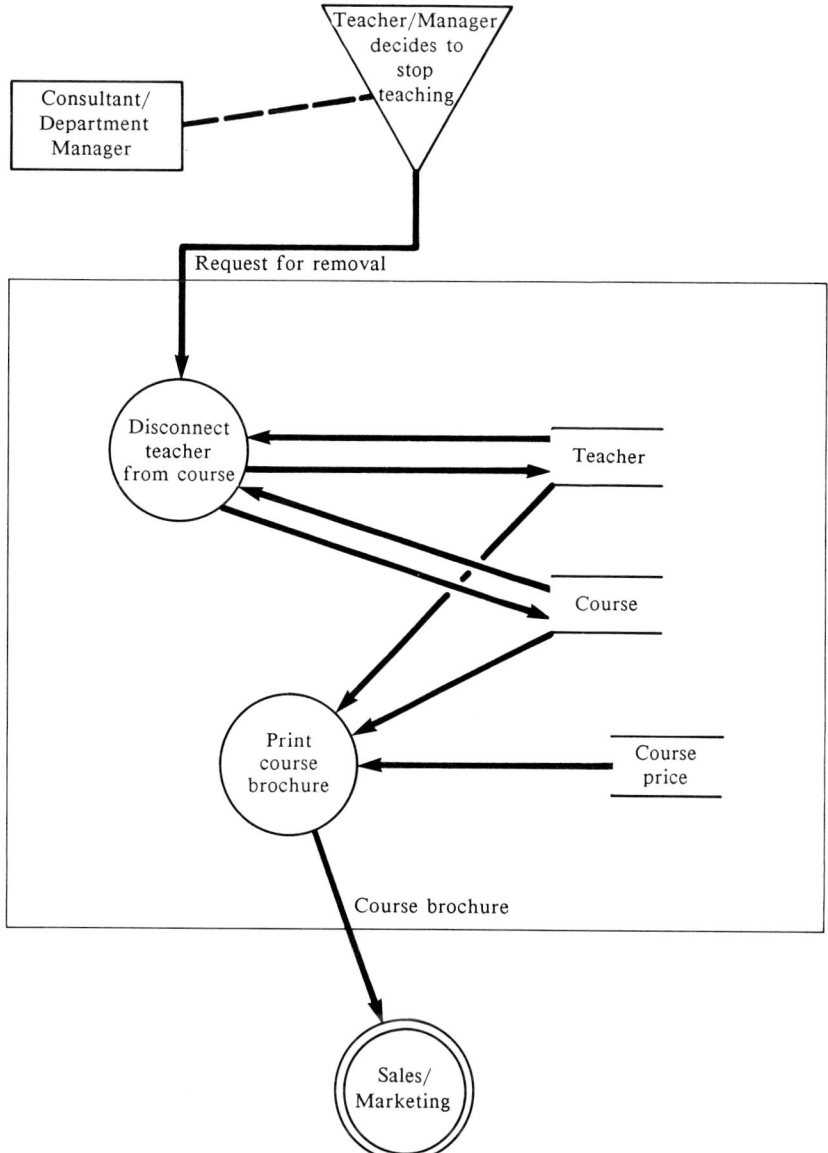

Figure 5.46 Record removal

Step 7
Add the Activity Decompositions to the full Decomposition and search for any common Activity. This is shown in Figure 5.48. Again we have identified a common Activity.

Step 8
Produce the Activity Descriptions. These can be fleshed out by further consultation with the user, although the objective is to classify what is happening within each Activity in brief terms. The descriptions of the two new, simple Activities follow.

170 A Simple Introduction to Data and Activity Analysis

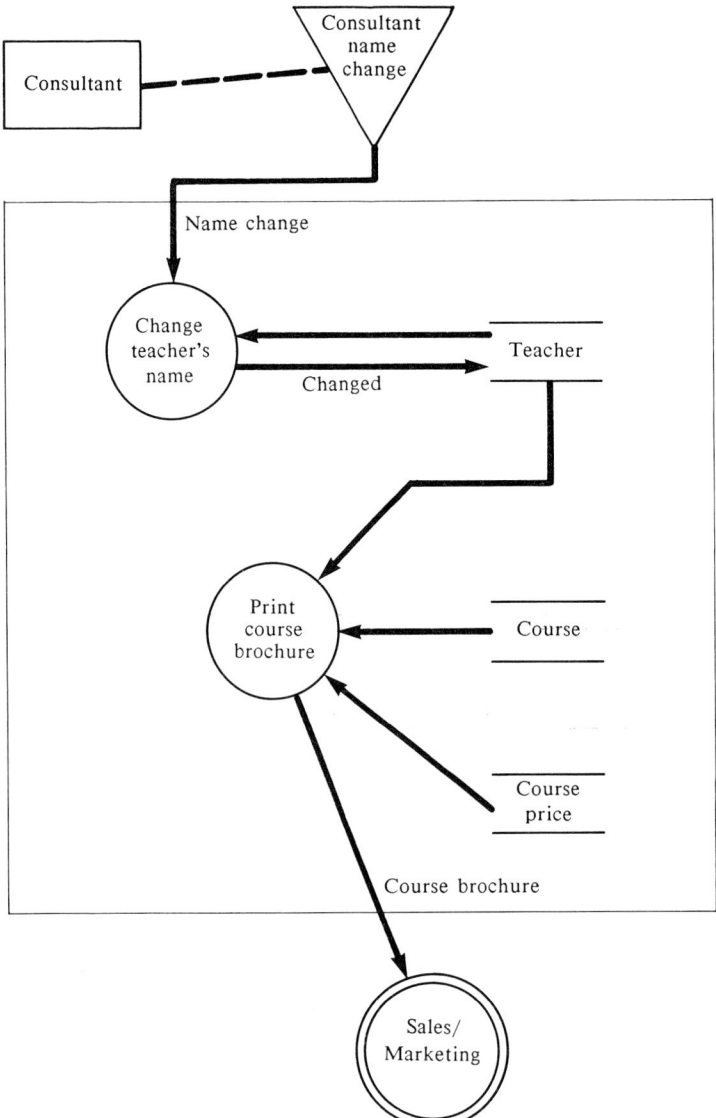

Figure 5.47 Handle consultant name change

Disconnect Teacher From Course
A request from a manager or consultant may be made to be removed from the list of teachers who can teach a course – this may be on the basis of lack of time or change of interest. The teacher is disassociated (or disconnected) from all courses.

Change Teacher's Name
A consultant may change his/her name or notice it has been recorded wrongly, in which case the name must be changed.

5.3 REFINING THE RESULTS
There are some very effective ways of refining your Data Flow and Activity Decomposition Diagrams, primarily to make them simpler, easier to understand and reduce the risk of error. Both the following checks should be made each time you draw a Data Flow Diagram.

Keep the "weight" of Activities the same
It is always difficult when doing analysis to produce diagrams which give similar levels of detail at each level. Very often, on your first try, you produce results where one or two Activities are too detailed for the level they're at in the Decomposition or are far too general, need more Decomposition and need to be moved 'up' a level in the Decomposition.

The Data Flow Diagram is the best indicator of incorrect "weighting". In Figure 5.49, we see an example. Activities 1, 2, 4 and 5 have only a small number of inputs and outputs, but Activity 3 has a

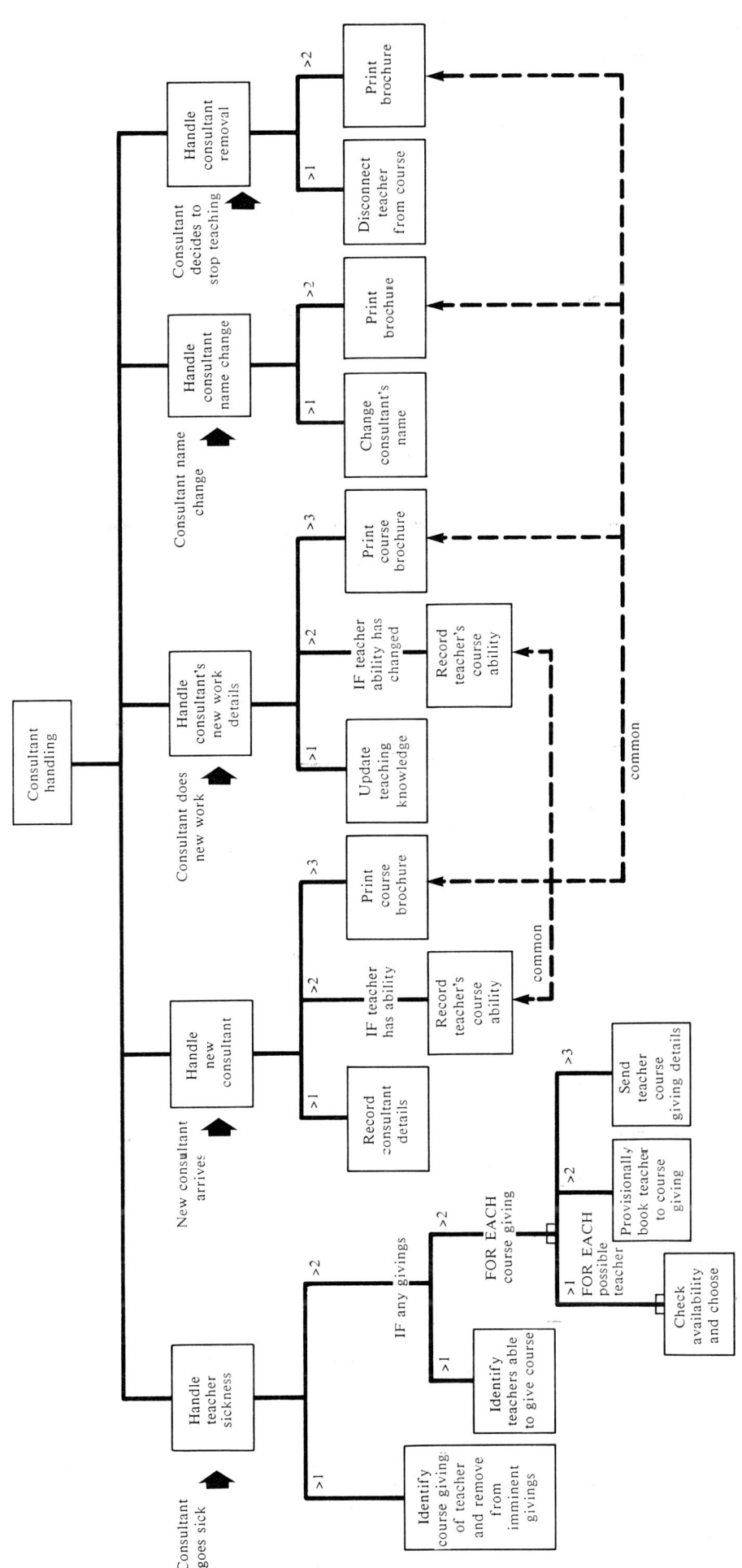

Figure 5.48 The full Decomposition

172 *A Simple Introduction to Data and Activity Analysis*

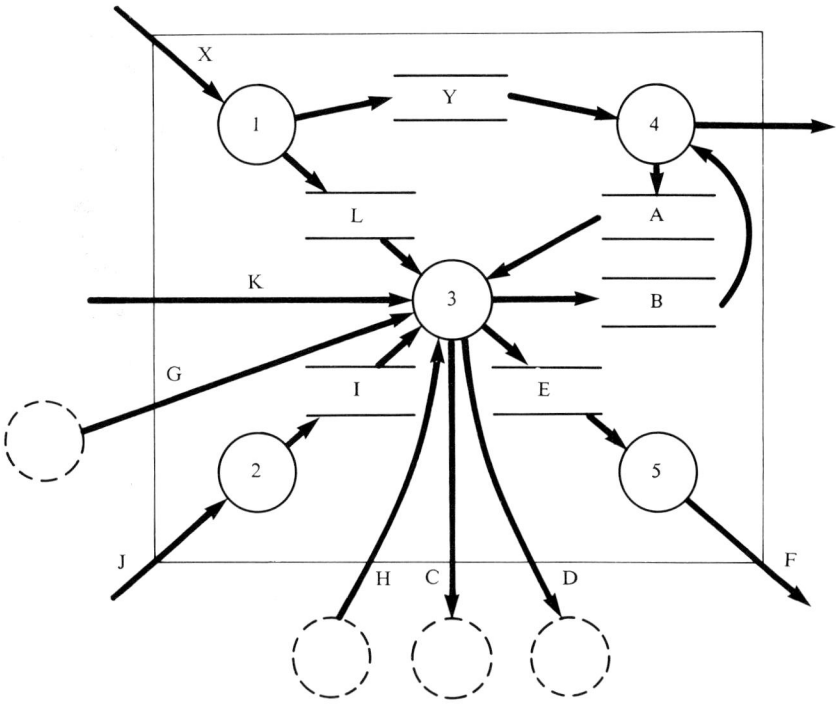

Figure 5.49 'Weighting of Activities'

lot. This should tell us that the 'weight' is wrong and Activity 3 is far too generalised for the level it is at. We must move the Activity up at least one level and redraw the Data Flows.

The number of sub-activities
There is no right or wrong way to decompose Activities. We could produce a Decomposition having hundreds of sub-activities spilling out of the main Activity (a sort of 'pancake' structure), as shown in Figure 5.50, or the opposite, a Decomposition having only two or three sub-activities, as in Figure 5.51.

In the latter case, the only disadvantage will be the number of levels we get and the probable increase in unnecessary documentation. In the former case, however, we are far more likely to make an error, if we plunge into that level of detail straight away. We will probably miss Activities and the Data Flow Diagram will look horrendously complex. G.A. Miller in a Psychological Review in 1956 found that when dealing with any sort of concept, the number of errors increased after about 7. If you keep your Decomposition round about this number (say 7 +/−2) then your Decomposition is less likely to be wrong and will be easier to handle in terms of levels.

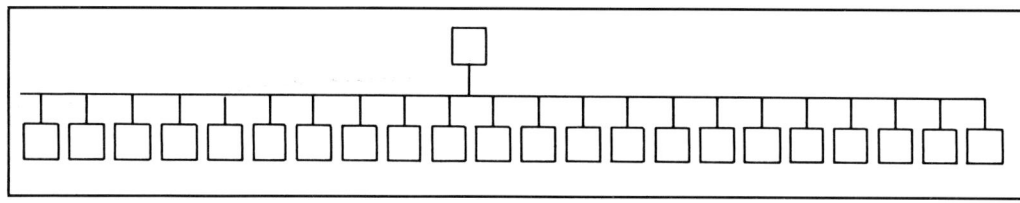

Figure 5.50

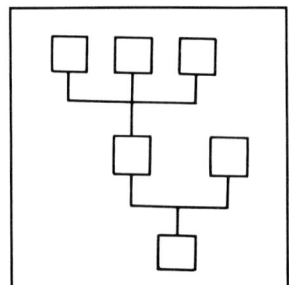

Figure 5.51

5.4 VERIFICATION METHODS

There are many methods we can use to verify the results of the analysis, but roughly they fit into two broad camps – those we do on the results to check inner consistency and those we do to check 'outer' consistency: whether our Model matches the "Real World". The former are generally quite mechanical, in fact some are being done by computers now in Analyst Workbenches (of which I will say more in the last chapter).

The following section lists some of the inner consistency checks you can apply. The list is not exhaustive.

Inner Consistency Checks

(i) **Ensure that no Activity is directly triggered by more than one Event**
   This is invalid. The Activity needs to be split. I am not including *decomposed* Activities in this rule.

(ii) **Ensure no Activity has two different Data Flows coming from the same source**
   An Activity should not have two or more separate Data Flows coming from the same Source to the same Activity. If they have been recognised as distinct, there must be distinct Activities to deal with each of them separately (see Figure 5.52).

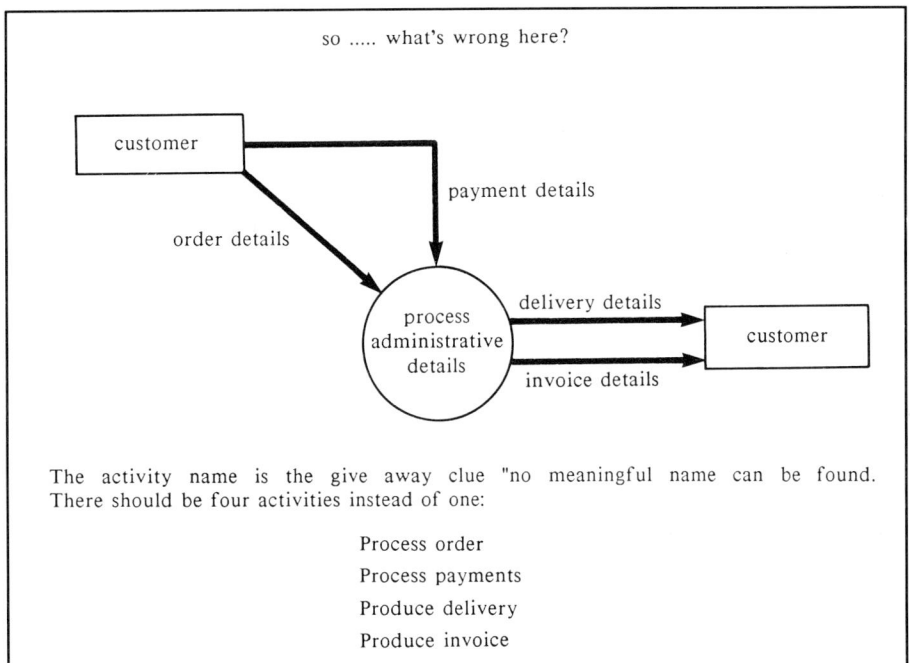

Figure 5.52 Activities must not describe mixed Objectives

(iii) **Ensure Events and Activities do not have the same name**
   If an Event has the same name as an Activity in the system, an error has been made. Perhaps the Event is really an Activity in another leg of the Decomposition.

(iv) **Remove forbidden words**
   The following words should not appear in your diagrams. Remove them and replace them with a more meaningful logical name:
   report, file, record (noun not verb), miscellaneous, parameter, table, utility, load, tape, dummy, database, annual/daily/monthly/ad hoc (and any other time periods), program, system, transaction.

(v) **Check that Activities having one input and one output are correct**
   An Activity having only one input and one output is unusual and should be checked to ensure no data has been missed.

(vi) **Remove forbidden references**
The following references are forbidden and should be removed. User names (e.g. Doug Smith), place names, equipment references e.g. terminal, computer.

(vii) **Check that Activity names are of correct form**
All Activity names must be of the form verb object or verb object link word object, or for more generalised Activities, object verb (e.g. consultant handling).

(viii) **Check that only one Event occurs per Data Flow Diagram**
A series of Activities in a Data Flow Diagram should be handling only one Event. No Data Flow Diagram should show more than one Event. If any do, split the DFDs.

(ix) **Check that all Activities have input and output**
All Activities must have at least one Data Flow input and at least one Data Flow output. (See Figure 5.53.)

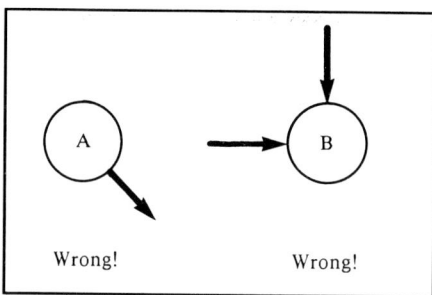

Figure 5.53

(x) **Ensure Activity names are meaningful**
Check all Activity names to ensure they are meaningful from a logical (business) viewpoint. Hence 'process customer **record**' would be rejected as the word 'record' has slipped through.

(xi) **Ensure all Data Flows are meaningfully named**
Data Flows to and from Sources and Sinks, and Data Flows between Activities, must be named and must be meaningful in logical terms, i.e. not 'Form x' or 'Record y'. Naming Data Flows between Data Stores and Activities is optional, but again they must be meaningful.

(xii) **Ensure Activity name does not imply mixed objectives**
The Activity name should not be of the form –
    'Do this and this'
nor should different unrelated output result. In both cases the Activity has been wrongly classified and should be split into either separate Activities based on the different outputs or one or more Activities implied by the term, 'this **and** this'.

(xiii) **Ensure Data Flow use is consistent**
Ensure that every Data Flow flows from or to

– A Data Store
– A Source or Sink
– Another Activity

(xiv) **Ensure that the data is conserved between levels**
This check is one most frequently provided by Analyst Workbenches. All data going into and out of an Activity must go into or out of its sub-activities. Data can be decomposed, but it must not be lost or suddenly gained.
Figure 5.54 illustrates this check. Activity 1 has been decomposed to the Activities shown at level 2. Some new 'internal' Data Stores have appeared, which is fine, but when we look round the boundary we see inconsistencies. B and E are OK, but H has appeared from nowhere and F as an output has been lost. In this case, either level 1 or level 2 is wrong. Either H should be at level 2 and level 1 or it should be in neither.

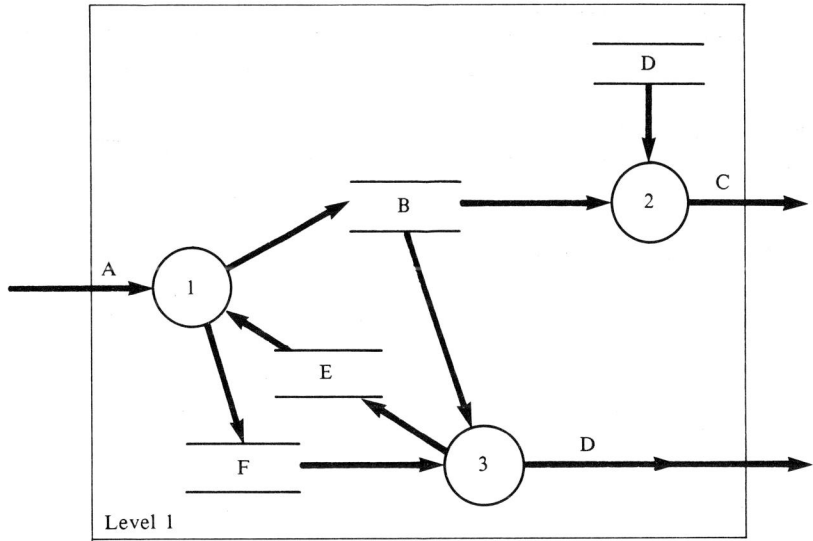

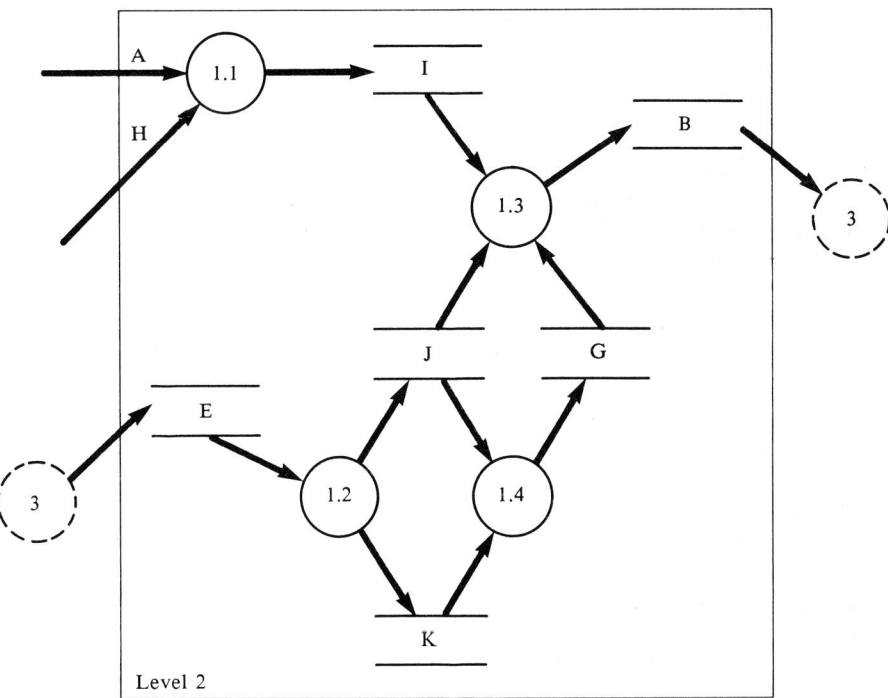

Figure 5.54 Data conservation

When you get errors like this make sure you keep all the levels consistent and add data and remove data from higher levels where necessary. You may find that the error affects other parts of the Decomposition.

There are two more checks which, although 'internal' consistency checks, are far less mechanical and rely more heavily on the **logic** of what we're trying to do.

(xv) **Check that sub-activities contribute to the Activity**
Check each sub-activity to ensure it can **logically** be thought of as a part of the 'owning' Activity. Ask if it contributes to it? And, 'does it contribute towards the **objective** of the Activity?'

(xvi) **Check that output can logically be derived from the input**
Every output must be capable of being derived from the input by manipulation and

176 *A Simple Introduction to Data and Activity Analysis*

derivation. This test is obviously one of pure logic and so is not easy, especially at fairly "generalised" levels. It is extremely important as a test, however, since the most common error is missing out data needed to achieve an Activity. (See Figure 5.55.)

You cannot calculate the pay of a person from details only about the person – even if those details include the tax code and salary. You also need monthly additions and deductions, tax to date and so on.

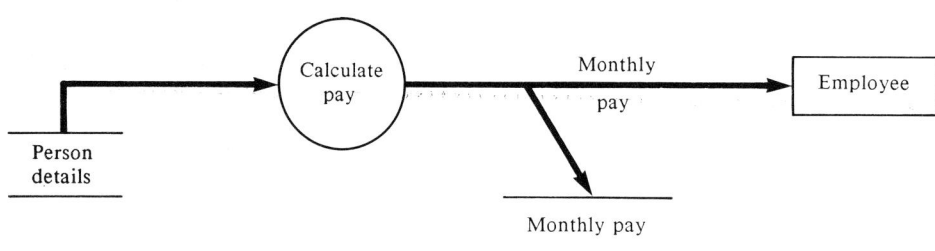

Figure 5.55

The most effective way of checking consistency for a whole level of Decomposition is by using matrices which show the use of the data by the Activities. These matrices are extremely powerful and help to show up all the inconsistencies we may have missed between the Data Model and the Activity Models.

We can produce 3 matrices when we are doing very detailed analysis, but at other stages the Entity/Activity Matrix suffices. This is one area where Analyst Workbenches could help enormously, but don't (at the moment). The three matrices are:

Entity/Activity Matrix
Relationship/Activity Matrix
Attribute/Activity Matrix

In Figure 5.56 an example from the Course Administration area is shown where Entities and Relationships have been listed across the top of the matrix and all the Activities listed down the page. In each intersecting box the **use** of that Entity, Relationship (or Attribute) by the Activity is shown classified by type of access. As you can see the letter D means delete or 'disconnect' in the case of a Relationship; U = use, look or read; A = amend, modify or change and C means create or in the case of Relationships, 'connect'. There is no reason why you can't have more than one type of Action in the box, and this is shown in the example. When we update company details we can create, amend or delete the company location.

This matrix isn't so easy to read if we want to check for inconsistencies, so we can help ourselves by summarising the contents in another form. This is shown in Figure 5.57.

In this table the Activities numbered E1 to E40 from the previous page have been classified under column headings according to the type of Action they perform on the Entity or Relationship. All we have done is reorder the results to highlight inconsistencies. Activity 1 creates (adds) the teacher Entity, Activity 2 amends the teacher, Activity 3 creates a company and so on.

Look down the column headings. Are there any Entities used but not created, modified or deleted? Are there any created, modified or deleted but not used? Similarly for Relationships, are there any Relationships created but not used and so on. If there are there **may** be inconsistencies in our analysis. If we are sharing data with other systems (our ideal) then we may well be using data we don't create, amend or delete. Similarly, we may be creating, amending and deleting data we don't use (although this is less likely). Basically, this table highlights those possible inconsistencies which need to be checked.

'Outer Consistency' Checks

The only way we can make sure that our analysis results are a true picture of the existing system is to use the method used by the police – "corroboration of evidence". We get as many versions from different sources as possible and compare until we start to get agreement. This takes time – it is often what causes many projects to take 3 or 4 times their estimated time at the analysis stage. You should only ever compare results after analysis. It is only at this stage that you have similar deliverables to compare. Many people are spending a lot of time and money trying to produce programs which are an accurate translation of their specification. I can't help thinking what a waste of effort it is when I compare the magnitude of errors made because we simply didn't get a true picture of what was needed in the first place.

How to do Activity Analysis 177

Summary of Usage (1)	Teacher	Company	Location	Course	Hotel	Course giving	Student	Course price	Invoice	Course-Course price	Course teacher	Course-Course giving	Course giving-Teacher	Student-Course giving	Course giving-Hotel	Course giving location	Course giving-Invoice	Invoice-Company	Company-Company location	Course giving manual sent location	Student company	Course-Course	Company-Course giving
1. Record consultant details	C																						
2. Update teaching knowledge	A																						
3. Record company details		C	C																		C		
4. Record skeleton course details		U		C																			
5. Update company details		A	CAD																		CD		
6. Record provisional course giving details		U	U	U	U	C					C		C	C		U							C
7. Obtain student list		U		U		U	AC				U		C								UC		
8. Confirm provisional course giving		U	U	U		A					U					U	C						
9. Record teacher course detail	U			U						C													
10. Update course details (final)			A				C	C													C		
11. Confirm teachers	U			U		U					U	CD											
12. Identify teachers able to give course	U			U		U					U	U	U										
13. Provisionally book teacher to course giving	U			U		U					U	C											
14. Identify teachers with necessary experience	U			U							U												
15. Record course giving details		U		U		A	C				U	CD									C		
16. Produce invoice		U	U	U		U	U	U	C	U	U		U				C	C	U	U			U
17. Record hotel details					C																		
18. Update hotel details					A																		
19. Update teachers' course schedule	U			U																			U
20. Send teacher course giving details	U	U	U	U	U	U	U			U	U	U	U	U		U	U	U		U
21. Print course brochure	U			U			U	U												U		
22. Produce secretaries' work plan		U	U	U		U	U				U		U							U	U		
23. Record improvements to course				A																			
24. Change teacher's name	A																						
25. Remove teacher	D					A						U											
26. Update course details		U		A			A	CD													CD		
27. Archive course giving	U	U	U	U	U	D	U		U		D	D	D	D	D	U	U	D	U				D
28. Archive student		U				U	D							D							D		
29. Archive invoice		U	U	U		U	U		D		U		U			D	D	U		U			
30. Record change of location		U	U	U	U	U						U					DC	DC		U			
31. Record teacher's course ability	U			U						C													
32. Identify course givings of teacher and remove	U			U		A						U	U										
33. Record date change				U		A						U											
34. Disconnect teacher from course	U			U						D													
35. Record change of manual location		U	CU	U		U					U									U	CD		
36. Archive course details				D			D	UD		UD											UD		
37. Archive hotel details					D									UD									
38. Archive company details		UD	UD													U		U	UD	U			
39. Send teachers course giving details	U	U	U	U	U	U	U				U	U	U	U		U	U	U					U
40. Identify other teachers able to give course giving	U			U		U					U	U	U										

D = disconnect/delete   U = use   A = amend   C = create/connect

Figure 5.56 Summary of usage

178 *A Simple Introduction to Data and Activity Analysis*

Entities	Add	Amend	Archive Delete	Use
Teacher	E1	E2, E24	E25	E31, E32, E34, E9, E11, E13, E27, E30, E12, E14, E20, E21, E39, E40
Course	E4	E10, E23, E26	E36	E13, E33, E15, E27, E29, E30, E12, E16, E34, E20, E21, E32, E6, E7, E8, E9, E31, E22, E11, E38, E39, E40
Course price	E10	E26	E26, E36	E16, E21
Course Giving	E6	E19, E8, E33	(A) E27	E7, 11, 13, 14, 22, 25, E12, E16, E19, E20, E35, E32, E28, E29, E30, E39, E40
Student	E7, E15	E7	(A) E28	E16, E20, E22, 27, 29, 30, 39
Hotel	E17	E18	E37	E20, E6, E27, E30, E39
Company location	E3, E5, E35	E5	E5, E38	E6, E8, E27, E29, E30, E38, E39, E16, E20, E22, E35
Invoice	E16	--	(A) E29	(E16), 27
Company	E3	E5	E38	E15, E16, E26, E29, E28, E16, E19, E20, E29, E38, E4, E7, E8, E22, E30, E35, E39

Relationships	Connect	Transfer	Disconnect	Use
Course-Course price	E10	E26	E26	E16, E21
Course-Teacher	E9, E31	--	E34	E12, E40
Course-Course giving	E6	--	E27	E7, E8, E11, E13, E33, E36, E12, E35, E16, E20, E32, E15, E29, E30, E22, E39, E40
Course giving-Teacher	E13	E11	E27, E32	E12, E14, E20, E25, E32, E39, E40
Student-Course giving	E7, E15	E15	E27, E28	E16, E20, E29, E22, E39
Course giving-Hotel	E6	E30	E27, E37	E20, E37, E39
Course giving-Location (held at)	E6	E30	E27	E20, E38, E39
Course giving-Invoice	E16	--	E27, E29	E16
Invoice-Company	E16	--	E29	E27, E38
Company-Company location	E3	E5	E5, E38	E6, E8, E27, E29, E16, E20, E22, E35, E30, E38, E39
Course giving manuals sent to location company	E8	E35	E27	E20, E22, E38, E39
Student-Company	E7, E15	--	E28	E16, E20, E27, E29, E38, E39
Course-Course	E10	E26	E26, E36	E21, E36
Company-Course giving				E16, E19, E39, E20

Figure 5.57

5.5 SUMMARY
The main steps I have shown you in this chapter are those of

* Analysing the raw data
* Refining the results

and * Verifying the results

I have chosen not to include the merging of the Activity Analysis results for the simple reason that it is fairly obvious and needs no explanation.

When analysing the raw input, we are reliant, as in Data Analysis, on the type of raw input available to us. Where we used 'Design Abstractions' (transactions, exchanges, clerical tasks and so on) we used a method of bottom-up analysis. When using Real World Occurrences or 'Actions' we used another method of bottom-up analysis. Only when using Real World Abstractions could we use the "top down" method.

This should highlight the usefulness of the methods of analysis in the various stages of a Systems Development Cycle. During Strategy and Feasibility or Tactical Studies, the top-down method is the only one we can use. It is only at the detailed requirements stage that the other two methods become suitable.

This makes both Strategy Studies and Tactical Studies dependent on one method and, although it is a good one, it does have its limitations, the main ones being the inability of a large number of people to think 'top down' and the impossibility of ever devising any good ways of checking the results are correct. You are more reliant on people's word and interpretation using this method than with any other. This apart, it can produce good results. I have often found that these results can only be obtained by experienced systems people who are very business-orientated. Furthermore, they must be working in discrete areas of study or be in a small team. Top-down Decomposition using big teams does not work – you get too many arguments because there is no right or wrong answer.

Activity Analysis using Actions can produce good results, if you get a good, representative sample of input. Be careful not to let it take too long. It is especially good for ferreting out rare Events and Activities – the sort the user may forget in an interview.

Activity Analysis using Design Abstractions can produce good results if the documentation is up-to-date, available and easily understood. One of the most common reasons for wanting a new system is because the old one has become a mess and is not understood – even by the people who have to operate it. In these circumstances, other methods should be used, because if the people who operate it don't understand it, you never will.

As we can see no method is perfect or foolproof. Used in combination, however, they can produce very good results and it is this we must bear in mind. Variety brings greater resilience and variety of methods means less chance of error.

6 Improving a System Using Analysis Deliverables

6.1 INTRODUCTION

Once we have analysed an existing system and obtained the Data and Activity Models which describe the system, our efforts should not stop. The next step we must take is to evaluate that system and seek to improve it, not by using new mechanisms – computer rather than person or disc rather than paper – but by questioning the logic of the way things are being done.

Probably 75% of all the Problems with existing systems I have come across are because of faults in the logic rather than with the mechanisms. Doing things faster or more accurately is a laudable objective, but doing the wrong things faster is not!

The way we evaluate an existing system is by first studying the Problems with the existing system and then studying the Objectives of a system, its Obligations and the Events it has to deal with. Events we have already seen: Objectives, Obligations and Problems we haven't, but all are interrelated and all have a fundamental impact on what systems we need and how we go about inventing them.

6.2. PROBLEMS, CAUSES AND EFFECTS

Problems

A Problem is an undesirable 'situation' or 'state', something the business does not want.

For example: My business is losing money
We have too high a staff turnover
We always seem to lose good employees

Problems aren't confined to businesses, as we know. We can apply the same analytical techniques to our own Problems.

e.g. My car won't start
I'm not paid enough!

A Problem within a business itself is only a Problem because the business (or you) has Objectives. For every Problem there is an underlying but unstated Objective. (See Figure 6.1.)

By studying Problems we get a very good idea not only of what is wrong with the business and hence what needs to be put right, but also what the business really wants, what it would like us to aim for, or in other words what 'right' actually means.

We can't put something 'right', however, until we know what it is that is causing the problem and this we term the 'Cause'.

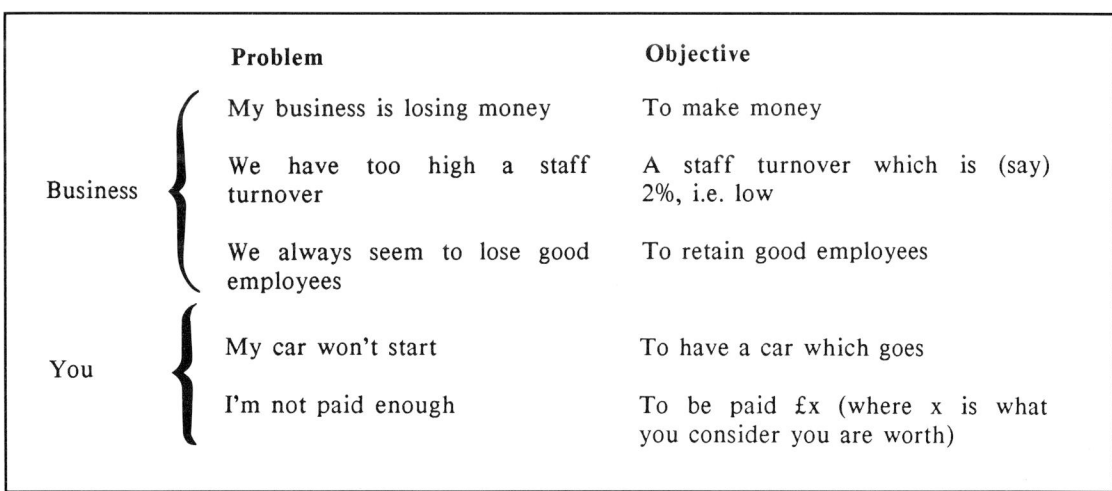

Figure 6.1

182   *A Simple Introduction to Data and Activity Analysis*

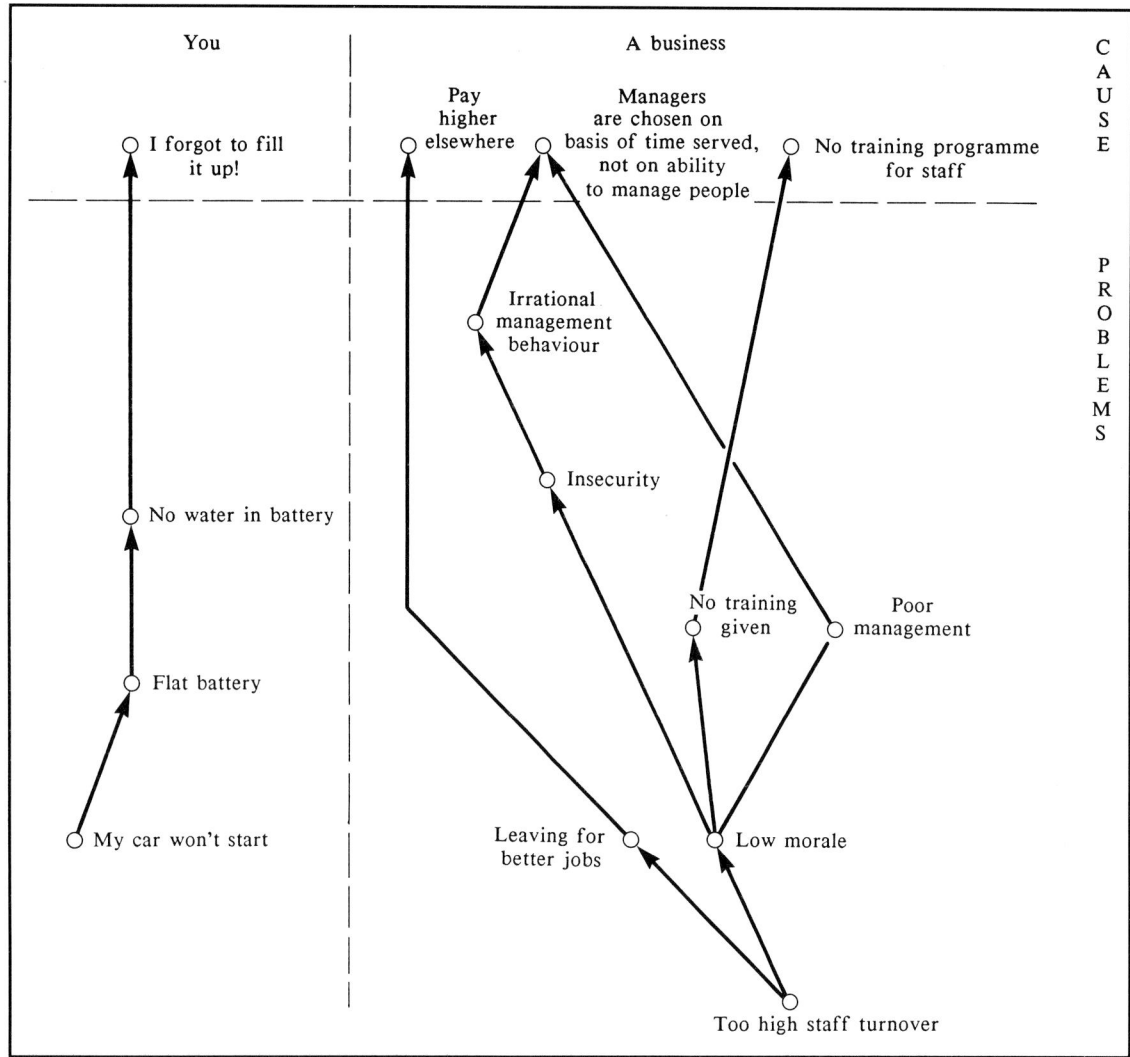

Figure 6.2   Problem/Cause network

Cause

The Cause is the 'Root Problem' or the situation which has caused the Problem, the reason for the undesirable situation. A Cause can be the Cause of many Problems, a Problem can have more than one Cause; the Relationship can be quite complex.

Our Objective is always to treat the Cause, not the Problem. In other words, treat the disease not the symptom. A useful way of tracing Problems back to what we think might be their Cause is by using a network approach. This is shown in Figure 6.2. Once each Problem is stated we then simply ask **why** that Problem has occurred until we reach a Cause – something we can correct.

Recently, many firms have introduced the idea of 'Problem Groups' to their organisation in an attempt to solve business Problems which are costing them money. This idea has been developed independently of the analysis techniques in this book. The Problem Group is formed by pulling people out of their jobs and giving them a Problem to study and solve. They stay in the group until they have solved it. A surprising number of serious Problems addressed by groups like these have found simple and easily cured Causes. In one well documented case the Cause of a faulty machine lay with a part supplied by another firm. The group had to work back in the manufacturing cycle to test out each hypothesis they had about the Cause. These techniques are therefore as applicable to 'manual' systems as they are to information systems.

Effect

The Effect is the final undesirable outcome from the 'mess' of Problems discovered. From the business point of view it normally relates in some way to money or to Effects which are money-related. On a personal basis, money isn't always our top priority and undesirable Effects can be related to other things, quality of life being an important one.

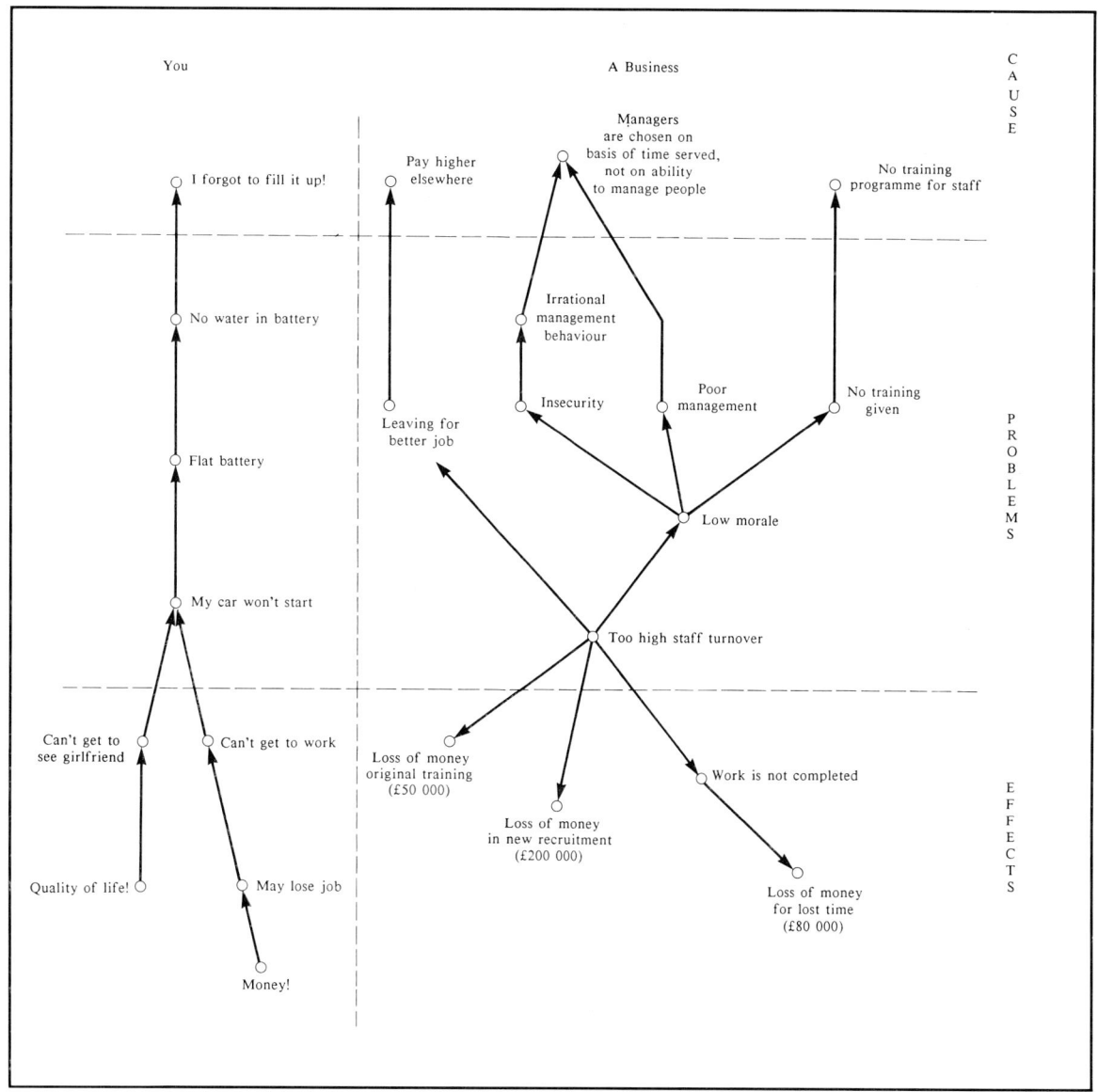

Figure 6.3 Problems/Causes and Effects

We can add Effects to our network of Problems and Causes. You find Effects by asking the simple question.

"and what will happen as a result?"
or "and what if that were to happen?"

This is shown in Figure 6.3.

It should be clear from the table that Problem, Cause and Effect aren't mutually exclusive. In fact, all the things shown are Problems – what we have done is to isolate those we think we can do something about – the Cause and those factors which give us some idea of how serious the Problems are if we don't treat them, and this is the purpose of the Effect. Effects are what we use to decide whether or not we need to solve the Problem and what effort we need to devote to solving the Problem. Serious Effects indicate that considerable effort should be devoted to solving them; minor Effects indicate that only a corresponding amount of effort needs to be spent. If the solution is simple, all well and good. If it doesn't come easily to mind perhaps we can learn to live with the Problem if the Effects are minimal.

As an example from the Course Administration System I have concocted an interview with one of our users about the system. Mixed in are details of the Activities used to handle an Event and the Problems it causes, and their Effects.

184 *A Simple Introduction to Data and Activity Analysis*

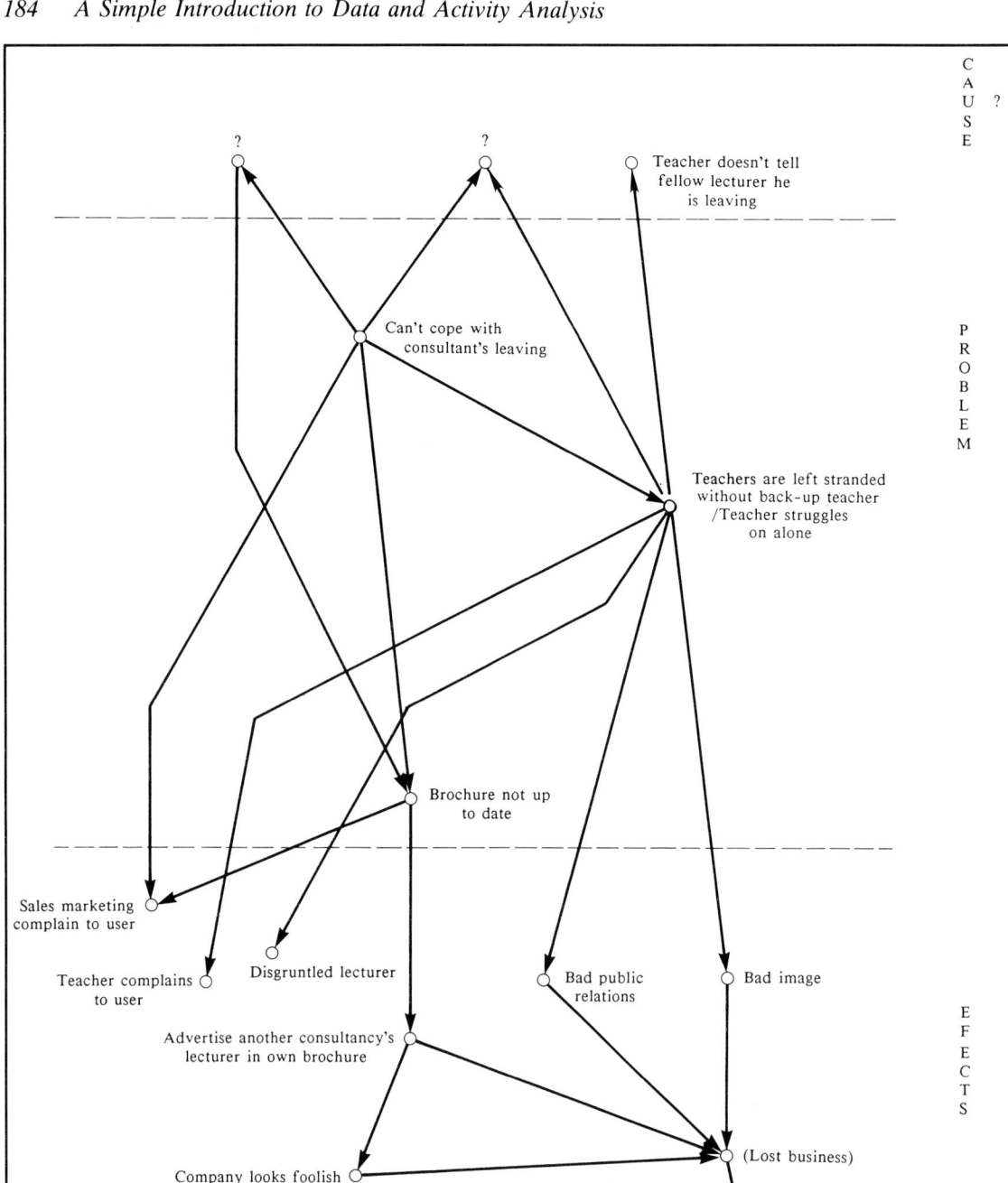

Figure 6.4 **The Problems from the example**

Analyst : I believe some of the things the consultant does can cause you Problems. Would you explain these to me please?
User : Oh... Yes. Blumin' consultants. The worst is when they leave.
Analyst : I believe they do give you plenty of notice.
User : Oh yes, a month, but we never seem to be able to cope with it.
Analyst : What do you do when a consultant leaves?
User : Well, we just remove his details from the files.
Analyst : That's all?
User : Yes.
Analyst : But what goes wrong?
User : Oh, all sorts of things – there are teachers left stranded without the back-up teacher – the consultant never thinks to tell his fellow lecturer he is off – you know, it's scandalous.

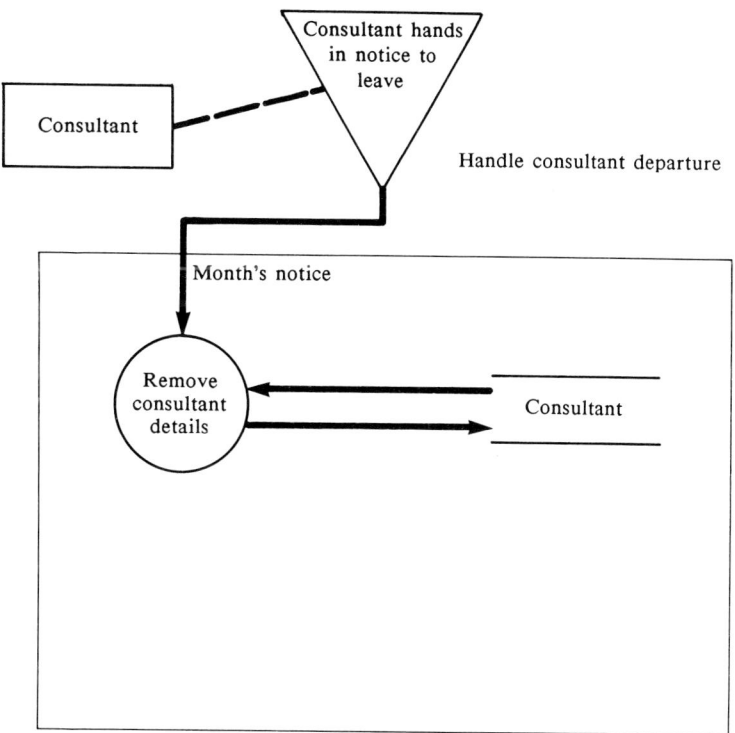

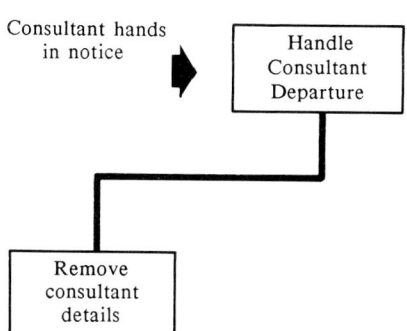

Figure 6.5 The Data Flow Diagram and Activity Decomposition Diagrams

Analyst : Um, terrible, what else?
User : Well, of course the sales/marketing people come down on us like a ton of bricks because their brochure isn't up to date
Analyst : And this is important?
User : It is to the sales and marketing people – they have specified that the brochure must always be bang up-to-date in all respects.
Analyst : What effect does this have?
User : Well, apart from everyone getting onto me – it isn't my job you know – it reflects badly on our courses when one lecturer struggles alone – bad public relations, bad image and pretty disgruntled lecturer is the overall effect.
Analyst : This isn't the sales brochure is it?
User : No, no, I mean the other problems – no, basically if sales and marketing have an out-of-date brochure they may be advertising another consultancy's new lecturer and we look extremely stupid.

In Figure 6.4, I have shown the results of analysing the Problems expressed in this interview. In Figure 6.5, we see what we have gleaned of the Activities and data.

The example illustrates quite well the sort of reply and attitude you will find in many users beset by Problems. First, it isn't their fault, next it isn't their job and finally it somebody else's fault. The network, however, helps to show very firmly that the fault does lie in his area and it isn't anybody else's 'fault'. The two main Problems are that the teacher is left attempting to give a course on his own and that the brochure is not up-to-date. It was made very clear in the interview that this Problem did indeed relate to a clear, well-stated Objective of sales and marketing that the brochure "must always be bang up-to-date in all respects" and it is also clear from the Effects why they have set that Objective. If it is not up-to-date – particularly as far as teachers are concerned – they can advertise another consultancy's lecturer, look foolish and ultimately lose business.

I have added the lost business and loss of money effects myself, because although they weren't explicitly stated they are the obvious consequence of the Effects the user mentioned. We haven't been able to follow through what Effects a disgruntled lecturer has on the company, but quite possibly he may leave or give the course badly, both of which ultimately will cost the company money. The fact that both the teacher and sales and marketing complain to the user are negligible Effects and can be ignored. Looking back up the network, asking 'why' each time, we can see that despite the user's attempts to blame the consultant for not telling his fellow lecturer, the true Causes for the Problems of the brochure not being up-to-date and the teacher being left stranded were never understood by our user.

It follows that our Objectives and Obligations must be:

* To have an up-to-date brochure
* To ensure teachers always have a back-up teacher on a Course Giving.

We will now look at Objectives, Obligations and Events to see what solutions we need to apply.

6.3. EVENTS, OBLIGATIONS AND OBJECTIVES

Objectives

An Objective is usually expressing one of two things – a state we want to attain or something we would like to do. For example:

I want to be **rich and famous**   { is a state I'd like to attain
I want to **fly**   { is an Activity I'd like to be able to do

We may have 'qualifiers' which give us some idea how we'd like to perform the Activity, given the chance.

For example:
I want to fly like a bird
I want to sing like Elvis Presley

These give us clues about the way we need to go about inventing Activities to get us to these states or to enable us to do these things in the way we want to do them.

For example:
If I want to fly like a bird, there wouldn't be much point in me booking on an airplane as I obviously intend open-air free flight. Hang-gliding might be a better alternative.

Obligations

An Obligation is a rule or law, written or unwritten, legal or moral, to which we must adhere.
As a person we are under many Obligations:

– we have to submit tax returns at the end of the year (legal)
– we are not allowed to steal (moral and legal)
– we shouldn't tell lies (moral)

Businesses are also faced with as many, if not more Obligations, to their customers, shareholders, Government and the public as a whole.

– the company must comply with the Safety at Work Act (legal and moral)
– the company must ensure its products are safe (legal and moral)
– the company must comply with the Company Acts

and so on. Most of a company's Obligations are legally enforceable, as Government has long since realised that the morality of a company, unlike a person is a rare phenomenon. Companies don't have a conscience and what might be considered moral Obligations have to be enforced by law.

Events

Events we have already covered. They are the Activities of other businesses and things in the

Improving a System Using Analysis Deliverables 187

system. Note that Events don't always have to be 'negative'. They can be 'positive' and we know them then as 'Opportunities'.

If we think of Activities from our own viewpoint for a moment, it might become clear why 'Activity' exists. If I ask the question of you, "Why do you do anything", your answer will undoubtedly be

- Because I want to
- Because I have to

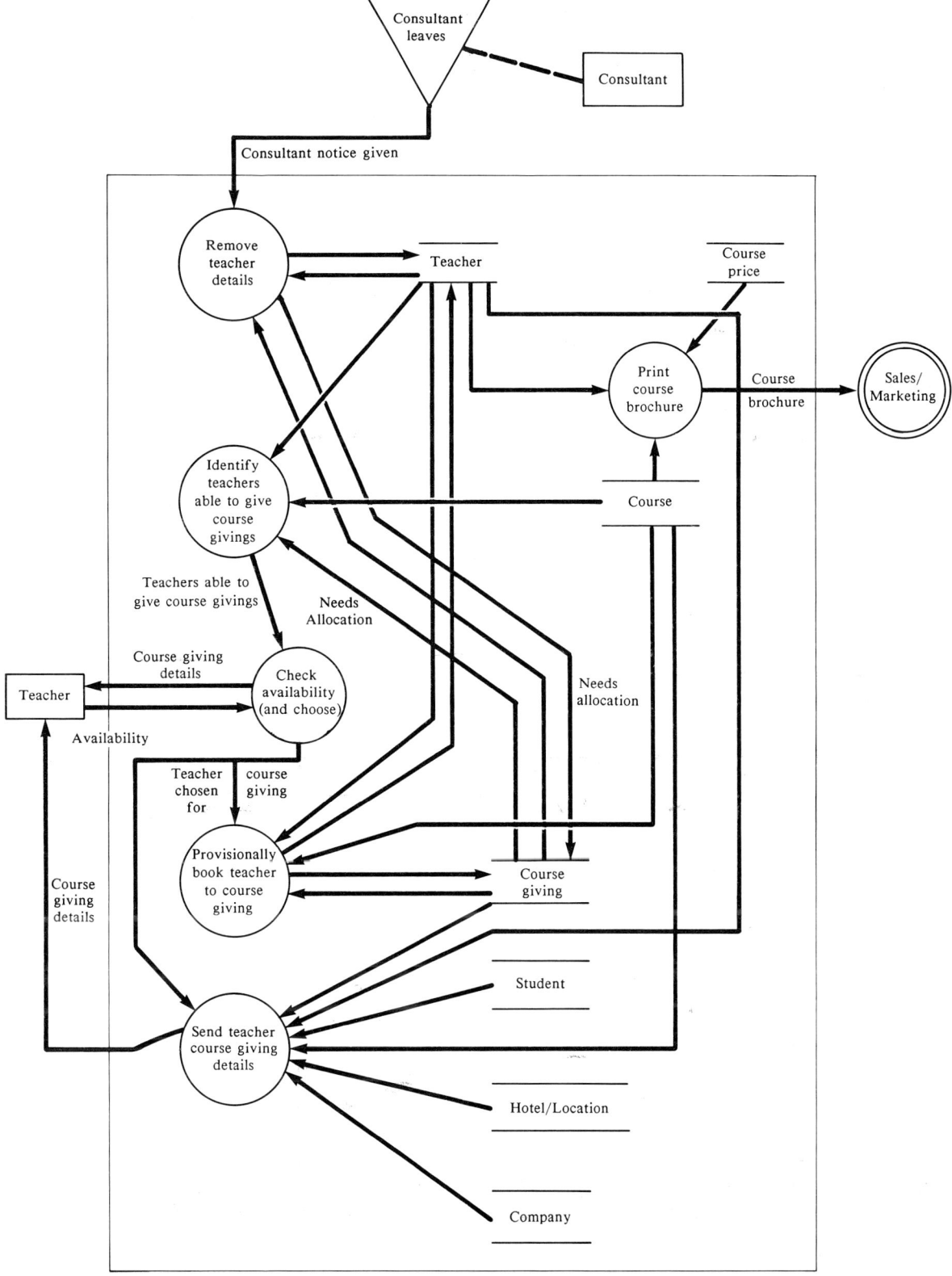

Figure 6.6 Handle departure

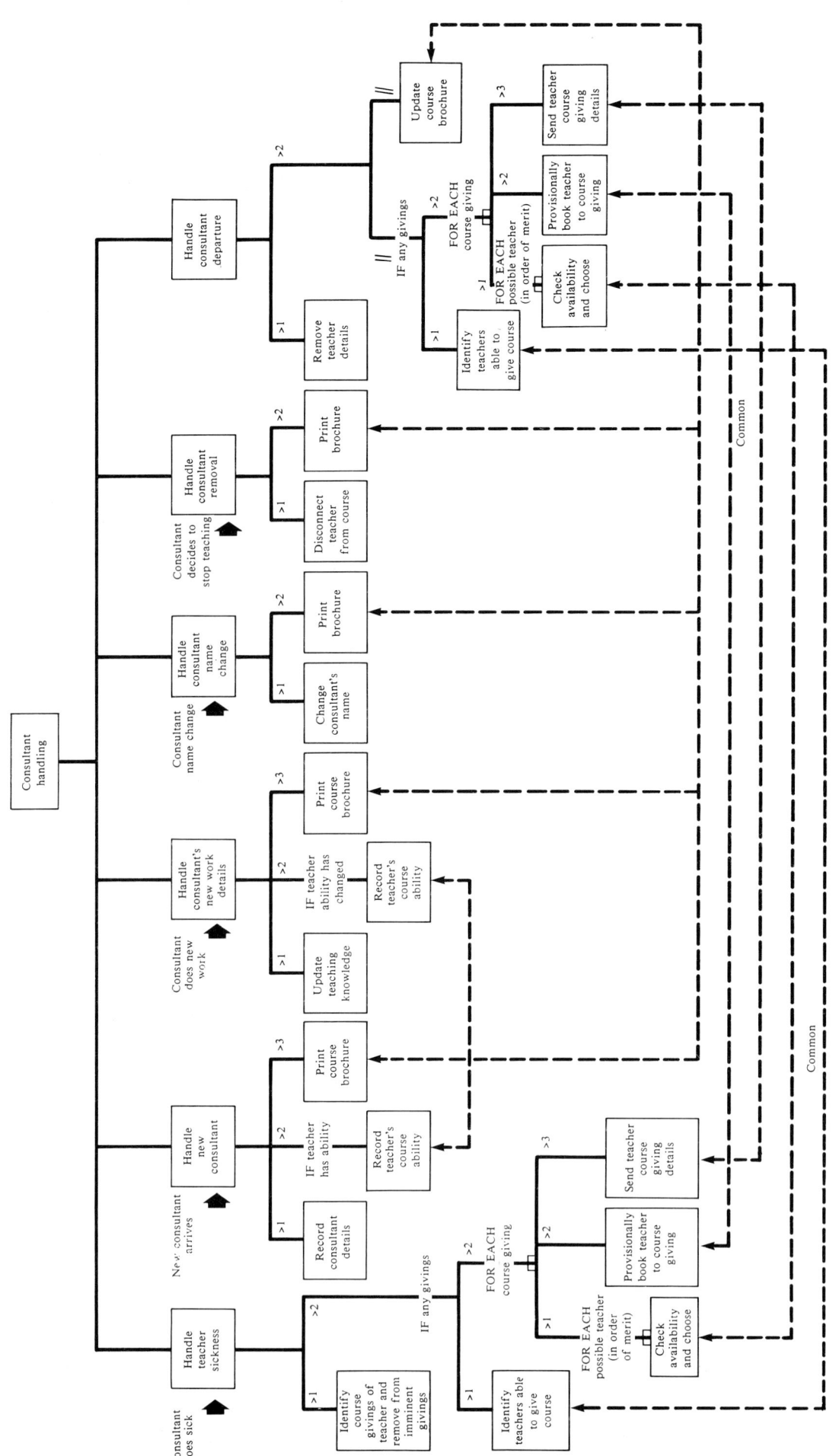

Figure 6.7 Activity Decomposition

Improving a System Using Analysis Deliverables 189

and if I then ask 'and why do have have to?', the reply would be

- Because I must do it
- Because I had to react to something happening

When we **want** to do something or **be** something we have Objectives or are presented with Opportunities (Positive Events). When we **have** to do something because we must do it, we have an Obligation and if we have to do it because we must react to something happening we are dealing with Events (they are negative, if we have to do it).

There are thus only three reasons why Activities are performed, whether by people or business:

- Because of the Objectives it has
- Because of the Obligations it is under
- Because of the Events it has to deal with (Positive Opportunities or Negative Events)

So when we evaluate a system, we need to establish all these things so that we can assess whether the Activities in place:

- Meet the Objectives
- Handle the Obligations
- Handle the Events/take advantage of the Opportunities

Sometimes we find **missing** Activities; sometimes we find Activities which don't do the job properly. A Problem's Causes and Effects Analysis is there to help us to highlight this; it will show us where there are missing Activities by showing up Events, Obligations and Objectives which are not handled or are not handled properly.

We can thus see that by extension, Problems can also be related to Obligations and Events.

Example	**Problem**	**Obligation/Event**
	We can't cope with consultants leaving	Consultant leaves
	Teacher struggles on alone	To give teacher support (moral Obligation not to overwork)

When improving a system we therefore seek to ensure that all the business Objectives, Obligations and Events are handled, and in the way it is obliged to handle them or wants to handle them (fast, accurately, efficiently and so on).

There is no 'method' available for inventing better ways of doing things. A bit of creative thinking by you and your users, brainstorming and similar techniques have all been successful under different circumstances. Another way is to look around to see what others have done in the same circumstances where they have been successful (and the latter point is important). Basically, intelligence is needed.

If we now look back at the results of our Problem analysis and Activity Analysis, we can see that Objectives and Obligations have not been satisfied.

       To provide an up-to-date course brochure
and   To provide the teachers with a colleague on a Course Giving

Thus the **Cause** is that there are missing Activities. The corresponding Activities must therefore be put in place to handle these two things.

Departure is not dissimilar to sickness in many respects from the systems point of view, so I have re-used those Activities from the 'handle sickness' Activity which dealt with any Course Givings the teacher was due to give.

To handle the Objective, all I need do is add the 'update course brochure' Activity to the Data Flow Diagram.

The resultant Data Flow Diagram is shown in Figure 6.6. The Activity Decomposition is shown in Figure 6.7 and the Activity Description of the one new Activity, 'remove teacher details' is shown below. Note that this would also have had to be changed from its original state by the changes we have made.

Remove Teacher Details
When a consultant leaves, it is important that their CV is removed so that they are no longer considered for teaching. If the consultant was due to give any Course Givings these are marked as needing reallocation.

6.4 SUMMARY
Problems, Objectives, Obligations and Events are all interrelated. By studying all but the first we are not only able to see what the business wants to do, should do and has to do, but by studying them

at the same time as the Problems we can also see where a businesses' Activities are incorrect or missing, given the stated needs.

When treating Problems we search for their Cause. The Cause during the analysis task will be related to missing data, poor data, incorrect logic, the wrong data or Activities and so on. In other words, the Cause will be related to deliverables of analysis. You find the Cause after each Problem has been stated by asking the simple question, "Why?"

Effect is the undesirable outcome of a Problem and in business terms will nearly always eventually be related to money. For a person, undesirable Effects may relate to many other things – health, happiness and, in general, the 'quality of life'.

Effects are determined by asking, "And what is the result/are the results of that?" They are used to determine how much effort should be spent solving the Problems.

Once we have put the business back on course by seeing what Activities it should be doing, we can start thinking about how those Activities ought to be done – using people or machines – but not before.

As a parting thought about Objectives, Events and Obligations, we hear people mention the 'culture' of a company. Culture is very often determined by how a company views these three phenomena. If it is strongly Objective-driven, it will appear ruthless. It may be successful if it dominates a market, but otherwise it could fail. It may well have staff Problems and Problems with customers and the general public. A company which is wholly Event-driven will never succeed – it will appear alert, but disorganised and incapable of making a profit. A company in a dominant market position which balances Objectives with moral Obligations is more likely to be successful both in business and with its staff and customers. Its "mission" statements may well include those about its Relationship with the general public and its staff. A company in a highly volatile market will have an equal balance between Event and Objective. It will be able to respond to new Events while satisfying its own Objectives. Every 'Problem' becomes an "Opportunity".

Perhaps in the end this is a definition of a successful company: one which is able to respond to Events by turning them to its own advantage and satisfying its Objectives, while retaining the ability to satisfy its Obligations whether legal or moral.

7 Elementary Activities

7.1 INTRODUCTION

In chapters 5, 6 and 7 we saw how Activities can be decomposed or broken down into more and more detailed Activities, using the techniques of Activity Decomposition and Data Flow Diagramming. There is an obvious question which arises in the heads of all analysts using these techniques, and that is: 'When do I stop?'.

The answer is: 'When you have found an Elementary Activity'. In this chapter we will see what an Elementary Activity is, how it can be recognised and how it can be described. We will also look at some other deliverables of an Elementary Activity which are useful in design.

7.2 DEFINITION AND PURPOSE

We use Activity Analysis Techniques for Strategy Studies, Tactical Studies and Detailed Requirements Studies.

In Figure 7.1, an Activity Decomposition Diagram shows what happens pictorially. During a Strategy Study you will be dealing with very generalised Activities. When you have decomposed the Activities to a level of detail where you feel confident that a strategy can be proposed, stop. Suggest areas where mechanised help or change of organisation would benefit the company and also suggest application or 'project' areas which should become the subject of a Tactical Study.

These are given a priority. These application areas are then further decomposed during the Tactical Study. In other words, for the one Strategy Study several Tactical Studies may result, tackled in the order identified during the Strategy Study. Activity Decomposition stops during a tactical study when enough is known of the Activities to suggest more detailed mechanisms and to apply cost/benefit and feasibility criteria to those mechanisms.

In both cases, there are no rules about the number of 'levels' you may need to decompose to. In a company or project with a limited number of Activities, three of four may well be enough, but large companies and large projects could require many more.

When doing a Detailed Requirements Study, however, stop when you recognise that you have an Elementary Activity. At this point, you can cease 'analysis' and start 'design' (but within the framework identified during the Strategy and Tactical Studies).

An Elementary Activity has a specific definition and this we will be exploring in more detail later on. It helps however, when doing analysis, to know how to recognise an Elementary Activity, so that you can see if the definition applies.

Basically, Elementary Activities are recognised by having a name which contains obvious and definite Actions:

e.g. *Match* delivery and invoice
Cancel patient appointment
Check stock quantity

The name often also contains the name of Entities. Furthermore, the Data Flows or Outputs it uses can be easily decomposed to Attributes and Attribute values.

Definition of Elementary Activities

An Elementary Activity has two definitions depending on whether it updates data or simply manipulates and outputs data. The update definition is more clear cut.

"An update Elementary Activity is one which if decomposed further would produce sub-activities, which if actioned independently would destroy the logical consistency and integrity of the Data Model".

In other words an Elementary Activity is a sort of data integrity or consistency unit.

"An output Elementary Activity is one which, if further split would produce sub-activities which do not produce the collection of data required by the Objective and demanded by the next Activity or Sink as a unit".

For example, a pay slip without tax details, tax returns with no tax code, an invoice without the invoice lines.

192 *A Simple Introduction to Data and Activity Analysis*

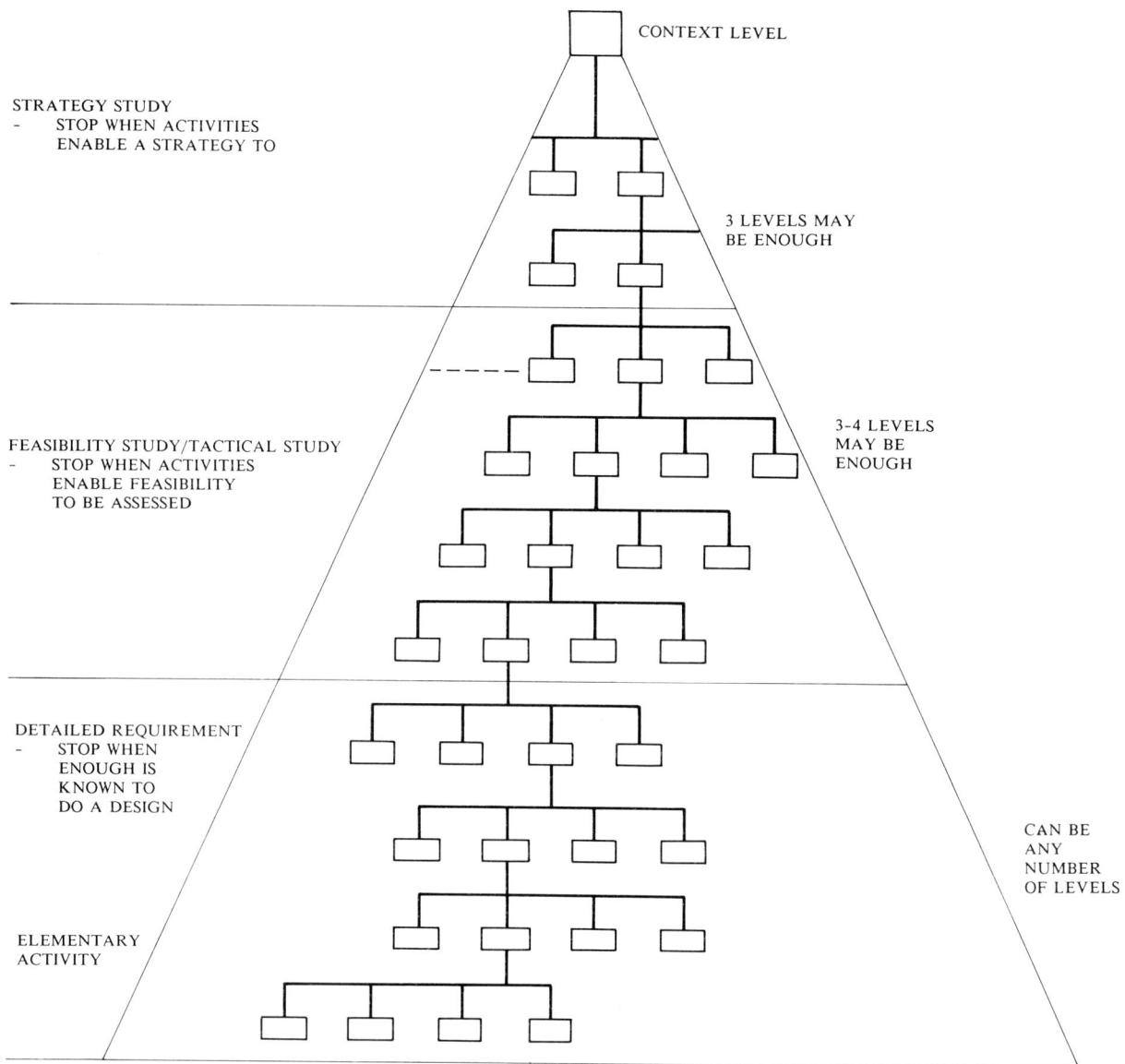

Figure 7.1

Elementary Activities do not attempt in one fell swoop to keep the Data Model consistent with the 'real world'. A string of Elementary Activities may be needed to do this.

In other words, to handle an Event or a Data Flow of new data we may need many Elementary Activities. Our Objective is to make Elementary Activities as small a unit of processing as possible while keeping the data consistent so that our "units of rollback" (for that is what they will become in the design) are also small. This way we save the user and the computer from wasted effort in rolling back an unnecessarily long way in processing if anything goes wrong. This is why we look for consistency units. An 'integrity' or 'consistency' unit is also a unit of rollback.

Integrity units can be defined by the patterns of Entities and Relationships on the Data Model, by the Attributes and how they are logically related.

Example 1 If I delete an A
my model tells me I
must also delete all the
Bs. Similarly creation
of an A must involve creation
of at least 1 B.
(See Figure 7.2.)

Elementary Activities 193

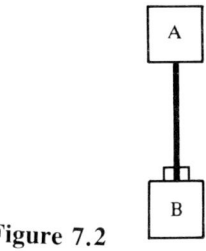

Figure 7.2

Example 2   When I create a B
I must link it to a D, A
and C. But creation of D,
A and C does not need to
involve any Bs.
(See Figure 7.3.)

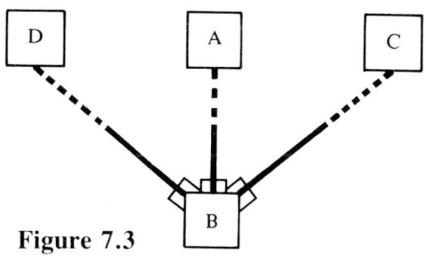

Figure 7.3

Figure 7.4 shows the integrity needed logically for Entities and Attributes, not just that dictated by the Data Model pattern. In this example, we have a hospital with patients. When a patient recovers we must *as one Action* -   RECORD THE DATE OF RECOVERY
- CANCEL BED BOOKING(S)
- CANCEL APPOINTMENT(S)
- RECORD WHICH TREATMENT CAUSED
  THE RECOVERY (IF ANY)

Example 3   (See Figure 7.4.)
If any of these things is *not* done we will destroy the *consistency* of the Data Model – in real-world terms:

  – we still have appointments for a person who has recovered
  – we will have bed bookings for a person who has recovered

Logically, looking only at the Data Model, we would have created inconsistency in the data.

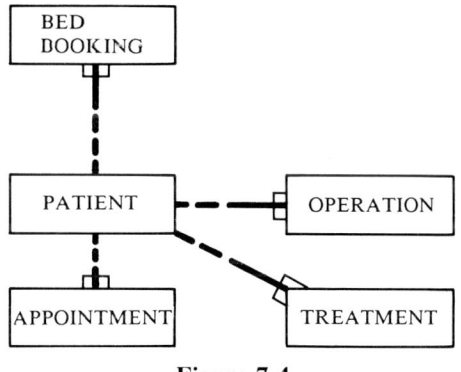

Figure 7.4

7.3. STRUCTURED TEXT AND ACCESS PATHS
We can describe an Elementary Activity using ordinary English a sort of semi-structured English or fully structured English.

The ideal is either of the last two as we are seeking a clear and unambiguous description of what needs to be done – ordinary English is open to ambiguity.

194 A Simple Introduction to Data and Activity Analysis

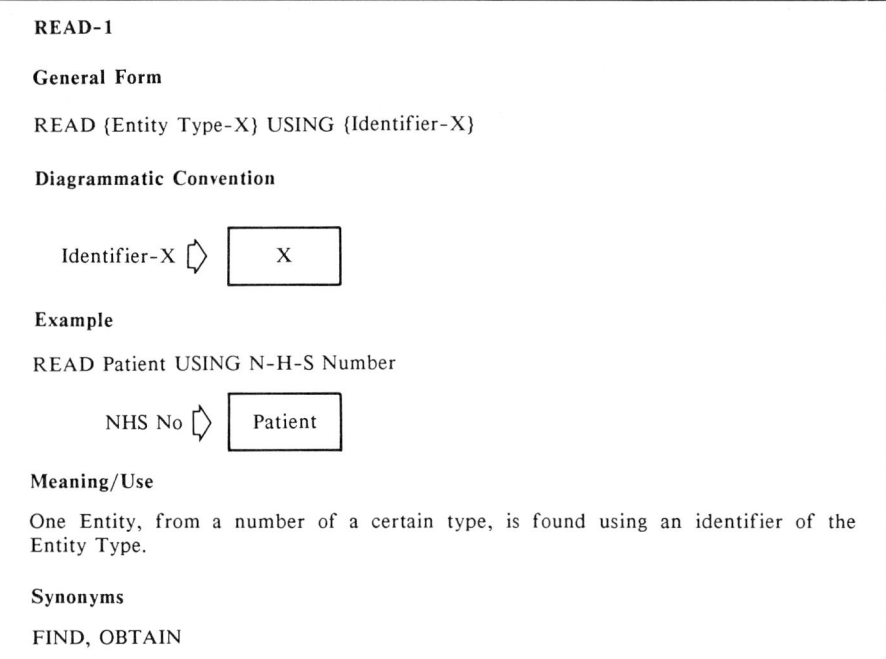

Figure 7.5

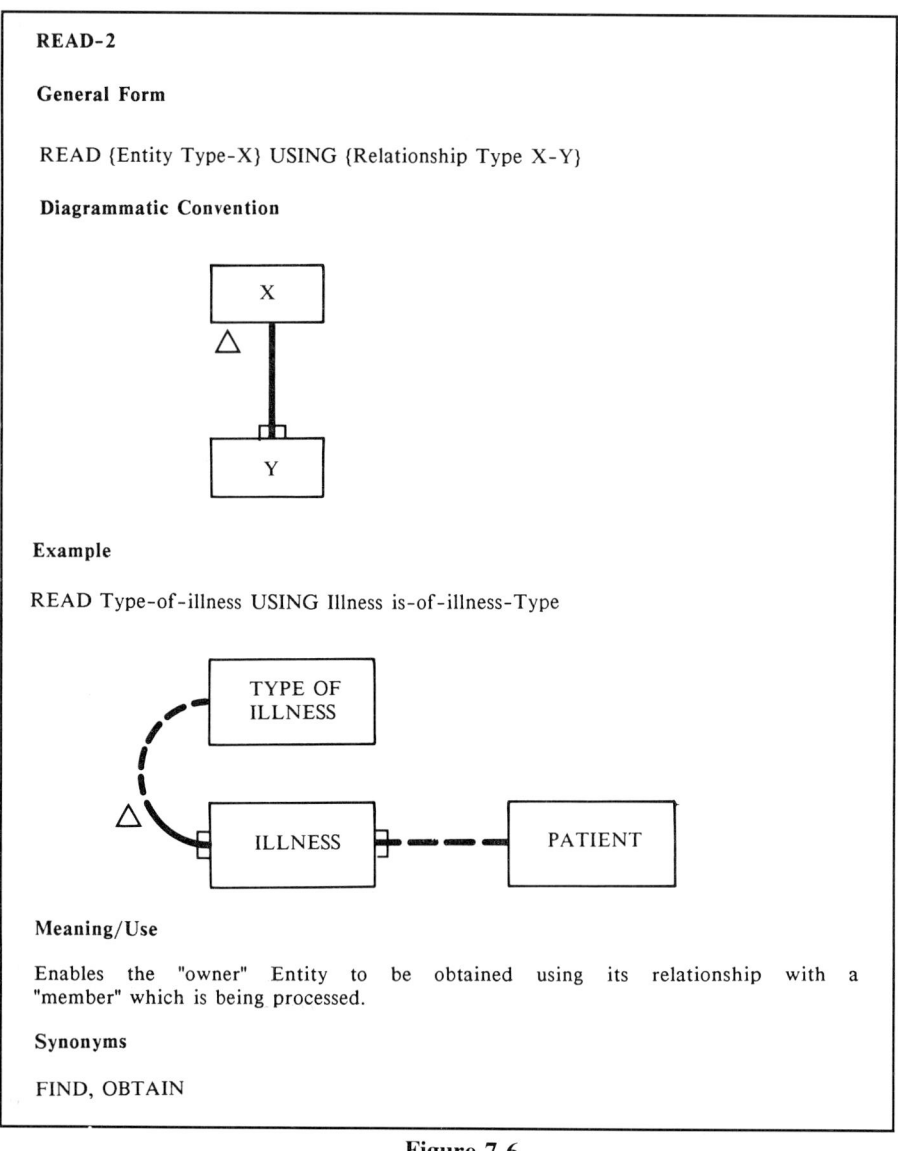

Figure 7.6

Elementary Activities   195

At the same time as we describe our Elementary Activities using structured English, we should be showing how the Elementary Activities use the data in the Data Model.

The use made of the Data Model by an Elementary Activity is called an "Access Path". It shows logically how the Activity 'walks around' the Data Model manipulating, creating, deleting and changing data, and we can show it using a picture.

Example Commands to Describe Elementary Activities

On the next few pages (Figures 7.5 – 7.24), I have provided some example commands you could use to describe Elementary Activities together with how they are pictorially represented on the Data Model (if they are).

I look forward to when we can point at a Data Model using a mouse, light pen or similar and generate this type of structured logic, as its format is totally dictated by the Data Model. Many Analyst Workbenches are moving in this direction, some are nearly there.

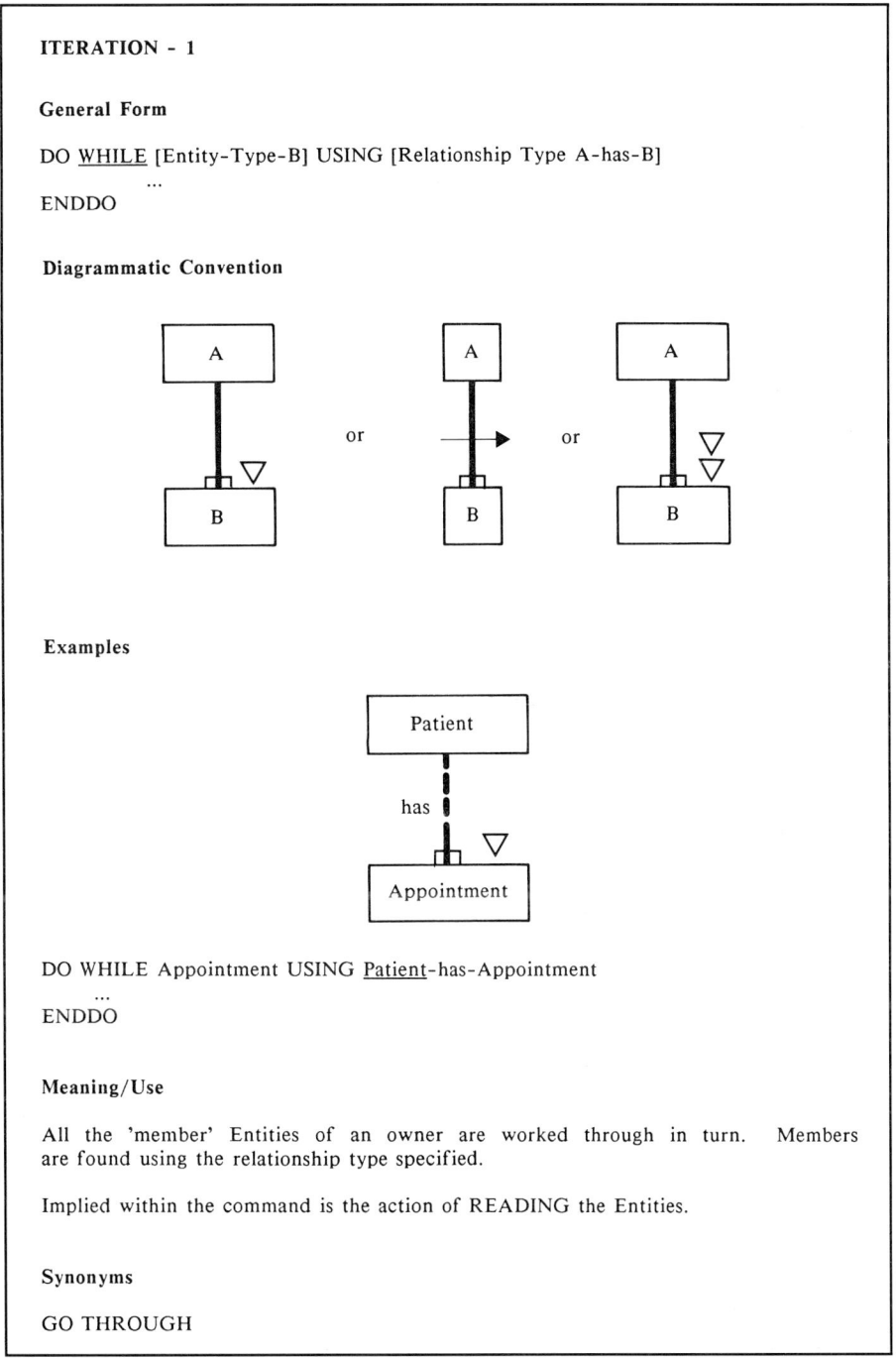

Figure 7.7

196 *A Simple Introduction to Data and Activity Analysis*

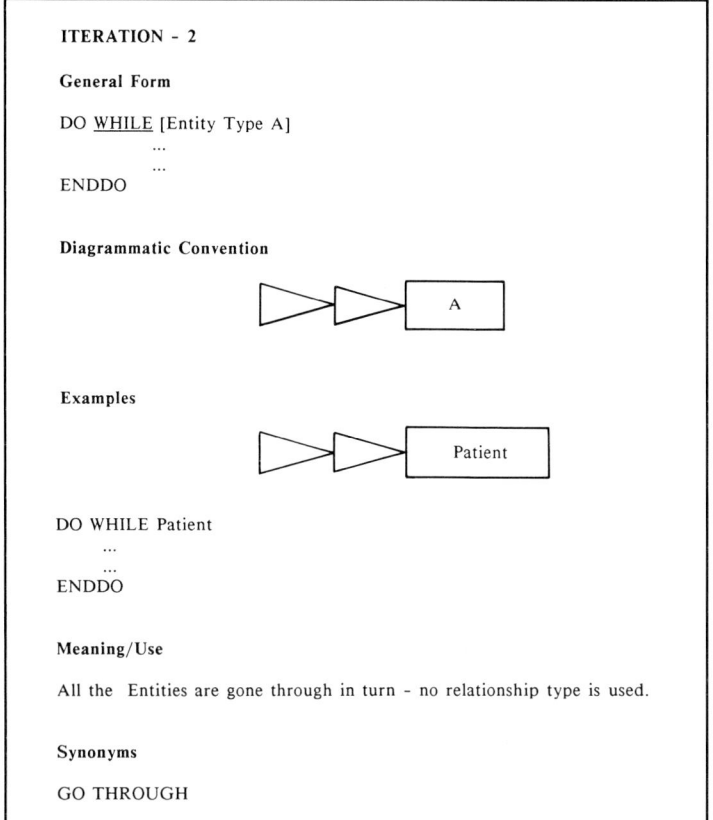

Figure 7.8

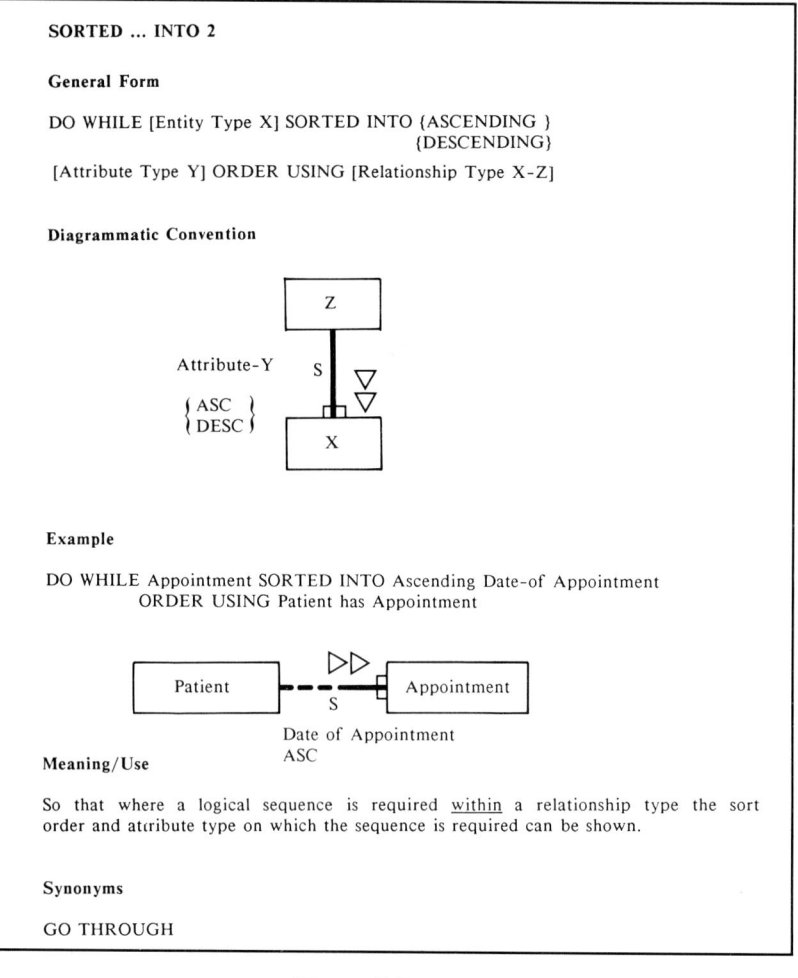

Figure 7.9

SORTED ... INTO ... 1

General Form

DO WHILE [Entity Type X] SORTED INTO {ASCENDING } [Attribute Type Y] ORDER
{DESCENDING}

Diagrammatic Convention

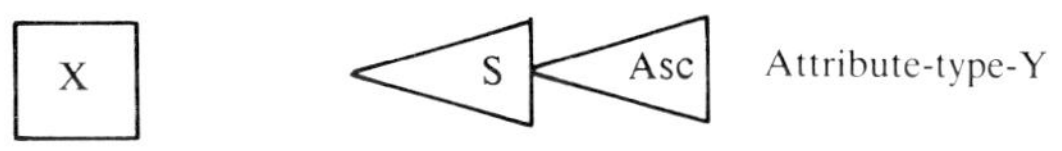

X S ◁ Asc   Attribute-type-Y

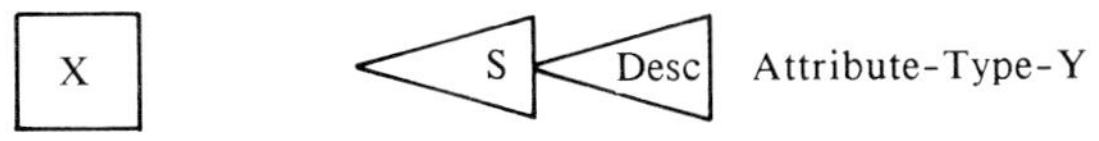

X S ◁ Desc Attribute-Type-Y

Example

DO WHILE Patient SORTED INTO ASCENDING N-H-S-No ORDER

Meaning/Use

So that where a logical sequence is required, both the fact that the entities are required in some sort of order <u>and</u> the Attribute Type in which the order is defined can be described.

Synonyms

GO THROUGH

Figure 7.10

DO WHILE ... UNTIL

General Form

DO WHILE {Entity Type} USING {Relationship Type} UNTIL {Condition}

eg

DO WHILE Order USING Customer-has Order UNTIL Order-Date=Today's Date

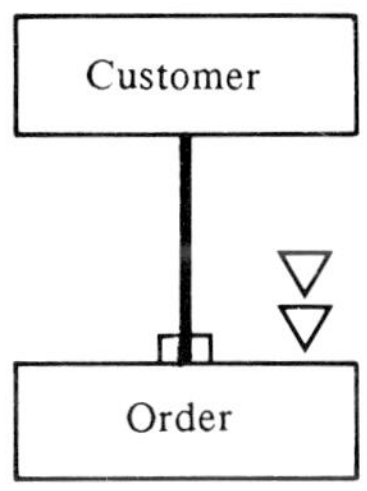

Customer
  |
Order

Meaning

Go through all the B entities related to the A entities until the condition is satisfied and then stop. Any entities after the condition is satisfied are not included in the processing which follows <u>including the entity which Stopped the processing</u>.

Synonym

GO THROUGH

Figure 7.11

198 *A Simple Introduction to Data and Activity Analysis*

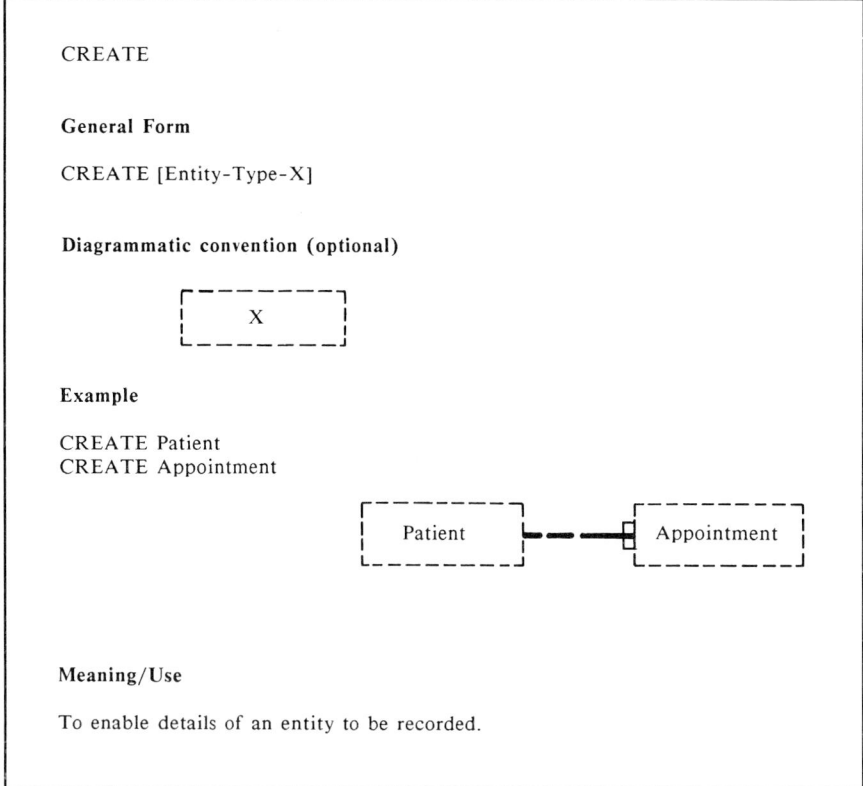

Figure 7.12

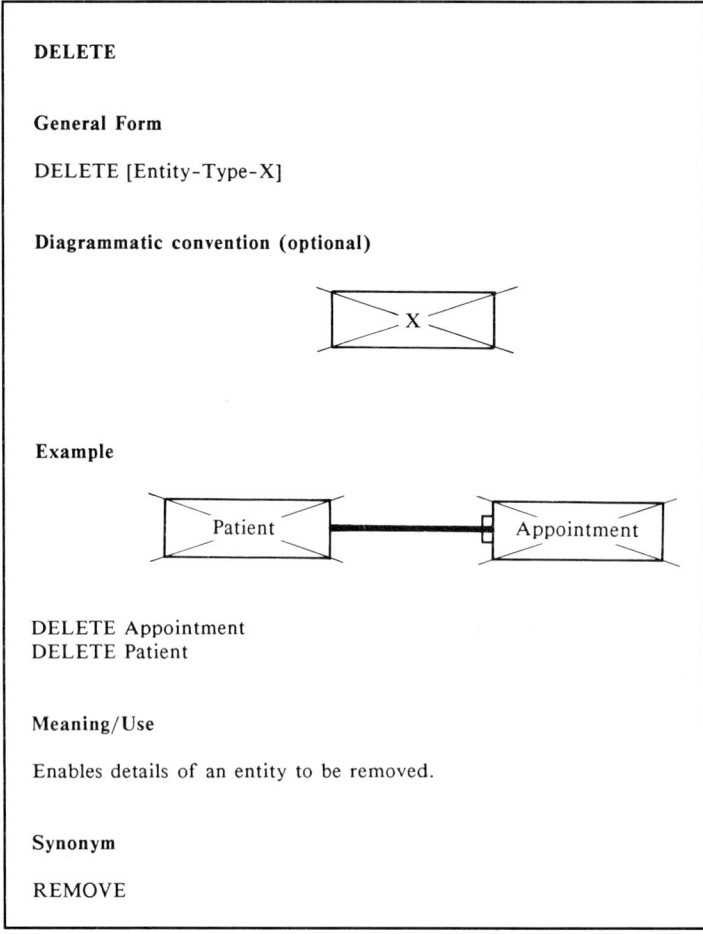

Figure 7.13

CONNECT/DISCONNECT

General Form

CONNECT [Entity-Type-X] TO [Entity-Type-Y] USING [Relationship Type X-Y]

DISCONNECT [Entity-Type-X] FROM [Entity-Type-Y]
                          USING [Relationship Type X-Y]

eg:

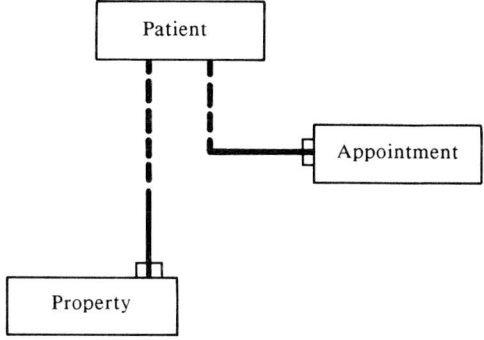

CONNECT Patient TO Appointment USING Patient-has-Appointment

DISCONNECT Patient FROM Property USING Patient-has-Property

Meaning/Use

Enables relationship types to be established and removed.

Synonym

REMOVE, DELETE, CREATE

Figure 7.14

COMPLEX SELECTION

General Form

CASE 1 (condition)
...
CASE 2 (condition)
...
CASE 3 (condition)
...
CASE N (condition)
...
ENDCASE

Example

CASE 1 Appointment-Date LESS THAN Today's Date
...
CASE 2 Appointment-Date EQUALS Today's Date
...
CASE 3 Appointment-Date GREATER THAN Today's Date
...
ENDCASE

Meaning/Use

This command is used when more than two mutually exclusive alternatives exist for selection. It allows a choice of more than two sets of actions where selection must be made. No alternative means of expression exists.

Figure 7.15

GET

General Form

GET {Attribute Type}

Example

GET Name-of-Patient
GET Sex-of-Patient

Meaning

Describes the case where input is obtained (say) <u>from an outside Source</u> and it must be obtained from that source. It is the opposite construct to the command 'PRINT'.

Synonym

ACCEPT

Figure 7.16

DISPLAY/PRINT

General Form

DISPLAY [Attribute Type - X]
or
DISPLAY [Message-Number-N]

Example

DISPLAY Date-of-Birth
DISPLAY Sex
DISPLAY Name
DISPLAY M1963   [M1963 = Here are the Patient's details]

Meaning/Use

To enable Attribute values of an Entity to be "output"

Synonyms

PRINT, SHOW

Figure 7.17

```
┌─────────────────────────────────────────────────────────────────────┐
│  SET ... TO (1)                                                     │
│                                                                     │
│  General Form                                                       │
│                                                                     │
│  SET Date-of-Birth                TO Today's Date                   │
│  SET Operation-Cancelled-Indicator TO '1'                           │
│                                                                     │
│  Meaning/Use                                                        │
│                                                                     │
│  Allows an Attribute Type to be set to a specific Value within the  │
│  logic of the activity.                                             │
│                                                                     │
│  SET ... (2)                                                        │
│                                                                     │
│  General Form                                                       │
│                                                                     │
│  SET [Attribute Type-X]                                             │
│                                                                     │
│  Example                                                            │
│                                                                     │
│  SET Patient-Sex                                                    │
│  SET Patient-Name                                                   │
│  SET Patient-Height                                                 │
│                                                                     │
│  Meaning/Use                                                        │
│                                                                     │
│  Enables an Attribute Type to be set to whatever value has been     │
│  input to the activity from the "outside".                          │
└─────────────────────────────────────────────────────────────────────┘
```

Figure 7.18

MANIPULATION COMMANDS

COMMANDS	EXAMPLE	OTHER ACCEPTABLE FORMS
EQUAL TO	IF Date-of-Birth EQUAL TO Today's Date	=; IS EQUAL TO; ARE EQUAL; EQ
NOT-EQUAL-TO	IF Date-of-Birth NOT EQUAL TO Today's Date	≠ ; IS NOT EQUAL TO; ARE NOT EQUAL TO; NE
IS LESS THAN	IF Patient's Age IS LESS THAN 50	<; LT; LESS THAN
IS LESS THAN OR EQUAL TO	IF Patient's-Age IS LESS THAN OR EQUAL TO 50	≤; LE; LESS THAN OR EQUAL TO
IS GREATER THAN	IF Patient's-Age IS GREATER THAN 16	>; GT; GREATER THAN
IS GREATER THAN OR EQUAL TO	IF Patient's-Age IS GREATER THAN OR EQUAL TO 16	≥; GE; GREATER THAN OR EQUAL TO
IS NOT LESS THAN		≮; NLT; NOT LESS THAN
IS NOT LESS THAN OR EQUAL TO		≰; NLE; NOT LESS THAN OR EQUAL TO
IS NOT GREATER		≯; NGT; NOT GREATER THAN
IS NOT GREATER THAN OR EQUAL TO		≱; NGE; NOT GREATER THAN OR EQUAL TO

Figure 7.19

ARITHMETIC

COMMAND	EXAMPLE	OTHER FORMS	NOTES
MULTIPLY {Attribute Type X} {Attribute Value X} BY {Attribute Type Y} {Attribute Value Y} TO GIVE {Attribute Type Z} ROUNDED UP ROUNDED DOWN ROUNDED	MULTIPLY Hours-Worked-in-Week BY Hourly-Rate TO GIVE Total-Basic-Pay-for-Week MULTIPLY Monthly-Salary BY '12' TO GIVE Annual-Salary	None	The 'rounded' clause enables the result to be rounded according to the requirements as expressed by the attribute type deliverables "Rounding"
DIVIDE {Attribute Type X} {Attribute Value X} (BY INTO) {Attribute Type Y} {Attribute Value Y} TO GIVE {Attribute Type Z} ROUNDED UP ROUNDED DOWN ROUNDED	DIVIDE Annual-Salary BY 12 TO GIVE Salary-This-Period DIVIDE No-of-Patients BY No-of-Doctors TO GIVE Patient-Doctor-Ratio ROUNDED UP DIVIDE No-of-Teachers INTO No-of-Students TO GIVE Student-Ratio ROUNDED DOWN		

Figure 7.20

MANIPULATION - ARITHMETIC

COMMAND	EXAMPLE	OTHER FORMS	NOTES
SUBTRACT {Attribute Type X} {Attribute Value X} AND {Attribute Type Y} {Attribute Value Y} FROM {Attribute Type Z} {Attribute Value Z} TO GIVE {Attribute Type A} ROUNDED UP ROUNDED DOWN ROUNDED	SUBTRACT Total-Deductions-This-Month AND Total-Tax-This-Month AND Total-National-Insurance-This-Month FROM Total-Gross-Pay-This-Month TO GIVE Total-Net-Pay-This-Month	None	Rounding as explained before
SUBTRACT {Attribute Type X} {Attribute Value X} FROM {Attribute Type Y} {Attribute Value Y}	SUBTRACT 1 FROM No-of-Passengers-in-Queue		
ADD {Attribute Type X} {Attribute Value X} AND {Attribute Type Y} {Attribute Value Y} TO GIVE {Attribute Type Z} ROUNDED UP ROUNDED DOWN ROUNDED	ADD Basic-Salary-This-Month AND Bonus-Payments-This-Month AND Total-Allowances-This-Month TO GIVE Total-Gross-This-Month	None	
ADD {Attribute Type X} {Attribute Value X} TO {Attribute Type Z} ROUNDED UP ROUNDED DOWN ROUNDED	ADD '1' to Total-No-of-Enquiries		

Figure 7.21

204   *A Simple Introduction to Data and Activity Analysis*

SIMPLE SELECTION

General Form

IF {condition}
   ...
OTHERWISE
   ...
ENDIF

Example

IF Sex-Code = Male
   ...
OTHERWISE
   ...
ENDIF

Meaning/Use

This command is used when only two alternatives exist for selection. One set of actions or the other is then done.

Figure 7.22

ABANDON

General Form

ABANDON [Message Number]

Example

ABANDON M1963   (M1963 = Patient cannot be found)

Meaning/Use

When an error is found or no action is required if a condition is met, this command enables the activity to be terminated - with a message to say what has happened.

Synonyms

EXIT, STOP

Figure 7.23

END

General Form

Signifies the end of the elementary activity.

Purpose

Self-explanatory

Figure 7.24

7.4. COMMON PROCEDURES, MESSAGES AND EMBEDDED ELEMENTARY ACTIVITIES

Common Procedures

Even after we have reached Elementary Activity level, our search for common Activities does not stop. Within the logic of an Elementary Activity we may still find blocks of text which are common with blocks in other Elementary Activities.

We give these common blocks of logic the name "Procedures".

Procedures can be common because they perform the same action on an Entity,

- e.g. Cancel operation
  Find customer
  Validate product data

or they may be common because they perform the same Action on an Attribute,

- e.g. Validate customer code
  Validate date

Elementary Activities can often be built up from building blocks of common logic, and this has enormous advantages. It saves us effort in analysis and it also ensures consistent action. During design and construction we save effort yet again, by using reusable "modules" in the design or controlled copied code. We may also find that common screens, listings or input documents can be used. We define and describe Procedures no differently to the way we would Elementary Activities. In Figure 7.25 a simple example is shown of a Procedure description, defined using structured English.

Many DBMSs, which have their own 'active' or driving Data Dictionary, allow you to record Procedures which validate Attributes or data items (as in the example) 'connected' to the record descriptions. This means you don't have to worry about invoking the Procedure in your logic.

If the data item or Attribute is input it is validated by the DBMS using this logic.

```
VALIDATE TEACHER NUMBER

IF TEACHER NUMBER NOT NUMERIC
    ABANDON M02

OTHERWISE
    IF TEACHER NUMBER = ZERO
        ABANDON M03
    OTHERWISE
    ENDIF

ENDIF
```

Figure 7.25 Example of a procedure

EXECUTE

General Form

EXECUTE "Procedure"

Example

EXECUTE "Validate N-H-S Number"

Meaning/Use

The execute command enables the analyst to specify which section of logic he would like to be executed at that step in the activity without having to repeat the steps themselves. This then saves him time and ensures consistent action when the 'sub-activity' is actioned.

Synonym

DO

Figure 7.26

If you don't have software which does this for you, you will need to specify in your Activity logic when these Procedures are to be used.

A special structured English command exists for this – the "Execute" command whose format is shown in Figure 7.26.

Messages

You will notice that in the Procedure example, whenever the processing was 'abandoned' because an error was found, a code was given – 'M02' and 'M03' being the two in the example.

These are the codes of Messages. It can help enormously, saving effort in writing and consistency in Message use if the analyst specifies what the Messages he wishes to appear at that stage are, gives them a (non-meaningful) code and refers to the code in the logic.

The Messages can then be provided to the designers as a list, to which they can add design-specific Messages,

e.g. 'Please Press PF1 to confirm'
'Please press Return'
'Move mouse up to Bin Icon and Click'

An example of a Message list from our Course Administration system is shown in Figure 7.27.

MESSAGES	
M01	TEACHER CODE ALREADY IN USE
M02	TEACHER NUMBER NOT NUMERIC
M03	TEACHER NUMBER MUST BE NON-ZERO
M04	TEACHER CANNOT BE FOUND CODE DOES NOT EXIST
M05	COMPANY CODE ALREADY BEING USED
M06	TEACHER NAME IS MANDATORY
M07	TEACHER EXPERIENCE DESCRIPTION IS MANDATORY
M08	COMPANY NAME IS MANDATORY
M09	ACCOUNT NUMBER NOT NUMERIC
M10	ACCOUNT NUMBER MUST BE NON-NUMERIC
M11	ACCOUNT NUMBER ALREADY IN USE
M12	ADDRESS IS MANDATORY
M13	TELEPHONE NUMBER MUST BE NUMERIC
M14	TELEPHONE NUMBER MUST BE NON-ZERO
M15	COURSE NUMBER ALREADY IN USE
M16	COMPANY CODE CANNOT BE FOUND
M17	COURSE NAME IS MANDATORY
M18	NUMBER OF SESSIONS MUST BE NUMERIC
M19	PUBLIC COURSE ORGANISER MUST BE 'Y' OR 'N'
M20	DATE REQUIRED BY NOT NUMERIC
M21	NUMBER OF DAYS MUST BE NUMERIC
M22	COMPANY NUMBER MUST BE NUMERIC
M23	COMPANY NUMBER MUST BE NON-ZERO
M24	COURSE NUMBER MUST BE NUMERIC
M25	COURSE NUMBER MUST BE NON-ZERO
M26	PROVISIONAL END DATE NOT NUMERIC
M27	COURSE CODE CANNOT BE FOUND
M28	COMPANY LOCATION NOT FOUND
M29	HOTEL CODE NOT NUMERIC
M30	HOTEL CODE CANNOT BE FOUND
M31	HOTEL CODE MUST BE NON-ZERO
M32	PROVISIONAL START DATE NOT NUMERIC
M33	PROVISIONAL START DATE MUST BE IN FUTURE
M34	PROVISIONAL END DATE MUST BE IN FUTURE
M35	PROVISIONAL END DATE MUST BE LESS THAN START DATE
M36	COURSE GIVING MUST BE EITHER P (PUBLIC) OR H (IN-HOUSE)
M37	A COMPANY MUST HAVE AT LEAST ONE ADDRESS
M38	
M39	
M40	INVOICE ADDRESS LOCATION MUST BE 'Y' (IT IS INVOICE ADDRESS) OR 'N' (IT IS NOT INVOICE ADDRESS)
M41	INVOICE ADDRESS HAS NOT BEEN RECORDED
M42	MORE THAN ONE INVOICE ADDRESS IS NOT ALLOWED
M43	
M44	CURRENCY CODE NOT VALID
M45	PRICE PER PERSON MUST BE NUMERIC
M46	PRICE PER PERSON MUST BE NON-ZERO
M47	PRICE FOR IN-HOUSE COURSE NOT NUMERIC
M48	PRICE FOR IN-HOUSE COURSE MUST BE NON-ZERO

Figure 7.27

Embedded Elementary Activities

It is possible for one Elementary Activity to contain one or more other Elementary Activities.

For example, if we are in a hospital, to handle a patient's recovery we might have to cancel the operations a patient has, cancel the appointments and so on. These Activities may be actioned as a result of another Event in a "standalone" capacity.

Effectively, we have Elementary Activities which are themselves Procedures in other Elementary Activities – a rather special case.

It helps considerably in systems design if we show this special case diagrammatically and the way we do this is by using the Activity Decomposition Diagram.

In Figure 7.28, two alternative diagramming methods are shown – the 'spotlight' symbol and the "cocked hat" symbol.

In Figure 7.29, the example described above is shown diagrammatically.

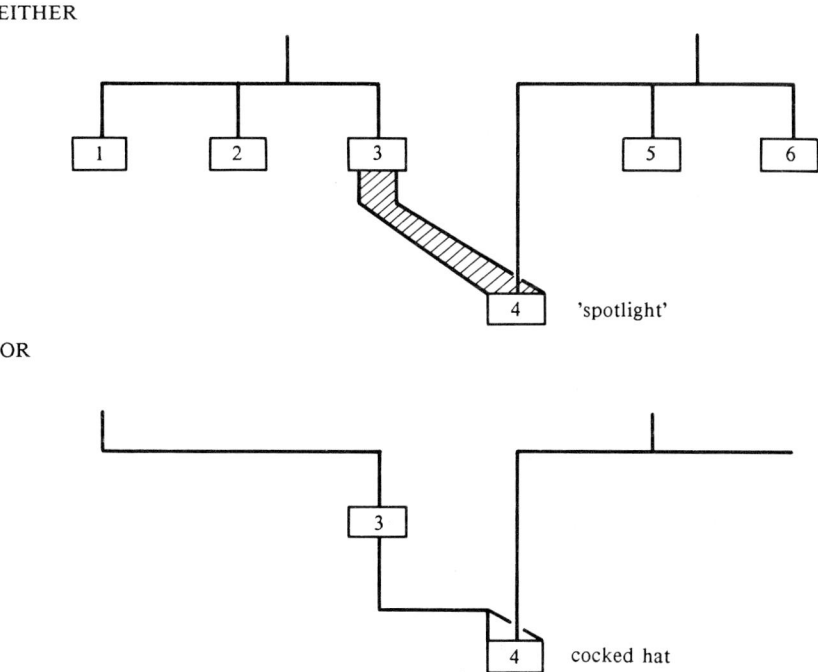

Figure 7.28 How to show embedded Activities on the Decomposition

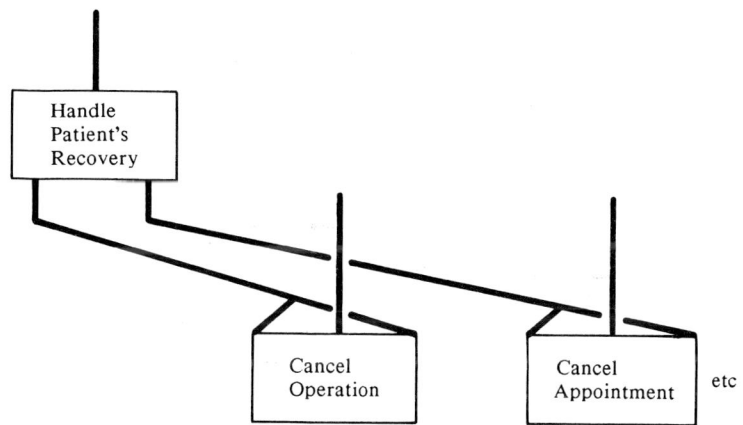

Figure 7.29 An example using the 'cocked hat' symbol

7.5. EXAMPLES OF ELEMENTARY ACTIVITIES

In the next few pages I have provided Access Paths and structured text for the examples from our Course Administration system.

The semi-structured text (which I haven't shown) would simply have been halfway between the two.

Fully structured text has many advantages, not least being the precision with which the analysis requirements are specified. Precision at this stage saves considerable time during design and

208 *A Simple Introduction to Data and Activity Analysis*

construction. It makes both tasks easier and less prone to error. Precision during analysis avoids the endless 'looping back' which occurs in most systems development departments as errors are found and attempts made to correct them, often without realising the impact of the error made.

The examples which follow are the Activities we discovered in the Activity Analysis chapter. In fact, these are all Elementary Activities.

From this structured text it is possible to improve the 'unstructured text' description used as the start point. This can be done by adding filler words to the structured text, removing the indentation and changing the wording slightly.

For example, using the first Activity,

"The teacher number is obtained
A check is made to make sure the teacher number is valid
The consultant details are found using the teacher number
If the details can't be found, processing stops with a Message to say they can't be found, otherwise the teacher name is displayed.
The courses are gone through in ascending course number order and the course number, name and abbreviated name are shown. If an indication is given that the teacher can teach the course, this is recorded."

This may seem a waste of time, but if user approval is being sought for each Activity, this form of presentation may be necessary. It is easily generated from structured text and could be achieved verbally rather than needing to be written down.

7.6. UPDATING THE DATA MODEL FROM THE ACCESS PATHS AND STRUCTURED ENGLISH (CONSISTENCY CHECKING)

The Access Paths and the structured English provide us with perhaps the most precise and important input in determining whether our Data Model is complete and correct. If we get the Data Model 'right' at this stage, it will save us many hours of wasted effort during design trying to hit a moving target, as we struggle with a changing model (caused by imprecise analysis results) and the complexities of a DBMS.

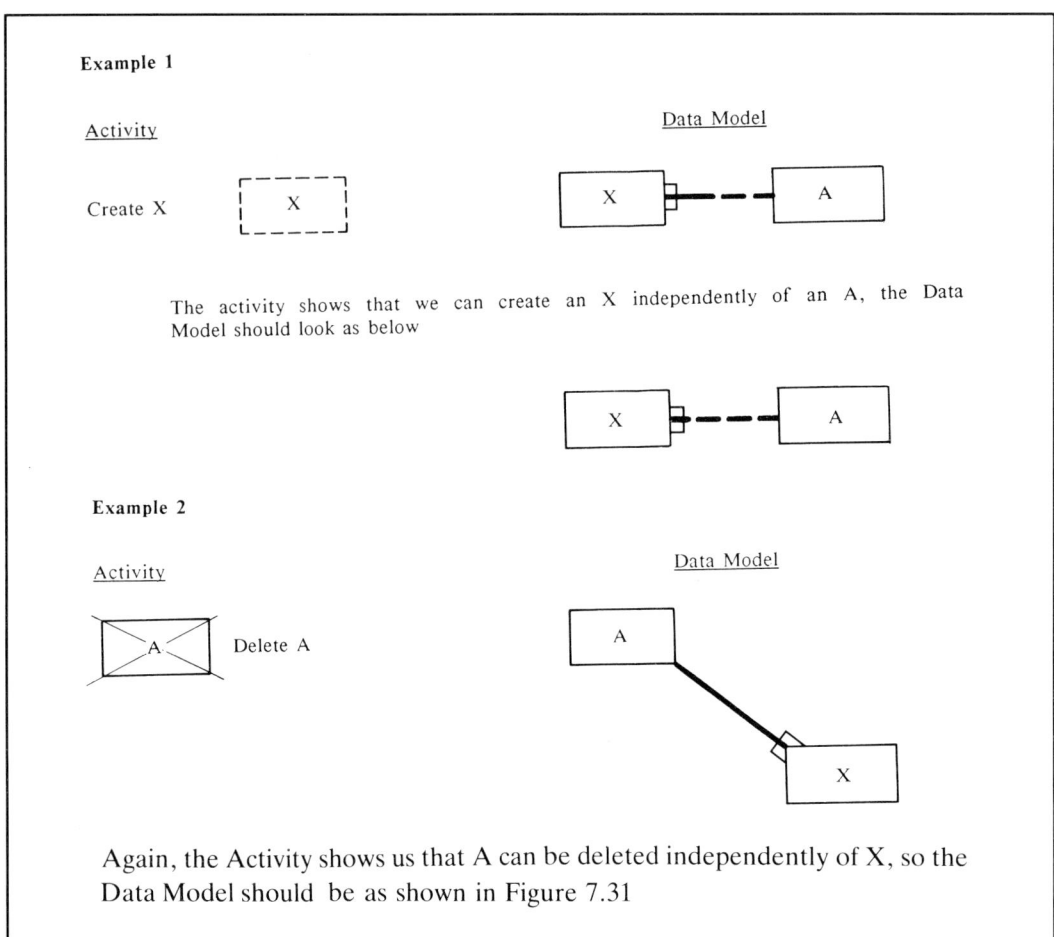

Figure 7.30

Elementary Activities 209

Each Access Path should be a sub-set of the Data Model. If it is not then either the Data Model or the Activity logic is wrong, and one or both should be changed. We may find missing Relationships and even missing Entities (particularly 'derived' ones). Another thing we may find is that a Relationship is optional where before we thought it to be mandatory or vice versa.

The Activities which *delete* and *create* data in the Data Model should be used to verify optionality. See Figures 7.30 and 7.31.

Figures 7.32–7.49 show how the access paths and structured logic from our Course Administration example might have looked.

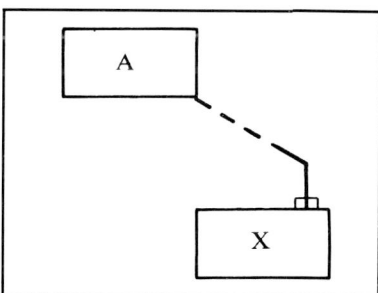

Figure 7.31

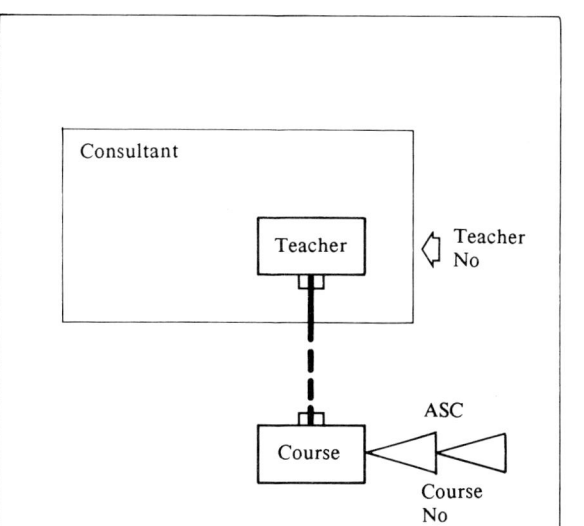

Record Teacher's Course Ability

When a consultant arrives, and is able to teach, the courses which he/she are able to give are recorded.

[The courses are selected from a list of those the company provides, rather than the user having to type in the course number. He prefers to select from a list.]

```
GET Teacher-Number
EXECUTE "Validate Teacher-Number"
FIND Consultant USING Teacher-Number
IF not exists
    ABANDON M04
OTHERWISE
    PRINT Teacher Name
    DO WHILE Courses in Ascending Course Number Order
        PRINT Course Number
        PRINT Course Name
        PRINT Abbreviated Name
        GET Can-Teach-Indicator
        IF Can-Teach-Indicator = 'Y'
            CONNECT Teacher To Course
        OTHERWISE
        ENDIF
    ENDDO
ENDIF
END
```

Figure 7.32

Disconnect Teacher from Course

A request from a manager or consultant may be made to be removed from the list of teachers who can teach a course - this may be on the basis of lack of time or change of interest.

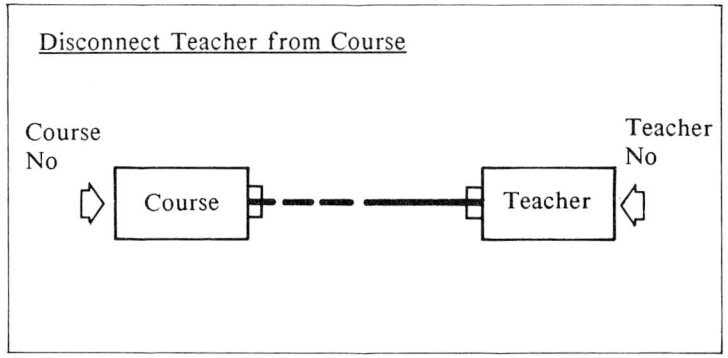

```
            GET Teacher-Number
            EXECUTE "Validate Teacher-Number"
            GET Course Number
            EXECUTE "Validate Course Number"
            FIND Teacher USING Teacher-Number
            IF not found
                 ABANDON M04
            OTHERWISE
                 PRINT Teacher Name
                 FIND Course USING Course Number
                 IF not found
                      ABANDON M27
                 OTHERWISE
                      PRINT Course Name
                      DISCONNECT Teacher FROM Course
                 ENDIF
            ENDIF
            END
```

Figure 7.33

Change Teacher's/Consultant's Name

A consultant may change his/her name or notice that it has been recorded wrongly, in which case the name must be changed.

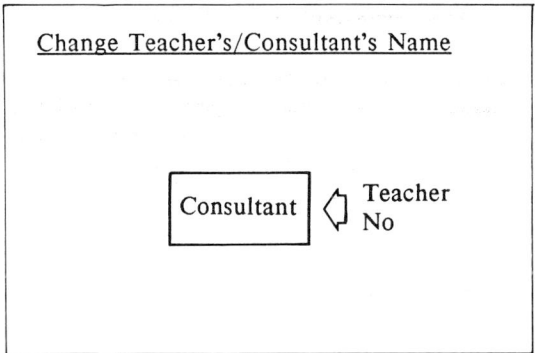

```
GET Teacher-Number
EXECUTE "Validate Teacher-Number"
FIND Consultant USING Teacher-Number
IF not found
     ABANDON M04
OTHERWISE
     PRINT Teacher Name
     GET Teacher Name
     IF Teacher Name = Blank or Zeros
          ABANDON M06
     OTHERWISE
          SET Teacher Name
     ENDIF
ENDIF
END
```

Figure 7.34

212 *A Simple Introduction to Data and Activity Analysis*

Record Consultant Details

When a new consultant joins, details about his/her previous experience, both in teaching and consultancy work, are recorded for use in selecting teachers for courses. This is in addition to his/her name (which is mandatory).

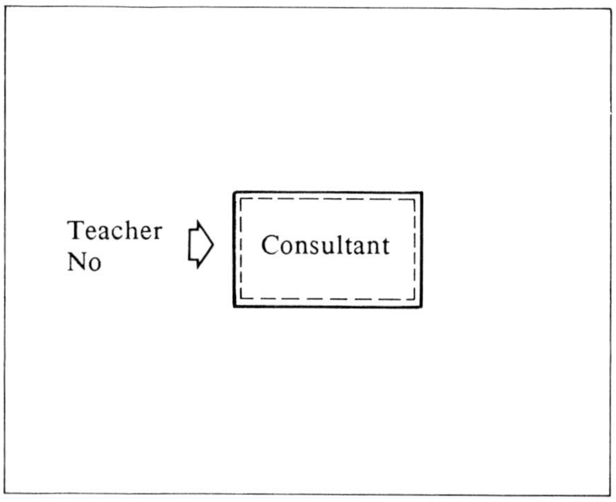

Teacher No ⇨ Consultant

GET Teacher Number
EXECUTE "Validate Teacher Number"
FIND Consultant USING Teacher Number
IF already exists
    ABANDON M01
OTHERWISE
    GET Teacher Name
    IF Teacher Name = blank
        ABANDON M06
    OTHERWISE
    ENDIF
    GET Description of Teaching Experience
    IF Description of Teaching Experience = blank
        ABANDON M07
    OTHERWISE
    ENDIF
    CREATE Teacher
ENDIF
END

Figure 7.35

Update teaching knowledge

When any teacher has done new consultancy work or gained extra teaching experience, their CV (curriculum vitae) is updated.

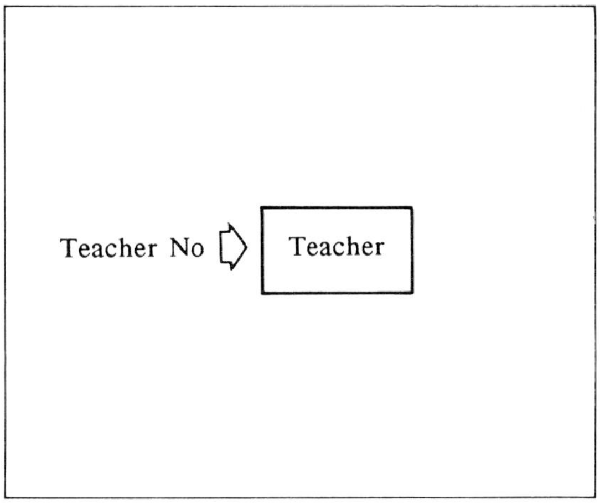

Teacher No ⇨ Teacher

```
GET Teacher Number
EXECUTE "Validate Teacher Number"
FIND Teacher USING Teacher Number
IF NOT EXISTS
    ABANDON M04
OTHERWISE
    GET Description of Teaching Experience
    IF Description of Teaching Experience = blank
        ABANDON M07
    OTHERWISE
        SET Description of Teaching Experience
    ENDIF
ENDIF
END
```

Figure 7.36

Send Teacher Course Giving Details

The teachers due to give a certain course giving are sent details of the course giving itself.

The details are:

- A list of students and their previous experience

- The location of the course

- Details of the course giving
  - dates etc

- The other teacher(s)

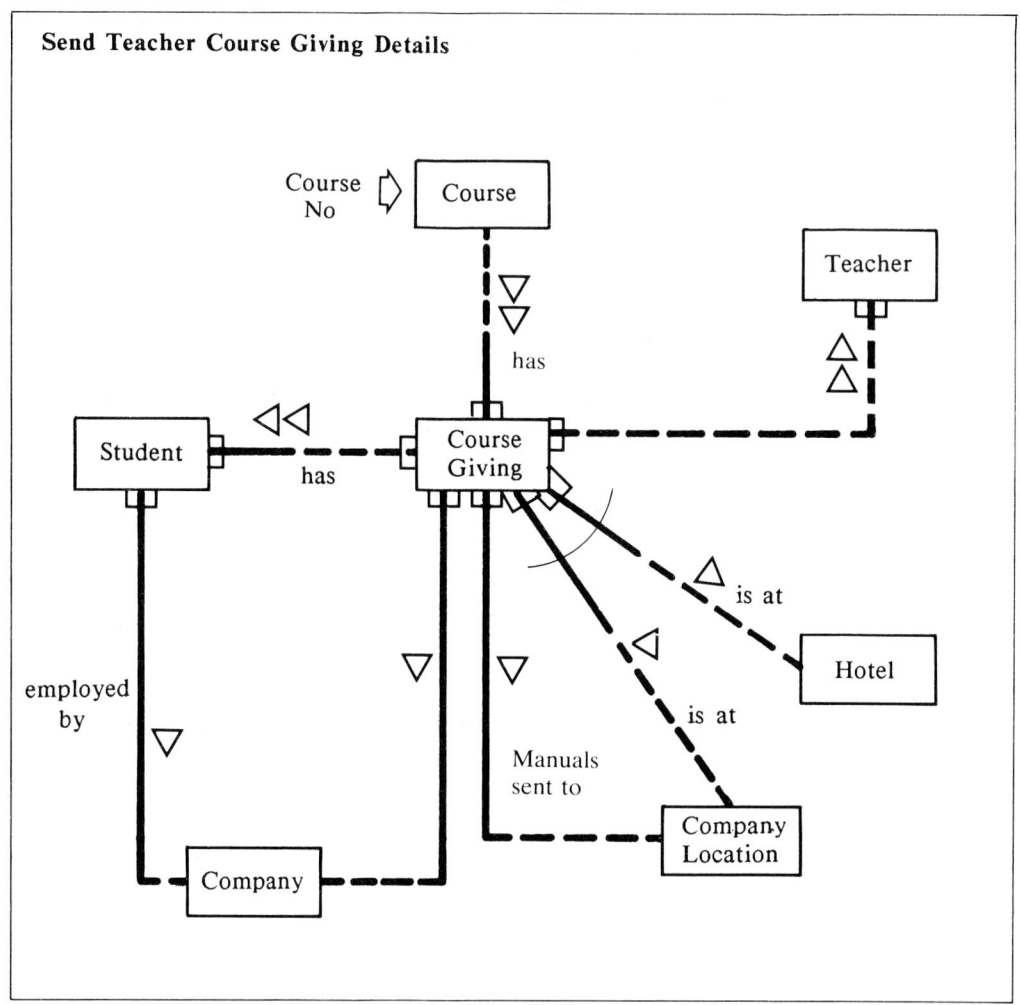

Figure 7.37

Send Teacher Course Giving Details

```
GET Course No
EXECUTE "Validate Course No"
FIND Course USING Course No
IF not found
      ABANDON M27
OTHERWISE
    PRINT Course Name
    DO WHILE Course Giving USING Course has Course Givings
        PRINT Provisional Start Date
        PRINT Provisional End Date
        PRINT Final Start Date
        PRINT Final End Date
        PRINT Public/In-house
        GET Course-Giving-found-indicator
        IF Course-Giving-found-indicator = 'Y'
            PRINT Manuals taken or Sent
            FIND Company Location USING Manuals sent to Company
                 Location
            PRINT Address of Company Location
            IF Course Giving is at Hotel
                FIND Hotel USING Course Giving is at Hotel
                PRINT Hotel Name
                PRINT Hotel Address
                PRINT Hotel Tel No
                PRINT Extension No of Booking Clerk
                PRINT Representative room cost per night
                PRINT Currency of Room Cost
            OTHERWISE
                FIND Company Location USING Course Giving is at
                     Company Location
                PRINT Address
                PRINT Description of Facilities
                PRINT Telephone Number
            ENDIF
            FIND Company USING Course Giving requested by Company
            PRINT Company Name
            DO WHILE Teacher USING Course Giving has Teachers
                PRINT Teacher Name
            ENDDO
            PRINT No of Students
            DO WHILE Students USING Course Giving has Students
                PRINT Student Name
                PRINT Student Job Title
                PRINT Experience
                FIND Company USING Student Employed by Company
                PRINT Company Name
            ENDDO
        OTHERWISE
        ENDIF
    ENDDO
ENDIF
END
```

Figure 7.38

216 *A Simple Introduction to Data and Activity Analysis*

Identify Teachers able to give Course Givings

The Courses are gone through in turn for all course givings requiring teachers. All the teachers able to give the course are identified and a check made that for the particular course giving they are not already booked for another course giving held at the same time.

A list of potential, suitable and free teachers is produced. When the list is produced a summary is also provided of the marks the lecturer obtained on past courses.

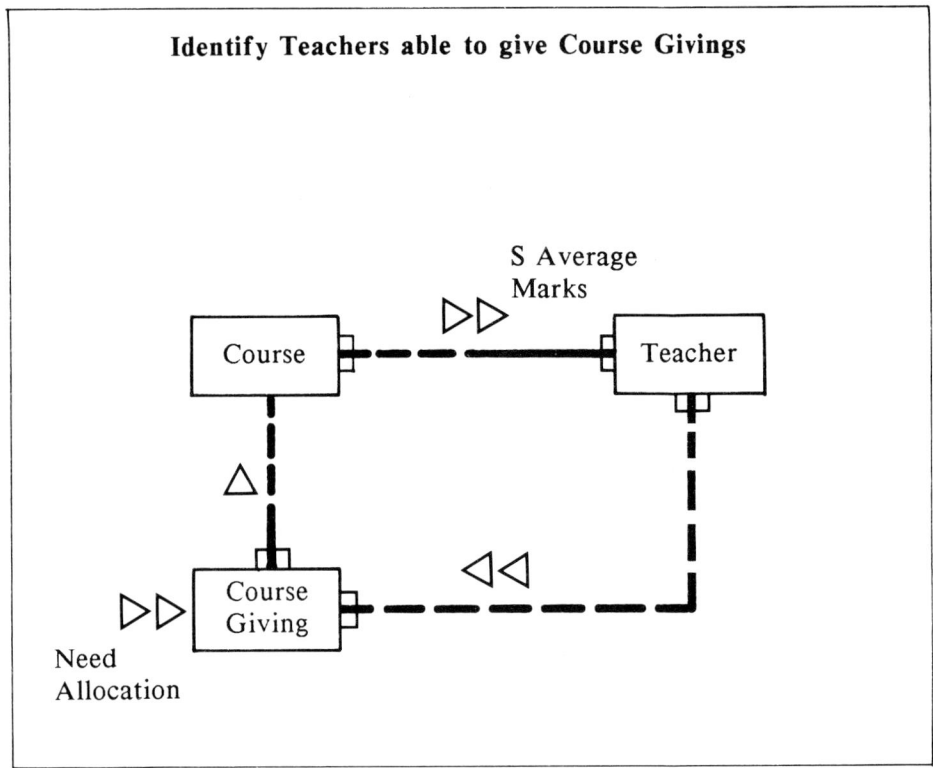

Figure 7.39

Identify Teachers Able to Give Course Givings

```
DO WHILE Course Giving
  IF Needs to be Allocated = Y
    PRINT Final Start Date
    PRINT Final End Date
    PRINT Provisional Start Date
    PRINT Provisional End Date
    FIND Course USING Course Giving is for Course
    PRINT Course Name
    DO WHILE Teacher USING Course has Teacher IN Descending
                                            Average Mark ORDER
      DO WHILE Course Givings USING Teacher will teach
                                    Course Giving (EXISTING)
      IF Finalised Start Date (of Existing Course Giving) ≠ 0
        IF Finalised Start Date (of Proposed Course Giving) ≠ 0
          IF ((Finalised Start Date (Proposed)≤
               Finalised End Date (EXISTING) AND≥
               Finalised Start Date (EXISTING)) OR
               (Finalised End Date (Proposed) ≥ Finalised
               Start Date (EXISTING) AND ≤ Finalised End
               Date (EXISTING))) GOTO 1
          OTHERWISE
            CONTINUE
          ENDIF
        OTHERWISE
          IF ((Provisional Start Date (Proposed) ≤
               Finalised End Date (EXISTING) AND ≥
               Finalised Start Date (EXISTING)) OR
               (Provisional End Date (Proposed) ≥
               Finalised Start Date (EXISTING) AND ≤
               Finalised End Date (EXISTING))) GOTO 1
          OTHERWISE
            CONTINUE
          ENDIF
        ENDIF
      OTHERWISE
        IF Finalised Start Date (of Proposed Course Giving) ≠ 0
          IF ((Finalised Start Date (Proposed) ≤
               Provisional End Date (EXISTING) AND ≥
               Provisional Start Date (EXISTING)) OR
               (Finalised end date (Proposed) ≥
               Provisional Start Date (EXISTING) AND ≤
               Provisional End Date (EXISTING))) GOTO 1
          OTHERWISE
            CONTINUE
          ENDIF
        OTHERWISE
          IF ((Provisional Start Date (Proposed) ≤
               Finalised End Date (EXISTING) AND ≥
               Provisional Start Date (EXISTING)) OR
               (Provisional) End Date (Proposed) ≥
               Provisional Start Date (EXISTING) AND ≤
               Provisional End Date (EXISTING))) GOTO 1
          OTHERWISE
            CONTINUE
          ENDIF
        ENDIF
      ENDIF
      ENDDO
      PRINT Teacher Number
      PRINT Teacher Name
      PRINT Average Marks
    1.Continue
    ENDDO
  OTHERWISE
    Continue
  ENDIF
ENDDO
PRINT "End of Course Givings"
END
```

Annotations:
- Course Giving Details used for asking teachers.
- Final Dates of Course Givings clash
- Provisional and Final Dates of Course Givings clash
- Provisional and Final Dates of Course Giving clash
- Provisional dates of Course Givings clash
- Teacher Details of teachers able to give course who are free on dates

Figure 7.40

218 *A Simple Introduction to Data and Activity Analysis*

Identify Course Givings of Teacher and Remove him from Imminent Givings

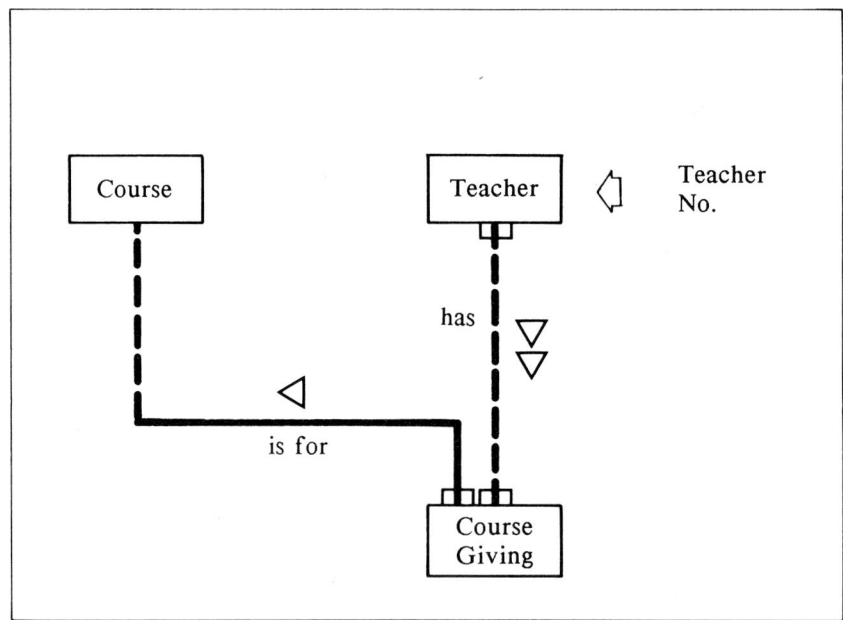

All the course givings a teacher was supposed to be giving (in the future) are listed. For each one, if the date of the course giving is imminent (i.e. near), the teacher is removed (disconnected) from the course giving and the course givings requiring allocation are marked.

Figure 7.41

Identify Course Givings of Teacher and Remove him from Imminent Givings

```
GET Teacher No
EXECUTE "Validate Teacher No"
FIND Teacher USING Teacher No
IF not found
      ABANDON M04
OTHERWISE
      DO WHILE Course Givings USING Teacher has Course Givings
            PRINT Provisional Start Date
            PRINT Provisional End Date
            PRINT Final Start Date
            PRINT Final End Date
            FIND Course USING Course Giving is for Course
            PRINT Course Name
            GET Course-Giving-Imminent-Signal
            IF Course-Giving-Imminent-Signal = 'Y'
                  DISCONNECT Teacher FROM Course Giving
                  SET Needs to be Allocated? = 'Y'
            OTHERWISE
            ENDIF
      ENDDO
ENDIF
END
```

Figure 7.42

Provisionally Book Teacher/Consultant to Course Giving

A provisional booking of the teacher to the course giving is made. The course is used as the start point and the course giving found by reference to the course. The list of willing and able teachers, is used to record which teacher will give the course giving.

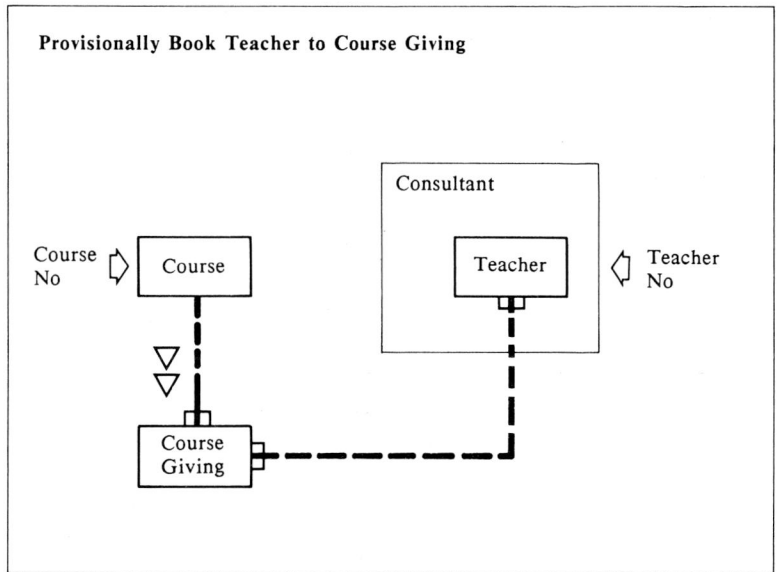

Provisionally Book Teacher to Course Giving

Figure 7.43

```
GET Course No
EXECUTE "Validate Course No"
FIND Course USING Course No
IF not found
      ABANDON M27
OTHERWISE
      PRINT Course Name
      DO WHILE Course Giving USING Course has Course Givings
            PRINT Provisional Start Date
            PRINT Provisional End Date
            PRINT Final Start Date
            PRINT Final End Date
            PRINT Public/In-house
            GET Course-Giving-Found Indicator
            IF Course-Giving-Found Indicator = 'Y'
                  GET Teacher Number
                  EXECUTE "Validate Teacher Number"
                  FIND Consultant USING Teacher Number
                  IF not found
                        ABANDON M04
                  OTHERWISE
                        PRINT Teacher Name
                        CONNECT Teacher to Course Giving
                  ENDIF
            OTHERWISE
            ENDIF
      ENDDO
ENDIF
END
```

Figure 7.44

Print Course Brochure

As new courses and teachers are added the "course brochure" must be updated. This means a new brochure must be produced showing both course details and course precedence details. A list of all the teachers who can give the courses is included, and their backgrounds are added at the end of each brochure (photos are added later).

(This brochure is used to send to clients or to take on consultancy/sales calls when an enquiry is made about a course.)

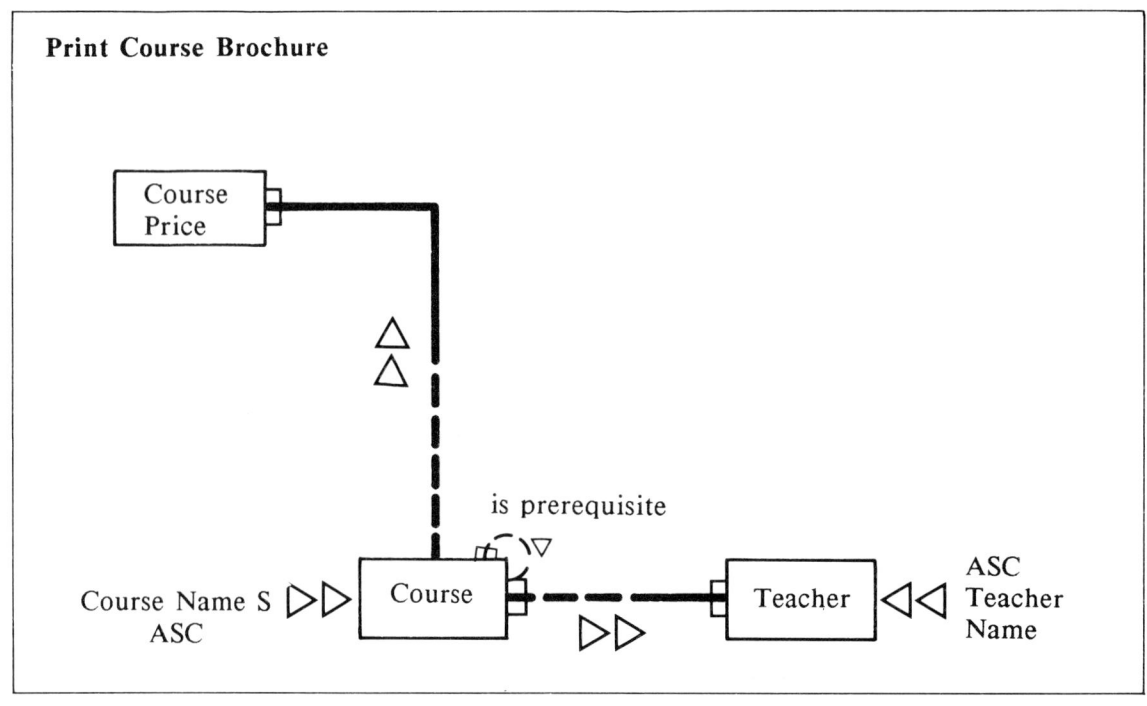

Figure 7.45

Print Course Brochure

```
SET Date Brochure Produced = Today's Date
PRINT Date Brochure Produced
DO WHILE Course IN ASCENDING Course Name ORDER
     PRINT Course Name
     PRINT Course No
     PRINT Type of Course
     PRINT No of Days of Course
     PRINT Abbreviated Name
     PRINT Description
     PRINT Course Objective
     PRINT Course Suitable for
     FIND Course USING Course is Prerequisite for Course
     PRINT Course Name
     PRINT Course Code
     DO WHILE Teacher USING Course has Teachers
          PRINT Teacher Name
     ENDDO
     DO WHILE Course Price USING Course has Course Price
          PRINT Currency
          PRINT Price per Person
          PRINT Price in house
     ENDDO
ENDDO
DO WHILE Teacher IN ASCENDING Teacher-Name Order
     PRINT Teacher Name
     PRINT Description of Teaching and Consultancy
                                         Experience
ENDDO
END
```

Course Details are printed first

Teacher Details are printed

Figure 7.46

Remove Teacher Details

When a consultant leaves, it is important that their CV is removed so that they are no longer considered for teaching. If the consultant was due to give any course givings they are marked as needing to be reallocated.

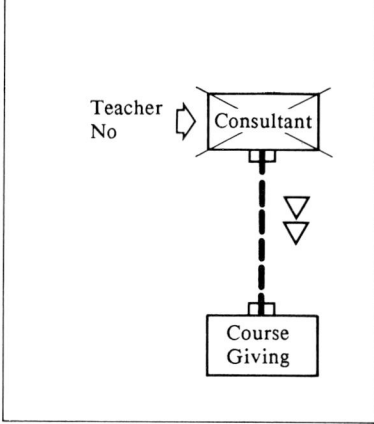

```
GET Teacher No
EXECUTE "Validate Teacher No"
FIND Consultant USING Teacher-No
IF not found
     ABANDON M04
OTHERWISE
     DO WHILE Course Givings USING Teacher has Course Givings
          SET Needs to be allocated? = 'Y'
     ENDDO
     DELETE Consultant
ENDIF
END
```

Figure 7.47

In our Data Model (Figure 7.48) we have been able to make a number of improvements. I have shown the part of the Model used by the Activities and added the accesses. A new Relationship has been added in – "Course Giving manuals sent to company location". Other Activities outside our particular area of study have shown that hotel details are recorded independently of the Course Giving and that the Course Giving is always requested by a company. This Relationship must be present and mandatory, otherwise we are unable to "produce the invoice".

The Elementary Activity logic has thrown up some interesting Attribute Synonyms,

'Final start date' and 'finalised start date'
'Final end date' and 'finalised end date'
'Out of a possible for this giving of' and 'out of'
'Name of lecturer' and 'teacher name'
'Number of lecturer' and 'teacher number' and 'teacher code'
'Description of teaching and consultancy experience' and 'description of teaching experience'
'Description' and 'full description of course for brochure'

There is also an Entity Synonym

'Course price' and 'Course price in currency'

A new Attribute is needed describing the Course Giving, 'needs to be allocated?' which shows that a Course Giving has lost one or more of its teachers through sickness or departure and needs to be reallocated to one or more new teachers.

There is also a new derived Attribute, 'average mark' which is calculated from the average marks the course giving obtained and what the marks were out of [the marks are all scaled to a comparative figure].

Four 'temporary' Attributes used in processing were also specified,

Can-teach-indicator
Course Giving found indicator
Course-Giving-imminent-signal
Date brochure produced

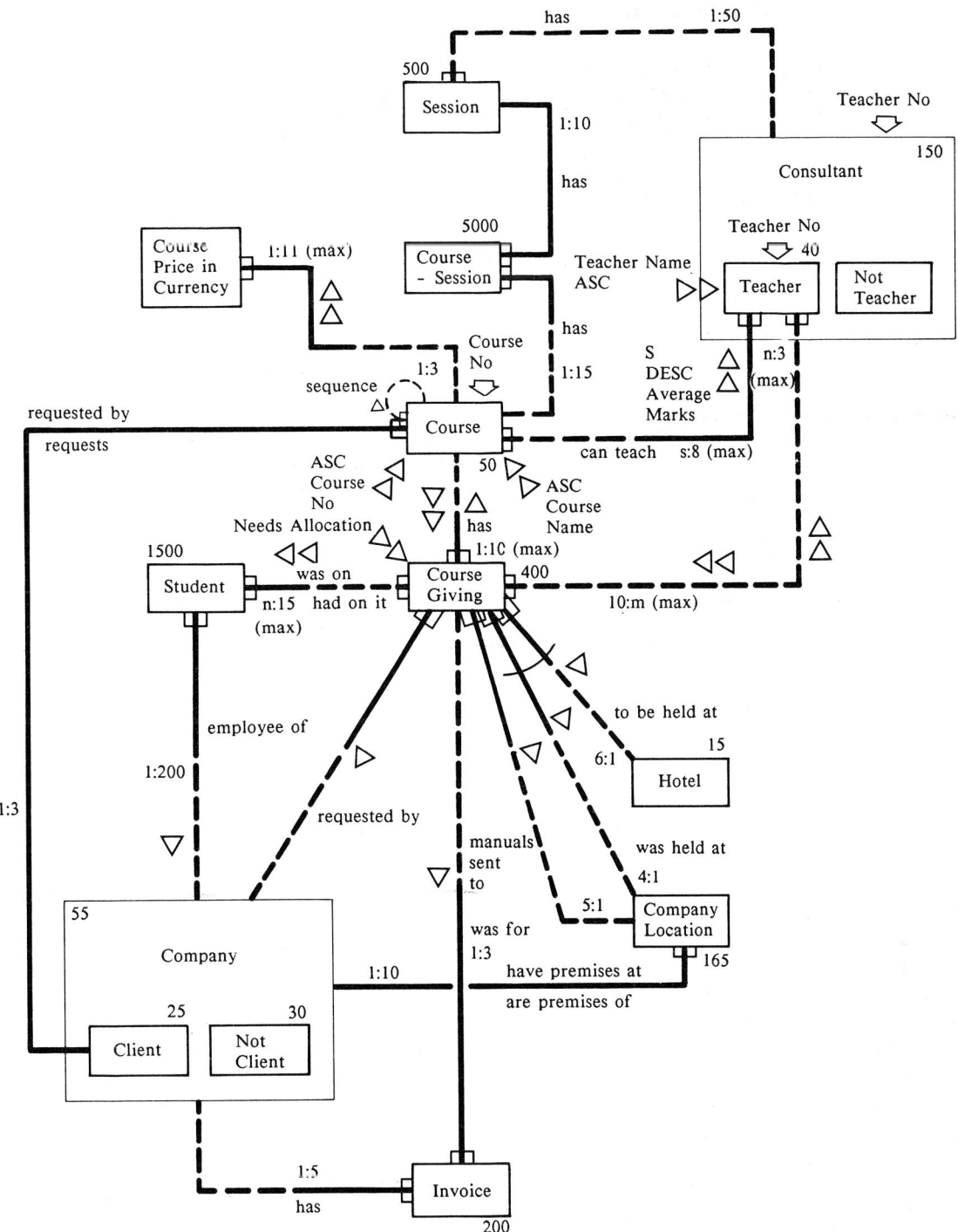

Figure 7.48 The Data Model showing improvements, accesses and quantifiable data

The list of Attributes in Figure 7.49 shows which Attributes were used by the Activities.

To help with the next step I have added some quantifiable information to the Data Model. The figures in the Entity boxes show maximum (in this case) volumes; the figures by the Relationships show the 'degree' of the Relationship, or how many of the one Entity are related to how many of another. In this case maximum degrees are shown.

The Data Model with the accesses on is the one we need for our particular Activities. It is, as it were, the Data Model in our sub-system or scope. Other Activities – those dealing with invoices, courses and Course Givings for example will use other parts of the Data Model and will probably use it in different ways.

Note that once all the Elementary Activities have been described, we should also produce the matrices described during 'Verification' in Chapter 5. Entity/Activity, Relationship/Activity and

List of Attributes

Hotel

Hotel Name
Hotel Address
Hotel Tel. No.
Extension No. of Booking Clerk
Representative room cost per night in currency
Currency of room cost
Hotel Code

Course Giving

Provisional Start Date
(Final) Start Date
(Final) End Date
Provisional End Date
No. of Students
Public/In-house
Overall Marks given
Out of a possible for this giving of
Manuals taken or sent?
Needs to be Allocated?

Invoice

Invoice Number
Date of Invoice
Amount Charged
Currency
Date Payable
Date sent

Company

Company Name
Account No.
Company Number

Course

Course No.
Course Name
No. of Sessions in Course
Abbreviated Name
Course suitable for
Full description of the course for the brochure
Date last updated
Type of Course (W, S, C)
No. of days of course
Course Objective
Date Produced
Date Required by

Session

Date Allocated to Consultant
Date Session created
No. of Slides in Session
Length of Session, average/mean time

Course Price in Currency

Currency of Course Price
Price per person
Price in-house

Company Location

Address
Invoice Address?
Description of Facilities
Telephone number

Course-Session

Length of Session on Course
Sequence of Session on Course

Student

Name
Job Title
Experience

Consultant

- Lecturer/Teacher

  Name of Lecturer
  Number of Lecturer
  Description of teaching and consultancy experience
  Average Mark (derived)
- Not-Teacher

Figure 7.49

Attribute/Activity Matrices should be produced to make sure that the end result is absolutely consistent.

7.7 OTHER USEFUL DETAILED DELIVERABLES OF AN ELEMENTARY ACTIVITY

There are three useful pieces of information which can be collected about an Elementary Activity. Each has a specific use during design – both system and database design.

The three deliverables are,

* The 'Response' required
* User/Activity responsibility and frequency
* Usage figures

Response required

The Response required does not have the definition normally associated with it when we discuss the design of a system. Response, when used to describe an Elementary Activity, is an indication of how quickly the user(s) of the Activity wish the Activity to be executed in relation to the Event which triggered it, the Objective they wish to satisfy or the obligation they must fulfil.

There are only two types of Response required as far as we are concerned – immediate or not immediate.

This deliverable is used in design to decide what sort of transaction is needed batch, real-time, on-line or on-line initiated with batch background.

User/Activity Responsibility

Each Elementary Activity needs to be the responsibility of one or more users. By 'user', I mean a

EVENT USER/ACTIVITY RESPONSIBILITY MATRIX

Event: ....   Consultant Goes Sick

ACTIVITY \ User	Identify Course Givings and remove	Identify Teachers Able to Give Course Giving	Check on Availability and choose	Provisionally book Teacher to Course Giving	Send Teacher Course Giving Details					
Department Managers										
Accounts										
Consultants										
Training Manager	13	13		26						
Training Administrator			208							
Secretaries					26					

(maxima per month)

Figure 7.50

226 *A Simple Introduction to Data and Activity Analysis*

job not a person. The current responsibility for the Activities should be known from your "raw input". If a user in an interview describes what he does then we know those Activities are his responsibility. Similarly, user job descriptions will tell us the same thing.

The results can be expressed as a matrix, and an example is shown in Figure 7.50. The users are listed on one axis, the Elementary Activities on the other. If that user is responsible for that Activity then either a cross can be put in the intersection box or, as has been shown in the example, the frequency with which he currently executes that Activity can be shown. It is most important that one matrix is produced *per Event*, as the frequencies are Event frequency dependant. Notice how the iteration and optionality of the Activity has affected the frequency figures. Figures 7.51 to 7.55 provide more examples.

EVENT USER/ACTIVITY RESPONSIBILITY MATRIX

Event: ....   New Consultant Arrives

User \ ACTIVITY	Record Consultant Details	Record Teacher's Course Ability	Print Course Brochure							
Department Managers	10									
Accounts										
Consultants	4									
Training Manager		6								
Training Administrator			6							
Secretaries										

Maximum times per month

Figure 7.51

For critical systems or Activities, for example an airline reservation system, we need to express frequency as a histogram over time per user and Activity and Event. In other words, show as a graph the frequency with which that particular Activity was executed by that user over the time span, for the event.

   e.g.   User A executed Activity 1 400 times on 10th May 1987 as a result of Event X

This gives us the information on critical times needed to plan for distribution, work out manning figures and a host of other important design tasks.

My four books on Analysis (see Preface on page vii) give more details about this.

Elementary Activities 227

EVENT USER/ACTIVITY RESPONSIBILITY MATRIX

Event: .... Consultant Decides to Stop Teaching

User \ ACTIVITY	Disconnect Teacher from Course	Print Course Brochure									
Department Managers											
Accounts											
Consultants											
Training Manager	3										
Training Administrator		3									
Secretaries											

Maximum times per month

Figure 7.52

EVENT USER/ACTIVITY RESPONSIBILITY MATRIX

Event: .... Consultant Does New Work

User \ ACTIVITY	Update Teaching Knowledge	Record Teacher's Course Ability	Print Course Brochure								
Department Managers	20										
Accounts											
Consultants	1										
Training Manager		12									
Training Administrator			12								
Secretaries											

Maxima per month

Figure 7.53

228   *A Simple Introduction to Data and Activity Analysis*

EVENT USER/ACTIVITY RESPONSIBILITY MATRIX

Event: ....   Consultant leaves

User \ ACTIVITY	Remove Teacher Details	Identify Teachers Able to Give Course Giving	Check on Availability and choose	Provisionally book Teacher to Course Giving	Send Teacher Course Giving Details	Print Course Brochure					
Department Managers											
Accounts											
Consultants											
Training Manager	7	7	224	28							
Training Administrator					7						
Secretaries			100		28						

Maxima per month

Figure 7.54

EVENT USER/ACTIVITY RESPONSIBILITY MATRIX

Event: ....   Consultant Name Change

User \ ACTIVITY	Change Teacher's Name	Print Course Brochure									
Department Managers	1										
Accounts											
Consultants	2										
Training Manager	1										
Training Administrator	1	5									
Secretaries											

Maxima per month

Figure 7.55

Elementary Activities 229

User Responsibility Summary Matrix

Elementary Activities	Department Managers	Consultants	Secretaries	Training Administrator	Training Manager
Record Consultant Details	10	4			
Update Teaching Knowledge	20	1			
Send Teachers Course Giving Details			54		
Print Course Brochure				33	
Identify Teachers Able to give Course Givings					20
Provisionally Book Teacher to Course Giving					54
Change Teacher's Name	1	2		1	1
Remove Teacher details					7
Record Teacher's Course Ability					18
Identify Course Givings of Teacher and remove him from Imminent givings					13
Check Availability and Choose			100	208	224
Disconnect Teacher from Course					3

Max Times per month

Figure 7.56

The sort of histogram we might use to record frequency is shown in Figure 7.57.

The Activity name, Event name and the user job name are placed at the top to show which user and Activity is being measured and if any restrictions on the times of access to an Activity must be imposed these too can be entered. This provides a useful check on the frequency figures entered, as the times of access and frequency in the histogram need to be consistent. If the times of access are restricted to weekdays for example, no frequency figures will be shown for Saturdays and Sundays.

The histogram is filled out using actual figures collected by measurements. They are thus historical and the 'time' axis will show past dates and times,

e.g. Saturday 10th August 9 a.m. – 10 a.m.

The time intervals shown depend on how critical the Activity is. The more critical the Activity the smaller the time intervals should be.

Figures can be projected into the future, if you wish to predict growth and therefore future use. This will be particularly important if the system is being studied because growth is predicted.

USAGE FIGURES

In Figure 7.58 is a table which can be used to collect and calculate usage figures. These figures show – by user – how *many* Entity Occurrences are accessed at each stage of the processing.

The figures are the basis for distribution planning, database design and systems design.

The 'name' is the name of the Elementary Activity, the 'description', is the description in semi-structured or structured text of the Activity. The 'users' are those users (there may only be one or two) responsible for the Activity. (This deliverable was collected in the last step.)

Each user may be interested in a different "partition" of the data. For example, a clerk in the 'tool division' of a company may be interested only in 'tool orders'; a clerk in the 'pipe division' may be

USER/ACTIVITY DETAIL

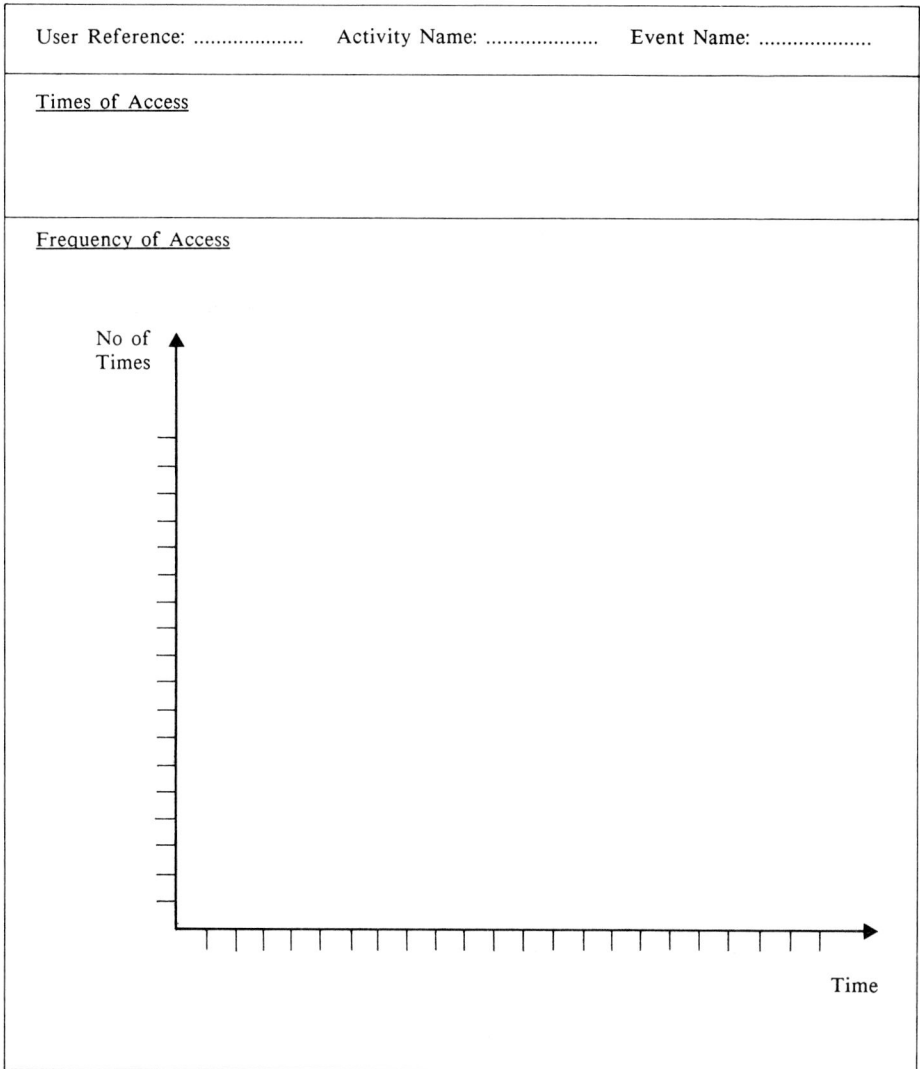

Figure 7.57

interested only in 'pipe orders'. The *population* of each type may be different, so there is a need to keep the calculations separate by user – if they are in different parts of the organisation.

The number of logical accesses being made on the Entities of a certain type for a particular user are entered for each step which accesses Entities.

The following rules apply:
- (i) Where *all* Entities of a type are being accessed (DO WHILE): Use the *mode* (most frequently occurring) or *maximum* (if the volumes are increasing) number of Entities of that type which occur in the "partition" in which the user is situated. (See Figure 7.59.)
- (ii) Where some Entities of a type are being accessed (DO WHILE with selection): Use the mode or maximum volume as above as a start point and using Entity sub-type or user input, assess what percentage of these basic volume figures will be hit.
- (iii) Where Entities of a type are being found using a Relationship type (DO WHILE USING): The *mode degree* (most frequently occurring) of the Relationship type is used or the maximum degree (if no mode exists). (See Figure 7.60.)
- (iv) Where Entities of a type are being found using a Relationship type (as above), but with selection then the users must be asked to assess what percentage of the basic mode or maximum number will be hit.
- (v) Where the type of access is "FIND" – the number of logical accesses is always 1.

Elementary Activities 231

ELEMENTARY ACTIVITY ACCESS PATH USAGE

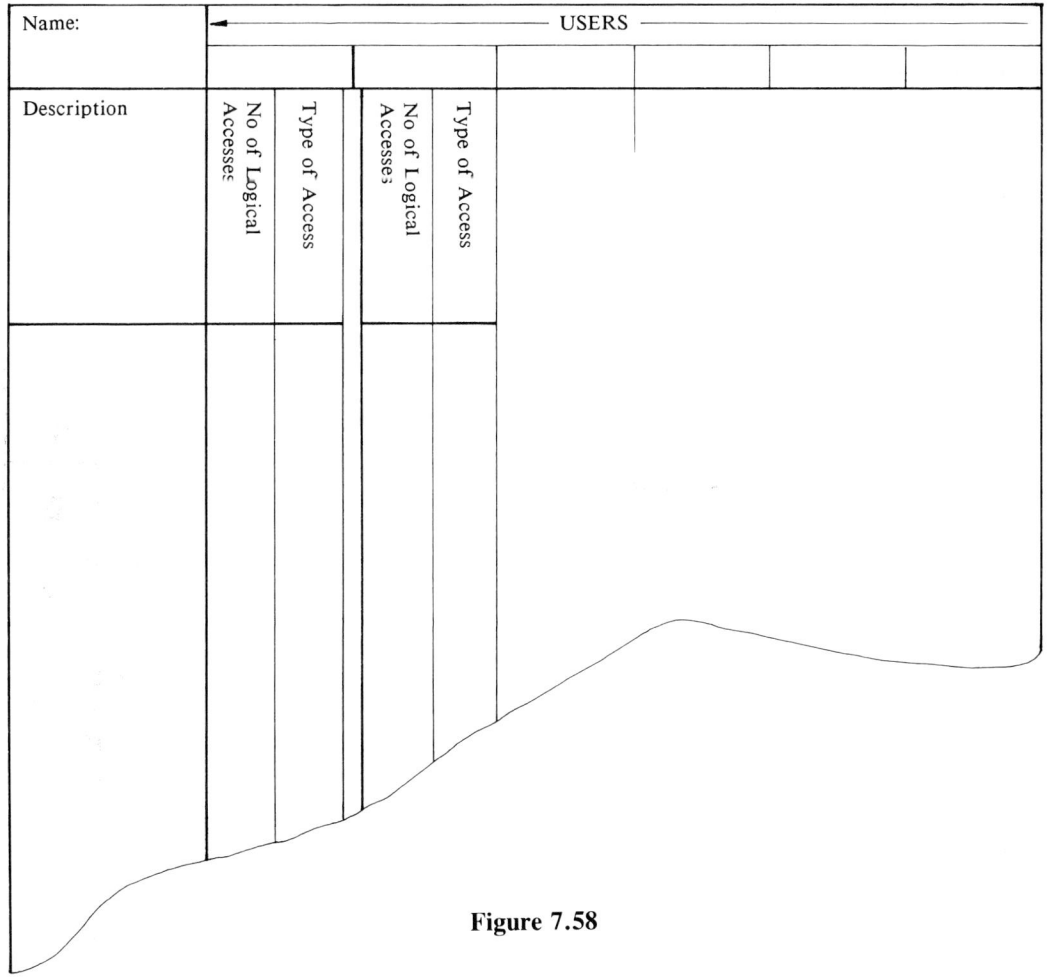

Figure 7.58

Entity X-Volumes

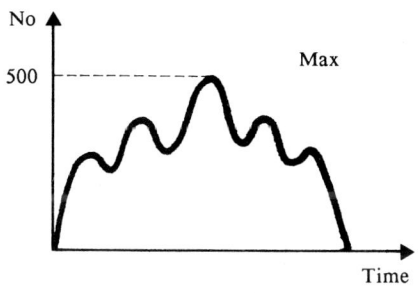

Figure 7.59

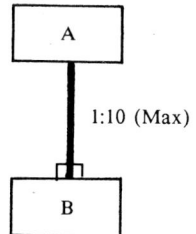

Figure 7.60

232 *A Simple Introduction to Data and Activity Analysis*

The type of access simply describes the kind of logical access being made on the Entity at that stage,

e.g. L = Look (FIND)
    D = Delete
    C = Create
    M = Modify/Amend (= Find and Amend).

This may seem a trifle complicated but in practice is easy to work out. (Again, my four books on Analysis give more detail on these deliverables and their uses).

In the following pages the examples used up to now for the Course Administration System are shown and explained. (See Figures 7.61–7.66.)

Examples of Elementary Activity Access Path Usage

Name: RECORD TEACHER'S COURSE ABILITY	Training Manager	
Description	No of Logical Accesses	Type of Access

GET Teacher-Number
EXECUTE "Validate Teacher Number"
FIND Consultant USING Teacher Number
IF not exists
    ABANDON M04
OTHERWISE
    PRINT Teacher Name
    DO WHILE Courses IN Ascending Course Number ORDER
        PRINT Course Number
        PRINT Course Name
        PRINT Abbreviated Name
        GET Can-Teach-Indicator
        IF Can-Teach-Indicator = 'Y'
            CONNECT Teacher TO Course
        OTHERWISE
        ENDIF
    ENDDO
ENDIF
END
	1
	
	50
		L
		
		L

Figure 7.61

Name:			USERS →						
CHANGE TEACHER'S/CONSULTANT'S NAME		Dept Manager		Consultant		Training Administrator		Training Manager	
	Description	Type of Access	No of Logical Accesses	Type of Access	No of Logical Accesses	Type of Access	No of Logical Accesses	Type of Access	No of Logical Accesses
	GET Teacher-Number								

	EXECUTE "Validate Teacher Number"
	FIND Consultant USING Teacher-Number
	IF not found
	  ABANDON M04
	OTHERWISE
	  PRINT Teacher Name
	  GET Teacher Name
	  IF Teacher Name = blank or zeros
	    ABANDON M06
	  OTHERWISE
	    SET Teacher Name
	  ENDIF
	ENDIF
	
	END
		L
		
		A
			1
			
			1
				L
				
				A
					1
					
					1
						L
						
						A
							1
							
							1
								L
								
								A
									1
									
									1

Figure 7.62

234 *A Simple Introduction to Data and Activity Analysis*

Name: DISCONNECT TEACHER FROM COURSE	Training Manager	
Description	No of Logical Accesses	Type of Access

GET Teacher-Number
EXECUTE "Validate Teacher Number"
GET Course Number
EXECUTE "Validate Course Number"
FIND Teacher USING Teacher-Number
IF not found
    ABANDON M04
OTHERWISE
    PRINT Teacher Name
    FIND Course USING Course Number
    IF not found
        ABANDON M27
    OTHERWISE
        PRINT Course Name
        DISCONNECT Teacher FROM Course
    ENDIF
ENDIF
END
	1
	
	1
		L
		
		L

Figure 7.63

Name: Update Teaching Knowledge	Dept Manager		Consultant	
Description	No of Logical Accesses	Type of Access	No of Logical Accesses	Type of Access

GET Teacher-Number
EXECUTE "Validate Teacher Number"
FIND Teacher USING Teacher-Number
IF NOT EXISTS
    ABANDON M04
OTHERWISE
    GET Description of Teaching Experience
    IF Description of Teaching Experience = blank
        ABANDON M07
    OTHERWISE
        SET Description of teaching experience
    ENDIF
ENDIF
END
	1
	
	1
		L
		
		A
			1
			
			1
				L
				
				A

Figure 7.64

236 A Simple Introduction to Data and Activity Analysis

Name: Record Consultant Details		Dept Manager		Consultant	
Description		No of Logical Accesses	Type of Access	No of Logical Accesses	Type of Access

GET Teacher-Number
EXECUTE "Validate Teacher Number"
FIND Consultant USING Teacher-Number
IF already exists
    ABANDON M01
OTHERWISE
    GET Teacher Name
    IF Teacher Name = blank
        ABANDON M06
    OTHERWISE
    ENDIF
    GET Description of Teaching Experience
    IF Description of Teaching Experience = blank
        ABANDON M07
    OTHERWISE
    ENDIF
    CREATE Teacher
ENDIF
END
		1
		
		1
			L
			
			C
				1
				
				1
					L
					
					C

Figure 7.65

SEND TEACHER COURSE GIVING DETAILS	SECRETARIES	
	Type of Access	No of Logical Accesses
GET Course No EXECUTE "Validate Course No"		
FIND Course USING Course No	L	1
IF not found ABANDON M27 OTHERWISE PRINT Course Name		
DO WHILE Course Giving USING Course has Course Givings	L	10
PRINT Provisional Start Date PRINT Provisional End Date PRINT Final Start Date PRINT Final End Date PRINT Public/In-house GET Course-Giving-found-Indicator IF Course-Giving-found-Indicator = 'Y' PRINT Manuals taken or Sent? FIND Company Location USING Manuals sent to Company Location	L	1
PRINT Address of Company Location IF Course Giving is at Hotel FIND Hotel USING Course Giving is at Hotel	L	1
PRINT Hotel Name PRINT Hotel Address PRINT Hotel Tel No PRINT Extension No of Booking Clerk PRINT Representative room cost per night PRINT Currency of Room cost OTHERWISE FIND Company Location USING Course Giving is at Company Location	L	1
PRINT Address PRINT Description of Facilities PRINT Telephone Number ENDIF FIND Company USING Course Giving requested by Company	L	1
PRINT Company Name DO WHILE Teacher USING Course Giving has Teachers	L	3
PRINT Teacher Name ENDDO PRINT No of Students DO WHILE Students USING Course Giving has Students	L	15
PRINT Student Name PRINT Student Job Title PRINT Experience FIND Company USING Student Employed by Company	L	15
PRINT Company Name ENDDO OTHERWISE ENDIF ENDDOENDIFEND		

Figure 7.66

Only one user performs this Activity. The Course Givings are searched until one is found, after which no others will be processed, so printing the details occurs once, but the search for the Course Giving required could take 10 accesses – the maximum number of Course Givings for a course.

There is a maximum of 15 students on any Course Giving and because the company of each student is required there will be 15 accesses on the Company Entity.

A maximum of 3 teachers teach a Course Giving.

PROVISIONALLY BOOK TEACHER TO COURSE GIVING	TRAINING MANAGER	
	No of Logical Accesses	Type of Access

GET Course No
EXECUTE "Validate Course No"
FIND Course USING Course No
IF not found
    ABANDON M27
OTHERWISE
    PRINT Course Name
	1	L

DO WHILE Course Giving USING Course has Course Givings
        PRINT Provisional Start Date
        PRINT Provisional End Date
        PRINT Final Start Date
        PRINT Final End Date
        PRINT Public/In-house
        GET Course-Giving-Found-Indicator
        IF Course-Giving-Found-Indicator = 'Y'
            GET Teacher Number
            EXECUTE "Validate Teacher Number"
	10	L

FIND Consultant USING Teacher Number
            IF not found
                ABANDON M04
            OTHERWISE
                PRINT Teacher Name
                CONNECT Teacher TO Course Giving
            ENDIF
        OTHERWISE
        ENDIF
    ENDDO
ENDIF
END
	1	L

Figure 7.67

See Figure 7.67 above. Again, we will need a maximum of ten accesses to find a Course Giving, but once found only one item will be of interest.

See Figure 7.68. There are over 400 Course Givings, but only a very small percentage need to be allocated because of sickness or consultant departure – at most three or four, and on average only one or two. Each Course Giving has one course hence as two Course Givings are accessed, two courses will be accessed. A course has a maximum of eight teachers able to teach it, hence the accesses will be 16. A teacher has a maximum of ten Course Givings, hence for the teachers a maximum of 10×16 accesses will result, assuming all Course Givings are gone through (the worst case).

Elementary Activities 239

	TRAINING MANAGER	
Identify Teachers Able to Give Course	No of Logical Accesses	Type of Access
DO WHILE Course Giving		
IF Needs to be Allocated = Y	2	L
PRINT Final Start Date		
PRINT Final End Date		
PRINT Provisional Start Date		
PRINT Provisional End Date		
FIND Course USING Course Giving is for Course	2	L
PRINT Course Name		
DO WHILE Teacher USING Course has Teacher IN Descending Average Mark ORDER	16	L
DO WHILE Course Givings USING Teacher will teach Course Giving (EXISTING)	160	L

```
                IF Finalised Start Date (of Existing Course
                                                      Giving) ≠ 0
                    IF Finalised Start Date (of Proposed Course ≤
                                                      Giving) ≠ 0 ≥
                       IF ((Finalised Start Date (Proposed)
                           Finalised End Date (EXISTING) AND
                           Finalised Start Date (EXISTING)) OR
                           (Finalised End Date (Proposed) ≥ Finalised
                           Start Date (EXISTING) AND ≤ Finalised End
                           Date (EXISTING))) GOTO 1
                       OTHERWISE
                          CONTINUE
                       ENDIF
                    OTHERWISE
                       IF ((Provisional Start Date (Proposed) ≤
                           Finalised End Date (EXISTING) AND ≥
                           Finalised Start Date (EXISTING)) OR
                           (Provisional End Date (Proposed) ≥
                           Finalised Start Date (EXISTING) AND ≤
                           Finalised End Date (EXISTING))) GOTO 1
                       OTHERWISE
                          CONTINUE
                       ENDIF
                    ENDIF
                OTHERWISE
                   IF Finalised Start Date (of Proposed Course
                                                      Giving ≠ 0
                       IF ((Finalised Start Date (Proposed) ≤
                           Provisional End Date (EXISTING) AND ≥
                           Provisional Start Date (EXISTING)) OR
                           (FINALISED END DATE (Proposed) ≥
                           Provisional Start Date (EXISTING) AND ≤
                           Provisional End Date (EXISTING)))
                                    GOTO 1
                       OTHERWISE
                           CONTINUE
                       ENDIF
                    OTHERWISE
                       IF ((Provisional Start Date (Proposed) ≤
                           Finalised End Date (EXISTING) AND ≥
                           Provisional Start Date (EXISTING)) OR
                           (Provisional) End Date (Proposed) ≥
                           Provisional Start Date (EXISTING) AND ≤
                           Provisional End Date (EXISTING))) GOTO 1
                       OTHERWISE
                           CONTINUE
                    ENDIF
                  ENDIF
                ENDIF
              ENDDO
              PRINT Teacher Number
              PRINT Teacher Name
              PRINT Average Marks
                  1 ......    Continue
           ENDDO
        OTHERWISE
              Continue
        ENDIF
      ENDDO
      PRINT "End of Course Givings"
      END
```

Figure 7.68

Name: IDENTIFY COURSE GIVINGS OF TEACHER AND REMOVE HIM FROM IMMINENT GIVINGS	TRAINING MANAGER	
Description	No of Logical Accesses	Type of Access

GET Teacher No
EXECUTE "Validate Teacher No"
FIND Teacher USING Teacher No
IF not found
    ABANDON M04
OTHERWISE
    DO WHILE Course Givings USING Teacher has Course Givings
        PRINT Provisional Start Date
        PRINT Provisional End Date
        PRINT Final Start Date
        PRINT Final End Date
        FIND Course USING Course Giving is for Course
        PRINT Course Name
        GET Course-Giving-Imminent-Signal
        IF Course-Giving-Imminent-Signal = 'Y'
            DISCONNECT Teacher FROM Course Giving
            SET Needs to be Allocated? = 'Y'
        OTHERWISE
        ENDIF
    ENDDO
ENDIF
END
	1
	
	10
	
	10
	
	2
		L
		
		L
		
		L
		
		A

Figure 7.69

As only one or two Course Givings of the teacher will be imminent, only two Course Givings will be amended.

PRINT COURSE BROCHURE

	TRAINING ADMINISTRATOR	
	No of Logical	Type of Access
SET Date Brochure Produced = Today's Date		
PRINT Date Brochure Produced		
DO WHILE Course IN ASCENDING Course Name ORDER	50	L
PRINT Course Name		
PRINT Course No		
PRINT Type of Course		
PRINT No of Days of Course		
PRINT Abbreviated Name		
PRINT Description		
PRINT Course Objective		
PRINT Course Suitable for		
FIND Course USING Course is Prerequisite for Course	15	L
PRINT Course Name		
PRINT Course Code		
DO WHILE Teacher USING Course has Teachers	400	L
PRINT Teacher Name		
ENDDO		
DO WHILE Course Price USING Course has Course Price	550	L
PRINT Currency		
PRINT Price per Person		
PRINT Price in house		
ENDDO		
ENDDO		
DO WHILE Teacher IN ASCENDING Teacher-Name Order	40	L
PRINT Teacher Name		
PRINT Description of Teaching and Consultancy Experience		
ENDDO		
END		

Figure 7.70

There are about 50 courses of which only 15 specify a prerequisite course which must be attended. A course has a maximum of eight teachers able to teach it, hence accesses are (50x8). Similarly, there are a maximum of 11 currencies in which courses can be quoted ($, £, DFl, Fr Francs, SWF, Belg Francs, German Marks, Lire, Spanish Peseta, Norwegian Kroner, Swedish Krona) giving a total number of accesses of (11x50). There are over 150 consultants, but only 40 are teachers.

Name: REMOVE TEACHER DETAILS	TRAINING MANAGER	
Description	No of Logical Accesses	Type of Access

GET Teacher No
EXECUTE "Validate Teacher No"
FIND Consultant USING Teacher-No
IF not found
    ABANDON M04
OTHERWISE
    DO WHILE Course Givings USING Teacher has Course Givings
        SET Needs to be allocated? = 'Y'
    ENDDO
    DELETE Consultant
ENDIF
END
	1
	
	10
	10
	
	1
		L
		
		L
		A
		
		D

Figure 7.71

7.8 SUMMARY

Elementary Activities are the Activities we will be using to 'map' or convert into the transactions in our design. If they update data, they are an integrity unit of processing; if they output data, they are units which provide all the output needed by the Sink or next Activity.

Elementary Activities can be described using ordinary text, semi-structured text and fully structured text. Ordinary text on its own – though acceptable as a means of gaining user approval – is unsuited to precise and unambiguous description, and the latter two forms, semi and fully structured text, are far more preferable.

The text is accompanied by Access Path Diagrams which show pictorially the accesses on the Data Model. These diagrams can be accompanied by additional quantifiable data about how many Entities are accessed at each step of the logic. These figures are used for many design tasks including database design, distribution planning and systems design. The figures are usually collected by User job.

The matrix of Activity/user responsibility can show not only which Activities are the responsibility of which user job, but also the frequency with which the Activity is executed – expressed either in simple terms or as a histogram for more critical Activities.

Other useful deliverables of this stage were the Common Procedure, Message and the Response required.

8 Summary

8.1 INTRODUCTION

In this chapter I will be summarising the contents of the last chapters, briefly going over the main concepts and the main steps of analysis. I am also going to give a brief overview of what I have called the "packaging" of the results – how the tasks of analysis and the deliverables can be supported or recorded using paper, Data Dictionaries, Analyst Workbenches or "CASE" tools. Finally, a brief mention will be made of what the next steps are in design: how the deliverables of analysis are used to produce a design.

8.2 PACKAGING THE RESULTS

This book has shown both some of the activities which need to be done to analyse the business and some of the end and intermediate deliverables produced by these activities.

Thus, collection, synthesis and verification are all Activities and the Data Model, Data Flow Diagrams and Activity Decomposition Diagrams are end deliverables. Intermediate deliverables included the forms we used as input in Data Analysis and the Semantic Networks produced during Data Analysis.

Analysis is like any other activity of the business. It can be supported in many ways using many mechanisms – paper, people, computers, drawing software, word processors, photocopiers and so on. For a long time (and possibly for a long time to come) the activities of analysis have been totally reliant on people with a small amount of machine support – mostly office machines. Within the past few years, however, we have seen more and more support being offered by software tools which help to record the deliverables.

The first software support to emerge, designed to enable a systems developer to record the deliverables on a computer rather than on paper, was the Data Dictionary.

Data Dictionaries tended to support design deliverables rather than analysis deliverables – in other words, records, data items, files and so on rather than Entities, Attributes or Activities. Some could be altered or adapted to support different concepts to those provided by the vendors and a fair number of Data Dictionaries still in use have been adapted to enable some of the analysis deliverables to be recorded in a basic way.

Data Dictionaries can loosely be classified as 'active' or 'passive'. Active Dictionaries are used by software products in the execution of the functions of those products. Many DBMSs – e.g. IDMS (ICL's and Cullinet's) and ORACLE – have a Data Dictionary which is used to store record definitions, data items, codes, screens and so on. These are also sometimes called Systems Encyclopaedias.

Passive Dictionaries act merely as repositories of data. They may have functions to provide the input for other software, e.g. generation of COBOL record descriptions, generation of IMS/DL/1 Segment layouts, but no function within the package actively uses the data for running systems. Many 'passive' Data Dictionaries have disappeared, Datamanager is one which is still going strong. Data Dictionaries do not have graphics capabilities.

The most recent set of software tools to enter the market which not only enable the analysis deliverables to be recorded, but also automate a few of the analysis activities are the Analyst Workbench and so called 'CASE' tools (Computer Aided Software Engineering). These tools are purpose-built to enable the analysis deliverables you have seen in this book to be recorded: they don't need adaptation. Furthermore, they have a 'graphics front end' – that is, they enable you to draw the diagrams as well. In true 'CASE' tools, the diagrams are integrated as you have seen in this book. Furthermore, the database which holds the information about all the things on the diagrams is also totally integrated with the diagrams.

Adding an Activity to a Data Flow will result in it appearing automatically in an Activity Decomposition Diagram as well as in the database which 'sits' behind these diagrams. Removing an item from the dictionary causes it to be removed from the diagrams, and so on. The new software tools can save a lot of time by ensuring that the results are kept consistent automatically and by automating many of the more mechanical verification checks we saw in earlier chapters. Some of them are also very attractive, with good colours and graphics.

244 *A Simple Introduction to Data and Activity Analysis*

Most of these products are PC based, although a few are mainframe and terminal-based. Some link to a mainframe or mini, where a central database may be shared. Some can be linked in networks; some are 'stand-alone'.

One the whole, it is still early days for these products. The database of the deliverables they contain is very weak, and the architecture of some is poor. In some cases the graphics are still a bit unattractive and restrictive. Having said that, however, they have a lot of potential and they will certainly be developed a lot more in the future.

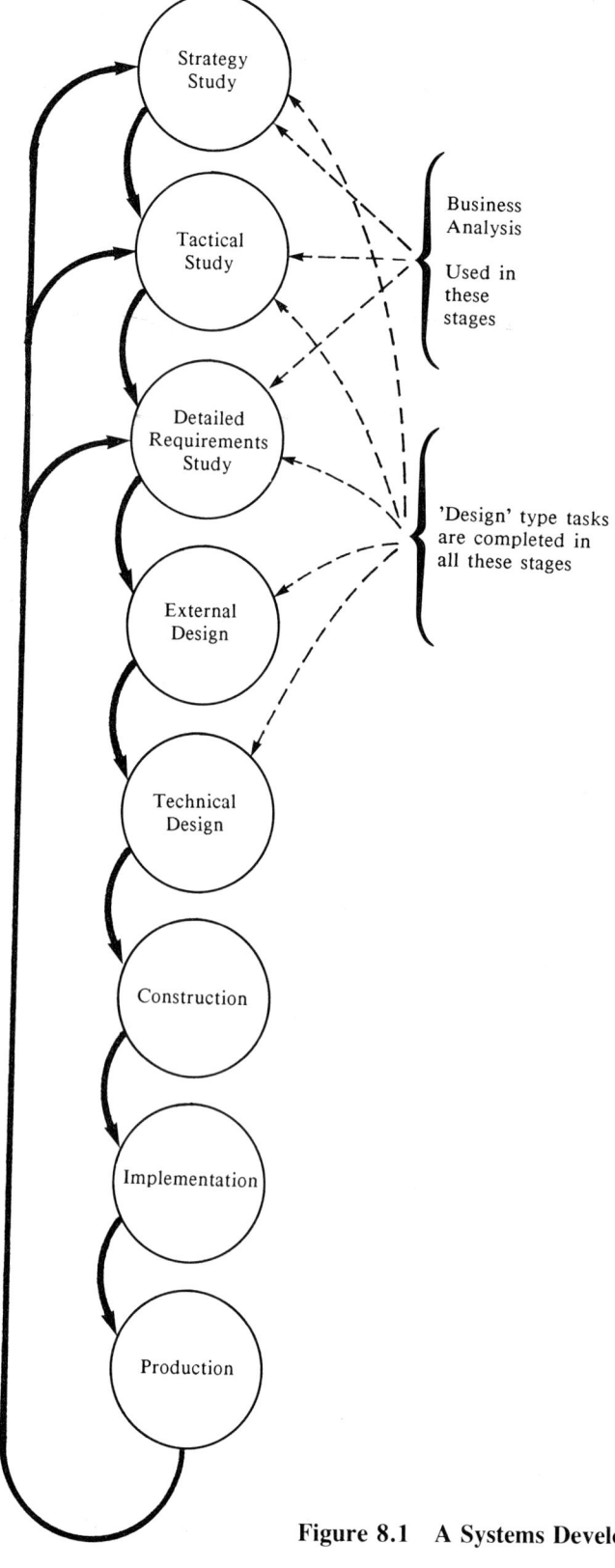

Figure 8.1 A Systems Development Cycle

Anyone interested in finding out more about the CASE and Analyst Workbench products may be interested in CASE: Analyst workbenches – A detailed product evaluation, published by OVUM and written by myself. It provides details of over seventy products.

If we look at these software tools in the context of the analysis task, they provide only a small amount of support to the task as a whole. Because intermediate deliverables are not supported, only end deliverables, and most of the activities are still reliant on people rather than the machine to do them, we must still accept that for some time to come analysis will be a task reliant largely on people and paper.

8.3 THE NEXT STEP – DESIGN

To understand what happens to the analysis deliverables during design we need to turn back to the explanation I gave of the Systems Development Cycle and where Business Analysis was used.

In Figure 8.1, I have repeated this picture but marked where 'design' takes place in the stages. It

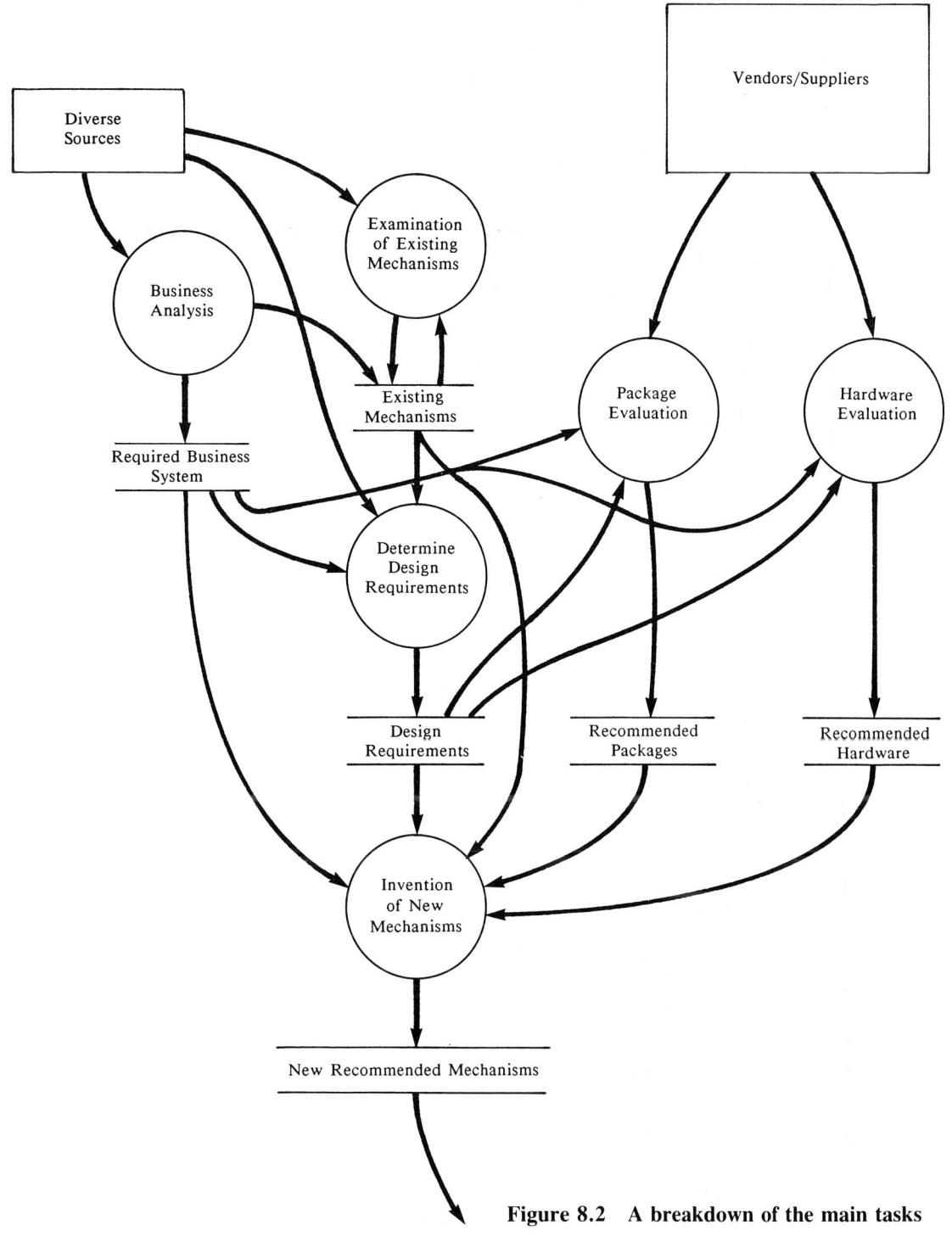

Figure 8.2 A breakdown of the main tasks

occurs in five. This may seem a complete overkill to anyone a little unfamiliar with the purpose of a Systems Development Cycle but a short explanation may help.

Systems Development Cycles were invented to help reduce the risk of system development, to enable priorities to be placed on projects and to enable a gradual reduction of design options to be made on a cost/benefit basis while keeping within a strategy or framework which took all the requirements into consideration. Furthermore, SDCs also aim to ensure that certain design decisions concerning the hardware in particular are made early in the development process because of the long lead times often experienced in the procurement and installation processes. Thus forms of design takes place a number of times during the various stages. A Strategy Study should place priorities on applications/systems and decide the telecommunication network and main hardware strategy, including the configuration. A Tactical Study will, for each application identified, determine the hardware, package and sub-system design components in more detail. As I mentioned in the introduction one solution is still not necessarily chosen, the cost-beneficial feasible solutions are carried forward for further investigation. During the detailed requirements study these solutions are investigated in depth and a choice made of one solution.

'Design', the choice of mechanisms to support the requirements, is being completed at each stage, but different design deliverables result at each stage.

A glance back at the introduction will also remind you of what external and technical designs achieve. Again the deliverables are different.

During Strategy, Tactical and Detailed Requirements Studies, the main tasks were those shown again in Figure 8.2. The design which takes place during all these three stages is part and parcel of inventing new mechanisms – new ways of supporting the activities and data, but in greater and greater levels of detail.

The main sub-tasks when inventing new mechanisms are to:

— Propose one or more new design solutions
— Plan and cost the solutions
— Choose one or more solutions for further development
— Specify Acceptance Criteria

In other words, because the choice of solution will always be based on cost, each solution must be costed. The cost will be based not only on hardware, software, people and operational cost but also development costs. The latter can be estimated by producing a plan for the subsequent SDC stages. Obviously, costs of hardware etc and the plan itself will be different for each solution.

To give you a feel for the main tasks of 'design' itself, I have provided in Figure 8.3 a breakdown of the design undertaken during the Detailed Requirements Study. The Data Flow Diagram shows the breakdown of the 'propose one or more new design solutions'. Basically, this same series of tasks is repeated for each possible solution.

Design at this stage revolves around transactions. The Elementary Activities are mapped to transactions – on-line, batch or real-time, or on-line initiated followed by background batch. (Package transactions may be used here). At this stage the need for fallback, recovery and contingency transactions is also considered. Transaction Access Paths are then produced using the mapping result and the Elementary Activity Access Paths. These are used to verify that the mapping has produced a 'consistent' system, eg no data on computer which isn't created, used, amended and deleted, and similarly for the 'human' paper based system.

The Data Flow and Activity Decomposition Diagrams are used to design the transaction network which shows what hardware or mechanism will be used to support the Data Flows. During this task user responsibility for transactions may be changed.

Once a decision has been made on who will perform each transaction, the distribution of data and transactions can be decided. It is largely based on where the user is located and what 'natural' partition of the data occurs in the organisation, together with the quantifiable data collected during analysis (which I called *usage*) and the frequency figures.

Once you know where data is going to be and how it will be partitioned or duplicated you can do a first cut design for your files or database. A choice is made on the software which will support the files (if it hasn't already been made) and then the Transaction Access Paths are used to build up an overall picture of what will go in the files/database and how it will be used. This adapted Data Model is further adapted to alter it according to the restrictions of the DBMS and the basic mapping rules applied to turn it into a first cut database design.

Finally, once the first cut design is known the conversion, interface and data capture transactions can be designed.

Once one of these solutions has been chosen, external design uses the details of transaction, transaction network, first cut database design, distribution, hardware and package use and simply expands it further into conversations, on-line transaction networks, batch processes, listings,

Summary 247

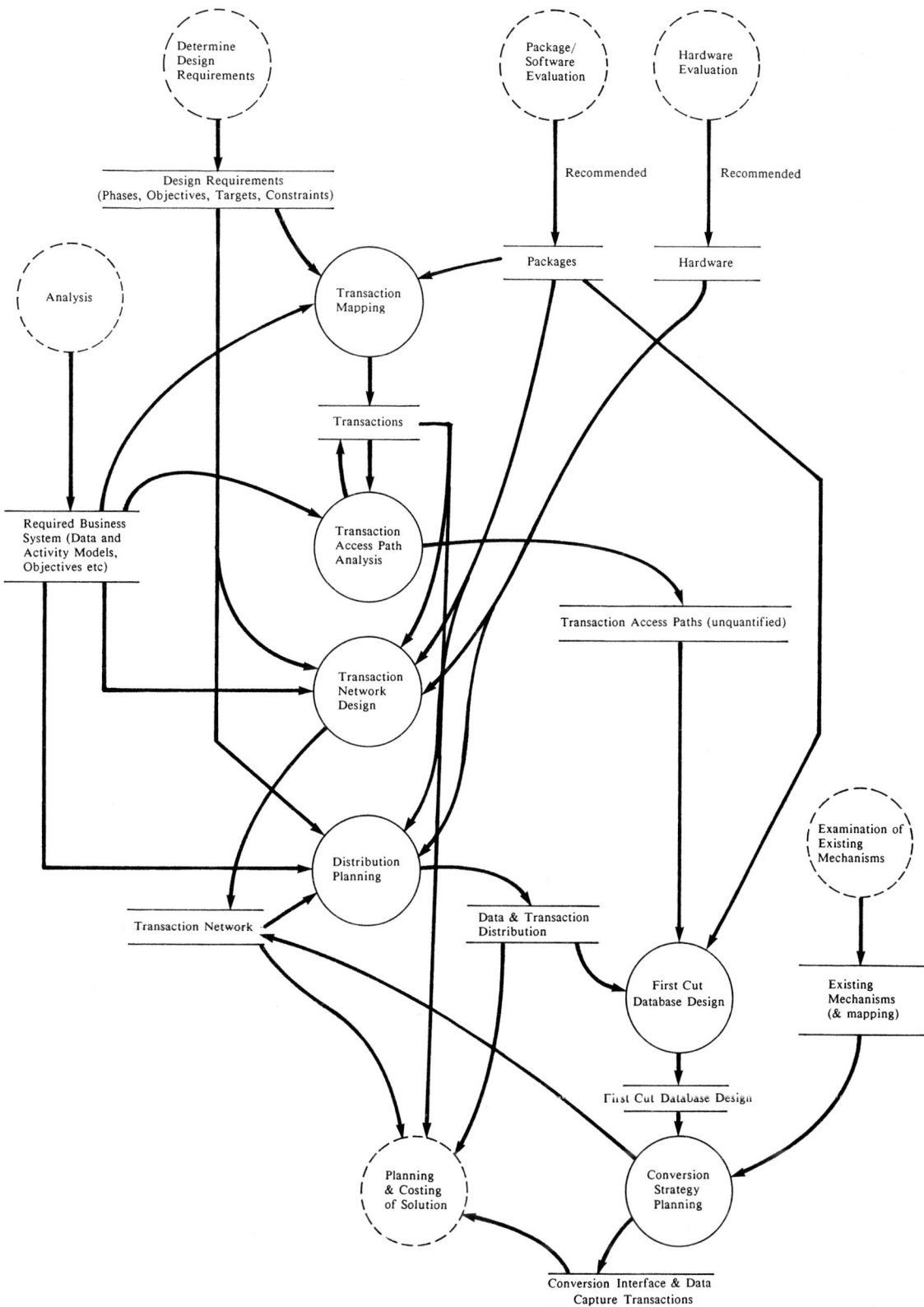

Figure 8.3 An example of the design task during the detailed requirements study

screens, forms and so on. Essentially, only enough design is completed during the detailed requirements study to enable a final choice of mechanism to be made.

Not every Systems Development Cycle has the design tasks I have shown at this stage. Some even delay database design until the technical design stage. I believe the one shown is a good balance between reducing the risk in terms of cost and infeasibility of the solution while avoiding unnecessary, detailed work at this stage.

In summary, design occurs at many stages of a Systems Development Cycle to varying degrees of detail. Unlike analysis, however, the deliverables tend to differ at each stage, for example, transactions during the detailed requirements stage, exchanges, screens, listings and batch processes at the external design stage and programs, jobs, blocks and files at the technical design stage.

8.4 SUMMARY OF RESULTS

Analysis is the study of what the business does now, wants to do and should be doing, together with the study of what data it needs to support these Activities.

The improvement of 'logical' business systems is part of the analysis process, where the study of Problems, their Cause and Effect can act as the driving force behind change, and the study of Objectives, Events (Opportunities or not) and Obligations shows where the change should be directed.

Activity Models and Data Models are used to describe what the business does now (together with its supporting data) and what it should be doing, wants to do and the data it will need.

A Data Model – as a generic term meaning "a model of the data needed" – is built from Entities, Relationships and Attributes. The Attributes do not appear on the Data Model Diagram which pictorially shows the Entities, their Relationships and some Relationship properties such as optionality and degree.

The Activity Model – again, as a generic term, meaning a model of what the business does or wants to do – is built from Activities, Events, Sources and Sinks, Data Flows and Data Stores.

There are two complementary diagrams used to represent the Activity Analysis concepts – the Data Flow Diagram and the Activity Decomposition Diagram. The Data Flow Diagram shows all the concepts. One diagram is produced for each successive level and 'leg' of the Activity Decomposition Diagram. The Activity Decomposition Diagram not only shows the Activities and Events, but also provides additional important information on sequence, selection and iteration, which cannot be shown clearly on the Data Flow Diagram.

The methods of analysis are entirely dependent on the type of input available.

If you have 'Design Data Abstractions', for example, you use the method geared to this form of input.

As a result of the types of input available to the analyst there are seven useful methods of analysis all of which are highly interrelated. The types of input on which these methods are based are:

* Design Abstractions – Data (records, forms, data items)
   – Mechanisms (transactions, user tasks, exchanges, programs)
* Design Occurrences – Data (form, records etc. but 'filled in' i.e. with data values to use)
* Conceptual or 'Real-World' Abstractions – Data
   – Activities
* Conceptual or 'Real-World' Occurrences – Data
   – Activities (actions)

The methods of analysis described showed how different types of input could be converted into the Data and Activity Models.

Along with methods for converting input into the models, methods were also described on how Data Models are merged and then subsequently refined, and how Activity Models are refined and verified using 'inner' and 'outer' consistency checks.

The matrices cross referencing data and Activity helped to verify both the Data Model and Activity Model.

One chapter was devoted to Elementary Activities, what they are, how they are described and what effect they have on the Data Model.

Elementary Activities are an essential stepping stone towards producing the transactions in design. They have a precise definition, one geared towards creating 'data integrity units' or 'data consistency units'. By using Elementary Activities to obtain transactions, a sound flexible design is more easily produced.

By using Elementary Activity Access Paths and the tables of data usage, the Data Model can be adapted until it supports all the Activities in the system, and consistency of data and Activities is assured.

The use of the data by Elementary Activities can be quantified. These 'usage' figures are used in both database and systems design.

The main message which should be clear from the book is that Data and Activity Analysis are highly integrated techniques and that together the deliverables they produce provide a complete picture of a business's logical requirements.

From this statement of logical requirements, one or more options on how the logical requirements could be physically implemented can be produced. The choice of mechanisms to support the logical requirements is based on a combination of cost/benefit and feasibility. The requirements, however, stay unaltered. The Data and Activity Models remain a clear and solid foundation for the decision on which technology is most suited to satisfying what is needed.

Index

Abstract things, method useful for analysing, 71
Access Paths, 193, 195
  updating Data Model from, 208–24
'Actions', using, 165–70
Activities
  adding, 168
  conditional, 120, 121
  Elementary, 191–242
Activity, 105–6
Activity Analysis
  main concepts of, 105–6
  meaning of, 1
  Techniques, 191
Activity breakdown
  Data Flow Diagram after, 136
Activity Decomposition, 106
  adapting, 120–21, 123–4
  addition of repetition to, 141
Activity Decomposition Diagram, 9, 109, 110–113, 115, 127, 170–72, 188, 192
  refining, 170–72
Activity Models, 132
Activity Occurrences, using, 165–70
Activity, types of, 111
Alternative Conventions, 122
Analysis techniques, 'modern', vii
Analysis within the Systems Development Cycle (published 1987), vii, 10, 26, 125
Analyst Workbenches, 174, 195, 243, 245
Applications/systems, 246
Attribute, 11, 12–13
  as 'adjective' of system, 13
  creating an, 57–60
  creation of one for each original Relationship, 89
  Duplication, checking for, 79
  representing existing or missing Relationship, 80–81
  type, 27
Attribute/Activity Matrix, 176
Automating the analysis process, 53, 243–5

Bachman, 9
Banking system, analysing, 71
BIS, 9
'Bottom–up' Decomposition of Activities, 110
BSP, *see* Business System Planning
'Building in situ', 8
Business, 'traditional' analysis of, 1–2

Business Analysis, 7
  meaning of, 1
  purpose of, 2–4
Business System Planning, 9

CACI, 9
CASE, *see* Computer Aided Software Engineering
'Cause', 182
CCTA, 110
Chen, 9
'Closed loops', 91, 92, 94
COBOL record descriptions, 243
'Cocked hat' symbol, 207
Codasyl DBMSs, 21
'Code only' Entities, removal of, 99–100
Codes of messages, 206
Common Activities, 110, 113
Common Procedures, 204–6
Complex exclusivity, 20
Computer Aided Software Engineering (CASE), 243, 245
  tools, 243
Computer, enhanced, system diagram, 151
Computer specification, extract from, 145
Computer System Specification, 143–5
Conceptual descriptions, using, 44–53
Conditional activities, 120, 121
Conditions, 119–20
  addition of, 137
Construction (stage in SDC), 6
Conventions, diagrammatic, 17, 19, 20, 23, 32, 33, 88, 91, 111, 113, 144
'Conversion', 132
CORE, 9
Cost/benefit grounds, 4
Cullinet, 243

Data Analysis (published 1981), vii
Data Analysis
  four methods of, 36, 37
  fundamental rules, 32–3
  how results are used, 8–9
  meaning of, 1
  term changed to 'Data and Activity Analysis', vii
Data conservation, 175
Data Design Abstractions, 143
Data Dictionaries, 205, 243
Data Dictionary/CASE, 100

251

252 *A Simple Introduction to Data and Activity Analysis*

Data flow deliverables, 128
Data Flow Diagram, 109, 113–19
  refining, 170–72
Data Flows, 12, 108
  adding, 138, 166
Data Model, 1–2, 12, 13, 15
  refining the, 77–101
  showing quantifiable data, 223
  updating from Access Paths and
    Structured English, 208–24
Data Modelling, 9
Data Models, merging, 72–7
Data Store, 108–9
Data–sharing, 3–4
Database design, 8
Database Management Systems, 8, 14, 243
  using different, 8, 14, 21
  validation checks, 100
Datamanager, 243
DBMSs, *see* Database Management
  Systems
DCE, 4, 7, 9, 110, 113
De Marco, Tom, 9, 110
Decomposition, 116, 171
Degree of relationships, 16–17
Degree verification, 100–101
Deliverables, vii, 15, 243
  collected during Data Analysis, 26–30
Descriptions, using conceptual, 44–53
Design, 245–8
  and design mapping, 29–30
  internal (stage in SDC), 5
  mapping, 130
  of system, 1–2
  solution, 4
  task during detailed requirements study,
    247
  technical (stage in SDC), 5
Design Abstractions, 35, 132
  using, 143–65
Design Occurrences, 36
  using, 60–71
Detailed Requirements Studies, 4, 6, 246
Detailed Systems Study, 4
Diagrammatic conventions, 17, 19, 20, 23,
  32, 33, 88, 91, 111, 113, 144
Diagrammatic Representation, 109
Diagramming methods, alternative, 207
Diary of Actions, 167
Duplication, removing, 77–9

'Effect', 182–3
Elementary Activities, 110, 125, 191–242
  commands to describe, 195–204
  definition of, 191–3
Embedded Elementary Activities, 207
Enhanced computer system diagram, 151
Entities, 11–12
  identified by relationships, 20–21
  removal of 'code only', 99–100

Entity
  as 'noun' of system, 12
  false, 81–2
  missing, 79–80
  state deliverables, 129
  sub–types, 21–5
  type, 26
Entity Occurrences, 165
Entity Relationship, 9
Entity State, 125
Entity/Activity Matrix, 176
Event deliverables, 127
Events, 106, 186–7, 189
Example model, 30–32
Exclusivity, 20–25
Exclusivity Case, 84–5
'Execute' command, 205, 206
'External design' (stage in SDC), 4

Factual sentences, reducing text to, 44
Feasibility Study, 4
File design, 8
Flavin, Matt, 9
Forms, using, 37–43
Function Analysis, 105
'Function', term changed to 'Activity', viii

Gane, 9, 110
Generalisation
  Entities, 83–4
  Relationships, 85–90

Hardware strategy, 246

IBM, 9
ICL, 243
IDMS, 243
IMAGE, 8
Implementation (stage in SDC), 6
IMS, 8
IMS designs, 21
IMS/DL/1 Segment layouts, 243
Inforem, 9
Information Engineering, 110
Information Engineering Method, 9
'Information Modelling Methodology', 9
Information Systems and Analysis of
  Change, 9
Inner Consistency Checks, 173–6
Inputs, types of, 131, 132
Internal design (stage in SDC), 5
'Intersection Entity', 93, 97
Interview
  analysing the Problems in, 183–4
  Attributes discovered during, 95
Interview notes
  deriving Data Model from, 46–52
  notes, using, 133–4
ISAC, *see* Information Systems and
  Analysis of Change

Jackson structured methods, 9
JMA, 9, 110

LBMS, 9, 19, 110
Logic Path, 125

Magazine articles, analysing, 44
Mandatory exclusivity, 20
Many Relationships, 88–90
Many–to–many Relationship, 16–17, 18, 40
    resolving, 92–7
Matrices, 176
Mechanism dependent processes, after
    removal of, 152
Merging the Models, 72–7
Merise, 9
Message deliverables, 129
'Message', 108
Messages, 206
Miller, G.A., 172
Model
    refining the, 77–101
    version, 28
Models, merging the, 72–7

Names, using to combine each Model, 45
Network, semantic, 92
Newspaper articles, analysing, 44, 53
Normalisation, 60

'O' symbol, 19
Objectives, 186
    mixed, 173
Obligations, 186, 189
Occurrence, removing single, 44
Occurrences, 131
    classifying, 56
    using, 53–71
One-to-many Relationships, 16, 38
    investigating, 98–9
Optional exclusivity, 20
Optionality, 17–19
ORACLE, 243
'Order Processing', 2
'Outer Consistency' Checks, 173–6

'Packaging' the results, 243–5
Parallel
    activities, 124, 125
    conventions, 125
Patterns, looking for, 84
Payroll system, analysing, 71
Pensions, analysing, 71
Permitted ranges, 12
Permitted values, 12
    and ranges, 28
Problem/Cause Network, 182
Problems/Causes and Effects, 181, 183, 189
'Procedures', 205
Process Analysis, 105
Production (stage in SDC), 6

Real World Abstractions, 35, 44, 131
    using, 133–43
Real World Occurrences, 35, 131
    using, 53–71
    vital role of, 91
Record
    layouts, using, 37–43
    removal, 169
Redundancy, removing, 91, 92, 93
References, forbidden, 174
Refining
    Diagrams, 170–72
    the Model, 77–101
Relationship, as 'verb' of system, 15
'Relationship degree', 60
Relationship/Activity Matrix, 176
Relationships, 11, 14–17
    degree of, 16–17
    identifying, 21, 22
    investigating one–to–one, 98–9
    many, 88–90
    many-to-many, 40
    one-to-many, 38
    removing redundant, 91, 92
    resolving many–to–many, 92–7
    type, 27
Removal of 'code only' Entities, 99–100
Repetition, 122–3
'Response' required, 225

SADT diagrams, 9
Sarson, 9, 110
SDC, *see* Systems Development Cycle
Semantic Network, 92
Sentence, drawing Data Model for each, 45
Sequence, 124
    conventions, 125
    looking for implied, 46
'Signal', 108
Sinks, 105, 106–7
Software
    support, 243
    tools, 243–5
Source, 105
Source/sink deliverables, 128
Sources, 106–7
    adding, 166
Specification Stage, 4
'Spotlight' symbol, 207
SSADM, vii, 10, 19, 26, 110, 125
'Stimulus' (Event Occurrences), 167
Strategy Studies, 4, 6, 110, 246
Structured English, updating Data Model
    from, 208–24
Structured Text, 193
Sub-activities, number of, 172
Symbols, 17, 19, 20, 23, 32, 33, 88, 91, 111,
    113, 144, 207
Synonyms, removing, 77–9
'Systems Analysis', how Data and Activity
    Analysis differ, 1–2

Systems Designers, 9
Systems Development Cycle, 4–8, 244–6
Systems Encyclopaedias, 243

Tactical Study, 4, 6, 110, 246
Technical Design (stage in SDC), 5
Tense, change of, 88
Terms, defined and summarised, 248
Text
  reducing to factual sentences, 44, 53–4
  used to record information, 2
'Top–down' Decomposition of Activities, 110
TOTAL, 8
'Traditional' analysis, 1–2

Usage, 246
  Figures, 229–32
  summary of, 177
User/Activity Responsibility, 225–9

'Validation tables', 100
Verification methods, 173–8

'Weighting', keeping correct, 170, 172
Words, forbidden, 173

Yourdon, 9

Notes

Computer Weekly Publications

Computer Weekly is the UK's leading weekly computer newspaper which goes to over 112,000 computer professionals each week. Founded in 1967, the paper covers news, reviews and features for the computer industry. In addition, *Computer Weekly* also publishes books relevant to and of interest to its readership.

Publications to date (obtainable through your book shop or by ringing 01-685-9435/01-661-3050) are:

Aliens' Guide to the Computer Industry by John Kavanagh

In a lucid and light style, leading computer industry writer John Kavanagh discusses how the various parts of the computer industry inter-relate and what makes it tick. Complete with extensive index, the book is invaluable for all who come into contact with the computer industry.

"Business professionals who worry about their grasp of the general computing scene and do not want to be bombarded with jargon and technicalities, will get good value . . . an excellent 'snapshot' of the companies, the current areas of interest and the problems" *Financial Times*

ISBN 1-85384-012-2   192 pages   Price £9.95

Computer Jargon Explained by Nicholas Enticknap

Following reader demand this a totally revised, expanded and updated version of our highly successful guide to computer jargon, *Breaking the Jargon*.

This 176 page book provides the context to and discusses 68 of the most commonly used computer jargon terms. Extensively cross-indexed this book is essential reading for all computer professionals, and will be useful to many business people too.

". . . a useful shield against the constant barrage of impossible language the computer business throws out" *The Independent*

". . . *a worthwhile investment*" *Motor Transport*

ISBN 0-85384-015-7   176 pages   Price £9.95

Women in Computing by Judith Morris

Written by an experienced editor of several computer magazines, this book reflects the upsurge in awareness of the important role women can play in helping to stem the critical skills shortage within the computer industry.

The book addresses women's issues in a practical and sensible way and is aimed at all business women who work in the computer industry or with computers.

ISBN 1-85384-004-1   c.160 pages   Price £9.95

Low Cost PC Networking by Mike James

The whole area of PC networking is taking off rapidly now. Can you afford to be left behind?

Mike James' *Low Cost PC Networking* shows how networking revolutionises the way we use PCs and the tasks that they perform. It also explains how networking goes further than simply linking PCs, and how it enables you to integrate your operations to transform your business.

Chapters cover every aspect of networking, from planning your network and selecting the hardware and software to applications, technicalities and contacts.

ISBN 0-434-90897-5   256 pages   Price £16.95

Open Systems: The Basic Guide to OSI and its Implementation by Peter Judge

We recognise the need for a concise, clear guide to the complex area of computer standards, untrammelled by jargon and with appropriate and comprehensible analogies to simplify this difficult topic. This book, a unique collaboration between *Computer Weekly* and the magazine *Systems International,* steers an independent and neutral path through this contentious area and is essential for users and suppliers and is required reading for all who come into contact with the computer industry.

ISBN 1-85384-009-2   192 pages   Price £12.95

Computer Weekly Book of Puzzlers Compiled by Jim Howson

Test your powers of lateral thinking with this compendium of 187 of the best puzzles published over the years in *Computer Weekly*. The detailed explanations of how solutions are reached make this a useful guide to recreational mathematics. No computer is needed to solve these fascinating puzzles.

"... a pleasant collection of puzzles exercises for computer freaks. Actually probably fewer than half the puzzles here need a computer solution..." *Laboratory Equipment Digest*

ISBN 1-85384-002-5   162 pages   Price £6.95

How to Get Jobs in Microcomputing by John F Charles

As micros proliferate throughout organisations, opportunities for getting jobs in the micro area are expanding rapidly. The author, who has worked with micros in major organisations, discusses how to get started in microcomputing, describes the different types of job available, and offers tips and hints based on practical experience. Ideal for recent graduates, and those already working with minicomputers or mainframes, who are looking towards a career in micros.

ISBN 1-85384-010-6   160 pages   Price £6.95

Considering Computer Contracting? – The Computer Weekly Guide to Becoming a Freelance Computer Professional by Michael Powell

Everybody in the computer industry talks of doubling their salary by going freelance. This book, written by a freelancer, explains how it's done. The topics covered, including how to form your own company, and handling your finance, also make this book useful for people in other industries considering going it alone.

"... is essential reading for anyone considering taking up contract work." *The Guardian*

ISBN 1-85384-000-9   156 pages   Price £10.95

Selling Information Technology: A Practical Career Guide by Eric Johnson

Selling in IT requires more skill and creativity than selling in any other profession. This essential handbook for IT sales people explains why and provides practical down-to-earth advice on achieving the necessary extra skills.

A collaboration between *Computer Weekly* and the National Computing Centre, this book discusses practical career issues, general IT sales issues, and key IT industry developments.

ISBN 0-85012-684-3   244 pages   Price £12.50

IT Perspectives Conference: The Future of the IT Industry

Many nuggets of strategic thought are contained in this carefully edited transcript of the actual words spoken by leading IT industry decision makers at *Computer Weekly's* landmark conference held late in 1987. The conference was dedicated to discussing current and future directions the industry is taking from four perspectives: supplier perspectives; communications perspectives; user perspectives and future perspectives.

"... makes compelling reading for those involved in the business computer industry" *The Guardian*

"... thought-provoking points and some nice questions put to speakers at the end" *Daily Telegraph*

ISBN 1-85384-008-4   224 pages   Price £45

The Computer Weekly Annual Guide to Resources '89

This extensively indexed book fulfils the computer industry's need for an independent, handy up-to-date reference review signposting and interpreting the key trends in the computer industry and how companies and their products are adapting to them. A key section is an in-depth independent discussion of 200 software and supplier companies, and of leading industry sectors and significant new products.

"In spite of a plethora of guides to various aspects of the computer industry, there hasn't been one readable, comprehensive overview of the current UK scene. Now Computer Weekly's first Annual Guide to Resources '89 has filled the bill . . . it's very good." *The Guardian*

ISBN 1-85384-014-9   352 pages   Price £45